Making Representa

Moira G. Simpson trained in art, museology and education. She has worked in the museum sector and most recently was a lecturer in the Institute of Education at the University of Warwick in England. She has travelled extensively in several countries conducting research into museum representation of cultures and has an extensive publications list. She has now moved to Adelaide, Australia, where she works as a freelance writer, museum consultant and educator.

For more information, see the author's website at URL: http://www.e-vocative.com

The Heritage: Care–Preservation–Management programme has been designed to serve the needs of the museum and heritage community worldwide. It publishes books and information services for professional museum and heritage workers, and for all the organizations that service the museum community.

Editor-in-Chief Andrew Wheatcroft

Architecture in Conservation: *Managing developments at historic sites*
James Strike

Development of Costume
Naomi Tarrant

Environmental Management: *Guidelines for museums and galleries*
Mary Cassar

Forward Planning: *A handbook of business, corporate and development planning for museums and galleries*
Edited by Timothy Ambrose and Sue Runyard

The Handbook for Museums
Gary Edson and David Dean

Hands-on Exhibitions: *Managing interactive museums and science centres*
Tim Caulton

Heritage Gardens: *Care, conservation and management*
Sheena Mackellar Goulty

Heritage and Tourism in the 'global' village
Priscilla Boniface and Peter J. Fowler

The Industrial Heritage: *Managing resources and uses*
Judith Alfrey and Tim Putnam

International Directory of Museum Training: *Programs and practices of the museum profession*
Edited by Gary Edson

Making Representations: *Museums in the post-colonial era*
Moira G. Simpson

Managing Museums and Galleries
Michael A. Fopp

Marketing the Museum
Fiona McLean

Managing Quality Cultural Tourism
Priscilla Boniface

Museums 2000: *Politics, people, professionals and profit*
Edited by Patrick J. Boylan

Museums without Barriers: *A new deal for disabled people*
Fondation de France and ICOM

Museum Basics
Timothy Ambrose and Crispin Paine

Museum Ethics
Edited by Gary Edson

Museum Exhibition: *Theory and practice*
David Dean

Museum, Media, Message
Edited by Eilean Hooper-Greenhill

Museums: A place to work – *Planning museum careers*
Jane R. Glaser with Artemis A. Zenetou

Museum Security and Protection: *A handbook for cultural heritage institutions*
ICOM and ICMS

Museums and the Shaping of Knowledge
Eilean Hooper-Greenhill

Museums and their Visitors
Eilean Hooper-Greenhill

Museum Volunteers: *Good practice in the management of volunteers*
Sinclair Goodlad and Stephanie McIvor

The Past in Contemporary Society: *Then/Now*
Peter J. Fowler

The Politics of Display: *Museums, science, culture*
Edited by Sharon MacDonald

The Representation of the Past: *Museums and heritage in the post-modern world*
Kevin Walsh

Towards the Museum of the Future: *New European perspectives*
Edited by Roger Miles and Laura Zavala

Making Representations

Museums in the Post-Colonial Era

Moira G. Simpson

London and New York

First published in hardback 1996
by Routledge
11 New Fetter Lane, London EC4P 4EE

Simultaneously published in the USA and Canada
by Routledge
29 West 35th Street, New York, NY 10001

First published in paperback 2001

Routledge is an imprint of the Taylor & Francis Group

© 1996, 2001 Moira G. Simpson

Typeset in Sabon by Florence Production Ltd, Stoodleigh, Devon
Printed and bound in Great Britain by
TJ International Ltd, Padstow, Cornwall

British Library Cataloguing in Publication Data
A catalogue record for this book is available from the British Library

Library of Congress Cataloging in Publication Data
A catalog record for this book has been requested

ISBN 0–415–06785–5 (hbk)
ISBN 0–415–06786–3 (pbk)

'We [the Aboriginal peoples] are well aware that many people have dedicated their time, careers and their lives showing what they believe is an accurate picture of indigenous peoples. We thank you for that, but we want to turn the page . . . '

George Erasmus, former National Chief of the Assembly of First Nations, in his opening address to 'Preserving Our Heritage: A Working Conference for Museums and First Peoples', Ottawa, November, 1988. (Cited in AFN and CMA, 1992: 7)

Contents

Illustrations

Acknowledgements

During the course of researching the material for this book, I spent several months overseas visiting museums and related organisations in Canada, the United States, Australia and New Zealand, and I would like to acknowledge my gratitude for the financial assistance which contributed towards the costs of these trips. Accordingly, I would like to thank the University of Warwick for the Research and Innovations grant which I was awarded in 1991; the National Museums and Galleries on Merseyside, Hapag-Lloyd (UK) Ltd, and W.R. Powrie for their financial contributions; and the Canadian Museums Association and the American Association of Museums for allowing me to attend their annual conferences in 1991.

In addition, I extend my thanks to all those whom I interviewed during my research trips (see appendix). They welcomed me warmly, gave me their precious time, shared their professional experiences and opinions with me, gave me tours of exhibitions and stores, and so provided much of the research material upon which this book is based. I would also like to thank those who shared a meal or their home with me, especially welcome during a lengthy overseas trip. Many other individuals, too numerous to name, responded helpfully to my letters of inquiry and provided comments or materials to assist me with my research; they also have my thanks.

Finally, I would like to thank my parents who have provided me with years of support, education, and encouragement. In particular, I would like to thank my husband Steve, who has patiently endured ten months of my absence overseas and untold expenditure of our personal finances in order to see this book completed. He has been fully supportive of my endeavours and a constant source of help and encouragement.

This revised edition of *Making Representations* includes an epilogue providing details of developments in repatriation issues over the five years since the first edition of this book was completed. Included in this epilogue is a description of research activities that I undertook on behalf of the Museums Association in the UK. I wish to acknowledge with gratitude the commitment of the Museums Association and, in particular, Assistant Director Maurice Davies, to addressing the issue of repatriation. I thank them for providing me with the opportunity to undertake the research work which led to the publication of *Museums and Repatriation: an account of contested items in museum collections in the UK, with comparative material from other countries* (Museums Association, 1997).

One of the recommendations that I made in *Museums and Repatriation* was for the publication of repatriation guidelines to provide guidance to museum staff in the handling of repatriation claims. The Museums and Galleries Commission commissioned Janet Leggett, a museum consultant, to write the repatriation guidelines and established a steering group to oversee the process. *Restitution and Repatriation: guidelines for good practice* was published in early 2000. The Museums Association, the Museums and Galleries Commission, and the Conference of Directors of National Museums also established the Museums Standing Advisory Group on Repatriation and Related Cultural Property Issues to explore the other recommendations and related matters. As a member of the MGC's Repatriation Steering Group and the Museums Standing Advisory Group on Repatriation and Related Cultural Property Issues, I would like to thank fellow members for their lively and informative discussions of repatriation issues.

In addition to the developments in the UK, the epilogue includes figures from the United States detailing the impact of the Native American Graves Protection and Repatriation Act (NAGPRA) after ten years, a date which occurred just prior to my submission of the revised manuscript in late November 2000. I would like to thank Tim McKeown, NAGPRA Team Leader with the US National Park Service, for his assistance in providing these figures before they were made publicly available. My thanks are due also to Deanne Hanchant, a museum curator and researcher of Aboriginal archive collections, for reading over and clarifying aspects of the section relating to recent developments in Australia.

Introduction

'The notion of western culture as inherently progressive, sophisticated and, above all, superior . . . remains firmly imbedded in the cultural institutions of western Europe, not least in its museums.'

(Tawadros, 1990: 30–1).

In Europe, the tradition of museums as institutions both reflecting and serving a cultural élite has been long established and, in many, is still maintained. The museum, the 'cabinet of curiosities', is the storeroom of a nation's treasures, providing a mirror in which are reflected the views and attitudes of dominant cultures, and the material evidence of the colonial achievements of the European cultures in which museums are rooted. The colonial origins of the museum remain an enduring influence upon these institutions and upon public perceptions of them. Taking the Louvre as an example, Giliane Tawadros has remarked that 'originally a bastion of western military and imperial sovereignty, the Louvre in its contemporary role as museum, functions as a bastion of western cultural and intellectual sovereignty' (Tawadros, 1990: 31). Aboriginal Australian writers have referred to the state of 'scientific colonialism' in which museums and anthropologists function and contend that cultural colonialism continues to control the representation of Aboriginal arts and culture (Fourmile, 1987: 60; 1990a; Marrie, 1989). Fourmile claims that 'most of (the Aboriginal) cultural property now in museum collections was acquired under distinctly colonial circumstances' (Fourmile, 1990a: 57).

Yet, despite the history of colonialism in which museums are inextricably enmeshed, museums are now undergoing a radical change in the way that they function and in their relationships with the cultures represented in the collections; a change which reflects shifts in the relationship between dominant western cultures and those of indigenous, minority, and suppressed cultures everywhere. There is recognition amongst museum professionals throughout the world that museums have not been providing adequately for the needs of culturally diverse communities, and that they must create profound changes in their philosophies and activities if they are to address these needs.

International interest in the issues associated with museums and cultural diversity is illustrated by the attention given to the subject in conferences held in many parts of the world in recent years – a testament to the global nature of the issues being addressed. Questions of ownership and representation, which arise out of the interactions of European and non-European peoples in the colonial era and the resultant plurality of societies, are now necessitating resolution in the vastly different relationships of the post-colonial era. The nature and histories of the collections themselves attest to the cross-cultural dimension of the debate surrounding the ownership and interpretation of material culture and require the development of new museological guidelines and international dialogue. Colonialism has played a significant role both in shaping the collections in museums and in shaping the audiences that might potentially use them. It is this colonial legacy that museums must deal with today.

The culture of change has progressed most assertively in those countries in which the colonial processes resulted in the indigenous population existing as a disempowered minority in its own land, outnumbered by an increasingly diverse population of immigrants: the non-European western nations. Hence, the museological issues in Canada and the United States are not dissimilar to those being experienced in Australia and New Zealand.

As former colonisers, now distanced somewhat from the problems they caused, there has perhaps been less pressure upon European nations to address the issues of concern to indigenous peoples; this can be reflected in the limited extent to which issues concerning human remains and sacred objects have been addressed and acted upon within European museums. However, the multicultural nature of contemporary society, resulting in part from immigration from the former colonies, has brought its own pressures to bear upon collecting and exhibiting practices, particularly in the fields of social history and anthropology. In Europe, as in North America, Australia and New Zealand, the plurality of contemporary, post-colonial society gives rise to complex issues in relation to museums: display and interpretation; the classification and values attached to objects; cultural bias in representing other cultures; the lack of representation of cultural diversity in local history collections; demands for self-representation and self-expression. In this respect, the issues which affect relationships between museums and indigenous peoples are very similar to those which influence museums and other ethnic groups.

Increasingly vocal expressions of dissatisfaction with conventional museological and interpretive methods have resulted in pressures being brought to bear upon museum curators to adopt more inclusive practices. This dissatisfaction has been demonstrated more forcefully in a series of confrontations over the past thirty to forty years. In this book, *Making Representations*, these issues will be examined in relation to recent developments in museum curatorial policy and practice in response to those criticisms and the needs of today's pluralist societies. The material for this book has been drawn from fieldwork conducted in Britain, the Netherlands, Canada, the United States, Australia, and New Zealand. The issues raised pertain generally to museums in the European tradition which are located in culturally diverse nations. They have relevance to all museums in all parts of those countries – despite what might be perceived as the homogeneity of the local community or the collections. For these issues are not just about displays in glass cases, but about relationships – between individuals, between museums and communities, and between peoples of different cultures – relationships which need to be built upon respect, tolerance, understanding, and appreciation of difference and similarity.

A note on terminology and the parameters of this study

Throughout the book I use terms such as 'cultural group' and 'community'. This is not intended to suggest that there is a homogeneous, identifiable community based exclusively upon ethnic background, but is merely a mechanism for facilitating discussion. The terms are used generically to apply to people who share some common bond in relation to the topic of discussion (ethnic origin/religion/tribal affiliation, etc.) although they may in many ways be very different and can often be re-classified into various sub-groups of communities defined in some other way: the gay community, the elderly community, the school-aged community, and so on. What I am concerned with here are the bonds of ethnicity that link otherwise disparate groups into a unit that, for convenience in discussion, is referred to as a community.

In some respects, the needs of ethnically diverse audiences bring new issues into play, questions concerning divergent perspectives, the authority of a dominant group not representative of those portrayed; yet at the same time, such issues affect other groups who have had little control over the representation of their cultures, including women, the disabled, the gay community, and so forth. Many of the questions that need to be addressed when examining the issues associated with museum representation and cultural diversity are also relevant to other cultural groups identifiable by class, gender, disability, and so on. However, the discussion in this book focuses specifically upon issues associated with ethnicity, and is therefore concerned with matters that relate to museums and their interaction with communities or cultural groups that share common cultural identity defined by racial origins, religion, nationality, or tribal affiliation.

Part 1 of *Making Representations* examines the cultural and political atmosphere which has placed these issues on the agenda of museum staff over the past thirty years. It examines the recent historical framework in which the criticisms and calls for change must be seen in order to unravel the complexities of intellectual and social conventions which pervade the academic disciplines in which muscums function; conventions which are rooted in the colonial era during which many collections were established, and which continue to influence contemporary museum practices. Dissatisfaction with those methods has resulted in mounting pressure upon museums to adopt more inclusive working practices and allow communities to participate in the process of cultural representation in museums.

The subjects of the exhibitions – the original makers and users of the artefacts – have traditionally been passive informants: observed, recorded, studied, and excluded from the planning processes – as much objects as the artefacts themselves. Western academic thinking, Eurocentric historical interpretation and scientific analysis, have too often reduced the traditional knowledge and material culture to little more than a subject of academic interest, curiosity or wonder. Academic study has tended to minimise the person and has often failed to provide an equitable working partnership between the exhibitor and the exhibited. Such exclusive practices by mainstream museums provided motivation for the establishment of museums by ethnic groups wishing to take control of cultural representation and develop museums which, while often based upon the traditional European model, are used to satisfy their own needs and can, therefore, adopt additional roles and functions.

In the contemporary context, the book draws upon many case studies to provide examples of innovative practice in exhibition planning involving community collaboration, more informed content, and increased accessibility and relevance for the cultural group represented. Specific case studies demonstrate ways in which indigenous peoples are beginning to develop new relationships with museums and with anthropologists, turning their work to their own advantage and ensuring that exhibition content can be better informed and more reflective of alternative cultural values and views.

Part 2 explores the growth of museums and cultural centres established by ethnic groups, such as Ukrainians, Mexican Americans, African Americans, Native Americans, and Aboriginal Australians, who have chosen to represent their own cultures and provide cultural services to their communities through the exhibition medium and related activities. Over the past thirty years or so, frustrated by under-representation in mainstream museums, many communities have sought to do this through the establishment of a community museum, cultural centre, or similar facility. Often motivated by a desire to preserve and interpret the past and document changes, the establishment of a museum enables historical and contemporary issues to be examined, discussed, and interpreted for the benefit of the community and visitors. Such initiatives can also provide a service for tourists and so generate employment and income within the community. Their agendas and activities are compared with those of mainstream museums.

The special problems of sacred objects and human remains are addressed in the third part of the book which explores the confrontations between western science and indigenous cultures over ownership, display and repatriation. It considers the ways in which museums are responding to these sensitive issues and examines policies which are being introduced by individual museums and professional bodies, and also discusses legislative developments in the United States and Australia which have a bearing on the issue.

The concluding chapter of the book looks to the future, identifying the most significant factors which lie ahead for museums in the light of the changes and pressures imposed upon them by society in the late twentieth century, raising questions about the future roles and activities of museums. It explores the future of representation in museums and their changing relationships with indigenous peoples and ethnic communities in the post-colonial era. It examines the implications for mainstream museums of the new methodologies which are being introduced in response to the cultural diversity of society and as a result of greater plurality amongst curatorial staff. It suggests that museums should adopt a more diverse range of interpretive activities if they are to ensure their relevance to the culturally diverse societies in which we all now live. It demonstrates the need for museums and anthropologists to re-examine their functions and suggests that museums, rather than merely recording, preserving and interpreting the past, should adopt a proactive role in social and cultural affairs and increase the beneficial roles that they can fulfil on behalf of the futures of indigenous people.

Research methods

This book is based upon research undertaken in Europe, North America, Australia and New Zealand. This included extensive interviewing of staff, community members and others involved in the planning and presentation of exhibitions, examination of the exhibitions themselves, and collection of documentation from museum files, libraries, archives, government agencies, community organisations, and other relevant sources. This provided evidence of a tremendous wave of change coursing through the profession, a catalyst for change resulting in some exciting examples of innovative practices and encouraging developments in the relationship between anthropologists and the peoples whose cultures they study. A new, more mutually beneficial relationship is developing, one which is resulting in a quiet revolution within museum anthropology, further enhanced by the freshness and uninhibited activities of new museologists who lack the culturally focused intellectual myopia of many curators trained in the European tradition. Museums are changing in many ways: their image as dusty, stuffy, boring and intimidating storehouses is slowly giving way to recognition that museums can be authoritative without being definitive; inclusive rather than exclusive; exciting, lively and entertaining while still being both scholarly and educational.

The following chapters examine the issues affecting cultural representation in museum exhibitions, the influences which have led to changes in museums, their responses to contemporary cultural concerns, and the developments of new research and exhibition practices, particularly in anthropology and social history. By using specific case studies, it demonstrates the extent to which museums have adopted new approaches in their exhibition planning and presentation, interpretive approaches, and dissemination methods, enabling communities to become actively involved in the representation of their own cultures. Such approaches give voice to members of cultures that were previously the subjects of anthropological study and public curiosity, but who were never given the opportunity or right to self-representation in mainstream museums.

Part 1
Cultural reflections

'Society will no longer tolerate institutions that either in fact or in appearance serve a minority audience of the élite.'

(Cameron, 1971: 23)

The politics of change

Over the past forty years or so, there has been a tremendous blossoming of cultural expression amongst indigenous peoples and other ethnic minority groups, resulting from a growing awareness of the importance of cultural heritage and the desire for free expression and civil rights. The decades since the Second World War have been years of upheaval and change in the relationship between European nations and those that they had dominated and exploited during the colonial era. Some of the most dramatic and violent were the struggles undertaken by the former colonial nations in their fights for independence. Following the end of the conflict in Europe, attention turned to political issues in countries in Africa and Asia where peoples were fighting for political and cultural autonomy and demanding independence. The determination to end centuries of colonial rule and exploitation in these countries was echoed by the political awakening of indigenous peoples and cultural minority groups in western nations.

This trend was particularly significant in North America where groups which previously had felt unrecognised, undervalued, or disadvantaged as a result of ethnicity, age, gender or sexual preferences began vocalising their frustrations, promoting their strengths, and demanding their rights. The 1950s and 1960s witnessed civil rights disturbances across North America with demonstrations and rioting as suppressed minority groups fought against inequality and racism inherent in every sector of society. In the United States, this period saw the emergence of the black civil rights movement, led by Martin Luther King, and the establishment of more forceful militant 'black power' groups, such as the Black Panthers, determined to achieve improved social and political rights for African Americans. Other groups were also struggling to attain basic civil rights in the USA: Mexican Americans formed El Movimiento and took new pride in their culture, turning the previously derogatory term 'Chicano' into a description they now embrace with pride. American Indians were reclaiming their cultural heritage and fighting for their rights after centuries of confrontation and exploitation of their land and resources, and decades of pressure to assimilate into American and Canadian society while being treated as second-class citizens. They formed pan-Indian organisations such as the American Indian Civil Rights Council (1969) and the National Indian Brotherhood (1969), (renamed the Assembly of First Nations in 1982), the Native American Rights Fund (1970), and the militant American Indian Movement (1968), to fight for self-determination, tribal recognition, the resolution of land claims and broken treaty agreements, and other issues effecting American Indian communities. As with the black civil rights campaign, there was a move from rhetoric to action during the late 1960s and the 1970s (Deloria, 1973).

In November 1969, American Indians took over Alcatraz Island in San Francisco, maintaining control for eighteen months despite the telephones, electricity and water being cut off by the US authorities (DeLuca, 1983; Horse Capture, 1991). Their action was an ironic allusion to the landing of Columbus and his crew in the Americas in 1492, described by George P. Horse Capture as 'a grand culmination of the civil rights decade' (1991: 86); a catalyst for much of the change that has followed.

> For the first time since the Little Bighorn, the Indian people, instead of passively withdrawing and accepting their fate, had stepped forward in the bright sunshine and let it be known that they were Indian and proud, and their present situation must and would change.
>
> (ibid.: 88)

Three years later, a group of Indians retraced the 'Trail of Tears' of the 1830s with their own 'Trail of Broken Treaties' which led to a seven-day occupation of the Bureau of Indian Affairs in Washington, DC, which they renamed the 'Native American Embassy'. In February 1973, members of the Oglala Sioux and the American Indian Movement returned to Wounded Knee, the site of the massacre of 300 Sioux by US troops in 1890, to draw attention to government violations of the 1868 Fort Laramie Treaty. There they were confronted by heavily armed government troops and a 71 day siege followed during which two Indians were killed.

This was a period of intense cultural activity, political fervour, and the emergence of an irrepressible determination to fight for political representation and the preservation of the identity of minority cultures as a distinct part of American society. Reflecting their desire to be American but also to acknowledge their distinct cultural background, there has developed a nomenclature of ethnic identity linked with American nationality resulting in terms such as Native American, African American, Italian American, Chicano, and so on. New federal legislation such as the Indian Self-Determination Act of 1972 and the

Native American Religious Freedom Act of 1978 provided tribal groups with greater autonomy. During the 1970s black studies and Indian cultural studies programmes flourished in American colleges and schools. Such movements have brought an end to the concept of the melting pot of US culture and established the importance of maintaining cultural diversity within a national framework.

American museums and the civil rights movement of the 1960s

Museums were not immune from criticisms and militant actions. Critics expressed dissatisfaction with the activities of mainstream museums and art galleries, and the ways in which black and other minority cultures were represented and interpreted in exhibitions. These institutions were perceived by many to be unsatisfactory: serving a cultural élite, staffed primarily by whites, reflecting white values, and excluding from the interpretive process the very peoples whose cultures were represented in the collections. Ethnic minority groups were poorly represented on museum staffs, and so felt they had little or no power over the content of museum exhibitions – a situation which was particularly frustrating for those who continued to suffer the effects of widely held misconceptions, stereotyping and inaccurate representation. Many artists of minority cultural backgrounds felt marginalised by museums and art galleries which were perceived to represent only the dominant white culture, and failed to provide equality of opportunity to artists of non-European origin. Museums came under increasing criticism for their Eurocentric approach towards the representation of cultures. They were seen to hold little relevance to the majority of peoples' lives and to be failing to meet the needs of minority communities in particular. While most criticisms of museums have been confined to the pages of professional journals or voiced at conferences and symposia, museums have not entirely escaped the protests and activities of political activists and occasionally have attracted more vociferous debate and censure including demonstrations, often noisy and sometimes violent.

The Black Emergency Cultural Coalition was established in the autumn of 1968 and, over the next few months, launched a campaign against the Whitney Museum demanding greater black representation amongst works purchased, artists exhibited, membership of the selection and purchasing committees, and on the museum staff (Glueck, 1969b: 24). They began by picketing the museum but settled down to meaningful discussions which resulted in agreement over increasing representation of work by black artists.

In January 1969, a group calling itself the Art Workers' Coalition was established in New York and launched an attack on the policies of the Museum of Modern Art (MoMA) (Glueck, 1969a). The Coalition, whose membership was composed of artists, writers, film-makers, and critics, urged the MoMA to have 'more cultural relevance' for blacks and Puerto Ricans and submitted a thirteen-point proposal, the demands of which included 'the extension of

MoMA activities into ghetto communities, the formation of an artists' committee to arrange shows at the museum, free admission at all times, and the opening of a gallery for black artists' work' (Glueck, 1969a). They also spilled cans of blood in the galleries, and demanded that the MoMA close until the Vietnam War was over and sell $1 million worth of its collection, giving the proceeds to the poor (Alexander, 1979: 227).

On the 18th of January in the same year, the exhibition *Harlem on My Mind* opened at the Metropolitan Museum of Art. The exhibition consisted of photos, slides, and videos of Harlem, the black neighbourhood in upper Manhattan. While the exhibition proved to be very popular in some quarters, it also attracted much criticism and anger leading to demonstrations and acts of vandalism. Anger was aroused amongst blacks by the fact that it did not contain works of art by black artists and therefore showed 'a white man's view of Harlem'. In January 1969, a group of demonstrators picketed a preview and a black-tie cocktail and dinner party at the museum. On the same day several paintings, including a Rembrandt, were slightly damaged by vandals who scratched an 'H' on them, referring to Hoving, the director (Arnold, 1969: 1). Two weeks later, paintings were defaced, obscenities were scrawled on the wall of the museum, and a guard injured while attempting to stop further vandalism (Anon., 1969: 74).

African Americans and Puerto Ricans expressed their anger and frustration of white museums and other cultural institutions at a *Seminar for Neighborhood Museums* held at MUSE in Brooklyn in 1969. In the spring of 1971, American Association of Museums meetings in New York City were disrupted by protesters who presented a manifesto and fought for the microphone on the platform, calling for reform in museums and art galleries (Cameron, 1971: 18).

The events of 1967–71 marked a climax to a period of social unrest and militant action which had addressed wide-ranging concerns from anti-war sentiment to the failure of US–Indian treaties, and from the unrecognised value of the elderly to the cultural inequities of the art world. The passions and resentments that such protests released, reflected frustration over decades of lack of self-determination, misinterpretation, marginalisation and exclusion, but served to draw attention to people's grievances and the need to address their differing cultural needs. In the United States, the civil disturbances and the cultural revival movement focused attention on the cultural needs of ethnic communities and disadvantaged inner city residents. Changing demographics, such as industrial and commercial growth or decline, population shifts from rural to urban areas and vice versa, changes in ethnic profile caused by immigration, and the growth of tourism bringing influxes of visitors, have caused communities to re-examine their past and present experiences.

In the late 1960s and early 1970s, museum curators in the United States gradually began to recognise that the needs of inner-city residents and minority groups were not being met and so began the growth of community museums and a rethinking of the traditional museum role. It was generally felt that museums were not relating to the urban poor; that many cultural programmes offered by museums were merely continuing the 'cultural colonialism' of the past and doing little to make museums more accessible or relevant to them. Instead museums needed to play a more socially significant role and respond directly to issues of concern to the public (Cameron, 1971; Noble, 1971b; Robbins, 1971; Kinard, 1972). In the face of the demonstrations which had so disrupted university and college campuses, Kenneth Hopkins recommended fifteen steps to deal with confrontation; recommendations which, unfortunately, remain as necessary today, demonstrating how much progress must still be made in democratising museums (1970: 123–4). During the 1970s and 1980s, exhibitions which focused more closely upon social concerns began to be presented by a number of museums in the United States, particularly the newly developed community museums such as Anacostia, MUSE, and the Museum of the City of New York (Kinard 1985).

In 1971 the Museum of the City of New York began to introduce a series of community orientated projects to serve the needs of the local population: primarily black and Puerto Rican groups living in Harlem. The Museum of the City of New York and Anacostia Neighborhood Museum presented exhibitions dealing with topics of social concern in urban residential areas such as drug addiction and the problems of rats (Noble, 1971a; Kinard and Nighbert, 1972). Such issues, while not the typical subject matter of museums, were of great interest and concern to the residents of the inner-city neighbourhoods which these museums served. These new museums were recognised as being very effective in providing relevant exhibitions, events and educational activities. Furthermore, community involvement was increasingly seen as being crucial to the successful implementation of programmes of exhibitions and activities which better reflected the cultural composition of society and the issues of relevance to the communities in which the museums were situated. John Kinard (1985: 220), the former director of Anacostia Museum, commented that 'the destiny of the museum is the destiny of the community; their relationship is both symbiotic and catalytic'.

Such political and cultural revival by peoples who had suffered years of oppression, subjugation and exploitation was not, of course, limited to the USA; it reflected a growing world-wide trend which saw indigenous and minority peoples in many parts of the world forming political organisations to fight for the settlement of old treaties, the resolution of land rights issues, and equality of opportunity in all spheres of social and political life. The developments in American museums had repercussions throughout the international museum community and were part of a widespread change in attitude towards the role of the museum in relation to the community. However, the museum profession has continued to be dominated by white staff, and the perennial problem of western-trained anthropologists and historians studying and representing 'the Other' continues to be a major issue, attracting criticism from indigenous peoples and those from other ethnic groups who still feel isolated and excluded from the process of representation. An Aboriginal Australian member of the committee involved in the establishment of a community-based Aboriginal research unit at the University of Adelaide expressed this frustration saying: 'We are tired of being researched; we want to be in the research ourselves, to have a say in what needs to be studied' (cited in Gale, 1982: 130). The involvement of members of ethnic groups, as partners in the planning process, as advisors, and as staff members, has come to be one of the major issues facing the museum profession in recent years.

Since the 1970s, issues of cultural diversity and related matters have featured prominently on the programmes of numerous regional, national and international conferences attesting to the growing professional concern. *The Role of Anthropological Museums in National and International Education* was a multinational seminar held in Denmark in 1974. *Preserving Indigenous Cultures: A New Role for Museums* was a regional seminar held in Adelaide, Australia, in September 1978 which presented a series of perspectives concerning the current and potential role of museums in assisting in the preservation of the material culture and cultural traditions of peoples across the Pacific region. Participants were drawn from many cultures throughout the region and represented museum staff as well as many other professions.

In 1986, the British Museum in London hosted an international conference entitled *Making Exhibitions of Ourselves: The Limits of Objectivity in Representations of Other Cultures*. The American Association of Museums and the Canadian Museums Association have addressed these issues as major themes of their annual conferences over a number of years. In 1990, sixteen museum curators from Europe and North America attended the *Taonga Maori* conference in Wellington, New Zealand. The conference was organised and funded by the New Zealand Government, but initiated by Maori elders following the successful US tour of the *Te Maori* exhibition in 1984. Invitations were issued to a number of curators in major overseas museums inviting them to participate in a discussion about Maori beliefs concerning *taonga* (treasures) in overseas museum collections. Lectures and comments by Maori speakers forcefully conveyed the strength of Maori feelings concerning the care, display and ownership of Maori *taonga* and had a profound impact upon several of the participants. Issues associated with the disposition of the dead were addressed by archaeologists at the *First Intercongress on Archaeological Ethics and the Treatment of the Dead* in Vermillion, South Dakota, USA, in 1989.

From these conferences and meetings have come a number of publications: edited collections of conference papers which document the discussions and concerns within the profession and the development of new approaches to museology, stimulating greater dialogue and fuelling the drive for change. Most notable amongst these have been the twin volumes *Exhibiting Cultures* (Karp and Lavine, 1991) and *Museums and Communities* (Karp, Kreamer, and

Lavine, 1992) arising out of two conferences held at the International Center of the Smithsonian Institution in Washington, DC: *The Poetic and Politics of Representation* in 1988 and *Museums and Communities* in 1990. The Association of Art Museum Directors (AAMD) has addressed similar issues in relation to American art museums in two symposia held in 1990 and 1991, the proceedings of which were published in *Different Voices* (AAMD 1992). Dealing with related issues in the field of archaeology, a major series of publications entitled *One World Archaeology* arose out of the proceedings of the World Archaeological Congress in 1986 at the University of Southampton in England.

Also emanating from the activities of the World Archaeological Congress were two documents which provided the most progressive examples of professional policy guidelines concerning the treatment of human remains and which have been influential in museological policy development in several countries. The Vermillion Accord, a paper drafted by Professor Michael Day, called for 'mutual respect for the beliefs of indigenous peoples as well as the importance of science and education' and received the full support of all the anthropologists and indigenous peoples represented at the Intercongress in 1989 (Day, 1990: 15–16). The following year, the World Archaeological Congress adopted the First Code of Ethics, listing the principles and rules which should guide professional practice when dealing with the archaeological material of indigenous peoples (WAC, 1990: 24).

Significant changes in ideology and practices have resulted from the social and political pressures of recent decades. Cultural diversity has come to be an issue of great professional concern and many curators have attempted to address criticisms and instigate new practices, involving communities much more closely in the research and interpretation process and addressing issues of concern to the communities themselves. In some instances this has involved trying quite radical or innovative interpretive approaches with varying degrees of success. Many others have been slow to adapt and have continued to use the culturally exclusive practices of conventional museology, and so have continued to alienate themselves from ethnic communities and attract criticism and sometimes vocal demonstrations of dissatisfaction amongst those represented. The following chapters of this book examine contemporary museological practices which are designed to address these concerns and increase community involvement in the museum representation process, while maintaining responsibilities towards scholarship.

1

History revisited

'To look back and detect the errors and the limitation of a previous era is a step forward, but it does not make one resistant to the conventions of one's own time.'

(Nooter, 1991: 79)

Many of the criticisms that activists in the 1960s aimed at museums are as valid today as they were thirty years ago. Many museums persist in their failure to represent adequately the presence and contributions of peoples of minority cultures in social history, and so their histories remain untold in exhibition texts, and their images absent from the accompanying photographic material. This is particularly noticeable with regard to non-whites or people of colour, whose exclusion from photograph material is plain to see, but white ethnic groups suffer the same discrimination. Little recognition is given to the contributions of a wide range of cultures in the fields of science, technology, and the arts. Exhibitions of labour history have frequently focused upon the traditional industries in an area but failed to document those of immigrant communities, even those established for considerable lengths of time. Exhibitions of military history rarely show much evidence of the roles of black servicemen, and displays of subjects such as costume have tended to present an image of homogeneity, despite long histories of immigration.

Several approaches are being utilised to address more controversial topics in museum–community relations and the process of making representations in which both artists and curators are professionally engaged. Aspects of this trend can be seen in exhibitions which seek to rectify the biases of history by addressing the activities of colonial nations in their early (and more recent) interactions with indigenous peoples. This includes highlighting the historical aspects of cultural diversity and the history and implications of the slave trade.

The black presence in Britain

The history of black presence in Britain is well documented in texts such as *Staying Power – The History of Black People in Britain* by Peter Fryer; *Black Settlers in Britain 1555–1958* by Nigel File and Chris Power; and *Ayahs, Lascars and*

Princes, by Rosina Visram. These contradict the commonly held assumption that black immigration is a post-1945 phenomenon and provide ample evidence that there have been significant sizeable black communities in Britain for hundreds of years.

A series of articles in the *Museums Journal*, the publication of the Museums Association in Britain, highlighted the frustration that black people feel over the failure of museums and others in the heritage industry to adequately reflect black history in Britain (Mehmood, 1990: 27–30; Poovaya Smith, 1990: 34–5; Ramamurthy, 1990: 23; White, 1991: 16–17; Agyeman, 1993: 22–3). Lenford White noted that one of the founding principles of Merseyside Museum of Labour History was to present a history of the working classes, 'the forgotten masses', yet it failed to present the history of another forgotten people: the black community (White, 1991: 16). Julian Agyeman, noting the failure of heritage sites to acknowledge the presence of black soldiers in Britain during Roman times, commented that 'Heritage is a powerful tool. It can inculcate a sense of belonging. It can be used to include or exclude, to give accurate or false impressions. It can also be used, as it has been at Vindolanda and Housesteads and countless other sites, to deny, cover up and sanitise the personal and community histories of a sector of British society (Agyeman, 1993: 23).

The museum staff at the Geffrye Museum in London were conscious that the displays in the museum were reflecting only a narrow cultural perspective. Nine room displays dating from 1600 to 1939 showed the changes in design and technology which had influenced domestic interiors and played a part in the lives of the British middle classes. However, the displays did not show the influences and contributions of other cultures upon the homes and lives of the British people, nor did they contain material relating to the immigrant communities who have settled in the area.

In January 1988, in order to revise and improve the displays, texts, and education programme so that visitors would gain a broader perspective of the culturally diverse nature of the museum's displays and collections, two black historians were commissioned to work on the Geffrye Museum Black History Project. *Black Contribution to History*, published in July 1988 (Fraser and Visram, 1988), reported the results of this research and the recommendations of its authors. They pointed generally to areas of black contribution to British history: in employment; politics; language; dress; food; literature; design; and the visual and performing arts. They suggested ways in which the museum could place such contributions in a variety of contexts using the displays and teaching techniques. Various themes were proposed: beverages and social habits, centred around the kitchen setting; wood, used in furniture making, highlighting the effects of trade and exploitation; decorative motifs and the influences from other cultures. Also, suggestions were made for focusing on individual people to illustrate black and women's history, using the museum collections, local archives, and oral history techniques. In 1990, the museum presented a temporary exhibition *Putting on the Style – Setting up Home in the 1950s* which described the overt racism which had been experienced by black immigrants seeking lodgings in London at that time (MacDonald, 1990: 33). Since the report staff have been redisplaying parts of the exhibition and developing collaborative projects with ethnic communities in the area (Hemming, 1992).

National Trust properties often epitomise the British upper classes and show little indication of their multicultural heritage. Like the Geffrye Museum, collections which seem to be the epitome of white British upper-class culture, taste and history, can be utilised to draw out a wealth of cross-cultural connections relating to matters such as design, social trends, trading activities, and so forth. Guides to the properties rarely give any indication of the heritage of black people yet the histories of many of them are frequently incontrovertibly entangled with that of the black British population. Wealth derived directly or indirectly from the slave trade funded the building of numerous stately homes while many of them had black servants, yet such histories remain hidden.

Of particular note has been the failure to address the subject of slavery, an especially significant omission in cities such as London, Liverpool and Bristol, in whose history slavery played a significant role (Fryer, 1984: 65–6; Gifford, Brown and Bundey, 1989; Mehmood, 1990: 27–30, Agyeman, 1993: 22–3). Slavery is a harsh reality of the past which should not be ignored or diminished, and yet a subject of great sensitivity. It is an area in which the histories of blacks and whites are inextricably bound, yet it is an issue which is only infrequently focused upon in museum exhibitions or heritage sites. Consequently there are conflicting views about whether the issue should be highlighted and explored, or whether attention should be concentrated instead upon the contributions and achievements of blacks and issues of immediate concern today.

In Britain, the most significant example of slavery as the subject matter of an exhibition is in the displays in the Wilberforce House Museum in Hull. The first floor galleries, devoted to the subject of slavery, are divided into two sections: *The Slave Trade* and *Wilberforce and Abolition*. The museum combines a focus upon local history with an examination of slavery and abolition, acting in part as a memorial to William Wilberforce, one of the most prominent figures in the city's history. *The Slave Trade* section provides a fairly detailed and graphic description of the actions of slave traders and the conditions of slavery, emotively reinforced by sound recordings of an actor in the role of a slave giving chilling accounts of the transportation aboard ship on the Atlantic crossing. While applauding the extent of the coverage of slavery in contrast to the cities of London, Liverpool and Bristol, 'the real historical villains of the piece', Gabriel Gbadamosi reproached its largely uncritical focus on Wilberforce and the abolition movement (1990: 25). It is all too easy for exhibitions about abolition of slavery to promote white abolitionists as heroes and blacks slaves as helpless victims, and so underplay the achievements of blacks themselves in the fight against slavery.

Much of Britain's wealth was generated through colonial activities, including slavery or the products of slave labour. Some of Britain's major institutions and manor houses stand silent testament to this history, an aspect which is seen only subtly, if at all, and rarely spoken of in the interpretation of such buildings. The ports of London, Bristol and Liverpool played major roles in the slave trade and profited enormously from it. It has long been recognised that Bristol and Liverpool were largely built upon the proceeds of the slave trade; as a result of their slave trading activities, they grew to become major seaports during the eighteenth century. Nineteenth-century historians said of Bristol and Liverpool that the bricks of which the cities were built had been cemented with the blood of slaves (Nicholls and Taylor, 1881–2, III: 165; and Corry, 1825, II: 690; cited in Fryer, 1984: 33). Ramsay Muir in *A History of Liverpool* (1907) commented that 'beyond a doubt it was the slave trade which raised Liverpool from a struggling port to one of the richest and most prosperous trading centres in the world' (cited in Fryer, 1984: 34).

Despite the major role that slavery played in the development and prosperity of these cities, their museums have failed to address the issue of slavery. Ironically, there are undoubtedly portions of the collections of these museums which originated from families who prospered from the slave trade. Liverpool was one of the most active European ports in the slave trade and, during the latter part of the century, merchants in Liverpool were responsible for more slaving voyages than any other European port (NMGM, 1994: 2). As Tariq Mehmood remarked in 1990 after exploring the city's museums in search of some evidence of its 'inglorious past, . . . the Maritime Museum barely acknowledges the city's wounding and bleeding of Africa, Liverpool Museum does not even do that' (Mehmood, 1990: 27–30). In 1988, responding to the concerns and grievances expressed by members of the black community, Liverpool City Council set up an Inquiry team to examine race relations in the city. *Loosen the Shackles*, the report of the Liverpool 8 Inquiry chaired by Lord Gifford (QC), criticised Liverpool's Maritime Museum in which the inhumanity of slave ships was referred to but Liverpool's role in the slave trade was given only cursory treatment. 'Modern Liverpool, while being aware of this shameful history, appears to try hard to gloss it over, if not forget it' (Gifford *et al.*, 1989: 26). This criticism drew attention to the failings of the museum service in Liverpool and consultation with the community in Liverpool exposed the concerns of members of the black community that their history was not being shown. They proposed the idea for a temporary exhibition that would document the presence of blacks in Liverpool over the centuries.

Over the next two years members of museum staff worked closely with members of the local black community to present an exhibition, *Staying Power – Black Presence in Liverpool* (1991), which documented nearly three hundred years of history. A steering group, consisting mainly of black members, was drawn from staff of the National Museums and Galleries on Merseyside; the City Libraries, Arts and Cultural Industries Unit; and members of the Liverpool Anti-Racist and Community Arts Association. The issues of slavery and abolition were 'central to the exhibition, both physically and intellectually because slavery and colonisation are seen as key to understanding the Black Diaspora and the formation of black communities in Western Europe' (Knowles and Helmond, 1991: 16). Members of the steering group were anxious that the exhibition, the first to attempt to document Liverpool's black history, should present a positive image and so most of the exhibition concentrated on the experiences of black immigrants, the establishment and achievements of the black community in Liverpool, and highlighted notable black Liverpudlians. Lenford White, one of the members of the exhibition steering group, commented that he hoped that the exhibition would 'let the white viewer be informed of the true nature of the Black experience and the Black viewer be aware of his or her historical position in the scheme of things' (White, 1991: 17).

Since then, the National Museums and Galleries on Merseyside have maintained contact with the black community working with them on a number of projects (Southworth *et al.*, 1993: 19, 21). In 1992–3, Liverpool Museum displayed an exhibition *Expressions of Belief* from the Museum voor Volkenkunde in Rotterdam. This was an exhibition of art from Africa, Indonesia and the Pacific which had little in the way of interpretive text with it. The staff of Liverpool Museum supplemented the exhibition with text panels which described the functional roles of the objects and provided information about the societies from which they originated. They also added an introductory video and a study area where visitors could examine books and other materials. The museum staff contacted the Liverpool Anti-Racist Community Arts Association (LARCAA) to consult with them about other activities to coincide with the exhibition, and they proposed an exhibition which would explore aspects of African heritage in European arts through the examination of artworks influenced by African arts. The NMGM provided a seconded curator to work with LARCAA and assisted in raising funds. The exhibition, *Out of Africa*, was only on show in the museum for a short time prior to the closure of *Expressions of Belief*, but was shown in a number of other community venues and was re-displayed in September and October 1994 as part of Black History month. In 1993, the NMGM negotiated with the Charles Wootton Information Technology Centre, a local black community training organisation and established two work placements in the archaeology and ethnology department, followed by others in other sections of the museum service.

A significant development has been the opening of the Maritime Museum's new permanent gallery *Transatlantic Slavery: Against Human Dignity* which explores the subject of transatlantic slavery and its consequences, and looks particularly at Britain's role. It covers a period of 500 years from 1500, with particular emphasis upon the eighteenth and nineteenth centuries. The project was funded by a grant of £500,000 from the Peter Moores Foundation in order 'to increase public understanding of the experience of Black people in Britain and the modern world through an examination of the Atlantic slave trade and the African Diaspora' (NMGM, 1994: 1). Peter Moores, in his speech to launch the project in 1991, said 'I have been conscious for some time that the subject of slavery and the slave trade is taboo. This barrier between historical events and our acceptance of their significance for ourselves must be removed. The results of this removal will be of benefit to everyone and I am very proud to be able to assist in this important step' (cited in NMGM, 1994: 1).

The project was co-ordinated by staff of the National Museums and Galleries on Merseyside who worked with an advisory committee chaired by Lord Pitt of

Hampstead. Membership was drawn from a range of black organisations, including academics whose research field is relevant to the subject, plus representatives of the NMGM and the Peter Moores Foundation. The text was written by a team of eleven guest curators who were all academics or museum professionals working in Britain, the United States, Barbados and Nigeria. Each brought the benefits of their individual research expertise to the project; for example, Dr Mary Modupe Kolawole, of Obafemi Awolowo University in Ile-Ife, Nigeria, contributed material on the subject of African women's resistance to enslavement and traditions of oral literature.

The project curator, Alison Taubman, and Maritime History curator, Tony Tibbles, wrote an outline brief of the project in 1992 which was circulated to black organisations and groups for comment and discussion. A series of meetings was held, which enabled members of the public to voice their opinions about the project. In fact, much of the comment received has been beyond the focus of the gallery but has served to highlight community concerns and turn the attention of the museum management to other issues such as equal opportunities and employment policy within the museum service. Resulting from this, the NMGM has established a number of trainee placements and, in November 1993, an outreach worker was appointed to increase public awareness and use of the gallery, and develop a programme of activities.

The exhibition opened in the Maritime Museum in Albert Dock, Liverpool on 25 October 1994. It incorporates a range of display methods: full scale reconstructions and dioramas, objects and text, sound recordings, video and computer technology. As is typical of the subject, artefacts relating to the daily lives of slaves are in short supply. NMGM does, however, have a fine collection of West African objects which have been used in the exhibition to illustrate the richness of cultures which existed in Africa before the period of the European slave trade. Extensive collections of documents from Liverpool slavers and eighteenth-century newspapers from St Vincent, Barbados and Jamaica provide further documentation of Liverpool's involvement in the slave trade.

The developments in Liverpool go some way toward rectifying the historical vacuum which has existed in interpretation of Britain's involvement with the slave trade but, although the exhibition deals with the subject of slavery covering 500 years and three continents, black history remains an under-represented area of heritage interpretation and one that needs to be addressed in the local history galleries of many other cities and towns throughout Britain.

Bradford Art Galleries and Museums and Leicestershire Museums, Art Galleries and Records Service both benefited from the establishment of Section 11 posts: permanent staff positions established with funding from the Home Office to provide services for members of the community whose origins lay in the New Commonwealth and Pakistan. Although most Section 11 positions were established in the education sector, five museum posts were established before the Home Office ceased funding such posts in museums. In Bradford, an Assistant Keeper (Ethnic Collections) was appointed, and this marked the start of a lively and varied range of exhibitions and activities utilising and developing the

Museum's own ethnographic and Asian collections. The post-holder, Nima Poovaya Smith, has also forged a strong working relationship with the Victoria and Albert Museum which holds very large and important collections of works from the Asian sub-continent. This has resulted in temporary exhibitions which have brought items from the Victoria and Albert Museum's magnificent Asian collection to Bradford and enabled the large Asian population there finally to gain access to some of the riches of their cultural heritage. In Leicester, the appointment of an Assistant Keeper (Indian Arts and Crafts) enabled the museum to begin to build a relationship with local South Asian communities and address their lack of usage of the museum service (Nicholson, 1989). A new post of Teacher Leader (Multi-Cultural Education) also enabled them to address the need for education concerning cultural diversity within the broader context of a multi-ethnic society.

The neglect of the history and cultures of minority groups is now widely recognised within the profession and over the past ten years there has been a series of exhibitions which have addressed this. A focus of some of these exhibitions has been the examination of immigration in an effort to correct the widely held view that immigration to Britain is a recent phenomenon. Several temporary exhibitions have dealt with immigration in relation to the local area including *The Black Presence* (1986), *Black Presence in Nottingham* (Nottingham Castle Museum 1993), *The Peopling of London: 15000 Years of Settlement from Overseas* (Museum of London 1993–4).

In 1986, the Ethnic Minorities Unit of the Greater London Council presented *The Black Presence*, an exhibition of photographs and documents which it hoped would:

> bring to the public attention the lost history of black people in London. The voices of the 15,000 strong black community of the late eighteenth century have been completely silenced. Prominent and well-known black figures have been omitted or neglected in the history books our children read. Their cries resonate loudly and demand from us that we reclaim their experiences and hence our own heritage.
>
> (GLC, 1986: 5)

The exhibition described the reasons for the presence of blacks in Britain and demonstrated that this history led back to the third century AD when an African division of Roman soldiers was stationed near Carlisle in defence of Hadrian's Wall. Through documents, letters, photographs, and reproductions of paintings, it documented the history of blacks in Britain and their participation in all walks of life. It documented the contributions of blacks in the work force: domestic service, military forces, education, politics, finance and in sports and the arts and continuing evidence of black history in features of the environment such as street names (Black Boy Lane) and pub names (The Black Boy). The exhibition was well-received and well-used by schools. It helped to draw attention to the omission of black history in heritage interpretation and since that time several museums have addressed the issue of local black history.

Local history galleries are also tending to devote more space to reflecting the history and impact of cultural diversity, although there is still much to be improved in this area. The London Boroughs of Brent and Hackney have made significant contributions in this regard while Blackburn Museum and Art Gallery in Lancashire, has opened an Asian Gallery which explores the background of the local South Asian population.

Throughout the 1980s and 1990s, the subject of cultural diversity has attracted a great deal of attention within the heritage and museum professions in Britain. Obviously museums in major urban centres, where there were larger numbers of ethnic minority communities located, tended to be those that addressed the issue. Initially, the matter was generally regarded as being an issue of race relating to the interpretation of those who were visibly different, such as those of Afro-Caribbean or Asian ancestry. Since then, however, there has been greater recognition of the more subtle aspects of cultural diversity and the need to address also the heritages of white minority groups.

African American history in US museums

> Museums have historically documented and exhibited artifacts and art which exemplify the best in human endeavour. Many African Americans have rejected museums as places of personal reflection and historical affirmation, for they have witnessed the continued omission of their contributions and an absence of their expressions.
>
> (Clay, 1994: 1)

Not surprisingly, African American history receives most of its coverage from the many African American museums and cultural centres which have been established across the country (see Chapter 4), although increasingly it is receiving attention in mainstream museums, such as the Chicago Historical Society, the Virginia Museum of Fine Arts and the Smithsonian Institution. In recent years, a number of exhibitions in African American museums and in mainstream museums have explored the African American experience from the earliest days of their enforced immigration to the present. Most have focused upon highlighting the richness of African American culture and the contribution of African Americans to American and world cultures, although some addressed the problems of racism and the experiences of blacks in the post-Civil War period. Exhibitions such as *The Real McCoy: African American Invention and Innovation, 1619–1930*, *Black Wings: The American Black in Aviation*, and *African American Artists: Selections from the Evans-Tibbs Collection, 1880–1987*, have highlighted little-known and unappreciated aspects of African American skills and influence upon wider society; while *Climbing Jacob's Ladder: The Rise of the Black Churches in Eastern American Cities, 1740–1877* and *Field to Factory: African American Migration, 1915–1949* have told previously untold stories of African American histories.

As in Britain, slavery and racism do not feature as a central focus of many museum exhibitions in America. However, any exhibition which deals with a subject or individual in African American history prior to the American Civil War will encompass slavery in some form, and certainly in recent years there has been an increase in the number of exhibitions which deal overtly with such issues. Racial segregation following the abolition of slavery was dealt with frankly in an exhibition at the National Museum of American History. *Field to Factory: African American Migration 1915–1949* traced the history of the migration of African Americans in the early part of the twentieth century. The exhibition presented visitors with the emotional conflict which African Americans faced in trying to decide whether to remain in the south or move to the north. It highlighted the effects of racism upon the lives of African Americans in the south and the challenges that migrants faced in the north. At the end, visitors were confronted by two doors leading into the train station at the start of the journey north: one door was marked 'White' and the other 'Coloured'. Visitors had to decide through which door they would step.

In 1990–1, the Afro-American Historical and Cultural Museum in Philadelphia presented the exhibition *Let This Be Your Home: The African American Migration to Philadelphia, 1900–1940* which explored the living and working conditions of blacks in the southern states, their journeys north, and arrival and new lives in Philadelphia. Illustrating the bigotry blacks faced, was a sign entitled 'Colored Waiting Room' and nearby, a Ku Klux Klan robe. Through its educational programmes, the museum has examined the Underground Railroad Movement, which organised the escape of slaves from the South to the Northern states and Canada, and featured major figures in the movement, such as Harriett Tubman and Frederick Douglass.

Dealing more explicitly with slavery were two recent exhibitions. The political context and debate surrounding slavery were discussed in the Chicago Historical Society's exhibition *A House Divided: America in the Age of Lincoln*, a Civil War exhibition which explored the issue of slavery as a central issue of the war. *Before Freedom Came: African American Life in the Antebellum South, 1790–1865* at the Museum of the Confederacy, in Richmond, Virginia explored the lives of slaves and their resilience to the dehumanising experiences of the slavery system. Focusing upon the working and domestic lives of the slaves themselves, it highlighted the richness of the lives they were able to create for themselves in the face of hardship and brutality. It included 250 artefacts of clothing, furniture, toys and quilts made by slaves, and artefacts which were used in working life on the plantations.

The lives of slaves and freed slaves are now the subject of a variety of programmes in Colonial Williamsburg, Virginia, the preserved and restored site of the eighteenth-century town of Williamsburg. A variety of interpretive methods are employed to interpret the history of Williamsburg in the 1770s: historical interpreters or guides; costumed character interpreters who role-play in first person; and skilled craftspeople who work and interpret in third person, producing the artefacts or providing the services of the appropriate eighteenth-century tradesmen. Colonial Williamsburg tries to provide authentic historical interpretation, yet the limited presence of black interpreters creates a quite inaccurate picture of the black presence in Williamsburg in 1770: during the eighteenth century, half of the population of Williamsburg was black, both slaves and free. For many years the subject of slavery was avoided in the interpretation of the site, to the frustration of some and the relief of others: efforts to interpret the lives of slaves had proved fraught with difficulties. However, Colonial Williamsburg has extended its interpretive programmes in recent years, adding black interpreters to what was previously an unrepresentative, mostly white interpretive staff, and black costumed interpreters now play the characters of slaves and free blacks, many of whom worked as tradespeople in the city.

Throughout its history as an interpretive site, the Colonial Williamsburg Foundation has employed a small number of black interpreters, and others have worked as volunteers; however, from the early 1960s until 1979, the subject of slavery was addressed through the use of sound recorded texts and publications but was omitted from the interpretive programme. In 1979, black actors were hired to write scripts and role-play slave characters: these began as theatrical monologues but later developed into first- and third-person character interpretations (Ellis, 1990). Initially this was done completely in first person, but the actors found the experience demoralising, feeling that the characters that they portrayed were being used to confirm the prejudices of visitors. They began introducing the characters in third person, role-playing them in first person, and then breaking out of role to discuss the issues with the audience. Since that time, various programmes have been introduced which interpret black history, in each case being valuable educational activities rather than merely entertaining. These include musical events, demonstrating the importance of music in reinforcing traditional values and preserving cultural heritage, and *The Other Half Tour*, which covers West Africa, the middle passage, and the lifestyles of slaves and free blacks in colonial times.

The Foundation now has a Department of African-American Programs including fifteen black interpreters and has specialists in African-American history on staff to advise about various aspects of exhibition and interpretation throughout the Foundation's sites. In addition to the main Historic Area, there are three museums and Carter's Grove, a mansion house, plantation, and reconstruction of the slave quarter. This latter area has recently become the focus of a new interpretive programme in which black staff communicate to visitors something of the lives of the slaves who lived and worked at Carter's Grove. While the composition of interpretive staff is still not representative of that of the population in the 1770s, efforts have been made to tell the stories of the slaves who played such a significant role in the history of Williamsburg and the goal is to ensure that in coming years, the teaching of black history is incorporated into all areas of the Foundation's interpretive programmes.

Racism in the modern era is the subject of the new National Civil Rights Museum in Memphis, Tennessee, located at the site of the assassination of Dr Martin Luther King in 1968. The project was initiated by a group of Memphis residents and received strong political and financial support from state and local government. The museum was designed to be strongly educational and, while it examined the constitutional issues which the civil rights movement fought to change, it contained a series of narratives designed to highlight and interpret specific events. The format of the exhibition was designed to convey the emotions and conditions of the events and included audio recordings, documentary footage, photographs, life-sized models, as well as artefacts and reproductions. Through these methods, Gerard L. Eisterhold, the exhibit designer, allowed 'the emotional intensity of the movement to speak through the exhibits' and succeeded in effecting the conversion of 'a site of a national tragedy into a culturally significant site' (Eisterhold, 1992: 52–3).

Just as slavery and black history have not been adequately addressed, so the interaction of colonisers and colonised has remained largely ignored in museum exhibitions. Ethnographic displays have tended to focus upon the material culture of indigenous peoples, but have largely failed to discuss the actions and attitudes of the colonialist era. Likewise, the issues surrounding the acquisition and ownership of cultural material are rarely discussed in museum exhibitions, yet the attitudes and actions of the colonialists and the deleterious effects of expansionist policies are a part of the history of the objects in museum collections and also part of the history of both colonised and coloniser.

However, in recent years, attempts have been made to interpret those periods of history in a more honest light, analysing the motives of colonisers and the effects of their actions upon the indigenous population. The historical context of the collections as collections, rather than as material culture, has become a subject of interest to museum curators and has been explored in a number of exhibitions such as *Images of Africa* at the Museum of Mankind in London, England; *Into the Heart of Africa* at the Royal Ontario Museum in Toronto, Canada; and through an interactive video programme in Gallery 33 of Birmingham Museum and Art Gallery in England. These endeavour to draw attention to the issues surrounding the history of the collections: their acquisition, their place in museums, their status. Such discussions help to portray more accurately the nature of colonialism and raise questions concerning ownership and power. Who collected the objects and why? Why were only certain types of objects collected? Why was the collector there? What effect did their actions have on the local people? What does this tell us about the attitudes and values of the times? What purpose did the objects serve in their society? What purpose do the objects serve now? How might descendants of the original owners feel about their presence in a museum? Such questions about the objects can be used to stimulate discussion of historical and contemporary issues of local and global relevance: attitudes and values, prejudice, racism, political repression, poverty, wealth and repatriation.

As exhibitions become more contemporary in outlook, and make more attempt to address issues of political intent, racial bias, and inaccurate historical representation, they inevitably become more controversial. By their nature, these exhibitions have challenged popular beliefs, national ideologies, and the images of some national heroes: consequently they have not always been well received by critics and the public. This may draw some unexpected public responses to exhibitions which were intended to be sensitive, innovative and inclusive,

25

even when efforts have been made to incorporate the views of community groups. The most significant example of this was the reaction to the exhibition *Into the Heart of Africa* which led to a court injunction against demonstrators, cancellation of the exhibition's tour to other venues, intimidation and threats to the guest curator, and ultimately her resignation from her post as a university lecturer.

In 1989, the Royal Ontario Museum (ROM) in Toronto opened the exhibition, which was scheduled to tour to four other venues in Canada and the United States over the following two years. The exhibition attempted to combine a presentation of African art with an examination of the colonial history of Canadians in Africa. The publicity leaflet described it as a celebration of 'the rich cultural heritage of African religious, social and economic life', and indeed the exhibition did set out to show the beauty, richness and diversity of the artefacts in the ROM's collections. However, due to the fragmentary nature of the collection and its age, most of which dates from 1875 to 1925, it was impossible to provide a detailed study of any particular group or area, or address issues such as urbanisation and industrialisation in contemporary Africa. Jeanne Cannizzo, curator of the exhibition, therefore decided to utilise the nature and period of the collections to determine the themes of the exhibition. It was her intention to address the effects of colonialism upon African cultures by providing 'a critical examination of the role played by Canadians in the European colonisation of Africa in the nineteenth century', and an exhibition which would be 'a reflexive analysis of the nature of the museum itself and an examination of the history of its African collection' (Cannizzo, 1990b).

The layout of the exhibition was designed to take visitors on a journey through time, beginning with Victorian Ontario, and leading through the Military Hall, the Missionary Room, and into the Africa Room (Cannizzo, 1989; 1991). It was Cannizzo's intention that the exhibition should examine the attitudes of the Canadian missionaries and military personnel who were involved in British endeavours to colonise and convert the African nations, 'a seldom-remembered aspect of Canadian history', and so illustrate the ignorance and 'cultural arrogance' of the white missionaries who failed to recognise the complexity and sophistication of the African peoples whom they encountered. Cannizzo used period photographs and quotations to convey 'the European view of the continent at that time' (Cannizzo, 1991: 152). In the text, inverted commas were used to identify phrases such as 'barbarous' and 'savage customs' as quotations from nineteenth-century sources. It was a sophisticated message which was not, apparently, successfully communicated to many of the visitors. Despite the punctuation, it soon became clear that many of those who criticised the exhibition appeared to be unable to distinguish between the views of the museum itself, and the views of the nineteenth-century colonialists being conveyed in the photographs and texts. Indeed, the use of inverted commas in this context is highly ambiguous: the incorporation of a quotation does not exclusively indicate opposition to the quoted views, but can indicate entirely the opposite. It should, perhaps, not be surprising then that this subtle message was not understood by those whose experiences of twentieth-century racism may have led them to expect little more than nineteenth-century views from a predominantly white institution with little or no record of liaison with the black community.

The second half of the exhibition examined African artistry and the complexities of world views, utilising more conventional museological methods to display the fine artefacts from the museum's African collection. Initially, the exhibition attracted praise from critics and the media, with descriptions such as 'fascinating African exhibit' and 'a revealing journey through space and time'. However, four months after it had opened, a group of black protesters began to organise weekly demonstrations outside the museum. They complained that artefacts, seen as the souvenirs of missionaries and soldiers, were to them 'the spoils of war' (cited in Todd, 1990), 'art objects that have been stolen from the African people' (Asante, 1990). They also complained that the exhibition did not tell their story, a concept that it was in no way intended to address; neither was it intended to provide a definitive interpretation of nineteenth-century African art and culture. The exhibition was primarily an examination of the attitudes, values and motives of white Canadians in Africa between 1875 and 1925.

The black Canadian protesters established the Coalition for the Truth about Africa, an umbrella group for a number of local black organisations. They produced a leaflet criticising the exhibition, stating that it 'glorifies and rationalizes Canada's Racist, Colonialist past of PLUNDER, RAPE AND RACIST ECONOMIC AND CULTURAL EXPLOITATION OF AFRICAN NATIONS' *(sic)* (CTA, nd). Weekend visitors to the exhibition had to face the banners and chanting of pickets outside the museum. The ROM took out an injunction to restrict the demonstrators from entering the immediate vicinity of the museum. Demonstrations outside the museum became violent as demonstrators and police clashed. Extensive and detailed press coverage gave the impression that the demonstrations were larger and more frequent than they were. The Toronto Board of Education School Programs Committee deemed the exhibition unsuitable for pupils at primary and junior secondary levels. The venues to which it was due to tour in other parts of Canada and in the United States cancelled their bookings. Whereas Cannizzo had set out to expose the racist attitudes prevalent amongst nineteenth-century colonialists, *Into the Heart of Africa* was, as Robert Fulford wrote in *Rotunda*, 'accused of the crime it depicted' (Fulford 1991: 21).

Sometimes such adverse reactions to an exhibition may be caused by underlying political intentions on the part of the protesters. It is strongly felt by many who were close observers of the incidents, or actively involved with *Into the Heart of Africa*, that the exhibition was used as a political platform by black activists, just as three years earlier, *The Spirit Sings* was unashamedly used by the Lubicon Lake Cree to attract international attention to their grievances. One of the complaints about the planning of *Into the Heart of Africa* was that there had been little consultation with the black community in Toronto, yet Cannizzo and other ROM staff insist that this was not so, and that dialogue took place with several groups. It has been suggested that local community politics were such that certain individuals or groups, resentful that they had not been consulted, provoked the reactions which followed for their own political ends. Cannizzo (1991: 157) considers valid the suggestion that 'the political context partially determined the demonstrators' reactions to the exhibition', referring to the current tensions between police and the black community in Toronto following the shooting of a young black.

Although some reviewers have been critical of the exhibition (Asante 1990; Crean, 1990; Drainie, 1991), most have supported Cannizzo (Cannon-Brookes, 1990; Hume, 1990; Lucs, 1990; Fulford, 1991; Ottenberg, 1991). They, and other observers, have offered a variety of explanations for the controversy: inappropriate publicity material issued by the ROM; the failure of the demonstrators to understand the ironies of the exhibition's text and imagery; failure to view the show at all; deliberate manipulation of the situation by black protesters. A black professor of African history has also expressed the view that the protesters, many of whom were 'involved in a new black identity movement', wanted a quite different type of exhibition which 'presents a glorified view of African history' (cited in Cannizzo, 1991: 159).

Da Breo, however, questions the extent of the consultative process and suggests that 'the ROM was not really seeking assistance or wanting input' but was looking only for 'approval and support' and that discussions with focus groups took place after the exhibition was basically complete (Da Breo, 1989/90: 33). Her explanation for the response of the black community suggests that it was the history of the collection itself and the absence of any prior relationship between the museum and the black Toronto community which resulted in the hostility towards the exhibition. The ROM's African collection had virtually never been seen by anyone other than staff and researchers, and the history of its acquisition, which was inextricably entwined with the history of colonial appropriation and the slave trade, caused its presentation in an exhibition about cultural imperialism to be seen as a further example of white imperialism in which white curators were once again interpreting black art history from a white perspective. When Dr John McNeill, Acting Director of the ROM, published a letter in March 1991, he acknowledged that the context of the exhibition could have been clearer. The ROM, he said, had 'missed an opportunity to bond with an important part of the community' and that 'some well-meaning people were hurt and angered'. He particularly noted the comment of a young protester who said 'All my life I've been looking for my roots; I came here looking for them and you've shown me nothing' (McNeill, 1991).

There is no doubt that the themes of the exhibition were culturally and academically ambitious and in a different social and museological context this exhibition might well have been successful. However, given the history of the museum–community relations (or lack of them) in Toronto, it proved to be too much, too soon. Yet, if the reproach of the missionary and military activities had been less subtle, more outspoken, it would perhaps have communicated a stronger historical message which would have proven more satisfactory to those who feel that their history has been silenced for long enough. Freedman, (1990: 40–1), while applauding the curator for including colonial perspectives, claims that the exhibition failed to provide adequate commentary on the nature of the conquest of Africa and left several crucial questions unanswered.

> What about this conquest? Was it brutal, violent, shameful? Or should we, when passing the soldiers' suits and the prizes the soldiers stole from sovereign African kingdoms, swell with pride and admiration for men who braved great distances and terrible dangers to subdue fierce natives? The exhibition is strangely silent here, as if there were no moral or political issues involved. As if nations did not take sides in war and conquest. As if there were no blame or judgement or responsibility in history. The exhibition simply records this conquest for posterity and displays the booty behind glass cases.

Such subject matter leaves the curator treading a tightrope between offending one sector of the community or another: for no matter how warranted a revisionist approach may be, it almost certainly cannot fail to offend those who prefer the nostalgia and glories of heroic myths to the realities of the past.

In the United States, two major art exhibitions have addressed the issues of politics and ideologies in cultural representation. In *Facing History: The Black Image in American Art, 1710–1940*, curator Guy C. McElroy explored ways in which American art has reflected changing attitudes towards African Americans and helped to reinforce stereotypes. *The West as America: Reinterpreting Images of the Frontier, 1820–1920*, addressed similar concepts with regard to portrayals of Native Americans and white American Western expansion. When William Truettner, curator of painting and sculpture at the National Museum of American Art in Washington DC, presented this exhibition he expected that it might attract some criticism, but little did he think that it would cause such a public uproar that the matter would be taken up in the US Congress.

Truettner presented revisionist interpretations of images of the American West which illustrated the political ideologies and the religious beliefs with which nineteenth-century Americans justified their continued expansion westward and their treatment of the Native American population. Through a series of themes, Truettner demonstrated how the political and social needs of white Americans prejudiced the treatment of the native population. His analysis of individual paintings included comparison of a portrayal of Kit Carson with depictions of Christ (Truettner, 1991: 326–8), and likened an image of Daniel Boone leading settlers through the Cumberland Pass to 'a latter-day Moses en route to the Promised Land' (ibid.: 114).

By re-examining the context and underlying purpose behind the art of the American West, the exhibition and the accompanying book (Truettner, 1991) challenged the romantic and glorified images of the American Western expansionist movement of the nineteenth century and the belief in Manifest Destiny; notions which lie behind many of the paintings. It also provided a vivid illustration of the ways in which images of Native Americans changed over time, reflecting the shifting attitudes towards the indigenous population as they were viewed as the Noble Savage living in harmony with nature, ruthless savages attacking innocent settlers, heathens ripe for conversion to Christianity, a doomed and vanishing race, or passive and dependent reservation Indians. Opposition to the exhibition came, not from the Native American population, but from white Americans for whom the exhibition challenged popular beliefs in the legitimacy and heroics of the settlement of the West and questioned the ideological motives of some of America's most popular painters. Truettner's interpretations proved injurious to the American sense of pride in its past and the exhibition became the focus of outrage by critics, the public, the media and by members of the US Senate.

Comments by hundreds of upset and angry visitors eventually filled three comments books during the sixteen weeks of its showing. Historian and former Librarian of Congress, Daniel J. Boorstin, described it as 'a perverse, historically inaccurate, destructive exhibit. No credit to the Smithsonian'. The matter was raised at an appropriations hearing when two senators accused the Smithsonian Institution of having a political agenda and called for cuts in the Smithsonian's public funding. Media coverage (Foner and Wiener, 1991; Masters, 1991; Ringle, 1991) ranged from supportive reviews which described it as the 'True West: A realist's guide to America's frontier' (Bell, 1991: 70) to charges of zealous political correctness and the accusation that the exhibition 'effectively trashes not only the integrity of the art it presents but most of our national history as well, reducing the saga of America's Western pioneers to little more than victimization, disillusion and environmental rape' (Ringle, 1991: G4).

The strength of this reaction vividly demonstrates the failure of many Americans to realise or, at least acknowledge, the truth concerning Western expansionism. Elizabeth Broun, Director of the National Museum of American Art, felt that the 'Desert Storm fever [which] was sweeping the country' at that time was a strong contributory factor in the angry and outraged reaction which the exhibition provoked in many white Americans. She also suggested that a Westward shift in American political power was a factor in creating tension in a 'a pluralistic society dominated . . . by a white establishment in the East' and proposed that 'the exhibit invites a comparison of the historical events of the nineteenth century and changes happening in our society today' (1991: 78).

The killing time – Europeans in Australia

In the Aboriginal Gallery of the Australian Museum, the section on European settlement of Australia is entitled *Killing Time*, a reference to the Warlpiri term for the early period when

> the best land was taken over by Europeans for cattle and sheep and the Aborigines had only the desert land to live in. In 1928, a severe drought forced the Warlpiri people from the desert. Some tried to get food and water on the better land and fights broke out. A large group of Warlpiri people were killed by Europeans.

In the exhibition *The Aboriginal Peoples of Tasmania* which opened at the Tasmanian Museum and Art Gallery in 1981, the curator, Julia Clarke, utilised stronger language than had normally been seen in exhibitions about Aboriginal–European relations. The section dealing with the arrival of the Europeans in Tasmania was titled *Invasion and War*, and a later section, titled *Heroes of the Resistance* gave details of Aboriginal peoples who had fought against dispossession by the Europeans. In *Invasion and War*, Clarke sought to explain the differences in concepts regarding ownership of land and property which, from the start of European settlement, caused problems and resulted in the wars that followed. The text reads:

> Aboriginal society is based on sharing and exchange. In return for allowing Europeans to share their resources, Aboriginal people expected dogs, tea, sugar, blankets and other European goods. This expectation became more insistent as Europeans hunted out traditional foods.
>
> European society is not based on this kind of sharing but on private ownership of property: Europeans did not understand what was expected of them. They saw the Aboriginal people as beggars and thieves and abused them when they came to claim what they believed they were owed.

The terminology used caused some controversy at the time, a reaction which reflects the general lack of awareness amongst many white Australians of the reality of European invasion of Aboriginal lands, or perhaps an unwillingness to accept it.

The Migration Museum in Adelaide also refers to the invasion of Aboriginal lands and addresses the clash of cultures which occurred when Europeans began to settle in Australia. In *The Immigration Story*, the text refers to the acts of atrocity which were perpetrated against the Aboriginal people by settlers – poisoning of water wells and flour, hunting and shooting by raiding parties – and the genocide of whole communities, such as the Kaurna who used to inhabit the area where Adelaide now stands. It refers also to the devastating effects of introduced diseases, such as smallpox, and the destructive impact of relocation upon a culture so completely integrated with the land. European efforts to Christianise and civilise the Aboriginal population resulted from a failure to recognise the validity of Aboriginal culture and religious beliefs, and often resulted in children being removed from their families to be brought up in white society. Those who resisted were treated like criminals. These two approaches are graphically contrasted in two nineteenth-century photographs. A photograph shows a group of Aboriginal Australians in European clothing seated with two missionaries, while below, a large panel shows a line of Aboriginal men shackled together.

Brambuk, the Aboriginal Living Cultural Centre in Victoria state, Australia, has also highlighted the atrocities committed against Aboriginal peoples during the colonial era. The exhibition includes details of the massive population decline resulting from disease and violence during the first twenty years of European settlement, and quotations from the letters and journals of white settlers in the nineteenth century describing the murder of Aboriginal people. These are presented on wooden poles erected in a grouping to resemble trees in a forest. The simple white text panels each record an excerpt from a journal or book written

Figure 1.1   The tragic truth: in *The Immigration Story* at the Migration Museum in Adelaide, Australia the effects of European colonisation are graphically portrayed in these nineteenth-century photographs. Europeans tried to Christianise and civilise the Aboriginal population; those who resisted were treated like animals.

Source: M. Simpson, July 1993, with permission of the Migration Museum, Adelaide, South Australia

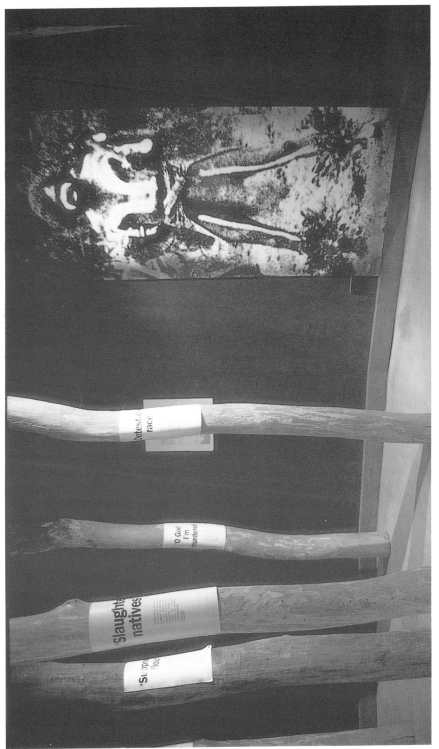

Figure 1.2 Brambuk Living Cultural Centre, Hall's Gap, Victoria, Australia. Many European settlers treated Aboriginal people like animals and thousands were poisoned or hunted down and shot. This display presents excerpts from the diaries and letters of nineteenth-century settlers which tell of these atrocities.

Source: Photo by M. Simpson, July 1993.

33

between 1836 and 1843, describing the brutal mistreatment or killing of Aboriginal peoples by white settlers, who regarded them as little more than savages.

From the journal of Neil Black, 9 December 1839, there is a telling comment concerning the appropriation of land: 'the best way to procure a run [a tract of land] . . . is to go outside and take up a new run; provided the conscience of the party is sufficiently seared to enable him without remorse to slaughter natives left and right'. Another describes the suspected poisoning of a group of Aboriginal people by a white settler:

> Mr Robinson . . . had sent away into the bush to some natives . . . a quantity of what was supposed to be flour. Of this they partook, and were immediately seized with burning pains in the stomach, vomiting . . . and on the following morning 3 men, 3 women, and three children were dead. I also find that a few months ago Mr Robinson received from Port Fairy two pounds of arsenic.
>
> (Watton to Robinson, 10 December 1842. P. Corris,
> *Aborigines and Europeans in Western Victoria*)

A panel entitled 'The Killing Times' describes how the population was decimated by 'killing, disease, and starvation. . . . Of an estimated 28,000 Koories in this region, approximately 25,000 died during the first twenty years of white settlement.' Such stark and haunting reminders of historical events are not often seen in exhibitions but these, and other aspects of colonialism, need to be explored in order to understand the political and cultural views of indigenous peoples in the post-colonial era.

2

The controversy continues

'Even though museums may aim to be cross-cultural in scope and to challenge ethnocentrism, they are also arenas in which one culture displays
another. The power to display another, as 'other', is considerable.'

(Grimes, 1990: 239)

Exhibitions concerning traditional or tribal societies have frequently been
criticised for their failure to show them as dynamic, living cultures. Rather, they
portray them as they were seen in the past, thereby giving the impression either
that the cultures had indeed vanished, as many Europeans in the late nineteenth
century had believed they would, or that their lifestyles persist, unaltered, in the
manner of their nineteenth-century ancestors.

This problem has arisen in part due to the nature of the collections and in part
due to the methods of display. The nature of the collections reflects the attraction and fascination that unfamiliar artefacts held for collectors and their desire
to gather material representative of the cultures they encountered. Within the
museum, it was formerly the objective of the curators to try to represent a
culture in its pure form with an emphasis upon traditional values and styles,
and authentic artefacts and practices. Displays tended to exclude evidence of
western influences and modern accoutrements and so perpetuated an image
of unchanging societies. Due to the predominantly historical nature of many
ethnographic collections, ethnographic material must be clearly placed in its
historical context to avoid creating an inaccurate impression of contemporary
cultures. This does not mean that it should only be shown in dioramas or environmental reconstructions, but rather that the historical context needs to be
stated, either in the object labels, or in a clearly defined statement of the exhibition's focus. By extension, such exhibitions also commonly failed to address
contemporary issues, particularly the problems facing many traditional peoples
today: problems which might threaten the continuation of the traditional culture or even the survival of the people. Instead they portrayed a romantic and
exotic, often nostalgic, image of small-scale societies which, superficially at
least, seemed to live in harmony with nature.

Hidden Peoples of the Amazon, an exhibition presented in the Museum of
Mankind (1985–6), was criticised for such failings by Amazonian Indians and

by Survival International (now known as Indigenous Survival International). The exhibition was described as being about the life and culture of the Indian peoples of the South American tropical rainforest but was felt by critics to give a totally inaccurate picture. They particularly noted historical inaccuracies and failure to address adequately the crisis being faced by contemporary Amazonian Indians: deforestation and land clearance, intimidation and genocide (Bourne, 1985: 380–1; Harris and Gow, 1985: 1–2; Jones, 1987: 103–10; Moser, 1986: 26).

The exhibition was constructed in two galleries divided into three main sections. In addition to an area in which artefacts were exhibited in showcases, the exhibition included two visually dramatic and atmospheric installations: a forest walk beneath a canopy of fabric 'foliage' and past a canoe drawn up on the river bank, and a walkway through a Tukano communal house or *maloka*. Interspersed throughout these main elements were a number of smaller dioramas and open display areas, large photographic reproductions and a slide projection area. The first room described the environment, lifestyles, festivals and warfare, while the second room focused upon the Tukano Indians and comprised the reconstruction of the *maloka*, in which artefacts were exhibited in their everyday context.

Richard Bourne, of Survival International, described the exhibition as presenting a 'bland' and 'pretty' picture which failed to inform visitors of the true situation confronting these people: threatened by extinction through illness, and from the impact of technical progress in the rest of the country which has led to the destruction of the rainforest and the ecology of the environment, and even genocide. As visitors left the *maloka* they passed through a small contemporary section consisting primarily of photographs and some text, which hinted at cultural influences affecting the Amazonian Indians. The contrast between this small space and the much larger exhibit areas was stark, accentuated by the low lighting and dramatic reconstructions of the main galleries. Consequently the brightly lit, clinical presentation of the contemporary section failed to attract the attention of many visitors. The central image in the final section was of a Panare Indian on a motorbike, an image which Survival International claimed failed to communicate the plight which threatened most of the tribal peoples in the area, as the Panare, unlike other groups, had adapted well to industrialised society. Survival International complained that 'to give visitors this, rather frivolous, image as a parting shot renders a grave disservice to the public' (cited in Houtman, 1985: 3).

Gustaaf Houtman, writing in *Anthropology Today*, remarked that, to the museum, Survival International's attack upon the Amazonian exhibition was 'an unexpected intrusion on its territory which is not a routine occurrence with exhibitions on other areas'. While noting that Survival International's role had changed 'from protector to broker for the native Indian issue', he nevertheless attributed their stance in part to a decreased dependency upon academic anthropologists and greater accountability to the native Indians and to the public (1985: 2–4). He noted that the increase in fieldwork in industrialised societies would mean that anthropologists would be unable to avoid becoming accountable to those studied. Anthropologists might, he suggested, have 'to focus on issues demanded by these communities, and present these in a language that community understands and approves' (ibid.: 4). It is precisely this process which has wrought such changes within academic anthropology and museology, extending the accountability of anthropologists and museums to indigenous and minority groups in western countries and the rest of the world. Contemporary social and political issues, such as those raised by Survival International, should be included in such an exhibition in order to inform people of the conflicting demands upon the resources of the environment between technological societies and tribal peoples. As Bourne asked, 'shouldn't an exhibition about these threatened tribal peoples speak up much more vigorously on their behalf?' (Bourne, 1985: 380).

In 1990, the Mexican Fine Arts Center Museum in Chicago presented an exhibition entitled *Vestido Con El Sol: Traditional Textiles From Mexico – Guatemala – Panama*, which displayed the richness and beauty of the colourful and beautifully patterned textiles produced by the indigenous peoples of these countries. However, in a catalogue to accompany the exhibition, an essay by Maricela Garcia Vargas described the continuing political repression and genocide of the Mayan minority population of Guatemala. Introducing this essay, Vargas stated that 'to do an exhibit on textiles and not deal with the political reality of the killing of some of the indigenous groups that produce these beautiful works of art would be irresponsible on the Museum's part' (Vargas, 1990: 16).

Inaction can be interpreted as a political stance; therefore museums which attempt to remain objective by refusing to address political issues might be seen to be condoning the very actions they seek to avoid addressing. Des Griffin, Director of the Australian Museum in Sydney supports this view: 'Some museum management and museum people seem to think that it is possible for a museum to be non-political, to be objective. Nothing could be further from the truth. It cannot be claimed that a museum in Australia which does not show the conflicts between Aboriginal peoples and Europeans is non-political. The fact that such subjects are absent is itself a political statement. All decisions made by museums as to what they say or don't say, show or don't show, are political' (Griffin, 1993: 3).

Museums attempting to remain objective are, however, in danger of their actions being interpreted as bias. *Buddhism: Art and Faith*, an exhibition at the British Museum (1985) and *The Sacred Art of Tibet* at the Royal Academy (1992) both included material relating to Tibet; but in both instances material was missing from the display due to disagreement about the manner in which Tibet–Chinese relations were to be explained. The Tibetan Liberation Organisation, which was to have lent objects, wished to have a notice displayed explaining the political situation surrounding the invasion and occupation of Tibet by the Chinese. These requests were refused with curatorial assertions that the museums must remain objective and not become involved in the politics of the situation, a decision which resulted in the loss of the material.

37

In this respect, government-funded museums may be in a more difficult position than independents. The stance taken by the curatorial staff of the British Museum and the Royal Academy was justified on the grounds of retaining political objectivity; however, such an action could be interpreted as bias in favour of the Chinese regime. On the other hand, a pro-Tibetan stance might have been seen as an anti-China statement by a government body and thus caused major political difficulties at a time when the British government did not wish to antagonise an important trade partner such as the Chinese government: a visit to London by the exiled Dalai Lama of Tibet was allowed only on condition that he made no statements about the political situation in Tibet. However, a small notice explaining the situation from the points of view of both the Chinese and the Tibetans would surely have provided a much more objective picture than that conveyed by total silence about the matter. Furthermore, it is not too difficult to communicate the basic facts while maintaining an impartial stance: the situation in Tibet was succinctly explained in the Ethnography Gallery of Brighton Museum:

> In the 20th century, Tibet has undergone two invasions . . . the first by the British . . . 1903–4. From 1911–50 the country was virtually independent. The second invasion was from the Chinese People's Republic which, together with the 1958 suppression of the Tibetans, . . . thoroughly destroyed the old Tibetan Buddhist culture. Tibet is currently a Special Territory of the Chinese People's Republic.

As pressures continue to grow from an increasingly culturally diverse society and from indigenous groups around the world, changing social values have markedly influenced curatorial practice. Ethnographic exhibitions now focus more frequently upon present-day peoples and there have been a number which are specifically designed to counteract the view that cultures have died out or remained unchanged. *I am Here: Two Thousand Years of Southwest Indian Art and Culture* was an exhibition presented by the Museum of Indian Arts and Culture in Santa Fe which was designed to demonstrate the continuity of cultures over a 2000-year period up to the present day. *Old Ways, New Ways* at the Heard Museum utilised interactive techniques in order to give visitors an insight into the traditional and modern cultural expressions of the Zuni of the Southwest, the Tsimshian of the Northwest Coast and the Kiowa of the Great Plains. In 1993, Milwaukee Public Museum opened *A Tribute to Survival*, a new introductory section to its North American Indian galleries which had as its centrepiece a pow-wow scene consisting of life-casts of Indian dancers in contemporary costumes participating in a pow-wow which is a symbol of modern Indian cultural expression.

Following the critical reception of *Hidden Peoples of the Amazon*, the Museum of Mankind presented *The Living Arctic: Hunters of the Canadian North*, an exhibition about contemporary life amongst the Indian and Inuit peoples of the Arctic. This was a collaborative project involving the Museum of Mankind, Indigenous Survival International (ISI) and the Assembly of First Nations, initiated by ISI, and partly funded by Native peoples from the region and by Canadian government departments.

For ISI and the native peoples, the exhibition provided an opportunity for them to present evidence regarding the importance of hunting and trapping within the contemporary economy of the region, and the detrimental effects upon traditional life of the actions of the anti-fur lobby and European import restrictions. The exhibition emphasised both traditional and contemporary aspects of Arctic life using historical, ethnographic material as well as contemporary material, much of it purchased for the exhibition; also videos and life-sized dioramas. The latter included a sectional view of an igloo representing housing in the 1920s, and the interior of a modern prefabricated house typical of the 1980s, with computer, television and other modern conveniences (King, 1989). The themes of the exhibition were further enlarged upon in two accompanying publications: a report and catalogue edited by the curator, Jonathan King (1989), and a book by Hugh Brody (1987) who quotes extensively the words of the Arctic peoples themselves. The exhibition was well-received by native peoples and by reviewers such as Nelson Graburn and Molly Lee (1988) who referred to it as 'doing what *The Spirit Sings* didn't'.

The Spirit Sings: Artistic Traditions of Canada's First Peoples caused a storm of protest when it was presented at Glenbow Museum in Calgary in 1988 and became the main focus of a land rights campaign by the Cree Indians in the lead up to the Winter Olympics, a time when such actions were guaranteed to receive international media coverage. Native opposition to the exhibition resulted from the involvement of Shell Canada Ltd, a sponsor whose activities in Canada were detrimental to the interests of the Lubicon Cree. Three years before *The Spirit Sings* opened, the Lubicon Lake Cree had called for a boycott of the Winter Olympics to draw attention to their land rights claim involving several companies, including Shell Canada Ltd, who were involved in destructive drilling activities on land the Lubicon claimed as their own. Shell had provided 1.1 million Canadian dollars of funding towards the cost of mounting the exhibition but the Lubicon felt that the sponsorship of an exhibition of native art work gave the impression that the sponsor supported native rights. They were thus angered by Shell's support of the exhibition; in their view, yet another example of the cultural heritage of native peoples being used by white Canadians purely as entertainment and promotion of Canada, while the concerns of the native people themselves were being largely ignored.

The exhibition was designed to highlight the rich artistic and cultural traditions of Canada's native peoples and displayed approximately 650 objects, the majority of which were on loan from more than ninety lenders in over twenty countries. The boycott drew much attention, nationally and internationally, to the exhibition and to the land rights campaign of the Lubicon Lake Cree; and a number of museums refused to lend objects out of support for the boycott. Reviewing the exhibition, Marjorie Halpin (1988) commented that the exhibition's approach reflected the concept of 'Us collecting and defining Them'. She felt that the exhibition, through the presentation of the objects, successfully illustrated how the relationship of the native peoples and their material world had changed between the sixteenth and nineteenth centuries, demonstrating how natural and imported material had been transformed into 'the necessities and finery of life'. She suggested that the curators might, however, have identified the collectors and their objectives, and used the beauty of the objects to consider the attitudes of the native peoples towards finery and adornment.

1492–1992: Celebration and protest

The Quincentenary of Columbus's landing in the Americas, provided an opportunity for the history and consequences of European and Native American encounters to be explored in a variety of forms. In 1989, the Florida Museum of Natural History presented *First Encounters: Spanish Explorations in the Caribbean and the United States, 1492–1570*. The exhibition traced the routes of expeditions by Christopher Columbus, Hernando de Soto, Tristán de Luna, and Pedro Menéndez. It examined evidence from archaeological sites, including both Native American and Spanish settlements, described in the exhibition brochure as 'time-capsules of artefacts and information documenting the first encounters between the Old and the New Worlds'. During the exhibition's presentation at this venue, it attracted some criticism from Native Americans and Hispanic Americans and became the focus for demonstrations by about forty protesters, including members of the American Indian Movement, who described the exhibition as racist and demanded that it be closed. Criticism focused primarily upon terminology: terms such as 'forced laborers' instead of 'slaves' to describe Indians who worked for the Spanish, and 'subdue' to describe Spanish control of Indians, were felt by some critics to be too innocuous to convey the reality of the horror and inhumanity of slavery. 'New World' and 'discovery' were felt to be Eurocentric and inappropriate from the Native American perspective, even though the curators had used inverted commas, and it was claimed that the exhibition glorified Spanish explorers (Acle, 1989; Porter, 1989).

Jerald Milanich, co-curator of the exhibition, agreed with protesters about the harsh treatment of Native Americans, but argued that the exhibition did convey the message that the deaths of millions of American Indians resulted from European colonization of the New World: 'Our ancestors pushed back the frontier, built railroads, killed thousands and thousands of Indians, placed the survivors on reservations, and committed genocide and ethnocide' (Milanich, 1989: 2). The exhibition guide, in a section entitled *Effects of Early European Contact on Aboriginal Societies: Disease, Disjunction, Depopulation*, refers to American society being 'built upon the graves of millions of Native Americans who lived in the New World in 1492' (Milbrath and Milanich, 1990: 52). These aspects of history are what Milanich refers to as 'the flip-side of the Columbian Quincentenary . . . those parts of the anniversary that clash with our commonly held beliefs about Columbus, the New World, and the founding and westward movement of the United States'. Milanich feels strongly that such aspects of history must be confronted:

> Individuals that seek to prevent activities associated with the Columbian
> Quincentenary, including the exhibit [*First Encounters*], are doing a
> disservice to the Native peoples who resided here in 1492 and their

descendants. If we are to understand the plight of many native groups today, we must be aware of what happened in the past, including those first decades after 1492.

(Milanich, 1989: 4)

First Encounters was just one of a plethora of exhibitions and events organised to mark the 500th anniversary of Columbus' landing in the Americas, while in Canada the year also marked the 125th anniversary of confederation. During preparations for 1992, museum curators who were organising exhibitions were well aware of the sensitive nature of the occasion. Most made particular efforts to take a fresh look at history and to adopt a sensitive approach which did not celebrate the occasion but which provided a perspective more sympathetic to the views and experiences of America's native peoples. For Native Americans, Columbus' arrival in the Americas has been variously described as discovery, encounter, invasion and conquest (Indigenous 500 Committee, 1992; McMaster and Martin, 1992). From their perspective Columbus' landing marked the start of 500 years of 'cultural conquest and disenfranchisement' (McMaster, 1990) during which time native peoples were subjected to genocide, exploitation and appropriation: rather than a time for celebration, 1992 was seen by many as 'a time of mourning' (Rose, 1990: 4).

For the most part, exhibitions such as *Circa 1492*, *Seeds of Change* and *Myth and Reality: The Legacy of 1492* examined wider aspects of the historical period, focusing upon the impact of European contact upon native cultures, and the exchange of ideas, goods, and resources which occurred during the following five hundred years. *Circa 1492*, an art exhibition at the National Gallery of Art in Washington, DC, surveyed the works of art being produced in various parts of the world during the fifteenth and sixteenth centuries. The exhibition included prints and drawings, paintings, sculptures, decorative arts, scientific instruments and maps, and was divided into three main sections: 'Europe and the Mediterranean World', 'Toward Cathay', and 'The Americas'. In the latter two sections, the exhibition focused, not upon the period of European contact, but upon the art being produced by the cultures and civilisations of Asia and the Americas as they existed prior to European contact. In this way the emphasis was upon the excellence and diversity of artistic achievement during that era.

Seeds of Change: Five Hundred Years of Encounter and Exchange, a Smithsonian Institution exhibition, examined the biological, agricultural and technological effects of the encounters between Europeans and Native Americans. Herman Viola conceived the idea for a natural history exhibition which would explain contemporary usage of plants and animals in parts of the world to which they are not native. His idea was stimulated by the book *Seeds of Change* by Henry Hobhouse which documented the history and contemporary usage of species which were exchanged between the Old and the New Worlds. The resulting exhibition surveyed positive and negative effects of contact, the spread of disease, the introduction of new crops, the exchange of ideas, materials, and technology, in order to demonstrate the lasting and extensive consequences which had world-wide implications. Five 'seeds or agents of change'

41

were selected: sugar, corn, potato, the horse, and disease, being those considered to have had the most immediate and enduring impact upon a wide range of peoples.

> The Columbian exchange, of course, reordered the ethnic composition of continents, changed the health and diet of people everywhere, and irrevocably altered the environment of the Americas . . . the dominant ethnic group would one day be African instead of Native American, New World plants like maize and potatoes would rival wheat and rice in countries as distant from the Americas as China and Russia, and mankind would benefit from a variety of wonderdrugs from a rainforest that now is being destroyed by the same motivation that 'discovered' it.
>
> (Sewell, 1991: 38)

Planners recognised that the exhibition would be dealing with contentious issues but held that the exhibition and the accompanying programmes would provide a forum for discussion and greater understanding of the complex and significant outcomes of the Columbian encounters.

Those curating such exhibitions were keen to avoid giving offence to native peoples, and hoped to present exhibitions which offered new perspectives and greater insights into the cultures of the period and the effects of the Columbian encounters. They also hoped that the Quincentenary would not result in the sort of scenes witnessed during other nationalistic celebrations such as the American Bicentennial in 1976, the celebrations marking the 200th anniversary of Cook's arrival in Australia, and the 500th anniversary of Bartolomeu Dias' landing on the Cape of Good Hope in South Africa. Such events highlight the vast difference in perceptions with regard to commemorative occasions when viewed by indigenous and non-indigenous peoples. For the non-indigenous population they are a celebration marking the birth of a new nation, a new national identity, and new lives for millions of immigrants, resulting in the prosperity and lifestyles that most now enjoy. For indigenous peoples, the occasions mark centuries of loss of freedom, land and independence, acculturation, racism, murder, mistreatment, injustice and inequality. As museums planned and presented exhibitions to mark the occasions, many indigenous peoples chose to boycott and demonstrate against such events, while others saw them as an opportunity to express their feelings and opinions through the arts.

In the United States a group of Native American elders formed the 1992 Alliance to respond to the Columbian Quincentenary. In Hull-Ottawa, Canada, approximately 700 native peoples and observers gathered at an international conference entitled *Strengthening the Spirit: Beyond 500 years*, which was convened by the Indigenous 500 committee, whose members came from seven national aboriginal organisations in Canada. Its aim was to 'commemorate Indigenous Peoples' resistance to colonisation in the Americas since the arrival of Europeans in 1492' and to enable indigenous peoples from all over the world to discuss their visions of the future. 'Solidarity is the capacity to "Strengthen The Spirit" of Indigenous self-determination, and non-Indigenous participation in the process of rebuilding Indigenous cultures' (Indigenous 500 Committee,

1992: 51). The 1992 conference resulted in a 'Declaration of the First Nations of the Americas' which laid down fifteen resolutions. These included demands that 'education at all levels respond to the preservation, promotion and development of the ancestral cultures of the First Nations and Peoples of the Americas, and that it be designed, implemented and operated by them' and that 'Nation-states respect the ancestral religious practices of the First Nations and Peoples of the Americas' (Indigenous 500 Committee, 1992: 49).

On such occasions, others have utilised the political power of the arts to provide a vehicle for protest or political expression (Megaw, 1988; Mundine, 1990: v-vi; McMaster and Martin, 1992; Roberts, C.A., 1992). In the year of the Columbus Quincentenary, exhibitions such as *The Submuloc Show/Columbus Wohs* and *Indigena* provided the views of native artists on the past 500 years of North American history. Such exhibitions of contemporary Native American art are a powerful demonstration of cultural continuity and contemporary artistic trends; and also provide a means of conveying native viewpoints through the eyes of artists, giving opportunities for political commentary, new perspectives on history, and reflections of cross-cultural reciprocation of ideas, images and techniques.

Crisis management

The events surrounding controversial exhibitions have highlighted the need for museums to develop strategies for avoiding unnecessary controversy and dealing with public criticism and controversy when it does occur. In the first instance, curatorial staff need to be very specific in stating clearly the aims and objectives of the exhibition. In the cases of *The Spirit Sings* and *Into the Heart of Africa*, it appears that the messages transmitted visually and verbally in publicity material did not accurately reflect the intended message of the exhibition, and contained imagery which members of the First Nations and African Canadian communities found offensive.

The curator of *Into the Heart of Africa* used period photographs and quotations to convey the attitudes of Canadian missionaries and service personnel during the colonial period. The aims of the exhibition and the use of period photographs and quotations throughout the text were clearly too subtle for many people. As a result, the exhibition, which set out to explore the issues of racism, was itself accused of being racist. Careful use needs to be made of period material, such as quotations and photographs, which might be misunderstood, with clear differentiation made between the views of the curator and any contemporaneous material, whether visual or textual.

A similar problem occurred when the Tropenmuseum in Amsterdam presented an exhibition entitled *White on Black* which was intended to address issues of racism in advertising, comics, illustrations and so forth. The exhibition conveyed such powerful racist imagery that some visitors were drawn past the all-important introductory panels, which explained the dangers of stereotypical imagery, and incorrectly concluded that the exhibition itself was racist in intent.

To overcome this an additional section was added with large title panel and dramatic illustrations which attracted visitors and explained the concepts with which the exhibition dealt. The text and illustrations dealt with slavery as a product of racism and drew attention to the continuing presence of racist attitudes which are all too evident in many forms of media today, as seen in the examples in the exhibition. The exhibition gained a better reception from visitors following these changes.

Inviting criticism

In 1986 the Field Museum in Chicago received a letter of complaint from a sociologist about a diorama showing the Morning Star sacrifice which used to be practised by the Skiri Pawnee. The writer believed that the diorama was unsuitable for a family museum and asked that it be removed. She described it as racist and sexist, displaying 'appalling' sexual overtones and the 'torture, burning and killing of a woman' (Throckmorton, nd). The Field Museum installed a 'talk-back kiosk' next to the diorama and asked visitors for their responses. More than 3,500 responses were received over three years (Dillenburg, nd).

Although some parents called for it to be removed because it had upset their young children, the vast majority of the comments were supportive with many visitors remarking that historically accurate events should be interpreted. Just as aspects of European history which are regarded as offensive today are now being interpreted in an effort to address the past, so it was felt by some visitors that cultural traditions which might be offensive to those from other cultures should be interpreted in an effort to increase understanding of the practices. As one visitor commented 'The behaviour and actions of our past cannot be glossed over or ignored. Should we not have an exhibit of slavery or Nazi atrocities because they "violate cultural taboos" central to our own American culture? I should say not!' Another remarked that 'the truth of history should teach; it can't if it is hidden'. Several commented that more information is needed in exhibitions to avoid visitors evaluating displays in Euro-American terms. R. Skyhawk, a member of the Blackfeet nation, stated that 'There is enough ignorance about our culture. The exhibit of Pawnee sacrifice is educational and should be viewed by all people who are interested in preserving history as it was.'

Many respondents requested that further information be provided to explain the context and function of the sacrifice. As a result of this, further research was carried out and changes were made to the diorama which provided more information for visitors and corrected some inaccuracies in the display. Those who responded to Ms Throckmorton's views generally appreciated the opportunity that they had been given to express their opinions, it was suggested that all exhibits should be open to questioning, and the response booth should remain.

November 1993 saw the opening of the Field Museum's major new African exhibition entitled *Africa*. Planning had involved a number of strategies for gaining feedback from the public in order to identify the expectations and concerns of the African American population as well as those of whites and people of colour. Front-end analysis was conducted to identify public perceptions of Africa and expectations concerning a major exhibition about the continent (PPDR, 1991). In addition to the attitude survey, they conducted live television discussions and phone-ins. By identifying stereotypical views of African cultures and history, the curatorial staff were able to specifically address these matters in the exhibition and so challenge incorrect perceptions. They were also able to respond to the particular interests expressed by substantial numbers of respondents and so focus on subjects designed to appeal to visitors as well as increase public knowledge.

Consultation and participation enable alternative perspectives to be presented, frustrations to be voiced and reconciliation to take place. Following its showing in Florida, *First Encounters* was booked to tour to ten other museums in the United States, including the Museum of Science and Industry in Tampa, Florida. According to co-curators Milbrath and Milanich, the Museum of Science and Industry 'welcomed the controversy as a means to call attention to the exhibit and bring in the public' and invited the protesters to make camp on the grassy space outside the museum (1991: 36). Later that year, the *First Encounters* exhibition was due to be hosted by Albuquerque Museum in New Mexico, an area with a high number of Native American residents. Dismayed that it had caused such adverse reactions, the staff nevertheless decided not to cancel their booking. Instead they planned a series of strategies which they hoped would pre-empt demonstrations by alleviating any concerns the local Native American population might have about the exhibition and demonstrating to critics of the exhibition, the desire of the Albuquerque Museum staff to hear and respond to the views of Native Americans.

Native Americans were invited as speakers and delegates to participate in a series of open forums entitled 'American Indian Perspectives'. Rick Hill, an Iroquois and director of the Institute of American Indian Arts Museum in Santa Fe, provided additional commentary from an Indian perspective and corrected or expanded upon some of the points raised in the text. His comments, which he emphasised were personal views and should not be seen as comments made on behalf of the Native American community as a whole, were available on a handout in the exhibition. As a precaution, in the event that demonstrations did take place after the exhibition opened in Albuquerque, museum staff prepared a notice supporting those who wished to express their opinions and exercise their rights of free speech and free assembly under the First Amendment of the Constitution. They stated that they welcomed discussion of the issues raised by the exhibition and invited visitors to enter their comments in the book provided at the end of the exhibition. In the event, it was not required. Their strategies appeared to have been successful, for the exhibition opened and ran with no adverse reactions or publicity.

The Science Museum of Minnesota also introduced a range of strategies to deal with the controversy of *First Encounters* which they exhibited in 1992. These included the development of a task force including members of the museum staff and of the community, the production of a ten minute video and a television public service announcement, and emergency phone lines to handle calls related to the controversy.

Recognising the potential for controversy, museum staff worked for over a year with a Native Views Community Planning Team drawn from Indian, Hispanic and black communities in Minneapolis-St Paul. Together they presented a parallel exhibition *From the Heart of Turtle Island: Native Views 1992* which depicted indigenous cultures prior to European contact and the contributions that they had made to world knowledge and cultural traditions. The Science Museum and the Native Views Community Planning Team had previously decided that they would use the exhibitions 'as a "teachable moment" in which to engage the many communities of the Upper Midwest region in a dialogue about the Columbian legacy and where we go in the next 500 years' (Science Museum of Minnesota, 1993). By engaging in dialogue they sought to avoid confrontation and focus attention upon the messages of the two exhibitions.

These actions did not entirely avoid confrontation and *First Encounters* became the focus for a dramatic act of protest by Vernon Bellecourt, a member of the American Indian Movement. At the opening of the exhibition on Friday 29 May, Bellecourt held a press conference in the gallery during which he climbed aboard the replica of the *Niña*. With a sudden and unexpected movement, he produced a container of blood which he splashed over the boat's sail and deck. In expectation of a protest that night, the museum management had discussed plans and prepared security staff for their responses to a number of scenarios that they envisaged might occur. They had decided that they would allow a protest to proceed as long as it did not endanger either people or artefacts. Bellecourt was allowed to complete his press conference and leave the museum, and the following week the Science Museum issued a press statement in which they announced that they would not be taking legal proceedings against him. In the statement they announced 'we choose not to indict the messenger because we respect the message – that the *First Encounters* exhibit contains elements offensive to native people. We have received that same message in far more constructive ways from other messengers.' The replica of the *Niña*, with its blood-stained sail, was allowed to remain in the exhibition as a visible manifestation of that message and a focus for the museum's education mission: 'We are very aware of [the *Niña*'s] powerful symbolism – both before and after this incident. We are very aware that it has potential both for healing and dividing' (Science Museum of Minnesota, 1992).

Museum staff moved swiftly to conduct a crisis management campaign that would build constructively upon Bellecourt's protest action. Following the incident, marketing and public relations staff issued the press statement and the curator and the museum vice president answered questions at a press conference. They drafted a memorandum from the museum president to museum staff explaining their response and desire to maintain their educational objectives. Emergency telephone lines were set up and handled over a thousand calls, while written responses were sent to the 300 or so letters which were received. The museum's senior vice president appeared on a local television programme in order to explain the museum's decisions and actions.

The museum also formed a protest response task force consisting of museum staff and members of the Community Planning Team. Arising from their recommendations, additional panels were placed in the *First Encounters* exhibit area using a question and answer format to address the issues raised by the protest. Within a week, a ten-minute video had been produced giving more detailed responses drawn from interviews with members of the Community Planning Team and the community. This was used in the gallery to communicate these views to visitors, and segments were also used to produce a thirty-second TV public service announcement which was shown on eight television stations across the state.

The cost of the crisis management campaign was put at $7,200 and 360 hours of staff time but museum staff regard the campaign as successful in enabling the institution to fulfill its educational mission, the success being evident from the comments of visitors recorded in the gallery and in letters sent to the museum. 'Arranged chronologically, these comments give a firsthand picture of the transition in the community from outrage on both sides of the issue to some kind of understanding for the need to move beyond ancient hatreds' (Science Museum of Minnesota, 1993). In recognition of the success of these initiatives, the museum was awarded a silver AMIE (Award for Marketing Institutional Excellence) by the Public Relations and Marketing Committee of the American Association of Museums (Griffin, 1994: 26) .

The Science Museum's crisis management campaign provides an example of museum actions that boldly confronted controversy by showing respect for the individual's right to protest, inviting dialogue, being receptive and sympathetic to the views and emotions of all parties, so creating something positive and constructive out of a symbolic act of vandalism. By addressing topical issues and providing information and alternative perspectives, museums can adopt a socially relevant role that engages the public in debate and demonstrates a democratic approach to the interpretive process, yet most curators continue to avoid such subject matter. Recent controversies, such as those which confronted *Into the Heart of Africa*, *First Encounters* and *The West as America*, have attracted international media attention and had some negative repercussions upon museum practice. Cannizzo suggests that, as a result of the reaction to *Into the Heart of Africa*, some curators are now more wary of producing thought-provoking, and therefore potentially controversial, exhibitions. Such reluctance is also felt by many curators and anthropologists who justify this stance on the grounds of maintaining their objectivity and political impartiality; yet this attitude to potentially controversial issues means that museums may miss out on opportunities for organising socially relevant and topical exhibitions.

Others, however, believe that museums should not avoid taking a potentially controversial stance: that such an approach can highlight subjects and events which need to be examined and discussed. This view was supported by many respondents when readers of the Museum News (September/October 1991) were asked 'Should museum exhibition planners adopt an interpretive strategy that is based on scholarly consensus?' This echoed an article in *Curator* in 1970, in which Kenneth Hopkins, Director of the State Capitol Museum, posed the question : 'Is Confrontation in your Future?' (1970: 120–4). Twenty-three years later when the same issue was raised again many museum curators responded strongly in support of controversial and issue-based topics. One anonymous Connecticut curator commented that:

> Regardless of one's politics, museums should provoke and coerce reaction precisely by taking a crisp and noncentrist position as the situation warrants. The left should not have a monopoly on provocation and there is no question that controversy attracts attention and public involvement.
>
> (Anon., 1991: 83)

Building upon this potential, the Australian Museum in Sydney established a 'Rapid Response' Project Team in 1993 to respond to issues of concern as and when they arise in the news. In the manner of the Milwaukee Science Museum's initiative in the early 1960s, the Project Team develops small, low-budget exhibitions addressing current, topical matters. In this way they hope to provide the public with factual background information from which visitors can consider the events from a better-informed standpoint; issues can be aired publicly giving alternative viewpoints in order to inform and encourage discussion. Since it was established in 1993, the 'Rapid Response' Project Team has presented exhibitions on a wide range of topics including: *1993 Year of Indigenous People*; *Sunburn*; *Battered Fish*; *Oil Spills*; *Gay and Lesbian Mardi Gras*; *GATT*; and *The Rabaul Volcano* (Tacon, 1995).

By taking the initiative, museums may avoid the controversy that can result when an exhibition is seized upon as an opportunity for a group to air its grievances, and by inviting such groups to contribute their views, museums can provide multiple perspectives on issues, rather than a single curatorial viewpoint. Providing inclusive, multivocal perspectives does not mean that a museum is actively involving itself in political issues, nor siding with any particular group, but such methods can help to inform members of the general public by providing background information to current events and counterbalancing the often biased reporting of the media. In this way, a curator can present visitors with a balanced picture and allow them to draw their own conclusions, presenting the museum as a forum for discussion. 'The view point of the museum is an unbiased one. It is not our purpose to think for the visitor but to present him with the facts upon which he can base his own conclusions' (Cameron, 1971: 11–24).

The demonstrations and events which have surrounded some exhibitions are the most visible and powerful expression of public opinion and demonstrate the strength of feeling that museum exhibitions can generate. They are a highly visible illustration of the pressures that have been brought to bear upon curatorial practices: influences which have successfully engendered change. Museum–community dialogue does not guarantee a smooth-running exhibition: within each community there are many factions with differing views based upon factors such as religion, political outlook, and status. It does, however, give people a feeling of ownership over an exhibition if they are involved in planning from the start, and a museum's community relationships will be strengthened if they are seen to value and seek the opinions of the community, particularly, those whose culture they will be representing in an exhibition.

3

Voices of authorship

'Learn what the community needs; fit the museum to those needs.'
(John Cotton Dana, Director, Newark Museum, 1917, cited in McNulty, 1992)

Although it is more than 75 years since John Cotton Dana, the Founder of the American Association of Museums, spoke those words, museums are still struggling to identify and meet the needs of the communities they serve. Curatorial staff have become much more aware of the need to address the social and cultural needs of diverse audiences and to explore the subject of cultural diversity through exhibitions and programmes. A major development in this regard has been the increased involvement of members of a community in the interpretation of their culture and history through various processes of consultation, guest curatorship and community exhibitions.

Exhibitions organised in consultation with the communities represented can provide a means of counteracting many of the problematic aspects of exhibitions which have drawn criticism in the past. They enable those represented to contribute information which reflects their perspectives and concerns and demonstrates their survival as a unique cultural group within a society which often shows little regard for the distinctiveness of cultural identity. However, the inclusion of the views and words of peoples of the culture represented is in itself a selective process: whom should the museum approach? What should be included/excluded? One of the problems facing curatorial staff when embarking upon such collaborative processes is negotiating the often difficult path through community politics and relationships to identify those who can speak for their communities. Leaders of community organisations are an obvious first point of contact, as are community workers who have wide contact with a large number of people. Exhibition subject matter will often provide further indications of appropriate lines of inquiry and community contacts.

Community involvement in the exhibition planning process can take a number of forms: participation in oral history recording, photographic documentation, and other forms of research; advice to museum staff who are curating an exhibition and ratification of plans, texts, images, etc.; guest curatorship by individuals or groups within the community; or curatorship in entirety by community participants. Depending on the length of the intended exhibition, the

51

nature of the collections and the subject of future exhibitions, museum staff may seek short-term participation by community members or wish to establish longer-term or permanent relationships in which the views and advice of community members form an integral part of the museum's policy-making procedures.

Various feed-back methods are used in museums including comment books or comment boards for specific exhibitions. The Children's Museum in Boston regularly uses such methods to enable visitors to comment upon the content or wording of exhibits, and staff respond with changes to the exhibitions where warranted. The 'talk-back kiosk' installed in the Field Museum in Chicago to invite visitor feedback about the controversial Morning Star diorama resulted in more than 3,500 responses over three years. Such techniques enable visitors to express their views and also demonstrate the museum's willingness to listen to and act upon public concerns. Other methodologies include the establishment of focus groups or advisory boards as representatives of the subject group in the planning and presentation of exhibitions and supporting events.

Focus groups are used extensively in consumer and market research and, more recently, have been utilised in the field of museum visitor research. A group of participants is selected according to a set of criteria such as ethnic background, age, gender, profession, and so on. The groups are engaged in dialogue about the issues pertaining to the subject matter of the proposed exhibition. This enables museum staff to listen to the focus group discussing issues such as their expectations, and their pre-visit and post-visit attitudes to the exhibition.

Advisory boards consist of individuals invited to take part in discussions with museum staff to advise about the content of exhibitions, to approve plans, to read and comment on texts and so on. These may be academics or other professional people, but it is now quite common for museums to work in close conjunction with advisory boards consisting of individuals from the cultural groups represented by the collections. Advisory boards are often established when a museum is preparing a new exhibition but, more significantly, in some museums they have been assigned a permanent consultative role in museum management and interpretation structures.

As long ago as the mid-1950s, Gisborne Museum and Arts Centre (known then as the Arts Society) in New Zealand established a Maori Museum Committee to oversee the establishment of a Maori wing. The Committee also assisted in the compilation of the Maori collections by encouraging members of the Maori community to deposit their treasures or *taonga* in the museum. However, following completion of the Maori wing attendance dropped and, despite the efforts of the Honorary Director of the Museum, Leo Fowler, the Committee was disbanded after just four or five years' existence (Haldane, 1984: 26). Forty years later, most major museums in New Zealand are working towards the creation of bi-cultural museums to ensure that Maori views are incorporated and reflected in the exhibitions and other museum activities. Many museums work with Maori elders, *kuia* and *kaumatua*, who act as advisers and, in some museums, have roles as education staff as well.

Advisory boards are now involved quite extensively in museum planning processes in other countries too. Julia Nicholson, formerly Assistant Keeper, Indian Arts and Crafts in Leicestershire Museum Service, England, regularly worked with advisory groups consisting of members of the community being represented in an exhibition. This method proved very successful in the planning of several exhibitions including *Caribbean Focus* in 1986, *Jainism: Art and Culture – Twenty-five Centuries of an Indian Religion* in 1987, and *Traditional Indian Arts of Gujarat* in 1988–9. In fact, the exhibition about Jainism was organised as a direct result of requests from the Jain community in Leicester. They wanted the museum to present an exhibition to coincide with the opening of a new religious and cultural centre in Leicester and the museum staff worked with Jain community representatives to select and interpret exhibits (Nicholson, 1989).

The Boston Children's Museum has worked with a Native American advisory board since 1973. One of the main concerns expressed by the board was that displays often suggest that Indian cultures did not survive the nineteenth century, or that Indians today still live as they did in the past. When the Museum was planning a new exhibition entitled *We're Still Here – Indians in New England Long Ago and Today*, they worked closely with the advisory board to address stereotypes and correct misconceptions. The exhibition was designed to show both traditional and contemporary lifestyles of Native Americans in New England, to emphasise the continuity of native cultures and their modern lifestyle. It included a traditional wigwam and a modern bedroom and fully equipped kitchen. On the walls of the rooms were a poster of a pop star, a map of Indian lands, a Native American calendar, and a reminder note to attend a Tribal Council meeting and finish a beadwork order. An open-storage area adjacent to the exhibition enabled visitors to examine items more closely with the assistance of a Native American staff member. The exhibition also addressed the issue of the ownership, display and repatriation of human remains and grave goods, and asked the children 'What do you think?'

As part of its efforts to create a culturally diverse museum, Boston Children's Museum also organised a Multicultural Advisory Board which included members of museum staff and representatives from educational institutions, social and health services, the artistic community and the private sector. The Advisory Board examined the galleries, materials and activities of the museum in an effort to identify problems or areas for improvement. 'The exhibit center was scrutinized for stereotypes, cultural insensitivity, a dominant-culture only focus, and accessibility in terms of visitors' cultural learning styles, frames of reference and language'. As a result, the staff experimented with multilingual signage presented in a number of different formats, and floor staff who are bi- or multi-lingual now wear badges which identify their language proficiency. They also made changes to exhibits:

> A generic grocery store has been recast as El Mercado del Barrio, a largely Victorian doll house exhibit is becoming an exhibit of homes from many cultures, and the traditional Grandparents house was transformed over the course of a year into the home of an Irish-American family, a Jewish

family, an African-American family, and a Cambodian family. Multi-cultural mini-exhibits are popping up; our bathrooms showcase tooth-brushes from around the world, and act as soundbooths for cross-cultural recordings.

(Jenness et al., nd).

The Museum also has a Multicultural Education Project to work with teachers providing training, seminars and curriculum support materials.

When the Museum of Indian Arts and Culture (MIAC) in Santa Fe, USA, was planning a new 12,000 square foot permanent exhibition, it was their intention that it would be different from the usual anthropology exhibition and provide what they described as 'a humanistic, Indian view'. To facilitate this, they established a planning team of 31 consultants of whom sixteen were Indian (Bernstein, 1991b). One of the main concerns of the Native American consultants was that the exhibition should highlight the fundamental differences between Indian and non-Indian thinking about the creation. They also established a curatorial team of five people of whom three were Indian. At MIAC, these team members are brought in, paid and treated as full partners in the curatorial planning process. A fifteen-member advisory panel, with members representing most of the Indian groups in New Mexico, also enables them to obtain the views of members of the community about the intended content of the exhibition. Bruce Bernstein, Assistant Director of the Museum of Indian Arts and Culture, emphasises that these individuals should not be seen as representatives of their whole community, but as individuals who express their own views as Indians about the museum's proposals. Thus they are able to provide a Native American perspective and identify often subtle points which might potentially cause offence or raise difficulties.

Working with an advisory board is a process of two-way dialogue requiring negotiation, compromise and trust. The extent of the board's authority varies greatly from museum to museum but, while advisory boards have an important role to play, curatorial staff normally retain overall responsibility for the content of the exhibition. However, when Joan Lester, Chief Curator of the Boston Children's Museum, was asked what she would do if the advisory board objected to something she planned to do, she responded with the comment that 'If they do not agree with something you want to do, why on earth would you want to go ahead and do it?' (Lester, 1991). Nor does working with an advisory board eliminate dissent: even within one community there can be differing views between individuals. Joan Lester sent the floor plan of a proposed kachina exhibit to four Pueblo people for comment. Four years earlier, she had been told by a Pueblo consultant that the kachinas should be hung hierarchically with the kachinas of the ground, such as the mudheads and watermelon kachinas, hanging lower than the kachinas of the sky, such as eagle or sun kachinas. Now she found another Pueblo consultant was insistent that the kachinas of the ground must stand on the ground or on the pueblo structure; they must not hang in the air as had been planned. This resulted in a last-minute change to the display to accommodate this view (Lester, 1991).

The Head-Smashed-In Buffalo Jump Interpretive Centre in Alberta, Canada, interprets the site of a buffalo jump which was used during hunting by the Plains Indians as far back as 6,000 years ago. The site is rich in archaeological remains and is one of the best-preserved sites of its kind; in 1981 it was designated as a UNESCO World Heritage Site. Opened in 1987 by Alberta Parks, the planning and establishment of the Interpretive Centre involved extensive consultation with the local Blackfoot community in the representation of Plains Indian history. Tribal elders were consulted concerning the themes that were used in the exhibitions and interpretive programmes, and also upon the text and the choice of artefacts to display, and they continue to be involved in the care of the collections. Elders conduct appropriate rituals for the installation or removal of sensitive materials, and perform periodic purification ceremonies and blessings of staff members, of whom over half are native people (Sponholtz, 1988).

In a similar vein, the Burke Museum in Seattle has given a great deal of authority to its Native American Advisory Committee, which was first constituted in 1987 in order to work with the museum staff on the preparation of a major exhibition of Native American cultural heritage. During 1989, the Burke Museum presented *A Time of Gathering*, a major exhibition dealing with the native peoples of Washington State (Wright, 1991). The exhibition was conceived by a legislative body, the Lasting Legacy Committee, one of a number of committees established by the State Centennial Commission to plan and sponsor various events to mark the State's centennial. The Burke Museum was selected to host the exhibition and, in order to ensure that there was a significant amount of native involvement, staff members began building up a network of contacts within the Native American communities.

There was native participation from the very start amongst members of the Lasting Legacy Committee and, early in 1987, the Museum established a Native Advisory Board which, over the next two years, met on a monthly basis. This had a core group of about nine people, which included museum professionals from tribal museums in the area, as well as tribal elders and linguists. They held open meetings, which were advertised in advance, and specialists were also brought in according to the topics being discussed. The Advisory Board did not just have an advisory role, but was given the authority to make final decisions concerning the selection of artefacts and the methods that would be used to display them. The Burke Museum also hired two key native staff members: Roberta Haynes who, with Robin Wright, Curator of Native American Art at the Burke Museum, was the co-curator of the exhibition; and Cecile Maxwell who, as protocol officer, was responsible for providing links between the Museum and tribal governments.

The initial exhibit plan was to locate and display artefacts and works of art from museum collections around the world, treasures that had been removed from Washington State between 100 and 200 years ago, and to present an exhibition that would recognise and honour the original inhabitants of the State. It was also proposed that some historic environments would be constructed to represent the lifestyles of the native population of 100 years previously when the state was formed. Advisers and native peoples who were consulted immediately commented that they wanted to be represented as they are now not as they were in the nineteenth century, and so a contemporary component was added.

Extensive consultation was undertaken with communities across Washington state. Wright and Haynes undertook approximately 27 meetings with native groups, taking advantage of elders' luncheons, basketry classes, and any other meetings at which they could address participants. They showed slides of art works in collections in museums around the world and invited views and suggestions concerning what to include or exclude from the exhibition, what issues were sensitive, and comments that would assist in the interpretation of the pieces. During the course of planning, several sensitive issues arose upon which there were opposing views within the native community and these matters were referred to the Native Advisory Board for resolution (Wright, 1991).

The exhibition, which opened in 1989, was very well received and has been widely acknowledged as an excellent example of a partnership between a museum and Native American communities. Robin Wright feels that the dialogue with the native communities was one of the most significant aspects of the exhibition.

> It was really this process that we feel was the heart of the exhibition. The outreach process was almost more important to us than the end result in that the communication that occurred was what became the valuable part. So we were sharing information with people about what is housed in museums around the world that they may never have had a chance to see; they were sharing with us information about the meaning, really the heart and soul of what those pieces mean to them.
>
> (Wright, 1991)

Following this successful collaboration, the Museum formed a permanent Community Advisory Board in 1991 and extended membership to include representatives of Asian and Pacific communities in the area whose cultures are represented in the collections or are the subject of exhibitions in the Museum. Early in 1997, the Burke Museum will be opening a major new exhibition entitled *Pacific Voices* which will explore the cultures of the Pacific Coast region, looking specifically at aspects of cultural identity and the issues of change and continuity; once again community dialogue and liaison will be a very important component (Hutterer, 1995). These examples demonstrate the degree to which collaborative working methods can be extended to give an advisory board a role as a partner in the Museum's exhibition development team.

Collaborative projects involving museums and communities provide illustrations of a method of research and exhibition interpretation which is becoming increasingly common in museums as they develop new, more inclusive relationships working with communities which they have merely studied in the past. In many institutions, consultation work is now routinely undertaken in the planning of new exhibitions or in the development of new facilities and, as a result, many North American museums have developed close working relationships with native peoples. In other instances, as was the case with *A Time of Gathering*, exhibitions have been curated by, or in liaison with, indigenous peoples employed as guest curators. The Field Museum of Natural History has in its collections, a Maori meeting house named *Ruatepupuke* which originates from Tokomaru Bay in New Zealand. In 1905, it was purchased for the Field Museum collection from a German dealer and in 1925 it was erected in the Field Museum. When it was erected, changes were made to the structure to compensate for pieces which were missing when it was purchased. These alterations resulted in a display which, in the words of Field Museum curator, John Terrell, 'seriously compromised the historical, cultural and architectural integrity of Ruatepupuke' (Terrell, 1993: 35).

The meeting house is very important to the Maori; it is used for family and community gatherings and is both ceremonial in function and sacred in nature. Its various components symbolise Ranginui, the sky father, Papatuanuku, the earth mother, and their children, the Maori gods. The structure is also regarded as the body of the ancestor after whom it is named. Over the years, there had been periodic communications between the Museum staff and the Tokomaru Bay community, but in the mid-1980s Field Museum staff decided that the *Ruatepupuke* should be restored. To this end, Museum staff entered into dialogue with the Maori community through discussions with elders from Tokomaru Bay who were amongst the members of the official Maori delegation which visited Chicago in 1986 to conduct the formal, ceremonial opening of the touring exhibition *Te Maori: Maori Art from New Zealand Collections*. John Terrell then led a delegation of eighteen to Tokomaru Bay. The Maori elders were keen that *Ruatepupuke* should remain in Chicago and be fully restored as a living *marae* inside the museum so that it would enable non-Maori visitors to learn about Maori people and their culture. Restoration work was undertaken by Field Museum conservators and two Maori interns, and the project was co-curated by Arapata Hakiwai, a Maori curator from the Museum of New Zealand in Wellington. Several of the missing carved panels were found in the collections of the National Museum of New Zealand and, at the request of the elders of Tokomaru Bay, were transferred to the Field Museum on long-term loan. Other missing pieces were found in the collections of the Auckland Institute and Museum in New Zealand, and the Peabody Museum in Salem, Massachusetts, in the United States.

New *tukutuku* panels (decorative woven panels) were required, and their replacement involved the identification and gathering of traditional plant materials. Phil Aspinall, a member of the Maori community in Tokomaru Bay, commented afterwards that:

> Finding and gathering materials like *kiekie* and *kakaho*, the plants that our forebears used to make the fibers for weaving *tukutuku* panels, was a task enjoyed by all who took part; now that the project is completed we hope that the team in Tokomaru Bay will continue to revive the art of *tukutuku*.
>
> (Aspinall, 1993)

After the restoration work was completed, the meeting house was formally opened by elders from Tokomaru Bay on 9 March 1993. To provide further interpretation of the meeting house, Terrel and Hakiwai also produced a booklet describing the role of the meeting-house in Maori culture, its symbolism, and the protocol surrounding its use.

The increasing number of indigenous curatorial staff in museums creates opportunities for the native perspective to be heard, not just in the exhibition planning process, but in management and policy making as well. *Fluffs and Feathers* was a touring exhibition conceived and planned by Tom Hill, the director of the native-operated Woodland Cultural Centre, in Brantford, Ontario, and mounted by guest curator, Deborah Doxtator (Doxtator, 1992). The exhibition explored the various stereotypes of Indians that have been constructed in the imaginations of non-Indians and in the media, the use (and misuse) of Indian symbols, and concepts of 'Indianness'.

Control over the exhibition process enables indigenous curators to present the native view in the public arena. *Indigena: Contemporary Native Perspectives in Canadian Art* was an exhibition of art works by First Nation artists and was co-curated by two native staff of the Canadian Museum of Civilization, Gerald McMaster, curator of contemporary Indian art, and himself an artist, and Lee-Ann Martin, interim curator, Canadian Indian Art. The exhibition and accompanying book consisted of visual and written works produced by native artists in response to the Columbus Quincentenary and expressed the strong and passionate views of First Peoples' to the 500-year legacy of Columbus' arrival in the Americas (McMaster and Martin, 1992).

In Britain, it is not always practical to undertake collaborative work on this scale as the material in ethnology collections originates from former colonies in many different parts of the world. However, collaborative work can be undertaken with quite distant communities and can prove immensely valuable. Cambridge University Museum of Archaeology and Anthropology (CUMAA) commissioned Yarjung Kromchhain Tamu (Gurung), a practising Pachyu shaman from Nepal, to make a collection of Tamu shamanistic material on their behalf, then brought him to Cambridge to assist them with appropriate storage arrangements and to display the collection in a temporary exhibition (Herle, 1993).

This coincided with the visit of the Chief Minister of the Indian State of Nagaland, who was presented with a Naga videodisc and a player to be given to the Naga people and made available in a publicly accessible location in Nagaland. The videodisc was produced by the University's Department of Anthropology and drew together a wealth of material on the Naga and their culture, from collections in Cambridge Museum, the Pitt Rivers Museum, the Museum of Mankind, and Manchester Museum as well as a number of private collections. The material included music and approximately 50,000 images: historic photographs, pictures of artefacts, film clips, maps, and drawings (Herle, 1992). The Naga videodisc will provide a valuable research tool for academics and other researchers and will also enable the people of Nagaland to access information and images which remain in the collections of museums in this country.

The British Museum in London has also undertaken collaborative projects in recent years. The newly-opened Mexican gallery was the result of collaboration between the British Museum and the *Consejo Nacional para la Cultura y las Artes* (CNCA) and the *Instituto Nacional de Antropologia e Historia* (INAH). British Museum and Mexican curators, designers, and technicians worked together on the project and the gallery was designed by a Mexican architect, Teodoro González de León (McEwan, 1994).

During June to August 1987, four builders and carvers from the village of Baruppu' in Sulawesi undertook the construction of a Torajan ricebarn in the Museum of Mankind. Visitors were able to observe the men at work and watch the progress of construction and decoration. Curatorial staff also obtained a great deal of ethnographic information from one of these men, Nenek Tulian, a high priest of the traditional religion (Barley and Sandaruppa, 1991).

Perhaps the most extensive collaborative work undertaken by the British Museum has been the preparation and presentation of the *The Living Arctic* exhibition and activities in 1987–8. A small exhibition called *Inuit/Eskimo: People of the North American Arctic* opened in the Museum of Mankind in London in December 1984. This gave a very brief view of the cultures of the Inupiat Eskimo of Alaska, the Canadian Inuit and Greenlanders based upon the museum's holdings of nineteenth-century material. There was some criticism of the exhibition, due to its historical focus, criticisms which the museum staff acknowledged as reasonable. The following year the *Festival of Native American Artists* presented the Museum's Indian and Eskimo collections which date back over 300 years.

Aware of the danger of showing only this historic material, it was seen as imperative that contemporary aspects be conveyed. The exhibition planners decided to organise demonstrations by Native American artists to 'show more vividly than any conventional display how native traditions of design and technology still flourish in the United States of today' (British Museum, 1985). The demonstrations were given by Nathan Jackson, a Tlingit carver; his wife Dorica Jackson, weaving a Chilkat blanket; Robert Tenorio, a potter from Santo Domingo Pueblo; Barbara Jean Teller Ornelas, a Navajo weaver; Henry Shelton, a Hopi kachina doll carver; Ethel Santiago from Florida, making Seminole patchwork; Paula and Clara Tiulana, Inupiat Eskimo from Bering Strait, making a model whaling canoe and *mukluks*; and Ric Glazer-Danay, a Mohawk sculptor whose work demonstrated a non-traditional style of work.

Inuit/Eskimo and the *Festival of Native American Artists* both proved immensely popular with the public: *Inuit/Eskimo* drew an additional 1,000 people a week and, during May and June 1985, up to 1,000 people were visiting the *Festival of Native American Artists* each day. The success of these exhibitions led to plans for *The Living Arctic*.

While Georges Erasmus, Co-Chairman of Indigenous Survival International (ISI) and Chief of the Assembly of First Nations, was visiting Europe, campaigning to highlight hunting and trapping issues facing native peoples, he engaged in dialogue with the British Museum regarding the possibility of a major exhibition about the cultures of the far north of North America. The prospect of a major exhibition presented a valuable educational opportunity to provide the British public with information about contemporary life amongst the peoples of the Arctic. What followed was a collaborative project between the staff of the Museum of Mankind, Indigenous Survival International and northern Canadian peoples (King, 1989).

The exhibition was partly funded by money from the native peoples of the Arctic regions of North America who wanted to give their views of the importance that traditional industries such as whaling and seal hunting play in the economy of the region. They also wished to describe from their perspective the impact of cultural contact, new technologies, and non-traditional education on the cultures of the peoples of the Arctic. The completed exhibition focused upon Inuit, Métis and Indian cultures in urban and rural communities. As well as the descriptive text panels and object labels, the exhibition included quotations by people living in the Arctic region describing their lifestyles, and conveying their thoughts about whaling, fishing, cultural influences, and the changes occurring around them. It addressed contemporary issues as a central component of the exhibition, including peoples' expressions of fear and concern for the continuation of traditional lifestyles in the face of international opposition to the fur trade and limits upon fishing quotas and areas.

Funding from Indigenous Survival International enabled the museum staff to organise an extensive range of educational activities to support the exhibition, including three video programmes which combined existing footage with additional commentary by native peoples, an interactive video, a handling collection, and various activities for schools. The Museum employed Canadian staff to present the educational programme including David Serkoak, an Inuit teacher from Eskimo Point (Reeve and Bateman, 1991: 15–16).

The presentation of multiple perspectives in this way illustrates to visitors the diversity of perspectives which can be brought to bear in the interpretive process and helps to counteract the impression that the museum is the sole voice of authority. By using such methods, an exhibition can provide a more meaningful and relevant picture of traditional societies, inform the public of human rights issues, and provide a forum for debate in which members of the culture portrayed are also given a voice.

The British Museum has been fortunate that it has received substantial sponsorship for several of its recent exhibitions which have enabled such collaborative ventures to be undertaken particularly as part of the Museum's extensive educational programmes. Further funding has been obtained from the publishing and retail activities of British Museum Publications (Anderson, R., 1992). However, they too are finding their projects severely restricted by financial constraints, and collaboration with overseas communities is highly costly. Smaller, local museums, with their limited resources, have had even less opportunity to undertake collaborative activities with overseas communities although, due to the nature of their collections, it may not be as appropriate anyway. For these museums, it is perhaps more practical and appropriate to concentrate upon building stronger links with local communities, ensuring that they are relevant and effective in serving the cultural needs of the local population.

Museums in the life of a city: the Philadelphia initiative

Collaboration between museums and communities enables exhibitions to be developed which reflect the wishes and interests of communities themselves, but collaborative ventures are time-consuming and involve energy and commitment from individuals on both sides if they are to succeed. In 1988, the American Association of Museums (AAM) and Partners for Livable Places founded the *Museums in Service to Communities* programme to 'improve communities' social and economic well-being through use of cultural institutions, museums, libraries, botanical gardens, and zoos'. The following year the AAM, Partners for Livable Places, and the Pew Charitable Trust launched a three-year demonstration programme *Museums in the Life of a City: The Philadelphia Initiative* to explore 'the unique role museums play in the social and economic development of American cities'. It was decided that one of the most important factors in Philadelphia was that of cultural diversity and this became the focus of the pilot scheme (Hamilton-Sperr, 1992b).

During the first year, a museum committee was formed consisting of staff representing twenty-two institutions in the Philadelphia area. A Museums' Initiative Office was established in March 1990, and the two project co-ordinators, Portia Hamilton-Sperr and Cynthia Primas, began to establish a network of community groups and museum staff, forming a Community Advisory Council providing links between museums and the different ethnic groups in the city. They organised periodic meetings, forums for people to discuss their views and find out what resources were available, and carried out focus group discussions with different ethnic groups to identify people's attitudes towards cultural institutions. These highlighted the views that museums were alien environments which many people found uncomfortable. They also presented a series of educational meetings exploring topics such as collecting oral history, formative evaluation, and group dynamics.

Museums and community groups were invited to submit joint proposals for collaborative, year-long pilot projects. Each institution or neighbourhood group was asked to provide details of their function, current activities, and descriptions of multicultural activities which they would like to undertake. This information was provided to other groups from which partnerships developed, and proposals were then submitted for consideration by the project's evaluation committee.

Some community groups were suspicious of the motives and believed the whole project was merely a marketing ploy designed to attract more people into the museums. The project staff had to allay such fears and stressed that projects should be mutually beneficial and jointly co-ordinated, not simply part of an outreach programme. In brokering such collaborative relationships, Portia Hamilton-Sperr, the Project Director, identified the biggest challenge as that of power. The purpose of the project was to override the usual museum-led approach by bringing together the museum and neighbourhood communities in an equal partnership with benefits to both, to increase understanding and appreciation of the diverse cultural heritages of the Philadelphia population, and to initiate changes in museum practices. These would include greater involvement of the community and better reflection, in staff and activities, of the different races and cultures of the people of Philadelphia.

The project enabled both museums and communities to find out more about each other, identify the resources that each could provide, and present a wide range of views and ideas. From the museums' perspective, curators would make many more contacts within the communities and have a broader understanding of the local neighbourhoods and the resources within them. Although increased visitor figures might result from the projects, this was not a major aim. Members of the community were able to identify the resources and services offered by the different institutions and were given the opportunity to take an active part in projects in which they played an equal role, thus museums became less intimidating places.

The Pew Charitable Trust provided $200,000 for the projects. An executive committee of museum staff and community representatives devised the guidelines and criteria for the proposals, and formulated an objective evaluation process. They received 41 proposals which were considered by members of an evaluation committee consisting of six people from museums and the social services sector across the country. From these proposals, eleven were selected and each was awarded the maximum amount of $20,000 in June 1991.

Philadelphia Museum of Art and two Latino organisations, Taller Puertorriqueno and the Congreso de Latinos Unidos, collaborated on a project which provided ten Latino high school and college students with paid internships over the summer. These involved three weeks of training and five weeks of teaching and evaluation. The training gave the students an insight into the operation of museums and involved observation of museum activities and programmes, researching of the collections, visits to other museums, and lectures and demonstrations of teaching methods in galleries and studios presented by staff of the Philadelphia Museum of Art. They helped present the Museum's summer programme of activities for thousands of children and taught a printmaking workshop for forty-five children who were participating in the Taller Puertorriqueno's summer programme. They also taught a number of community workshops and planned a mural project, assisted by a Latino artist who was hired to co-ordinate the work.

The projects benefited all participants – the institutions and the community organisations – with each forging new links with the other. In one project, Khmer students and folklorists undertook research into the availability in museums and the community of information and materials relating to Cambodian culture. Through a series of meetings they explored various aspects of Cambodian culture: dance, drama, music, art, literature and cuisine. Offers of help in the translation of Khmer and the interpretation of Cambodian objects were made to three museums in Philadelphia (Hamilton-Sperr, 1992b:26).

Four of the projects involved the documentation of local history. In one of these, members of the Johnson Homes Tenant Council received training in oral history interviewing techniques from an oral historian from the Pennsylvania Historical and Museum Commission and production techniques from Scribe Video Center. They then initiated a programme of interviewing of residents of the James Weldon Johnson Homes, Philadelphia's first public housing development built over fifty years ago. They recorded the reminiscences of some of the earliest residents, charted the establishment of the tenants' rights movement, and produced a video to be made available through libraries in the area (Hamilton-Sperr, 1992b: 23).

This pilot project enabled the organisers to carry out action research with a positive benefit in the short term for those who participated, but the project is seen only as a starting point which it is hoped will initiate long-term collaborations. The Philadelphia initiative is intended to provide a model for other communities to establish networks of contacts between community organisations and cultural institutions, and thus enable greater community involvement and power in the cultural affairs of their towns and cities.

The natural question to ask is how can such partnerships be continued in the future without the funding that was provided during this pilot project? It is hoped that museums and community groups in Philadelphia will maintain their links and forge new ones, and that a more inclusive approach will become a permanent feature of museum organisation and planning reflected at all levels and through all activities. Museums would then be able to plan such collaborative ventures into their forthcoming programme of events within their current budgets. Cynthia Primas, Assistant Project Director, suggested that another possible link is between museums, communities and the business sector in projects focusing upon job skills and mentoring. She hopes that such links will lead to corporations taking a greater interest in such projects and providing funding; for them, the benefit would be to attract youngsters into employment in the science sector. For urban communities in particular, one of the most pressing issues is the education and vocational training of young people (Primas, 1991).

One of the pilot projects involved the Franklin Institute Science Museum, African American high school students from the Germantown Boys and Girls Club, the National Organization of Black Chemists and Chemical Engineers and the National Society of Black Engineers (Hamilton-Sperr, 1992b: 21). Members of these latter two groups, employed in a variety of companies in the science field, acted as mentors to the students providing role models and encouraging the youngsters to consider future careers in science and technology. The mentors worked with the students at the Franklin Institute while they undertook training workshops and then developed and taught lessons to younger visitors to the Franklin Institute.

This type of project is also seen as a way of encouraging community and education leaders to revise their attitudes to museums and to see them as valuable educational resources for urban populations which can supplement the traditional, and more formal, educational establishments. It also provides a means of increasing dialogue within the museum profession itself about the educational function of museums, in the hope that people from organisations which deal with community and training issues will enter into dialogue with museums and begin to develop liaisons in the future.

While there were some very positive outcomes from this project, it also became clear to all concerned that undertaking collaborative projects was not an easy task, requiring the commitment of considerable time and energy from all concerned. Many of those involved commented that it took time for participants to get to know each other and establish roles and methods; those with previous knowledge of each other were able to initiate their projects with more speed and fewer difficulties, emphasising the benefits of long-term relationships between museums, organisations and community members. Many of those involved in the pilot project expressed the desire to maintain the links and continue with the projects that had been initiated, although the discontinuation of the funding poses a serious obstacle to such plans.

Community galleries

As interest in museum–community collaboration has grown, some museums have shared or handed over control of the curatorial reins to the communities whose culture is being interpreted, enabling them to initiate and plan exhibitions themselves. The Migration Museum in Adelaide, Australia, has a community access gallery called The Forum which is available to community organisations living in the area (Migration Museum, 1992). Since the establishment of the museum in 1986, the museum has hosted exhibitions in this area by more than twenty-four community groups. These have included: *Serbs Down Under*, by the Serbian Orthodox Church; *Byelorussian National Artefacts*, by the Byelorussian Association in South Australia; *Ukrainian Embroidery in South Australia*, by the Ukrainian Women's Association; *The Sorbs (Wends) of Lusatia: Australia's Unknown Immigrants*, by the Australia–German Democratic Republic Friendship Society; *No Longer Strangers*, by the Catholic Multicultural Office and Justice and Peace Commission; and *America 500 Years*, by the Australian Spanish Latin American Institute. Each exhibition is in place for a period of three months.

The community groups are provided with the use of The Forum at no charge but cover all production costs themselves and provide the necessary items for the opening ceremony. The displays are produced as a co-operative venture between the museum and the community. The choice of subject matter is with the community group, though they must submit their proposal for acceptance by the Board of the History Trust of South Australia. The community group is responsible for writing the text and labels, selecting the artefacts and images to be used, and any supplementary information to be provided.

Figure 3.1 Ukrainian community exhibition in The Forum: Community Access Gallery of the
      Migration Museum, Adelaide, South Australia
Source: M. Simpson, July 1993, with permission of the Migration Museum, Adelaide, South Australia

The museum documentation makes it plain that 'the particular views expressed in displays are neither endorsed nor rejected by the museum' but also reminds the exhibition planners that, in line with the museum's multicultural agenda, the displays should not cause distress to other groups. The museum staff ensure that the subject matter is relevant to the museum's focus upon immigration and settlement history in South Australia, advise upon the language content and visual aspects of the display, and assist with installation. They also ensure that the content and presentation are of an appropriate standard and check the text for accuracy.

For the most part, the community groups are given total responsibility for the content, but occasionally museum staff have asked for changes to be made. While another museum in Adelaide, the Old Parliament House, has a community space called the Speakers' Corner where it encourages debate about controversial issues, the Migration Museum has a different aim, which is to display culture and history in a manner that engenders greater intercultural understanding and tolerance. The museum staff therefore need to be sure that comments in the texts do not inflame intercommunity tensions, but have only had to request minor alterations on a couple of occasions.

The Australian Museum in Sydney is also developing programmes which increasingly reflect the diverse nature of Australian society and has developed a close working relationship with indigenous peoples with regard to the research, management and interpretation of their collections. Musical and dance performances, plays, poetry recitals and so on are regular features of the public programming. During 1994, a new community gallery opened combining both temporary and permanent exhibition space, and a large performance area. The gallery has been named *Our Place: Australian People, Australian Identity*, reinforcing the sense of ownership and involvement that the initiative is intended to give to members of the public, and reflecting the shared national identity of the many ethnic communities which exist in contemporary Australian society.

It is intended that the gallery be used to focus upon the cultures of the peoples of Australia, and their relationship to the land and the natural environment. Exhibitions are topical and relevant to people's lives: topics include aspects of the cultural life of Australians, arts, sports, etc.; work patterns, employment areas; war as a factor in immigration, and as an event which can draw people together or create animosity between different cultural groups within Australia. The exhibitions draw heavily upon community involvement, using oral histories, video taped interviews, photographs and so on.

The planning for the gallery involved community collaboration and feedback from the outset. A community open day was held with invitations sent to over 50 different cultural groups within the city. Following presentations by Paul Tacon, Scientific Officer in the Division of Anthropology, and Lula Saunders, the Cultural Diversity Officer, in which the basic concept was outlined, the visitors were shown around the gallery space and then participated in group discussions about what they would like to see in the gallery. Their suggestions were incorporated into a more concrete proposal for submission to the Public

Programmes Committee. Following its acceptance, a second 'community day' was held, this time involving approximately 200 members of museum staff. A survey was also carried out to identify the specific wishes and ideas of staff and members of the community.

The gallery proposal was received with great enthusiasm and efforts to obtain community opinion and input provided valuable suggestions for the exhibition planners. People particularly voiced the desire that the initiative should not be restricted to that gallery alone but should be integral to the activities and services of other departments throughout the museum such as the restaurant, the shop, and other available temporary exhibition and performance spaces. Also arising out of the community consultation process was the concern that the museum should present a full picture of the issues it deals with, which did not play down the negative aspects. People emphasised that issues such as racism needed to be dealt with, but in a sensitive manner.

Community involvement is a continuing feature of the planning and presentation process. Projects are initiated either by museum staff or by members of the community, and those accepted are developed by the *Our Place* team in partnership with the community groups involved. The content of exhibitions is discussed fully with members of the community, although the museum retains final editorial rights over written and visual material. A wide range of programmes has been presented since the gallery opened, some incorporating exhibition material, others performance-based, including activities such as performing arts and fashions by Aboriginal children living in the inner city area; and performances of *wayang kulit* (shadow puppets) accompanied by Javanese gamelan musicians (Slarke, 1995).

Many programmes attest to the culturally diverse nature of the Australian population and some actively address issues associated with immigration, settlement and public attitudes. For refugees, the experience of being forced to leave their homeland and settle in a new country is a traumatic, frightening experience that can be eased or exacerbated by the reception that they receive in their new homeland. Often they are greeted with indifference, a lack of understanding, or even hostility.

Several of the programmes were designed to give insights into the experiences of refugees and to demonstrate how they maintain and reinforce their own cultures while living within Australian society. *Why We Had to Leave* featured the personal stories of refugees who have recently arrived in Australia and was designed to raise awareness of the circumstances that force people to flee their homes and seek a new life overseas. *Discoveries* was a community arts programme organised by a group of Indo-Chinese students who had arrived in Australia as refugees. It included photographic studies of Cabramatta, the area in which most of them lived, and a five-foot-long, cardboard boat, a model of the boats that had carried them to Australia. With sponsorship they were able to arrange for the programme to tour to Queensland and the Northern Territory, ending in Darwin. There the exhibits were ritually burned as a symbolic re-enactment of the final fate of the refugee boats.

*Croatian Australians * Australian Croatians* was initiated by the Croatian community in Sydney and focused upon the maintenance of cultural identity through such activities as clubs, sports, religion, celebrations, media, and the arts. To draw attention to the presence of African communities in Australia, the local African community worked in conjunction with museum staff to present a programme called *Treasures of Africa* which included live performances and material from the Museum's African collection (Slarke, 1995).

Young people have also been involved in the presentation of programmes. Highlighting broader aspects of cultural diversity, *Youth Identikit* involved 66 youth groups and individuals representing Aboriginal, disabled, and refugee youngsters, street kids, and technical college students. They addressed a range of topics of relevance to the lives of young people today including drugs, safe sex, homosexuality, Aboriginality, disabilities, identity, employment, street life, rock music, environment, employment, jewellery and fashion design. The techniques that they employed included the display of objects, art works and installations: and the use of videos, games, music, and performance. Another project by young people was *Our Families*, which was developed by children from a public school in Sydney, in order to highlight The Year of the Family. It incorporated written work, artwork, and video interviews with the children, and they also wrote poems, stories and comments about families and selected a family 'treasure' to write about (Slarke, 1995).

The Easter egg syndrome

Despite these developments, not all curatorial staff are convinced of the value of such interaction. Some curators wish to avoid the difficulty of dealing with the divergent views found within any community, while others simply prefer to retain control of the project, so maintaining the traditional role of curator. When preparing an exhibition about Ukrainian culture in Canada, Robert Klymasz, a curator at the Canadian Museum of Civilization, preferred to maintain the role of curatorial expert, a role he felt was justified in view of his own Ukrainian-Canadian background:

> Each culture has its own culture brokers. With the Ukrainian community, which I know best, if you let the community do the work, then you don't need me. I had ideas that I wanted to develop and I took advantage of celebrating the Ukrainian Centenary in Canada to do things on my own. We can't do this with every cultural group because we don't have a specialist for every cultural group.
>
> (Klymasz, 1991)

Another anxiety expressed about community collaboration in the exhibition development process concerns the nostalgia that people tend to experience when thinking of the past and the lifestyle which they or their ancestors left behind. Members of a community will often wish to show only the positive aspects of their culture, and may present or expect a romanticised vision of the past. Klymasz describes this as the 'Easter egg syndrome' in relation to

Ukrainian exhibitions in which people expect to see dozens of decorated eggs (Klymasz, 1991).

The European Village at Milwaukee Public Museum reflects the romantic attitude towards the past held by many immigrants and their descendants. Planned with input from the many ethnic groups living in Milwaukee, the gallery contains reconstructions of more than twenty houses representing the traditional architecture and furnishings found in their homelands. The exhibition focuses upon the artefacts and skills that were common within those communities. Scaled down and shown in only a small part, each house is a small catalogue of the objects most typical of each culture: Ukrainian eggs and embroidery; Swiss cheeses and clocks; English antiques. The displays convey nothing of the immigrant experience in a new land, but reinforce memories and images of the countries the immigrants left. This same phenomenon can be seen in a number of museums established by immigrant communities, in exhibitions which recreate elements of the traditional lifestyle left behind, but speak little of the immigration experiences or new lives of immigrants after settling in their adopted country.

The initiatives described in the preceding chapters demonstrate that a range of methods are being utilised to develop collaborative working relationships between museums and communities. In many museums a more inclusive approach is being adopted and the single authoritative voice of the curator has been challenged in exhibitions which incorporate multiple perspectives and so bring together the western anthropological perspective and the beliefs of those whose culture is the subject of the exhibition. The Canadian task force report on museums and First Peoples suggested that 'an equal partnership involves mutual appreciation of conceptual knowledge and approaches characteristic of First Peoples and the empirical knowledge and approaches of academically-trained workers' (AFN and CMA, 1992: 7). It seems likely that, after repatriation, this will become one of the most difficult issues for many museum staff to address. It involves acknowledging, not just that other world views and scientific models exist, but that they have equal validity as culturally defined concepts.

However, even in such instances the basic power relationship between the institution and the public remains the same. As Henrietta Fourmile has commented with regard to Aboriginal heritage interpretation: 'Aboriginal heritage committees, where they do exist are advisory committees adding a further insult. Such advisory committees merely emphasise the fact that ownership and ultimate authority over our heritage rests in non-Aboriginal hands' (Fourmile, 1989c: 5–6). Only through the training and employment of culturally diverse staff, and by ensuring that the governing boards and other positions of authority include representatives of various cultural groups within the community, will museums become truly pluralist and share the interpretation of heritage with those whose heritage it is. In this respect, a further development has been the establishment of museums and cultural centres by communities themselves, enabling them to take full control of their heritage interpretation and provide cultural services of direct relevance to their own communities.

69

Part 2
The 'new' museum paradigm

'Much of the acrimony perpetrated between Tribal people and historical societies, anthropologists, legislators, etc., is rooted in the collection, analysis, interpretation, and display of artifacts, objects, and specimens. Much of the negative discussion becomes moot when a community, through ownership, determines the ultimate placement, interpretation, and exhibition of its artifacts. When a community is comfortable with placement, analysis, and interpretation, it wants to share. From sharing, the whole society benefits.'

(Charles Carlyle, Ak-Chin, quoted in *Keepers of the Treasures*, Parker, 1990)

The past 30 years have seen significant changes in the field of museology, perhaps none as significant as the development of ecomuseums and community-based museums. These developments have enabled members of communities to become much more actively involved in the process of making representations and turned the focus upon those who, in the past, were so often neglected by collectors and curators of social history. They have also enabled indigenous peoples to develop the means to store and display materials in a culturally appropriate manner according to their own requirements concerning access and interpretation and, through these means, to convey their perspectives, world views, and concepts concerning the artefacts.

The ecomuseum concept developed in France and was pioneered by the French museologists Georges Henri Rivière and Hugues de Varine during the 1970s (Hudson, 1992). A number of community-based museums were established in parts of France which had a unique history and culture (Hubert, 1985). The ecomuseum was designed around and within the community in order to combine the natural and social environments, and extend the activities of the museum and the focus of its work beyond the actual museum building and into the community, often covering quite a wide region. The collections consist of the whole environment of buildings, artefacts and people. Indeed, the participation of members of the community is central to the ecomuseum concept; for the interactions of the museum and the various strands of the community are part of the functioning of the ecomuseum.

During the 1970s and 1980s, the ecomuseum trend spread to other parts of the world including Canada, Scandinavia and Portugal (de Blavia, 1985; Kinard, 1985; Nabais, 1985; Rivard, 1985; Bouchard, 1993). In Canada, the concept of the ecomuseum was adopted when thirteen villages in the southern Beauce region of Quebec co-operatively purchased a collection of objects relating to their cultural heritage. Forming themselves into a group and renamed as Haute-Beauce they established the Ecomusée de Haute-Beauce in order to care for and interpret the artefacts and to preserve their heritage as a unique entity (Fuller, 1992). Three other projects have been established in the Keewatin district of Canada's Northwest Territories, involving the Inuit communities in the development of innovative approaches to heritage conservation which emulate the ecomuseum (Bouchard, 1993).

Arising from a similar desire to create museums which better serve the communities in which they are situated, a related concept, that of the neighbourhood museum, developed in the United States during the 1970s. The earliest examples were often affiliated to mainstream museums but were established to serve very specific communities in the museum locality, primarily in urban areas. Ethnic-specific or culture-specific museums are independent institutions established and run by members of an ethnic or cultural group to interpret the history and culture of that group. In each of these categories, the museums have a mandate to serve and represent specific communities, whereas mainstream museums are intended to serve a broader, less specific audience. However, mainstream museums have failed to do this and have instead tended to serve a cultural élite and a narrow, ethnically-defined audience.

Cultural empowerment and the rise of culture-specific museums

The 1970s marked a dramatic period in the growth of community-based museums in North America as a result of the social and cultural revitalisation of that period. One of the most significant catalysts for the development of community museums in the United States, was the establishment of Anacostia Neighbourhood Museum by one of America's greatest cultural institutions: the Smithsonian Institution. A community museum, serving the low-income, disadvantaged, inner city population, was the dream of S. Dillon Ripley, who was Secretary of the Smithsonian Institution in the late 1960s. He was acutely aware of the failure of museums to reach 'the huge untapped public that has never entered a museum nor enjoyed any of the educational or aesthetic values that museums reflect' (quoted in Kinard, 1985: 220). In September 1967, Anacostia Neighborhood Museum opened in Washington, DC, with a crowd of 4,000 attending the opening ceremony. The first museum of its kind in North America, it provided a cultural centre for the residents of the predominantly black neighbourhood of Anacostia and served as a model and resource centre for similar projects throughout North America and the world.

In 1969 a three-day seminar on neighbourhood museums was held at MUSE, the Bedford Lincoln Neighbourhood Museum established in 1968 by the Brooklyn Children's Museum, in the Crown Heights section of Brooklyn, New York, where 60 per cent of the population is black. There were over 200 participants at the seminar who shared the concern that museums generally lacked significance and relevance to certain sectors of the population, in particular the ethnic minority communities living in inner city areas. Many agreed that the neighbourhood museum, as well as addressing itself to the social issues of direct concern in the lives of the residents, could also be most effective in helping people to develop a sense of cultural identity, to learn about their history in America, and the countries from which their ancestors originated (Robbins, 1971: 63–8). The success of Anacostia and MUSE provided motivation for similar projects across America and, as a result, the concept of the neighbourhood museum grew and flourished throughout the 1970s.

In other countries such as Brazil, Spain and Portugal, museums were developed in a variety of unusual locations including red-light districts, psychiatric hospitals, urban barrios, and other areas where the participation of residents was emphasised and the museums worked towards creating changes within the community. In Mexico, the Museo Nacional de Antropologia established community-based museums in poor city areas when the main museum closed for renovation. Since that time fifty-two community museums have been established across the country (Fuller, 1992: 329–30). These changes were highlighted by the 1972 ICOM meeting in Chile in which it was stated that museums should be integrated with society around them, and in 1974 the ICOM definition of a museum was changed to emphasise its role 'in the service of society and its development'.

Paralleling these developments was the growth of museums and cultural centres established by ethnic groups wishing to preserve and share their cultural heritage and counterbalance the ways in which mainstream institutions represented their cultures. They also provided a centre for the display, teaching and research of their cultures for the benefit of members of their own communities as well as other members of the public. In this way, communities could establish a venue in which they can take control of the representation of their cultures, provide a cultural centre for the promotion of traditional and contemporary arts, and a venue for a range of community activities otherwise unavailable in deprived inner city neighbourhoods. In North America there are now hundreds of museums and cultural centres devoted to the display and interpretation of the different cultural groups: African Americans, Chinese, Ukrainians, Italians, Poles, Hispanics and others.

A significant factor in the development of such projects was the growing pride in ethnic identity. Events such as the British Columbian Centennial celebrations of 1958 and those of the American Bicentennial in 1976 brought the concept of cultural diversity into sharp focus and provided a vehicle for many different ethnic groups to reassess their past and present cultural status. Government funds were made available for suitable projects and events in which cultural diversity was a strong feature, in some instances providing the capital funding for the establishment of museums.

For decades, the policy in the USA had been to try to assimilate all ethnic groups into the dominant Anglo-American culture, in the concept of the 'melting pot'. The 1976 American Bicentennial focused attention upon the previous two hundred years and the immigrant history of the nation. While promoting the nationalistic pride of the United States, the Bicentennial celebrations also fostered greater awareness of cultural diversity. This reflected the start of slow change in public and government attitudes as the limitations and culturally deleterious effects of the melting pot concept have come to be recognised, leading to a new approach in which differences between ethnic groups are celebrated with pride. 'In its promotion of homogeneity as a cultural ideal, the myth of the melting pot remains a powerful yet often silent and negative influence on our ability to deal realistically and positively with cultural diversity in contemporary America' (Roberts, 1990).

The idea of the melting pot is now giving way to a new concept, as yet undefined, in which shared culture is enriched by the unique qualities of each of the ethnic groups that constitute American society. The arts continue to provide an important focus for many ethnic-specific museums, not just for entertainment, but for the display of unique forms of artistic expressions and the continuation of cultural traditions. They also continue to provide a means of demonstrating political and cultural perspectives, particularly evident in many Hispanic, African American and Native American institutions.

Over the past 30 years, a number of possible sources of funding have been made available in the United States, providing financial support for those wishing to establish a museum or cultural centre or apply for grants to assist with the development of public programmes, educational activities, archiving, etc.; these include government agencies, foundations, and corporations.

Tribal groups wishing to establish a museum or cultural centre have been able to apply to the Labor Department's Division of Indian and Native American Programs, and to the Economic Development Administration who, in an effort to ease unemployment on the reservations, provided funds for such projects. State funding could be sought through the Departments of Tourism and Education, the National Assembly of State Arts Agencies and, in urban areas, Community Development Block Grants provided funding for community facilities. Museums would only be funded in conjunction with some other type of facility such as a tourism complex, neighbourhood services centre, community college, or youth centre. In the 1970s, this resulted in some unusual combinations of establishments such as a Slovakian Museum funded as part of a health clinic; and a Hungarian Museum funded in conjunction with a book bank.

In recent years, tribal archaeological projects and museums have received funding from the Administration for Native Americans (Department of Health and

Human Services) and the Bureau of Reclamation under the Reclamation Small Loans Act for activities such as archaeological data recovery and public education (Parker, 1990: 134). A number of agencies provides grants to support programmes and activities, some available only to Native American communities, others open to all sectors of the public. These include the Advisory Council on Historic Preservation, the Bureau of Indian Affairs (BIA), the Institute of Museum Services (IMS), the National Endowment for the Arts (NEA), National Endowment for the Humanities (NEH), the National Park Service (NPS). Grants may be available for the preservation of archives and staff training from the National Historical Publications and Records Commission. Funding for science-based projects can be sought from the National Science Foundation (NSF) (Smithsonian Institution, nd).

Private funding provided another major source of financial support for museums. The Congressional Research Service runs a Federal Program of Assistance to American Indians providing lists of federal and private organisations which provide financial or technical assistance, or research opportunities which would benefit Native Americans. Since 1917, the US tax code has offered tax deductions to individuals and companies encouraging them to make donations to charities and other organisations which benefit the public. For many years this has proved a significant factor in generating private funding in the USA, much of which comes from various private foundations.

New directions

What is particularly noticeable about many of these institutions is the rich variety of activities undertaken. Community-based museums often provide a broader range of activities than the traditional European model of museum, including the use of performing and visual arts as an integral part of the exhibitions, as a means of interpreting the collections, and as an activity for participation by visitors. They frequently provide a venue for many community activities, fulfilling the role of museum and community cultural centre. In some instances, the activities of these new museums go beyond this and deal with issues of social, political and economic importance to the community. Such areas are not the traditional subjects of museum exhibitions, but museums must change with the times and respond to the needs of the public. E. Barry Gaither, Director of the Museum of the National Center of Afro-American Artists, believes that

> culturally specific museums have a unique role to play in forging a new America. Grounded in historic heritages associated with particular communities, they provide intimate models for the partnerships and dialogue which museums and their communities may develop. Responding to social, cultural and educational needs, these museums participate simultaneously to affirm the worth and contributions of minority peoples.
>
> (Gaither, 1990)

Community-based museums rely upon the enthusiasm and generosity of members of the public to ensure their success, requiring the donation of objects, money and time. Many of the basic ideas behind the concept of the community-based museums which have been established by members of ethnic communities reflect those of the ecomuseum: community involvement in the establishment and running of the museum; the collection of material from local residents; and the cross-disciplinary approach. A strong motivational factor is the desire to educate the younger members of the community in the traditional knowledge, skills, beliefs and values of the religious or cultural group, and to preserve and promote a sense of cultural identity at a personal and community level.

Although ethnic communities in Britain share these concerns, the country has a long tradition of publicly-funded museums. There is not the same range of grants available, nor is there the tax incentive to encourage business sponsorship on the same scale as in America. This makes it even more difficult for community groups to establish their own museums. However, even in America grants are limited and most of the minority-run, community museums frequently function as non-profit organisations or charitable trusts, with very small budgets and a minimum of staff. Grants are limited and, although able to make applications for funding to various government sources, most community-run museums have had to struggle for many years without any substantial financial assistance from such agencies. Relying upon public donations and upon various fund-raising ventures, the sum needed to establish the museum can take many years to raise, reflecting the commitment, determination and desire of those concerned to see their dream of a museum become a reality.

The proposal to establish a museum can also be a valuable weapon in the fight for the return of cultural property. Frequent arguments voiced in opposition to repatriation centre upon the subject of material preservation, the conditions of storage and the question of ownership. These are questions which are being addressed by the establishment of tribally-operated museums in Australia and North America, developments which can serve to facilitate the repatriation of material culture under repatriation agreements which are contingent upon suitable storage and/or display facilities being available. The development of such facilities can ensure the safety and conservation of museum collections which are returned to communities and so lead to the realisation of a dream long held by the whole community.

Once established, continuing major expenditure is required if the facility is to achieve the appropriate levels of security and conservation requirements. Many community-based museums fail in these areas due to lack of money and trained staff, often relying heavily upon public donations and volunteer staff, and so are unable to conserve their collections, provide a changing programme of exhibits, or take advantage of touring exhibitions offered by mainstream museums.

As a consequence of their culturally focused mandates, tribal institutions may use unconventional methods to fulfill their specific cultural needs. The Makah Cultural and Research Center has an oral history programme used to record the oral traditions of the tribe through the words of the elders. Recordings are held in the tribal archives but are not made available to anyone unless specified by the elder. As in many traditional societies, some knowledge is restricted and is only passed on to members of the tribe holding certain positions according to age, sex, kin or clan. It is an anathema in such cultures that restricted knowledge should be shared with non-tribal members. Ann Renker, Executive Director of the Makah Cultural and Research Center, has explained the policy of this institution:

> Regardless of what the Society of American Archivists says, regardless of what the American Association of Museums says, we have the responsibility to protect the ancestral information management system and we do that in our facility today. When an elder agrees to do an oral history for us (he or she must specify) if the information is ever to be published.
>
> (cited in Parker, 1990: 55)

The restriction of knowledge runs counter to one of the central functions of mainstream museums: that of dissemination of information about the collections. Zuni councilman Barton Martza has also commented that 'white society must also learn that some of our traditional culture is for Zunis only' (quoted in Ferguson and Eriacho, 1990: 12). White society *is* learning and, as a result, some museums are now reviewing their policies with regard to the interpretation of certain artefacts.

Harry Walters, curator of the Ned Hatathli Cultural Center Museum in the Navajo Community College, in Arizona, is critical of professional and government bodies such as the Institute of Museum Services and the American Association of Museums which, he feels, fail to recognise that Native American museums may have different but valid priorities from mainstream museums. He feels that the continued underfunding of Native American museums is in part due to such attitudes and also accounts for problems in gaining accreditation. As an example of this he described the criticisms by some evaluators of a grant proposal, who objected to the Hatathli Museum's practice of lending valuable material such as medicine bundles. Such practices are culturally relevant and appropriate to the function of this particular museum and Walters counters such criticisms emphasising 'We are a Navajo museum and we serve the Navajo public'. Indeed, in recent years a number of mainstream museums in North America, Australia and New Zealand have been lending ceremonial items to the communities from which they originate for use in ceremonies. Such developments may provide a mutually acceptable solution to repatriation requests and demonstrate the benefits of a reciprocal approach.

In order to address these issues, a fundamental change in museological policy must take place, demonstrating an acceptance of alternative concepts of ownership rights and intellectual copyright. In *Keepers of the Treasures: a Report on Tribal Preservation Funding Needs*, produced by the US National Park Service in 1990, it was recommended that

> Federal agencies, State and local governments, museums, foundations, universities, and arts and humanities institutions that assist tribal preservation programs must recognize that basic program goals, standards, and approaches must be adjusted to accommodate the unique needs of grant recipients and program administrators in different cultures.
>
> (Parker, 1990: 174).

Other professional organisations have also recognised the value of community-based museums and cultural centres and have called for mainstream museums to provide assistance to such initiatives. The Council of Australian Museum Associations' *Policies for Museums in Australia and Aboriginal and Torres Strait Islander Peoples* stressed the responsibility of museums to provide assistance in management and preservation of cultural property, and training in research and documentation procedures (CAMA, 1993b: 9). A report into museums and First Peoples issued jointly by the Assembly of First Nations and the Canadian Museums Associations in 1992, gave support to the establishment of community-based museums and cultural centres and called for provisional and territorial governments to provide financial support for such initiatives. In the report it was stated that 'community-based cultural centres and programs can reinforce a positive identity, help to heal cultural dislocation and improve educational opportunities for children. These improvements in turn support the realization of socio-economic goals of First Peoples communities.' (AFN and CMA, 1992: 5–6). The Canadian Museum of Civilization has given its support to a project to establish a new museum on the Queen Charlotte Islands and has offered to transfer a significant portion of its Haida collection to the new museum on long-term loan (MacDonald, 1993: 13).

However, not everyone regards these developments as desirable: David Anderson, head of education at the Victoria and Albert Museum in London, blames museums in part for:

> accelerating the decline of practice of the popular arts and other cultural activities and an increased dependence on commodified culture . . . by emphasising passive, distanced appreciation rather than engaged practice. . . . The preservation and display of works of art of the past as timeless icons has made us self-conscious, has severed our links with our own cultures. The incentive for us to create for ourselves has been reduced. Museums have become centres, symbols and agents of cultural dissociation.
>
> (Anderson, D., 1992: 10).

He refers to the influence of western culture breaking the cycle of cultural renewal in Ladakh in northern India, but regards the idea of a museum being established as contributing to the decline: 'All that remains now is for us to help the government in Ladakh to open a museum in Leh, the capital, for the process of cultural alienation to be complete. . . . Perhaps the appearance of a museum is the surest sign of the death of a self-sustaining culture' (ibid: 10).

Anderson is correct in his view that museums can signify cultural decline: museums established by immigrant communities often serve little more function than to preserve history, providing a means of clinging to the past while contributing little to the future development of the culture or preservation of traditional skills and knowledge; but this is a worst-case scenario. Museums can provide resources for the rekindling of skills and knowledge which have been virtually lost in recent decades, providing visual and documentary evidence for the training and inspiration of new generations of artists and craftspeople. They can also provide venues for demonstrations of performing arts, domestic and trade skills, and educational facilities for ensuring that such skills are not lost, despite the enormous changes that immigrant and fourth world cultures have experienced. In this way, museums can help to revive and preserve cultural traditions and so can present interpretive activities which are not static memorials to the past, but demonstrations of dynamic, living cultures.

The following three chapters provide a brief overview of the histories, goals and activities of a number of museums which were established to cater for the needs of specific ethnic communities. These examples will demonstrate the ways in which such institutions are contributing vigorously to the active preservation of the cultures of their communities. The growth of such facilities is one of the most significant factors in the development of museology as we approach the new century. They provide communities with control in the process of representing their past and demonstrating their continuation as a distinct cultural entity, enabling them to counteract misconceptions and demonstrate their continuing vitality as a community. They also provide valuable resources for communities seeking to preserve and recover aspects of their past and educate the younger members of the community in the language, religious practices, artistic skills and other unique aspects of their culture. The best of them provide role models for the museum profession generally in the development of alternative approaches to interpretation, the inclusion of dynamic, living cultural practices in the normally static environment of the traditional museum, and the provision of community-focused activities.

Many of those examined are in North America, but examples from Australia and New Zealand are also included in the discussion. In the following chapters, the subject of culturally specific museums is divided into three distinct categories: museums and cultural centres established by immigrants or descendants of immigrants; those established by African American groups in the United States; and those established by Fourth World communities, that is indigenous populations who remain in their homeland but constitute a minority of the population of the modern state, specifically Maori, Australian Aboriginal and Native American communities.

Chapter 4 examines museums and cultural centres established by immigrants or descendants of immigrants including Chinese, Ukrainian, Jewish, Mexican-American and other ethnic communities who, although often forced by circumstances to leave their homeland, were voluntary immigrants to a new land. Institutions established by African Americans are also dealt with in this chapter, but separately, as their history of slavery (enforced immigration) necessitates the treatment of some distinct issues.

Indigenous groups in Australia, New Zealand and North America, while unique and diverse, share certain similarities with regard to their treatment historically at the hands of colonial powers, their status as disempowered minority communities in their own countries, and the history of their treatment by anthropologists and museum interpreters. Chapter 5 examines museums and cultural centres established by Maori and Aboriginal Australian communities and Chapter 6 explores the growth of Native American institutions. These categories have been utilised as a means of illustrating differences in the agendas of institutions which nevertheless also share certain characteristics as organisations seeking to address the needs of their own specific communities, while also addressing self-representation in the context of cross-cultural communication.

As a result of the failure of mainstream museology to address the needs of the broader community, Claudine Brown, the former director of the Smithsonian Institution's National African American Museum Project, rejects the term 'ethnic-specific museum'. As she has correctly remarked 'historically all American museums have been ethnic- or culturally-specific by virtue of their exclusionary practices' (Brown, 1993: 2). Instead, Brown uses the term 'community-focused' museums. She also argues that 'every museum should see itself as a neighbourhood museum' (Brown, 1990: 6).

While the term 'community-focused' seems to address accurately and appropriately the mandate of the institutions being discussed in the following chapters, it is now evident that many mainstream museums are becoming increasingly more community-focused as well. In recognition of these changing trends, and for the sake of clarity, I have utilised the terms 'neighbourhood museum' to refer to those museums which developed as outposts of mainstream American institutions in the 1970s, and 'community museum' to include museums established by immigrant populations and their descendants, as well as those established by indigenous peoples in North America, Australia and New Zealand.

4

Remembering the homeland

'We are the custodians of the community's heritage which by extension means that the community has ownership of our collections. Ownership and documentation go hand in hand as the way of preserving our heritage for history.'

(Dennis Ferguson-Acosta (1990) in 'Report of the Symposium on African American and Latino Museums and their Collections', p.11)

In the past, community-based museums established by immigrant communities have had a tendency to be nostalgic memorials to the past. Many peoples who emigrated to North America and other parts of the world did so as economic, political or religious refugees escaping hardship and persecution in their own countries; despite this, many harbour a deep love of the country from which they or their ancestors originated. The establishment of a museum can provide a means of recalling what has been lost, and attempting to preserve traditional skills and knowledge. Such activities can be important for immigrants as they seek to retain a sense of cultural identity and community in a new environment, and to share and take pride in those things which they feel makes their culture unique.

For members of immigrant communities and their descendants, the collection of early historical material to use in the museum presents a particular problem. Cultural treasures are rare in such museums. Although many individuals do still possess family heirlooms, objects of personal importance or mementoes of the traditional ways of the past, much of the important or valuable material of historical interest and religious significance has been lost to the communities which have resettled in other areas or other lands. Communities became greatly fragmented as people sought a place where they could make a new home, find employment and support themselves and their families.

Even in mainstream museums, the collections of material relating to the lives of immigrants may be sparse. Social history collections reflecting the lives of the poor are typically under-represented in museum collections; when early collections were being acquired, it was primarily the material culture of the wealthy and important members of society that was valued and preserved. They were more likely than the poor to have links with museums and they had more possessions to donate. Those who were poor had little, retained items for longer, and their material culture was of little interest to collectors. Many of those who emigrated were poor, while others left under circumstances which did not allow the transportation of many possessions; refugees, in particular, are likely to have few possessions from the home country. As a result, much of the material collected in community-established museums comprises documents, photographs, crafts, domestic and personal items, and some family treasures, while much of the valuable material may be found in the collections of mainstream museums or in the hands of wealthy collectors. The situation is particularly acute for black communities who, as a result of their slave history, have virtually no material relating to their African origins and little personal material of a historical nature other than papers and photographs documenting the arrival and life of the slaves in the North American continent. Collections devoted to the experiences of slaves reflect both the limits of personal possessions which they were able to own and, in the past, the general lack of interest in preserving the history and material culture of slaves.

As a consequence of these factors, many of the museums established by immigrant communities are historical in focus and dominated by artefacts which demonstrate movable cultural property: knowledge and skills. So, for instance, the Ukrainian National Museum in Chicago displays examples of folk arts and evidence of the skills people were able to continue to practise in their new homeland: embroidery, costume, wood-carving, *pysanky* (Easter egg decorating); and images of prominent individuals in Ukrainian history. The text is basic and factual, with little to convey to an outsider the reasons for departure, the realities of the life that was left behind, or the experiences being a Ukrainian American. There is no feeling in it, no sense of contact with individual people and their experiences, nothing to stir the imagination or sentiments of the visitor. The overall feeling is of gloomy melancholy, a nostalgic yearning for the past, a culture isolated from the passage of time, an environment tainted with a pervasive layer of psychological, if not real, dust.

Variations on this theme can be found in many small community museums across North America, Britain, and in other countries where immigrants have settled. Ossified and outdated, they struggle to exist with insufficient funding, accommodation problems, and volunteer staff with little or no museological training, all of which contribute to severely limiting the activities and potential growth of such museums. Exhibitions focusing upon the social and political aspects of the immigrant experience tend to be presented in major mainstream museums where, in recent years, the multicultural aspects of society have become a central focus of social history research and interpretation. However, the issues which are effecting change in mainstream museum interpretation techniques, are also influencing the practices in community museums, and certain examples stand out as innovative in their methods and outlook. Facing the same problems as described in the preceding paragraphs, these examples illustrate what is possible with creative thinking, energy and enthusiasm, and the determination to gain wider support.

The growth of ethnic museums has been most profound in the United States and Canada where there has been a tremendous rise over the last twenty-five years in the number of museums and cultural centres focusing upon the collection and interpretation of material relevant to the cultures of ethnic groups, both immigrant and indigenous. In addition to the many European immigrants who have settled in the United States, there are large Hispanic and Asian communities, and, of course, the African American population whose ancestors were subjected to a forced migration through the processes of the transatlantic slave trade. Like the Ukrainians, Poles and other European groups, they have established their own museums and cultural centres to enable them to take control of the interpretation of their history and the promotion of cultural activities for the community.

Mexican Fine Arts Center Museum, Chicago

The Mexican Fine Arts Center Museum in Chicago, Illinois, was founded in 1982 by members of the Mexican American community of Chicago. The Museum aims to demonstrate the richness of the arts in Mexican culture through the acquisition of a significant, permanent collection of Mexican art and the presentation of a full and varied programme of visual and performing arts events. It has a strong emphasis upon education, aiming to inform visitors about the historical and contemporary arts of Mexico and encourage the professional development of Mexican artists in the Chicago area. Located in the largely Mexican community of Pilsen, it also provides a cultural focus for the Mexican population of over 500,000 residing in the Chicago metropolitan area.

The Mexican Fine Arts Center Museum (MFACM) began by sponsoring exhibitions in other institutions and community venues around Chicago. Four years later the Chicago Park District provided a building in which the museum could be permanently based: the Harrison Park Boat Craft Shop in Pilsen. The building was converted into a multi-purpose arts centre and museum devoted to the presentation of Mexican visual and performing arts, becoming the largest facility of its kind in the country when it opened in March 1987. The centre consists of two galleries, a multi-purpose area with a stage and seating capacity for 325, a shop, and administrative offices and storage spaces. The Museum has a permanent collection of photographs, folk art, graphic art and contemporary art, including prints by Mexican artists living in the United States and by prominent Mexican artists such as Rufino Tamayo, José Clemente Orozco and David Alfaro Siqueiros. The Museum offers a lively programme of exhibitions and supporting events. Subjects have included *Fifteen Contemporary Artists of Mexico*, which toured to other venues in the United States and Mexico; *Vestidos Con el Sol: Traditional Textiles from Mexico, Guatemala, and Panama; Rufino Tamayo: Sculptures and Mixographs; Popular Toys of Mexico; The Art of Mexican Papier-Maché*; and *The Modern Maya: a Culture in Transition*. Texts are in Spanish and English (MFACM, 1991).

While some of the exhibitions provide reminders of the influences that Mayan, Aztec and other ancient cultures of Mexico still exert upon some Mexican artists such as Francisco Toledo, others highlight the influences of modern international movements, such as Surrealism and Abstract Expressionism. The annual *Dia*

83

Figure 4.1 Large papier mâché figures being installed in the *Day of the Dead* exhibition, Mexican Fine Arts Center Museum, Chicago, 1989

Source: Mexican Fine Arts Center Museum, Chicago, USA

Figure 4.2 Mexican artist Ricardo Linares painting an *alebrije*, fantasy figure, Mexican Fine Arts
   Centre Museum, Chicago

Source: Mexican Fine Arts Center Museum, Chicago, USA

de los Muertos exhibition frequently combines the traditional papier mâché and pottery artefacts with avant-garde art works. *The Barrio Murals*, an exhibition of '19 murals by 19 artists . . . a celebration of 19 years of mural painting in Chicago by artists from the Mexican community' illustrates the way in which murals 'have traditionally served as ethnic and racial billboards for historical and social messages' (Jimenez, 1987: 21). *The Modern Maya: a Culture in Transition* was an exhibition of photographs taken by American Macduff Everton which documents the changing lifestyle of today's Mayan Indians in the Yucatan as tourism increases and has an ever-greater impact. The exhibition also served to remind visitors of the continuing existence of Mayan Indians, descendants of the ancient civilisation decimated by the Spanish invasion.

Supporting these exhibitions were a variety of activities. Some provided insight into the skills and methods of the artists whose work is exhibited. For example, the 1989 and 1990 *Dia de los Muertos* exhibitions focused on colourful papier mâché and pottery items. The museum organised events such as demonstrations by potters Alvaro and José Antonio de la Cruz, showing how they make hand-built clay skeletons finished in bright colours, and by papier mâché artists Miguel and Ricardo Linares, showing the methods of making *alebrijes*, fantastic creatures, composites of animals, demons and dragons, and *calaveras*, brightly coloured and highly decorated skulls and skeletons.

Other exhibits have dealt with more serious aspects of life. The 1988 *Dia de los Muertos* exhibition included a display of *ofrendas* or altars, often with food offerings, and images and memorabilia of the individuals being honoured. An assemblage, made from rubble and wallboard and mixing Christian and Aztec imagery, was created in honour of the victims of the earthquake which hit Mexico City in 1985. During the 1989 *Dia de los Muertos* exhibition, a Californian printmaker, Ester Hernandez, created an installation dealing with the long-term use and effects of toxic pesticides on grape crops, which caused serious pollution in her hometown (Holbert, 1989: 53). The exhibition *Vestidos Con el Sol* presented beautiful handwoven garments produced by the indigenous peoples of Mexico, Guatemala, and Panama. Maricela Garcia Vargas, in an essay in the exhibition catalogue, stressed that museums have a responsibility to deal with and draw public attention to issues such as the killing of the indigenous peoples who had produced the exhibits (Vargas, 1990: 16–18). In addition to exhibitions, the museum presents lectures, artists' workshops, artists-in-residence, and musical and theatrical performances. It sponsored the first Nezahualcoyotl Poetry Festival and co-presented an outdoor Mexican Film Festival in Chicago.

The budget for the museum grew from $900 in the first year of operation, to $950,000 in 1991, with attendance reaching 75,000 for the year 1990. The museum receives its revenue from various sources including foundations and corporations, city and state funds, the National Endowment for the Arts, and income generated through contributions, membership, donations, and shop sales (MFACM, 1991: 3). The success of the museum has been acknowledged with several local awards including the 1989 Beatrice Foundation Award for

Excellence in Management, and awards from the Chicago Commission on Human Relations and the Chicago Council on Urban Affairs.

Museum of Chinese in the Americas, New York

The Museum of Chinese in the Americas is located in Chinatown in Manhattan's Lower East Side. It researches and documents the 150-year history of the Chinese in America and the changing face of New York's Chinatown, past and present. The Museum was established in 1990, developing out of ten years of work by the New York Chinatown History Project. Following the enthusiastic reception of an exhibition *Images from a Neglected Past: The Work and Culture of Chinese in America* sponsored by the Basement Workshop, a Chinatown cultural organisation, Jack Tchen, one of the exhibition organisers, and Charlie Lai, a community activist, established the New York Chinatown History Project in 1980.

Initially, the project focused upon photographic documentation of the local area, oral history interviewing of residents and presentation of exhibitions. Since then, the range of activities has expanded to include the creation of bilingual radio programmes, the presentation of slide shows, plays and roundtable discussions, and walking tours of Chinatown. It also has a library and archive containing materials relating to the history and culture of Asian Americans, runs a small Asian American bookshop, publishes *Bu Gao Ban*, a bilingual publication, and rents out travelling exhibitions, slides and videos. Staff have used unusual techniques to disseminate the results of their historical research. Building on the popularity of the Hong Kong soap operas, they used the soap opera format to present the stories of real people, gathered during oral history work, in radio docu-dramas.

By 1990, the idea had formed to create a Chinese American Museum. The New York Chinatown History Project (NYCHP) was housed in P.S. 23, a former public school in the heart of Chinatown. Rather than seeking funds to build a new purpose-built museum, members of the NYCHP decided to continue to use the school building which they recognised as 'an artifact in itself, meriting historic preservation' (Chew, 1990: 2). The building was also a focal point for the memories of many of the area's residents who had vivid recollections of their school days there. It therefore seemed natural and important to build the museum in the former classrooms, accepting that the structure of the building would inevitably impose physical constraints upon the use of space and the layout of exhibitions.

The NYCHP was renamed the Chinatown History Museum in 1991, and later became the Museum of Chinese in the Americas. It operates as a non-profit community education organisation with funding from membership and from various public and private sources, including grants from the Rockefeller Foundation and the National Endowment for the Humanities. Jack Tchen, one of the founders, recognises that the difficulties they face in fundraising reflect the competing social service needs which face the community as a whole, but he

87

sees the work of the history project as crucially important to the preservation of Chinese American heritage.

> Chinatown is not peopled by the famous, but by workers whose records are not usually the substance of history. Who will be considered part of this country's history? Are we going to have a democratic history for a democratic country? It's appropriate now and long overdue.
>
> (Tchen cited in Floyd, 1984: 11)

While little financial support is obtained from community sources, the history project and the Museum have consistently received enthusiastic response and endless assistance from the local residents.

Community involvement is central to all levels of operation in the Museum of Chinese in the Americas: it is the memories of the area's residents and their loaned or donated artefacts and personal memorabilia, which form the nucleus for exhibitions. Volunteer staff are required as oral historians, gallery guides, designers, archivists, and in many other areas of work, to supplement the efforts of the handful of permanent staff. Together, since the project began in 1980, they 'have been climbing into garbage dumpsters, foraging on construction sites, and searching laundries, garment factories, neighbourhood stores, schools, restaurants, and tenements to rescue and reconstruct a history of the Chinese Americans and the community they built in New York's Chinatown' (Cooper and Liu, 1991: 50). This philosophy is the basis for the development of what has been called 'the dialogue-driven museum' leading to the creation of 'a learning environment in which memory and testimony inform and are informed by historical context and scholarship' (Tchen, 1992: 286). However, the functions of the Museum are intended to extend beyond the interpretation of Chinatown's past and to actively benefit the future of the neighbourhood. As Tchen has stated, 'Ultimately, we seek to become an ever more resonant and responsible history center in which scholarship and public programs can help make a critical historical awareness a powerful factor in improving New York and the community for the future' (Tchen, 1992: 291).

The Museum's focus upon the development of Chinatown is wide and diverse extending beyond the Chinatown residents and Chinese American New Yorkers, to include non-Chinese residents of New York, the wider US population, and tourists from all over the world. The Museum staff engage in dialogue with individuals and organisations representing a variety of fields and cultural groups. These include scholars and museum professionals who have been involved with the Museum's planning group; members of the Chinese American and non-Chinese communities who have been involved in the documentation of the area's history; and Chinese and non-Chinese individuals whose enthusiasm has led them to continue to explore the history of their neighbourhood with training from, and in co-operation with, the Museum of Chinese in the Americas (Tchen, 1992).

By documenting Chinese American history in Manhattan and across America, the work of the Museum of Chinese in the Americas is intended to provide 'access to the previously silent historical record of lives lived in Chinatown' (Cooper and Liu, 1991: 50), to counteract demeaning stereotypes of Chinese Americans and of Chinatown, and 'to give dignity and respect to the history of Chinese Americans and other minority groups' (Yu, 1990: 4). Exhibitions have focused upon the lives of those who are often neglected in the official histories, such as laundry and garment workers. In Tchen's view, such exhibitions provide public validation of the efforts of workers whose contribution to the community is largely unrecognised (Tchen, 1992: 292).

In addition to this the Museum aims to 'fulfill a commitment to the ideal of a multicultural society to view the Chinese American community in its relation-ship to other ethnic groups.' (Chin, 1991: 2). To this end, projects do not just focus upon Chinese American experiences, but also involve collaboration with other communities. A temporary exhibition *School Days: Memories of P.S. 23* was based around memories of Chinese and Italian Americans who attended the school, while *Between Mott and Mulberry: Views of Italians and Chinese in New York City* was a workshop which focused upon the interaction of Chi-nese and Italian American students of P.S. 23 during the 1920s, 1930s, and 1940s. Other inter-cultural projects have included: the *Chinatown–Harlem–East Harlem* initiative; a panel discussion entitled *Other's Others: A Dialogue About Identities and Relations Among Asian and African Americans*; and a series of tri-lingual workshops in conjunction with an exhibition *Landscape of Labor and Love: Puerto Rican Women in the Garment Industry*, organised by the Center for Puerto Rican Studies. Another challenge will be to relate the con-cerns of the Museum of Chinese in the Americas with the needs and interests of new Chinese immigrants who have no prior history in the United States.

The museum has a strong community focus in all areas: audience, staff, research, exhibitions and activities. As stated in a publicity leaflet, the Museum 'reclaims, preserves, and shares Chinese American history and culture with a broad audience of visitors. Working together and talking with people of all backgrounds helps shape our exhibitions, programs, and collections'. The Museum's publicity brochures and the publication *Bu Gao Ban* are written in both Chinese and English, and both carry requests to members of the commu-nity not to discard artefacts and materials without first thinking of their potential historical value:

> An artifact can be ordinary everyday things like business cards, restaurant menus, store records, class photographs, or personal mementos like auto-graph albums, ticket stubs, diplomas, report cards, and graduation outfits. Often, the most exciting finds are those which people don't think are valu-able or useful, yet which provide important information or tell an almost forgotten story.
>
> (NYCHP, 1990: 11)

The *Bu Gao Ban* also lists the names of members and volunteers; those who have donated or lent items, provided financial support, or been interviewed as part of the oral history project; and gives details of exhibitions being planned, and materials or memories required.

From the start, it has been the intention of those involved in the development of the Museum to create 'a new exhibition format which will engage our diverse audience in an exchange of experiences and information' (Chew, 1990: 2). The museum's first permanent exhibition *Remembering New York Chinatown*, which opened in February 1991, utilised interactive techniques and changing components. As well as documenting the memories of residents and workers from various ethnic backgrounds, the exhibition explores ambiguities such as the paradox of the view of Chinese Americans as foreigners despite the history of the Chinese in New York over 160 years. It also explores the differing views of Chinatown, contrasting the perceptions of its residents with those of other New Yorkers and visiting tourists. Throughout the exhibition, the voices and faces of Chinese people reach out to visitors and speak of their experiences, memories and views. It is very much a museum about people and one which is clearly supported by the people within the community.

African American museums and cultural centres

The history of the African American people is very different from that of other immigrant groups. While many immigrants may have been forced to leave their homeland due to poverty, war, religious or cultural persecution and other social, economic or cultural pressures, most chose to settle and create a new home in the USA, seeing it as a land of new opportunities and hope for the future. In contrast, the African ancestors of the African American population were dragged from their homes, transported in appalling conditions across the Atlantic and forced into slavery for white owners in the Americas.

Until the 1960s, the history and culture of the African American population had been neglected within the education system and museums; African American artists were marginalised by the art establishment, and the cultural needs of African American communities were not being met by the primarily white, mainstream cultural institutions. Since that time there has been a tremendous growth in the number of African American museums and cultural centres reflecting a general rise in the number of museums, but also being an indicator of major changes in African American political and cultural status.

Many of the earlier black museums were established on university campuses with a strong black tradition: Hampton Institute in Virginia established a museum in 1867, and was the first organisation in the United States to establish collections of artefacts relating to African American history and culture (Orator, 1995: 9). The museum at Hampton Institute, now known as the Hampton University Museum, was established in 1867 by the Institute's white founder, General Samuel Chapman Armstrong, the son of American missionaries in Hawaii. He established the Institute to provide educational facilities for African Americans and later also Native Americans.

The museum was intended to provide the students with information concerning natural history and other cultures of the world. Armstrong developed collections originating from the Pacific and the USA and, in the 1890s, purchased and received donations of African material from William H. Sheppard, one of the Institute's graduates who had become a missionary amongst the Kuba in the Belgian Congo. During the twentieth century, the collections of African and Native American material continued to grow and were augmented with art works by nineteenth- and twentieth-century African American artists (Ruffins, 1991a: 519). Howard University and Fisk University also established collections prior to the Second World War (AAMA/AASLH, nd: 3), while others, such as the College of Charleston's Avery Institute for African American History and Culture, were established in mainstream institutions. While collections established within colleges and universities continue to provide a valuable resource for new courses in fields such as black history and culture, such collections are often less accessible to the general public.

The Civil Rights Movement provided the catalyst for new developments during the 1960s. Anger and frustration over racism and the resultant feeling of alienation from a society and institutions dominated by white attitudes and values boiled over. The political fervour of the period gave a new resolve to black Americans to take control over their lives and counteract the alienation that they experienced in relation to mainstream educational and cultural institutions which failed to promote their historical and cultural heritage. New pride in black culture led to a surge of interest in the promotion of black arts and the provision of educational and entertainment facilities for black inner city residents. Academic courses relating to the history and culture of African Americans were developed in schools and colleges. Black Americans wanted to see their history and culture documented and represented in a more accurate, thorough and sympathetic manner than was being carried out in mainstream museums and recognised that African American museums could provide the black community with a powerful forum for self-expression, education and cultural control.

These were the motivational forces that led to the establishment of many of the African American museums and cultural centres (Stevens, 1975; Austin, 1982). Museums became part of the process of politicisation and empowerment of the black community and, during this time, there was a rapid growth in the number of African American museums; the bicentennial celebrations in 1976 provided a further burst of enthusiasm and funding for many cultural projects including the establishment of museums.

The scale and activities of these black-oriented institutions varied considerably although, overwhelmingly, they have been established in the northeast and in urban areas where much of the African American population is concentrated (AAMA/AASLH, nd: xiii). Some devoted themselves to black history and culture at a local, regional or national level: the Museum of Afro-American History in Boston, Massachusetts; the Black American Museum at Niagara Falls, in New York State; the DuSable Museum of African American History in Chicago, Illinois; the International Afro-American Museum, Inc., in Detroit. Some were small concerns, established through the enthusiasm and efforts of individuals or a community group. The International Afro-American Museum,

Inc. which focused on 'black achievements in Africa and America' was established in 1965 through the efforts of a group of citizens. The activities of the museum included a mobile exhibition, an oral history programme, and films identifying career opportunities for black youngsters. Your Heritage House, Inc., established in 1969, provided arts classes and resources for children, using a collection of toys, books, musical instruments and historic artefacts collected by one of the co-directors who had gathered them during travels in many countries. The Adept New American Folk Gallery established in 1970 by Vivian Ayers, a black poet and educator, organised community arts projects aimed at the black community. One of these involved as many as 350,000 people in a variety of different arts activities (Stevens, 1975).

During the late 1960s and early 1970s efforts were made to establish a professional organisation to represent black museums and related institutions culminating in the formation in 1976 of the African American Museums Association (ibid., 4–5). By the mid-1980s, there were over 100 museums in the United States devoted to the collection and interpretation of material relating to Africa and African American history and culture (AAM, 1984). The African American Museums Association:

> fosters and promotes the celebration of African and African American cultural heritage through supporting Black museums and related institutions. . . . [It] is open to cultural organizations, historical societies and museums which not only collect, exhibit and preserve objects valuable to art, science and history, but also educational institutions, research agencies and cultural centers.
>
> (Gaither, in AAMA, 1988: 17)

Mainstream museums were also being forced to review their practices and began to recognise that they were failing to address the needs of the black community. As a result, some specialist facilities devoted to black history, art and culture were established by major institutions: the Schomburg Center for Research in Black Culture, a department of New York Public Library; Anacostia Neighborhood Museum, established by the Smithsonian Institution to serve the needs of the predominantly black population of the Anacostia area of Washington, DC; and the MUSE Community Museum of Brooklyn, established in 1968 by the Brooklyn Children's Museum as a pilot project for small neighbourhood museums in New York.

Anacostia is probably one of the best-known museums devoted to the interpretation of African American history and culture. Operated by the Smithsonian Institution in Washington, DC, Anacostia Museum of African American History and Culture was the first federally funded community museum in the United States. The museum collects, preserves, interprets and displays material relating to the history and culture of black Americans, and in particular the residents of Anacostia.

Initially, the museum provided activities and events specifically related to the experiences and needs of the people of Anacostia. Its exhibitions have dealt with issues not often covered in other museums at that time. Early exhibitions dealt mainly with historical subject matter and included: *This is Africa*, an exhibition of objects, art works, costume and fabrics from a number of African nations; *Black Patriots of the American Revolution*, which portrayed the role of black Americans in the American War of Independence; . . . *Towards Freedom*, about the Civil Rights movement; and *The Rat – Man's Invited Affliction*, an exhibition that dealt with rat infestation in the neighbourhood (Kinard and Nighbert, 1972: 102–19). This last exhibition in particular attracted public and media attention at a national level. It highlighted a problem which was very relevant to the people in the neighbourhood, and provided information concerning action necessary to deal with the problem. It was then decided that future exhibitions should continue to deal with contemporary issues of relevance to the residents of Anacostia; social, political and economic issues as well as cultural and historical.

With funding from the Carnegie Corporation of New York research was carried out into urban problems in Anacostia which reflected similar problems across the nation. This led to the production of educational materials; the presentation of *The Evolution of a Community*, an exhibition portraying the history of Anacostia from pre-contact days to the present; and to the establishment of the Center for Anacostia Studies to study the history of the area, contemporary issues affecting residents, and the future of the neighbourhood. In a survey carried out to identify the issues of most concern to Anacostia residents, the responses listed crime, drugs, unemployment, housing and education (Kinard and Nighbert, 1972: 106). This provided guidance for future development of the exhibitions programme.

Since the early days, the focus of Anacostia's exhibition programme has shifted somewhat. Although it still provides a focus for community activities and issues, its mission now includes the interpretation and dissemination of knowledge about African-American history and culture, and urban problems, in a broader national context. Over the last few years, exhibition subject matter has included *Black Women: Achievements Against the Odds*; *Blacks in the Western Movement*; *The Real McCoy: Afro-American Invention and Innovation, 1619–1930*; *Climbing Jacob's Ladder: The Rise of Black Churches in Eastern American Cities 1740–1877*; *Gathered Visions: Selected Works by African American Women Artists*; *The Renaissance: Black Arts of the '20s*; and *To Achieve These Rights: The Struggle for Equality and Self-Determination in the District of Columbia, 1791–1978*. In addition to exhibitions in the museum itself, Anacostia offers a variety of activities related to the theme of the exhibitions: films, lectures, panel discussions, concerts, plays, craft demonstrations, guided tours, and workshops. It also has a mobile exhibition unit and a library of over 11,000 volumes on African and African American history and culture (AAM, 1972).

Collections and activities in African American Museums

In 1986–7, the African American Museums Association commissioned a survey of black museums and other black organisations involved in collecting and exhibiting objects associated with the black experience to identify the categories, funding sources, spending, and activities of African American museums and related institutions. The survey results were based upon the responses of 52 museums in the USA and Canada. These showed that most African-American museums are run as non-profit organisations and obtain, on average, almost half of their income from federal, state and local funding, with significant amounts also being obtained through donations from individuals and local businesses. At that time annual budgets ranged from $2,000–$1,300,000 with a mean of $208,763 (AAMA/AASLH, nd: xiii). Endowments accounted for an average of only 4.70 per cent and admission fees 3.57 per cent. The main categories of governing authority were private 44 per cent, state 13 per cent, and university 13 per cent.

The survey results indicated that the categories of the museums are concentrated in the areas of history 42 per cent, ethnic cultural centre 19 per cent, art 15 per cent, and historic house or site 13 per cent. (ibid.: 22). Approximately a third function as art museums or cultural centres. Some acquired and displayed collections of black or African arts: the Museum of the National Center of Afro-American Artists in Dorchester, Massachusetts; and the Museum of African Art in Washington, DC. Others provided access to the arts through the provision of space, materials, and classes in everything from dance and music to printing and puppetry: Studio Watts Workshop in Los Angeles; the Studio Museum in Harlem; the Afro-American Cultural Arts Center; Neighborhood Arts in Akron; the Afro-American Cultural Development in Jacksonville, Florida; the New Thing Art and Architecture Center, in Washington, DC; and Your Heritage House, Inc., in Detroit, amongst others. Primarily concerned with responding to the cultural needs and deprivations of the urban black communities, these institutions have not always been strictly concerned with the activities of a museum as defined by professional organisations such as the AAM and ICOM. Indeed, a survey of black museums showed that more than half of those surveyed had no collections policy. The subsequent report recommended that collections policies and documentation procedures needed to be developed and greater effort put into conservation and preservation. It also emphasised the support that these institutions required in terms of staff training and the need for increased and wider funding sources and audiences (nd: 48). As Elizabeth Stevens (1975: 20) observed:

> The new institutions that have been established before or since the riots of the late 1960s have frequently turned in other directions. The trend is not towards collections, or even primarily, towards exhibitions. Instead, many fledgling, black-oriented organizations are concentrating on bringing art to the people in a variety of simple but extraordinarily effective ways.

While artistic activities form the central functions of many African American museums and cultural centres, almost half are devoted to the history of the African American people. African American museums often lack original artefacts representing the history of the African American experience and may have to rely primarily upon reproductions and two-dimensional material. The

AAMA survey showed that collections in black museums consisted primarily of photographic negatives, books, and manuscripts (AAMA/AASCH, nd: xiv). Social history collections reflecting the lives of the poor are typically sparse: when early collections were being acquired, it was primarily the lives of the rich that were valued and thought worthy of preservation. Likewise, collections devoted to the experiences of slaves reflect both the limits of personal possessions which they were able to own, and the general lack of interest in preserving the history and material culture of slaves.

Slavery is seldom the primary subject of an exhibition but is dealt with in relation to the biographies of notable black individuals such as Harriet Tubman, a former slave who led others to freedom on the underground railroad; Soujourner Truth, who nursed black soldiers during the Civil War and fought to have street cars desegregated; and Frederick Douglass, a leading abolitionist. However, the Black Holocaust Museum established in Milwaukee, Wisconsin in 1980 depicts 'the crimes committed by slave traders and organizations like the Ku Klux Klan'. It was established by James Cameron, reputed to be 'the only man alive known to have survived a lynching' (*Orator*, 1995: 9).

With a paucity of artefacts relating directly to the lives and experiences of the slaves themselves, curators may have to rely upon documentary evidence and a story-based approach in exhibitions and use material which reflects the reactions to, and outcomes of, slavery as witnessed by the society which sanctioned and profited from the trade. In addition, some curators have suggested that blacks do not want to be reminded of their slave history but wish to concentrate instead upon the achievements of black individuals. Indeed, social history exhibitions frequently focus upon the achievements and contributions of individuals, including the work of black artists, musicians and writers, politicians and social reformers, and notable figures in medicine, law, science and technology. They reflect the achievements and contributions of African Americans in almost every facet of life in North America, and often focus upon such prominent individuals in a celebratory fashion rather than providing a more analytical look at social history or the interaction between blacks and whites. This may be a result of the lack of attention paid in the past in the US school system, museums, and historical circles generally, to African American history and culture, and the achievements and contributions of black Americans.

The Black American West Museum and Heritage Center in Denver, Colorado, is a small museum which represents a little-known area of African American history: it is the only museum devoted to 'the contributions of African Americans to the American West' (Powers, 1995: 3). This small museum grew out of the personal collection of Paul W. Stewart and is now run by a board of directors and a group of community volunteers. It is located in a quiet residential street in the preserved and restored home of Dr Justina Ford, the first African American female doctor in Colorado. The Museum serves to preserve and interpret this historic landmark, as well as exploring African American history in the growth of the American West.

As a child, Stewart, like most other people, had been unaware of the existence of black cowboys. It was after meeting a black cowboy for the first time that Stewart decided to begin collecting African American cowboy memorabilia. He travelled the country meeting people who had lived in the West or whose relatives had lived there. He was given many items to add to his growing collection: guns, tools, clothing, photographs, household items, and so on. For many years, Stewart kept his collection in his barber's shop where it was a talking point with customers, including cowboys. Eventually the collection became too large for these premises. In 1971, Stewart founded the Black American West Museum and Heritage Center and the collection was moved to an old saloon in Denver, later being transferred to its present location in the preserved home of Dr Justina Ford (Powers, 1995: 3).

The Museum describes the westward movement of black pioneer families who worked in all areas of employment and helped establish towns throughout the American West. Its collections include the outfits of black cowboys and the uniforms of black soldiers in the US cavalry. In this way it tells the untold history of the roles that African Americans played in shaping the American West, providing facts which are often a surprise to visitors for whom images of the West tend to be dominated by white settlers, cowboys and cavalry pushing westwards, pitted against the American Indian population. It states, for example, that nearly one third of the cowboys in the West were black, and points out that African Americans were amongst the region's first millionaires, owning many valuable properties and prominent businesses.

Stewart's research uncovered many little-known facts and personal stories of endurance and achievements by African Americans and he is determined to make this material and the collections as widely available as possible. He travels widely giving lectures and has written two books: *Westward Soul* (1976) and *Black Cowboys* (1986). The staff of the Museum also prepare travelling exhibits on a wide range of topics including: *Black Pioneers of the West, The Early Black Denverites, Twentieth Century Black Political Firsts, Jazz: A History from Roots to Fusion* and *Baseball*, which features players from the Negro Leagues (Powers, 1995: 4). Stewart would like to expand the museum further so that he can create an educational resource centre for scholars and enable teachers and college lecturers to gain access to documentation and so enrich the teaching of African American history.

The lack of attention given to African American history in mainstream museums and educational institutions has been a major motivating factor in the establishment of African American museums. Although there are now many courses in African American history and culture, the lack of interest in collecting African American history and material culture in the past, has resulted in a dearth of artefacts and available material for educators to draw upon. Consequently, many African American museums and cultural centres have a very strong educational mission and were often established by individuals who were committed to fostering greater awareness of African American history, arts and achievements. Such institutions often function with very small budgets relying upon the dedication of a small band of staff and volunteers.

The DuSable Museum of African American History in Chicago, Illinois, is typical of this type of institution. The museum was founded in 1961 by a group of local people, headed by Dr Margaret Burroughs, who for many years wished to promote black history and culture. Eugene Feldman in *The Birth and the Building of the DuSable Museum* (1981) described Burroughs' efforts to establish a museum. In 1945, she opened her collection of pictures relating to black history and culture in her own apartment and, with a few other individuals, attempted to establish the National Negro Museum and Historical Foundation, an initiative which did not succeed. When she and her husband later purchased a house in South Michigan, they were able to establish the Ebony Museum of Negro History and Art in October 1961, using three rooms of that property (Feldman, 1981: 61–78). For the first few years it was run entirely by volunteers who staffed the museum, guided visitors, raised funds, gave lectures, produced publications, and so on.

During the 1960s, as demand for black history and black studies courses grew, the museum staff began offering courses to teachers, and outreach programmes for schools and community groups. They requested donations from the black community in order to build up a collection of artefacts relating to the lives of ordinary black people and received some income from fund-raising events, before receiving their first grant from the Wiebolt Foundation in 1966. During the 1970s, the DuSable Museum attracted grants from various sources including Chicago Community Trust, the Woods Charitable Fund, the Field Foundation and the Standard Oil Company (ibid.: 85).

In 1968, the Museum was re-namcd the DuSable Museum, in honour of Jean Baptiste Pointe DuSable, the black founder of Chicago, the city's first permanent settler. In 1972, the Museum was relocated to a larger building in Washington Park, its present location, owned by Chicago Park District. Appeals to the Park District for use of the building were supported by petitions signed by thousands of supporters. The new facility enabled the staff to expand the displays and cater for the increasing demands from Chicago school groups (ibid.: 61–78).

The central themes in the activities of the Museum remain the interpretation of black culture and history and the promotion of the achievements of blacks. In some of the visual imagery used around the museum, and in some of the content of educational presentations, an Africanist perspective is strongly evident. Its earliest exhibits consisted of portraits of important or famous black men and women in the fields of science, medicine, politics, social reform and so on, a replica of the shoe-making machine invented by Jan Maetzliger, and some dioramas of black history by artist Robert Jones. The museum was given a collection of 150 Bernard Goss paintings which had been commissioned for the Exposition of Negro Business and Culture and over the years has built up substantial collections of art works by African and African American artists, African artefacts, a library, and archives. Other displays have included African artefacts from the DuSable Museum collections; *Up From Slavery*, exploring African American experiences from slavery to the 1940s; and *Stereotypes/*

Realtypes, a small exhibition of commercial products portraying stereotypes of blacks with contrasting positive imagery. Activities have included mask-making workshops, a fashion show of traditional and contemporary African fashions, and an introduction to Swahili. An African American teacher, with experience of teaching in Africa, demonstrated differences between African and American schools in a presentation for family groups. The Museum has also organised study visits to the Caribbean and Africa.

From its inception, the Museum has relied upon the dedication and commitment of its volunteers and supporters who have given time and skills to ensure its continuation. Initially untrained in museology and many of the other skills required to run a museum, they developed the necessary skills and solicited aid from many others to assist in the realisation of their goals. The educational focus has remained strong and, in addition to lectures, schools programmes, teacher training workshops and so forth, they also ran a training programme for young people. Supported financially by the Sears Company, it was called the Sears Heritage Institute. Each summer, groups of 25 to 30 youngsters were given training as guides and studied black history and culture (ibid.: 87). Feldman was also involved in the establishment of a Black Studies Program at Pontiac Correction Center run jointly by Lewis University and the DuSable Museum. The Museum continues to provide an important educational and cultural facility for the black community in Chicago and maintains its endeavours to promote black history and culture to all.

African American museums vary considerably in size and financial status; some have been much more successful than others in attracting federal, state or corporate funding which has enabled them to acquire modern facilities which meet the highest museological standards, and to employ trained curatorial and educational staff members. In November 1993, the Museum of African-American Life and Culture in Dallas, Texas, opened a new facility which cost $6 million and was financed primarily with private funds. In 1994, the Connecticut Afro-American Historical Society (CAAHS) working in conjunction with Mystic Seaport was awarded over $2 million in state funds for a proposal to build a sea-going reconstruction of the *Amistad*, a nineteenth-century Spanish/Cuban slave ship on which a successful slave uprising took place in 1839 (Lusaka, 1995: 5).

In contrast, the Society for the Preservation of Weeksville and Bedford-Stuyvesant History (the Weeksville Society), in Brooklyn, New York has worked hard to develop an educational facility and museum with little outside funding. Four historic houses are being restored and interpeted, the oldest remaining evidence of the nineteenth-century African American community of Weeksville, named after James Weeks a black landowner who purchased land there in 1838. The buildings, dating from 1840 to 1883, were located on Hunterfly Road, an old colonial road which has all but disappeared, and today they stand at an angle to Bergen Street, opposite a multi-storey housing block. The tiny remnant of Hunterfly Road on which the houses stand is today no more than a small clearing, indeed the site was only identified in 1968 after historian

James Hurley began to explore the area from the air and noticed the wooden buildings and the lane sitting at an odd angle to the surrounding streets.

Hurley had been running workshops on Brooklyn neighbourhoods at Pratt Neighborhood College and students in his classes had decided to research the history of Weeksville, about which little was known. After the College workshop finished, the research was continued with the involvement of community groups and individuals who formed Project Weeksville in 1969 with Hurley as director. When work was due to begin on the construction of the Weeksville Gardens Houses, in the centre of old Weeksville, archaeological work was undertaken with members of the community, including children from the local school and members of the local Boy Scout troop, assisting with the dig. Local children have been closely involved in the project from the start; indeed it was their idea that the historic houses should be restored and become an African American history museum (Maynard, 1994). In 1970, the school children, their parents and teachers, along with members of the Weeksville Society, testified at the New York City Landmarks Commission hearing at which the historic houses in Hunterfly Road were declared landmarks and placed on the National Register of Historic Places in the United States (Maynard and Cottman, 1983: 12–18). Through the School Community Council, pupils of Weeksville School raised $1,000 by holding a fair in the school gym, and presented the cheque to the Weeksville Society at a school assembly (Maynard, 1988; Maynard, 1994: 78).

The Society for the Preservation of Weeksville and Bedford-Stuyvesant History (the Weeksville Society), was founded in 1968 by residents of the area in which Weeksville once stood. With the assistance of the Bedford-Stuyvesant Restoration Corporation, the Vincent Astor Foundation, the New York State Historic Preservation Office, and various fundraising initiatives, the four nineteenth-century buildings on Hunterfly Road were purchased by the Society (Maynard and Cottman 1983: 35). Funds from a Federal Community Development Block Grant enabled restoration work to begin on the rundown wooden structures and has transformed the buildings into attractive houses painted in soft yellows, greens and beiges. In recent years the Society has received financial assistance from the New York State Council on the Arts, the New York Landmarks Conservancy, the Brooklyn Downtown Development Corporation and other corporate and community sources (Maynard, 1994: 78).

The Weeksville Society has created a number of exhibitions; its first *Weeksville, Save the Memories of Self*, told the story of the origins of Weeksville and the attempts to rediscover the history of the community, leading to the establishment of the Weeksville Society and the continuing work by members of the community. The exhibition was displayed in a number of venues in greater New York and, following the acquisition and restoration of the buildings on the old Hunterfly Road, the Society in 1985 was able to present its first historical exhibition in one of the restored buildings. *Memories of Mrs Harriet Etta Lane* consisted of a small display of various household items, photographs and documents.

Figure 4.3 Four historic houses, dating from 1840 to 1883, which were located on Hunterfly Road, an old colonial road, in Weeksville, USA, 1980, prior to restoration. They provide the oldest remaining evidence of the nineteenth-century African American community of Weeksville.

Source: Society for the Preservation of Weeksville and Bedford-Stuyvesant History.

Figure 4.4 The historic houses on the old Hunterfly Road in 1984 after restoration work by the Society for the Preservation of Weeksville and Bedford-Stuyvesant History

Source: Society for the Preservation of Weeksville and Bedford-Stuyvesant History

Community involvement, which was so crucial to the initiation of the project, has continued throughout with enthusiastic participation in archaeological activities by adults and children alike. The development of educational facilities remains one of the primary concerns of the director, Joan Maynard, and others involved in the work of the Weeksville Society. Weeksville Family History Workshops have enabled members of the community to undertake research into their heritage in Weeksville and, working in collaboration, the Brooklyn Historical Society, the Brooklyn Children's Museum and the Weeksville Society have developed the Crown Heights History Project. Designed to explore the history of a culturally diverse neighbourhood, this project utilised a series of exhibitions and educational programmes, using objects, photographs and oral history materials collected from within the different communities living in the neighbourhood.

In recent years, the Weeksville Society has faced a number of set-backs: a drunk driver crashed his car into the front of the building in Bergen Street, where the Society's offices are located in a building adjacent to the historic buildings. Burglaries have resulted in the loss of computer, photographic and video equipment and other valuable materials. With only a handful of staff and very little financial support, the dedicated staff and supporters of the Weeksville Society have achieved much but face a continuing battle to see their task reach fruition. Their aim is to create a historical museum consisting of furnished period rooms and providing an educational facility within the community. While it is intended to attract audiences from further afield, the negative perceptions that many New York residents and visitors hold for the Bedford-Stuyvesant region of Brooklyn may prove a difficult obstacle to overcome.

A national African American museum?

African American museums provide visible evidence of African American heritage within the broader context of American history and culture. They are a visible manifestation of the pride that contemporary African Americans take in their heritage and culture, and their ability to communicate that through their own efforts rather than those of white historians and curators. In his introduction to the Survey of Black Museums, commissioned by the African American Museum Association (AAMA) and the American Association for State and Local History (AASLH), Edmund Barry Gaither, Director of the National Center for Afro-American Artists in Boston, and former president of the African American Museum Association (AAMA), commented that:

> black museums . . . are committed to gaining significant hegemony over the understanding and interpretation of Black cultural heritage and of Black contributions to world history. They are committed to the concept of the museum as an educational vehicle telling the story of the Black experience for all people, but especially for their own communities.
>
> (AAMA/AASLH, 1988: 4)

However, although there are now over 100 African American museums in the United States, there has yet to be established a museum dedicated to the history and culture of the African American population as a part of the complex of national museums on the Mall in Washington, DC. In the 1980s, efforts began to gain federal charter for a National African American Museum. The Smithsonian Institution appointed a Project Director and established an African American Institutional Study Board to submit recommendations which were published in 1991 in the *African American Institutional Study Final Report*. A National African American Museum project was established within the Smithsonian Institution in 1993 to begin the process of planning and organising the activities of the proposed museum.

The Museum's proposed mission and its relationship with the public have been debated extensively in discussions involving over one hundred scholars and museum professionals (Lusaka, 1993: 1). As part of the planning process, a number of task forces have been established in the areas of media, art history, performing arts, biography, history and the diaspora. Project staff have been building collections and archives, conducting reminiscence work, organising exhibitions, and building public awareness of the project and the contributions that they can make to it.

The Museum's collections and exhibitions will cover every aspect of African American life; the African American Institutional Study Advisory Committee recommended that 'the National African American Museum should celebrate the creativity and accomplishments of persons of African descent in their countries of origin and in the United States, and should strive to enhance our understanding of human culture and interaction' (Smithsonian Institution, 1991: 2). The report identified four areas for collecting which had previously been 'undercapitalized, inadequately researched or neglected'. These were:

> Images of African Americans in the print and non-print media; Archival material and material culture documenting African American history, invention and creative endeavours in the 20th Century, focusing specifically on the Civil Rights Movement and Blacks in the labor force; Art and material culture documenting the experiences of Africans in the diaspora; Collections of African American art – most specifically those collections which might be lost to the public sector because of their cost.
>
> (ibid.: 12)

One of the initial tasks facing Claudine Brown, the National African American Museum Project's former director, was to investigate sources of objects and documents. According to Claudine Brown, the survey of potential collections has brought to light a wealth of material in archives, collections, churches and family homes across the country and identified 30,000 objects to be acquired (Brown, 1993; Trescott, 1994: 1). While some sections of African American history are well represented, the material culture of antebellum African Americans was neglected. As a result the household goods, musical instruments, textiles, jewellery, baskets and pottery of the oppressed rural blacks of the eighteenth century are poorly represented in collections, although much material may exist unrecognised or inaccurately documented in private and public collections in the South (Ruffins, 1991a: 519–20). According to Fath Davis Ruffins, a historian with the National Museum of American History, 'the art and artifacts of African Americans before the 1840s is relatively sparse, these same kinds of materials dating from the 1880s and beyond are quite abundant. Most are still held within the attics, basements, and garages of Black American families' (Ruffins, 1991b: 16).

As well as the material culture of African Americans, the collections will include more sensitive material associated with white perceptions and treatment of blacks, such as media images, artefacts associated with segregation, and objects produced for the amusement of whites which show racial stereotypes caricaturing the perceived character and physical features of blacks. Such items are evidence of the bigotry and racism experienced by the black population and a part of African American history which cannot be ignored.

The legislation required for authorisation of the Museum successfully passed through the House of Representatives in June 1993. However, despite the recognised neglect of African American history, the National African American Museum bill failed to get through Congress before it was adjourned for the start of the election season in October 1994. Senator Jesse Helms opposed the bill on the grounds of cost and in fear that it may induce other ethnic groups to lobby for similar museum facilities. This concern, also voiced by others, has been addressed by the African American Institutional Study Advisory Committee (AAISAC) which, in its final report in 1991, stated that of all the immigrant groups in the United States of America:

> blacks are the largest of these racial minorities and the only people who came here by special invitation. Black people have a unique history in America of toil and trouble, of achievement and institutional development that cannot easily be translated into, or subsumed under a generalized American national experience. It is unique.
>
> (Smithsonian Institution, 1991: 9–10)

In February 1995, a bill was introduced to the House of Representatives and a companion measure was introduced in March to the Senate. Senator Lewis commented:

> Throughout American history, two racial groups – African Americans and Native Americans – have been consistently mistreated and under-represented. To help make up for this mistreatment, a memorial to the Native American experience has already been authorized. This legislation would commemorate the African American community and experience.
>
> (cited in *Orator*, 1995: 1)

During 1995, the project was re-named as the Center for African American History and Culture and it is now administratively a part of Anacostia Museum (Newsome, 1995: 1). In March 1999, Congressman John Lewis of Georgia again sponsored a bill, H.R. 923, to establish a National African American

Museum within the Smithsonian Institution. At this time, efforts continue to try to obtain authorising legislation to establish the Museum.

The National African American Museum is envisaged as a world-class museum which will work with, and support, the network of African American museums across the country. It will also augment and complement the work of other Smithsonian museums, so that African American issues will continue to be addressed in the other museums thus providing a variety of perspectives. In its proposed location on the Mall in Washington, DC, it will attract visitors from all over the world who will be able to learn the African American story as told by African American historians, curators and educators, as well as those whose personal stories are represented by the collections. Whatever the outcome of the proposals to build a National African American Museum, the Anacostia Museum and Center for African American History and Culture will ensure the continuation of the important work of collecting, documenting and disseminating the history of African Americans.

5

From treasure house to museum
. . . and back

'The longer one thought about the idea of the museum the more the custom house seemed like one already.'

(Sidney Moko Mead, Professor of Maori Art at Victoria University of Wellington, 1983)

In discussions concerning museum provision for culturally diverse audiences, it is often stated that the museum is based upon western ideology; that the concept of visiting a museum – a collection of objects removed from their arena of active participation in cultural affairs, to a place in which they are put on public display to be preserved for future generations – is unique to western cultures. This argument then proposes that museums are therefore alien to many of the new audiences which curatorial staff are seeking to attract, making it difficult if not impossible to succeed in these endeavours. However, this impression of museums as a purely western concept is not entirely accurate. Museum-like models have existed traditionally in other cultures for many years, and some facets of conventional museum practice conform to these indigenous models.

Furthermore, western museum curators often argue that the museums and cultural centres recently established by indigenous communities are not museums and do not function as museums, but this is not the case. As the evidence presented here will show, many of these indigenous models do indeed function as museums and, in some instances, lead the way in developing methodologies which are relevant to the communities they serve, yet conform to the basic philosophies of the museum. Other cases presented in these chapters provide examples of some of these philosophies being applied to the specific needs of a narrow group of people within the community to which the collection relates.

The non-public role of such facilities may run counter to the aims of museums, which are intended to disseminate information to the public; however, these examples are evidence of the concepts of collection, storage and preservation being applied within a particular cultural framework as an extension of earlier traditions, but with the adoption, in some instances, of modern museological environmental, security and recording methods. This, then, is an example of museological methods being adapted to suit the demands of current social needs within a particular cultural context; such developments have featured throughout the history of museums and continue to effect change in museological methods today. Indeed, the issues surrounding the display and possible repatriation of human remains and sacred objects have begun to effect quite radical changes upon museum practices in the latter part of the twentieth century, resulting in restricted access, non-display of sensitive materials and repatriation. While such changes run counter to the most basic museological principles of collection, preservation, and dissemination, they are gradually being accepted as necessary responses to concerns within contemporary society.

Various writers have documented the history of museums (Murray, 1904; Shelley, 1911; Wittlin, 1949; Impey and MacGregor, 1985; Krzysztof, 1990) and, if we look at museum history, we find that the concept and philosophy has changed dramatically over the period of their development; various forms and functions of museums can be identified prior to the development of the classic European model. Henry C. Shelley, writing in 1911, argued that prior to the establishment of the public museum:

> the Englishman of the dark ages, however poor and comfortless his own dwelling, . . . lavished all his skill and much of his wealth on the house of prayer. The churches of his villages and the cathedrals of his cities provided him with objects for the exercise of such aesthetic taste as he possessed; and that fact should lessen the surprise which is sometimes expressed when those sacred buildings are found to contain such articles as the modern mind usually associates with a museum. The fact is, the parish church was not only the store-house and armoury of the fifteenth century, where corn and wool were deposited in unsettled days and weapons hoarded, but it was also the only museum. Its shrines were hung with the strange new things which English sailors had begun to bring across the great seas – with the 'horns of unicorns', ostrich eggs, or walrus tusks, or the rib of a whale given by Sebastian Cabot.
>
> (Shelley, 1911: 8)

In some non-western cultures there have been traditions of having buildings or sites in which were stored collections of objects of religious or ceremonial significance, which are in some respects analogous to the western concept of a museum. In Aboriginal Australian communities, although much of the material culture and imagery was of either an ephemeral nature or made from organic materials which were fragile and liable to degenerate, sacred objects and some everyday items were stored away in caches in caves or rock shelters. Such caches were vulnerable, however, to discovery and theft by non-Aboriginal people who might regard them as abandoned (Anderson, 1990c). Today many Aboriginal communities maintain Keeping Places in which to store securely their secret/sacred materials with access restricted to initiated individuals.

In addition, the European model of the publicly accessible museum and cultural centre is also being adopted. These function as educational facilities which enable Aboriginal communities to interpret their history and culture to non-Aboriginal communities, and may also provide display facilities and a sales outlet for Aboriginal arts. Although the Keeping Places serve to preserve secret/sacred material, their role is to maintain the secrecy of the objects and so restrict access rather than widening it. In this they differ fundamentally from the classic European model which has at its heart, public education and the dissemination of information. However, it is significant, perhaps, that, as anthropologist Chris Anderson notes, 'in some parts of Central Australia, Aboriginal people use the term "museum" for bush caches of restricted items (Anderson, 1988: 24). Evidently, the museum's function in the preservation of material culture has been focused upon and applied to the bush caches of secret/sacred objects.

An additional type of Keeping Place has been developed out of the debate over the holding of human remains in museum collections: that of a secure storage area to ensure community control over the remains without taking the more radical and damaging step of re-burial. According to Mulvaney, the process of storing human remains in a Keeping Place, 'a suitably designed underground vault, entry to which is controlled (or denied) by the community, simulates the burial process' (Mulvaney, 1991: 19). Similar types of Keeping Places have been established in some of the state museums to provide a secure storage facility in which both human remains and cultural material can be stored with access limited and decisions concerning research made by the Aboriginal community concerned.

The carved meeting house of the Maori in New Zealand can also be compared to a museum in certain aspects, and in fact, those which are decorated are referred to by their owners as their museum or art gallery (Hakiwai, 1993; Whiting, 1994). Each Maori village has a *marae*, consisting of a ceremonial site (*marae atea*), in front of a meeting house (*whare whakairo)*, and a dining hall (*whare kai*). The meeting houses are usually carved or painted, and inside display carvings of the ancestors, woven wall panels (*tukutuku*), and photographs of deceased relatives. In some meeting houses, *heitiki*, feather cloaks and books are also stored.

Sidney Moko Mead, Professor of Maori Art at Victoria University of Wellington, has noted that 'painted identifications of the ancestors on the wall indicate that the Maori housebuilders of the late nineteenth century were already moving towards the idea of a museum. In some houses the photographs are all labelled and identified' (Mead, 1983: 98). Arapata Hakiwai, Curator of Maori Collections at Auckland Museum, has commented that:

> the whole concept of a meeting house is in essence a museum on its own. What a meeting house stands for, what it represents, the carvings, the *tukutuku* – they all tell stories, they are all meaningful. It is a living museum in the sense that it is an art gallery, it is a form of recalling past events, past history. It's everything, it's animate, it's inanimate, it's real, it's there.
> (Hakiwai, 1993)

Here, then, are contained many of the finest art works and most important treasures of a Maori community. In this sense the *whare whakairo* is not dissimilar to the western model of a museum, although the actual functioning of each differs. The primary function of the *whare whakairo* is not display; rather

Figure 5.1 *Haus tambaran* or spirit house at Korogo village on the Sepik River, Papua New Guinea

Source: Photo by M. Simpson, 1984

Figure 5.2 Haus tambaran at Korogo on the Sepik River, Papua New Guinea, used as an outlet
　　　　for display and sale of carvings and other artefacts
Source: Photo by M. Simpson, 1984

it is a meeting house which is used by the community for formal gatherings and ceremonies. It is here that the community can gather for discussions, conduct wedding and funeral ceremonies, ceremonially greet visitors, and join together in a meal to mark important occasions or extend hospitality to guests. The *whare whakairo* serves the Maori community and is accessible only to villagers and to guests who are first greeted and invited in, usually for attendance at a formal meeting or ceremony. Hakiwai points out that even on *marae* where *Pakeha* are welcomed and shown around in order to give them insight into Maori cultural traditions, Maori protocol and Maori tradition will supersede any other function that might operate (Hakiwai, 1993).

In contrast, the European museum is open to the general public as an institution which serves to instruct and entertain. The public display of the collections which the museum holds and conserves is a central focus of all other museum activities. There are, however, signs that the European model is also being adopted by Maori communities seeking to extend the function of the *marae* to include the interpretation of their culture to *Pakeha* or non-Maori through the preservation and exhibition of artefacts. Such developments will serve to reinforce cultural identity and also benefit the economic strength of the community.

According to Gavin Brookes, a Maori Anglican missionary involved in the development of a *marae* museum in Koriniti near Wanganui on New Zealand's North Island, the establishment of Maori *marae* museums reflects an enduring tradition within Maori culture in which Maori *taonga* were stored in caves. He believes that the adoption of the European museum model as the basis for the establishment of Maori *marae* museums is a modern development of this practice. Sidney Moko Mead (1983: 98–101) and Haare Williams (see Haldane, 1984: 26) have suggested that the Maori carved meeting house, *whare whakairo*, fulfills much of the function of a museum in Maori society.

Professor Mead (1983: 100) also noted similarities between the custom houses found in the Eastern Solomon Islands and western museums when he visited Santa Ana Island in 1973:

> In the context of the village the custom house served a valuable purpose in presenting to the carvers fine examples of the local carving styles. Through the structure the men were able to examine art works done fifty years earlier. The large house posts lasted longer and so provided a greater sense of continuity with the past. There was a wide selection of objects to observe and study. In fact, the longer one thought about the idea of the museum the more the custom house seemed like one already.

In Papua New Guinea, the *haus tambaran* or spirit houses of the Abelam and Sepik River regions have traditionally served a similar function. Objects were stored and preserved in the *haus tambaran*, in so far as the climate would allow, for future generations. Meanwhile they were also being utilised in ceremonies, and for teaching history, beliefs and cultural practices to younger members of the community. Today, a *haus tambaran* serves a similar function but may also provide storage and display areas for artefacts made specifically for sale to dealers and tourists from the *Sepik Explorer*, a tour boat which makes occasional journeys up the river. Often access to the *haus tambaran* is prohibited to women and to uninitiated males; however, outsiders are sometimes given entry privileges and female visitors from outside the community may be given honorary status as a man, so enabling them to enter. The *haus tambaran* and its contents then become a form of museum through which villagers guide visitors and explain the functions and stories of the artefacts, an appropriate means of interpretation in a society which has relied upon oral history for the recording and dissemination of its history and lore.

In their traditional forms, these types of building existed as an integral part of the village or community, in some ways akin to the church in medieval Europe, their function being inextricably linked to the religious and ceremonial use of the objects, and to the education of a non-literate society. Such cultural storehouses played a particularly important role in non-literate societies in which people relied upon oral traditions and the communicative powers of objects to educate the young and the uninitiated and to provide historical records.

Writing about Australian Aboriginal Keeping Places and museums, Margaret West (1981: 13) stated that 'the storage and contemplation of culturally removed objects is a peculiarly Western practice' and indeed it is true that these collections in the indigenous models tended primarily to represent only the community's own culture. This is in marked contrast to the encyclopaedic collections of exotica and natural history specimens gathered from throughout the world by European collectors in the eighteenth and nineteenth centuries. In the indigenous models, few objects from other cultural groups were displayed with the exception, in some cases, of trophies of war such as shrunken heads. Like many early European and American ethnographic collections, these were preserved and displayed to gain prestige or power for the owners, and demonstrate the successful domination of the enemy. They were a much more integral part of the daily and ceremonial life of the community than most European museums have been. In Europe museums tend to dwell on the past and cater for the cultural requirements of only a portion of society. Museums in Britain are, for example, frequently perceived by the public as a casual leisure facility, and by museum curatorial staff as a research facility for their own and other researchers' work, with the public services and education being secondary. The educational element is all too frequently centred upon schools, and left almost entirely in the hands of the education staff.

The traditional indigenous museum-like model differs most significantly in purpose; most of the objects continue to fulfill their original function, and indeed are frequently still in regular usage. Their location in the Keeping Place or 'museum' provides accessible storage and enables the context, function and symbolism of the artefacts to be communicated to others within the community through oral traditions such as storytelling, song, dialogue, and through events such as dances, rituals and ceremonies, but only within traditional cultural parameters and subject to restrictions of ownership, initiation and so on. However, the extension of many of these activities to cultural centres that function as museums provides the opportunity for the community to take control over its own representation and to facilitate cultural awareness amongst a wider audience including outsiders.

The contemporary European model of a museum is more static in concept but is more active in terms of collecting, with a wider, research-based remit, constantly acquiring more material, and with clearly defined collecting policies determining the direction and scope of the collecting. The European model has tended to be used by a narrower section of the community, and is seen by many people to be élitist. Curatorial concerns such as preservation and research have tended to take precedence over public usage and education.

It could be argued then that the museum – a centre of cultural storage, preservation, education and activities – is not a purely European concept but can be compared with a number of related cultural models which take various forms, and therefore it is inappropriate to assume that an unassailable gulf exists between museums and non-European peoples. As traditional cultures have undergone a process of cultural revitalisation and have sought to establish and promote their cultural identity, European-style museums have proven to be a useful means of doing this. In contrast, European museums have played a much less integral role in society than the traditional types of cultural storehouses or spirit houses.

Perhaps it is for this reason that in some societies, modern museums are evolving as centres of cultural activity in which community involvement, public education and social issues are at the fore of the museum's aims, making them a focus for community activities. They provide a showcase for cultural representation in a context which is neither insensitive to the host community nor alien to Europeans. They provide evidence of the community's ability to care for artefacts and therefore strengthen claims for the retention or return of cultural patrimony; and they present artefacts and information using formal interpretive methods and the written word, upon which so much emphasis is placed in western culture. The museum, then, is a useful and powerful tool for politicisation and promotion of culture.

In countries in which the European model of the museum was introduced by colonial powers, the museums have tended to adopt a slightly different role in the post-independence years, becoming more socially significant. They have grown with the newly independent nation in the post-colonial period as the people sought to preserve their cultural traditions and to develop a national identity, in some instances trying to draw together several different tribal, linguistic or religious groups. Their collections have concentrated mainly upon indigenous material and the active promotion of cultural traditions, education and the concept of the new nation. Kwasi Myles notes that, with regard to West Africa, museums were established by the British for purposes that were economic rather than educational, and that under the colonial administration, indigenous cultural activities were either ignored or discouraged. However, since independence, there has been a need to build up the national identity of these new nations, to make people aware of the variety of cultures which constitute the nation; and to rediscover and promote traditional cultural activities (Myles, 1976: 196–202).

In Papua New Guinea, in the period since independence in 1975, the traditional cultures of the many different ethnic groups living in the country have become expressions of the new national identity. The National Museums and Galleries of Papua New Guinea developed slowly from early origins under colonial rule, and have grown into a valuable mechanism for the preservation and display of the cultural heritage of the nation. As an Australian protectorate, efforts to create a national identity had threatened to subsume the individuality of the tribal communities. With independence came a new pride in the richness and diversity of the many traditional societies in the country; since then, the cultural expressions of the traditional societies have come to be the expressions of a new national identity.

Although the museum institution was introduced to Papua New Guinea by Europeans, G. Mosuwadoga, a former director of the Papua New Guinea Museum in Port Moresby, regards the modern museum as a continuation of traditional practices, noting that the concept of securing valuable cultural objects was a traditional one in Papua New Guinean societies:

> The necessity for building a communal type of house to secure and to house these objects is not a new or commonplace practice. Papua New Guinea was doing this long before the museum reached our country. The name and function of a museum can be looked upon in our society today as fitting into our basic ideals, which were with us long before any influence actually reached us.
>
> (cited by Smidt in Edwards and Stewart, 1980: 157)

In 1973, the government launched the Cultural Development Programme to include the establishment of the National Museum, the National Arts School and the Institute of Papua New Guinea Studies. The Museum has been active in assisting village people to retain their valuable cultural artefacts in the face of great demand from dealers and private collectors from overseas. It has also been instrumental in slowing the illegal export of valuable and culturally significant artefacts which have been declared Proclaimed National Property by the government. At the Museum's opening ceremony, the Prime Minister spoke of the importance of ensuring that the older villagers pass on traditional knowledge and artistic skills to the younger men in order to preserve the past, but also emphasised the need for cultural development so that culture continues as a living, dynamic force.

Similar motivation lies behind the establishment of many museums and cultural centres by indigenous peoples in Canada, the USA, Australia and New Zealand, countries in which they now live as minority groups. Striving to reassert themselves politically and culturally, they must fight to retain their cultural identity against domination by the mass culture. Often the older generation is striving to preserve the old ways and pass the knowledge and traditions of the community on to the younger generation, who are more likely to

Figure 5.3 Hikerangi: House of Preservation. The *marae* museum being established by the Maori community in Koriniti, Aotearoa New Zealand. The museum is the small white building in the centre.

Source: Photo by M. Simpson, 1993

Figure 5.4 Interior of the *Hikerangi: House of Preservation*, Koriniti, Aotearoa New Zealand. The museum collection is being gathered ready for display once repairs and improvements to the building have been completed

Source: Photo by M. Simpson, 1993

117

have adopted all the trappings of popular, mainstream culture. Museums can assist in this process, providing a secure storage facility for the cultural material and community archives, and a focus for community activities. Such facilities enable them to interpret their own cultures and so educate visitors from other cultural backgrounds. They may also be seen as a possible source of financial income through the promotion of tourism, though this often proves to be an attractive but unrealistic proposition.

Maori *marae* museums

This dual role lies behind the establishment of one of the first Maori *marae* museums, at Koriniti, in New Zealand, where the concept of a public museum established by a Maori community is in its infancy. Several others are in the planning stages and feasibility studies are being carried out to determine the economic viability of such projects.

Until recently, the only *marae* museum in operation was that at Turangawae-wae in Waikato, where the collection of gifts presented to the Maori Queen, Dame Te Atairangikahu, are displayed in the meeting house *Mahinarangi* (Whiting, 1994). However, the *Iwi* (Tribal) Trust Board of the village of Koriniti decided to establish a museum on the *marae* in order to develop the facilities within the village for the benefit of the people of the community, the *Ngati Pamoana*.

The village of Koriniti lies in an isolated area 47 km north of Wanganui, along a dirt road which winds around bends and over hills, following the river Wamanui. The *marae* museum is being developed as part of the *Ngati Pamoana* Strategic Plan which was drawn up between 1990 and 1992; this includes education (including a *kohangare* or language nest), health, recreation, building, farming and tourism. Being of such importance to community affairs, the *marae* is the focal point for the community and the natural site for the newly-conceived museum proposals. The museum at Koriniti will be called *Hikerangi: House of Preservation* and will be located in a small building on the *marae*, alongside the *whare whakairo* and the dining hall (*whare kai*).

Gavin Brookes sees the project as a way in which younger members of the community can fulfill the dreams of the elders by returning to the rural community some of the traditional skills and knowledge which were lost as people moved to the towns and cities. The museum will enable the community to preserve and interpret its collection for the benefit of younger members of the community as well as for non-Maori visitors. It is hoped that the *marae* museum will attract visitors to Koriniti and so generate income which will be used to develop the social amenities of the community. It will also provide an opportunity for the *Ngati Pamoana* to present their cultural heritage to non-Maori visitors. Tourism was the single biggest source of income to the *marae* in 1992 as a result of the development of one- and two-day package trips organised under a tourism exchange agreement with a firm in Auckland. Brookes believes that traditional

Maori communities are beginning to understand the importance of financial prosperity and seek ways of generating income in rural communities through initiatives such as this (Brookes, 1993).

The museum project is still in the early stages. The collection includes traditional *taonga* such as carved panels, ceremonial clubs and adzes, and a substantial quantity of material of European manufacture, such as a laundry mangle, a Singer sewing machine, pots and pans, and the wheel of a paddleboat which used to ply the Wamanui River. Staff of Wanganui Museum were consulted and wrote a report outlining essential repairs and improvements required to bring the small, single-room building up to a standard that satisfies basic levels of security and conservation; this included replacing the door, sealing the floor and affixing UV screens to the windows. By 1993 the building repairs had been carried out, the collection was being accumulated inside, and further assistance and financial funding were being sought from appropriate sources to enable the project to proceed with documentation, conservation, display and training.

Echoing the principles of the ecomuseum, Brookes described the museum concept as one which stretches beyond the building and into the rest of the community. He anticipates that the day-to-day running of the *marae* museum will be attended to by members of the community, which will bring visitors into direct contact with the villagers.

Aboriginal Keeping Places and museums

In Australia, Aboriginal peoples are also beginning to adopt the European museum model for their own uses and a substantial number of Aboriginal cultural centres and 'Keeping Places' have been established in recent years. Here, individual communities have adopted the aspects of museum provision that best suit their purposes and have developed two distinct entities: the Keeping Place, serving a traditional role, and the museum and cultural centre addressing contemporary educational and economic needs. In the central and western areas of the country, where Aboriginal communities live a more traditional lifestyle in remote locations, Keeping Places are specifically community-orientated and often embrace the traditional role of storehouse for sacred objects. Materials stored in traditional Keeping Places are of a sacred nature and access is restricted on the basis of gender and to those who have been initiated. In the south-east, in the states of Victoria and New South Wales, where Aboriginal peoples live primarily in urban areas, museums and cultural centres are seen essentially as educational facilities and tourist venues designed to generate jobs and income, to provide display facilities and retail outlets for artists, and to offer education about Aboriginal culture to non-Aboriginal people. Museums and cultural centres fulfilling both functions have been established amongst Aboriginal communities in the North where tourism plays a significant role.

Interest in the establishment of Aboriginal Keeping Places grew amongst Aboriginal communities in the 1960s and 1970s. Many of the earlier ones were simple, prefabricated stores for secret/sacred material continuing a tradition of storing caches of secret/sacred objects in caves and bush sites. The resettlement of Aboriginal communities on government reserves or missions far from their traditional sacred sites, and the increasing theft of secret/sacred objects, compelled the adoption of prefabricated storehouses in the vicinity of the settlement (Kimber, 1980: 79; West, 1981: 9–11). Paddy Roe, an elderly Aboriginal man, described the important role that museums could play for Aboriginal communities:

> to keep safe objects of great tribal significance; to show our young people that our cultural things are important to non-Aborigines – this in relation to things that can go on public display; for keeping tribal discipline, which keeps our culture alive; to preserve objects to be used in cultural ceremonies such as initiations.
>
> (Roe, 1980: 53)

However, Chris Anderson of the South Australian Museum questions whether such centralised stores are indeed more secure (Anderson, 1988: 25). Indeed, the practice of keeping certain items which in the past would have been destroyed after use, and the placement of a collection of sacred materials in one location, perhaps makes the risk of theft greater.

Support for Aboriginal Keeping Places

According to Margaret West, the first official Keeping Place in Western Australia was built at Twelve-Mile Reserve, Port Headland in North Western Australia. It was requested by ceremonial leaders who wished to obtain secure storage facilities for their ritual material. The earliest such Keeping Places were simple sheds which continued the traditional practice of storing secret/sacred materials. These sheds were originally supplied by the Western Australian Department of Native Welfare and, after the Department was disbanded, responsibility for this work was taken over by the Aboriginal Affairs Planning Authority and the Western Australian Museum (West, 1981: 10).

At the UNESCO Regional Seminar *Preserving Indigenous Cultures: A New Role for Museums*, held in 1978, it was recommended that 'established museums and galleries . . . support the development of local cultural centres by provision of display items and records (including films, tapes and still photographs) and by the return, where requested, of sacred and ritual objects derived from that group or area'. They were asked to 'initiate training courses for indigenous peoples in all aspects of museum management'. It was also recommended that the Aboriginal Arts Board in Australia 'extends its resource of knowledge on cultural centres' in order to undertake an advisory role and provide to 'Aboriginal and Torres Strait Islander communities seeking to establish cultural centres, draft articles of association for the establishment of incorporated bodies to operate local community cultural centres' (Edwards and Stewart, 1980: 13–15).

The Australian Archaeological Association (AAA) supported the establishment of Keeping Places as a means of safeguarding collections of human remains. A letter from the President of the AAA to the Victorian government in 1984 stated the AAA's support for the return of skeletal remains of known individuals, but argued that 'all other Aboriginal skeletal remains are of scientific importance and should not be destroyed by being re-buried or cremated'. In response to the growing threat of the repatriation and cremation or reburial of human remains collections, the AAA gave its support to the development of Keeping Places. These would provide a means of returning the human remains to Aboriginal control while ensuring their continued preservation, thus keeping open the possibility of future research. The AAA urged the Victorian government 'to instigate a programme enabling the construction of Aboriginal Keeping Places and the training of Aboriginal people in the skills necessary for employment in these Keeping Places as well as in the State's museums' (cited in Mulvaney, 1991: 16).

A paper presented to the Conference of Museum Anthropologists meeting in December 1986 by Cliff Samson of the Heritage Branch of the Department of Aboriginal Affairs (DAA), suggested that Government involvement might be in the form of funding for training courses for Aboriginal people and sponsorship of individuals to attend the courses run by the Canberra College of Advanced Education. He also called for support of the establishment of positions for Aboriginal Liaison Officers in each State Museum.

While supporting and encouraging the establishment of Aboriginal Keeping Places, the DAA policy particularly noted that 'initiatives for the establishment of Keeping Places should come from Aboriginals. Care must be exercised that Eurocentric notions of what is desirable in the field of curation of Aboriginal material are not imposed on Aboriginals' (Samson, 1988: 22). However, Chris Anderson, in response to the paper, noted that the DAA had stated that government policy would give priority to the Keeping Places established to preserve the security of secret/sacred material, yet also promised financial support for training in museology. Such training, as Anderson explained, is less appropriate to those establishing Keeping Places as traditional secret/sacred stores than those establishing Keeping Places as cultural centres which have much wider remits involving public display and education. He argues instead for financial support from the government to fund qualified museum staff going to the communities in order to provide advice and aid appropriate to their individual needs.

The establishment of a Keeping Place, cultural centre or museum may also enable a community to negotiate loans or the return of cultural material from the collections of state and other museums. Tiwi Keeping Place on Bathurst Island in the Northern Territory was built in order to provide the Tiwi people with access to cultural artefacts which could inspire and renew the artistic traditions. While the main exhibition space is used for the display of contemporary works, a smaller environmentally-controlled gallery space was also built with climatic conditions which would meet the stringent specifications of public galleries. It was hoped that this would enable them to receive important pre-contact material on extended loan or even permanent display (Myers, 1980).

Arrangements with Australian museums for the return of material or the loan of material for display have normally been dependent upon the provision of suitable accommodation to house materials. Furthermore, the Australian

Government, in its efforts to facilitate repatriation of Aboriginal material from overseas collections, had made it clear that such returns were contingent upon material being professionally curated and this factor has led to the establishment of a number of Keeping Places. The Government, while supporting the establishment of Keeping Places, therefore stated that 'priority should be given to projects primarily aimed at the return of cultural property to Aboriginal communities. Enterprises of a more overtly commercial nature should continue to seek funding from existing sources', such funding being from a variety of Commonwealth and State sources (Sampson, 1988).

The Keeping Place in the Western, Northern and Central Australian Aboriginal communities continues to serve a community function as storehouse for secret/sacred material, although the necessity for such museums and their long-term viability has been questioned. Chris Anderson has expressed reservations about the need for and the success of European-style Keeping Places, noting that their presence in centralised communities can become the focus for power struggles amongst groups within the community and they may end up being relevant to only one group (1988: 25). Lissant Bolton has suggested that, where the repatriation of artefacts is contingent upon the provision of a secure storage facility and professional curation, 'once the museum is built and open, interest in continuing to curate the collection may fall away'. This is not because the material lacks importance to the Aboriginal community, but rather they do not place such importance upon the long-term preservation of the artefacts. As Bolton has noted 'it is the symbolism of the possession and control of the material, rather than the material itself, which is significant' (Bolton, 1988: 27).

Tourism, education and Aboriginal culture

Over the past decade, there has been a very substantial growth in the number of museums and cultural centres established as commercial and educational facilities designed to develop in non-Aboriginal visitors a greater awareness of Aboriginal culture and heritage. Shepparton Aboriginal Keeping Place was the first Keeping Place to be established outside tribal land (Atkinson, 1985: 9). It was established as part of Shepparton International Village, an open air museum which was being developed in the City of Shepparton and was intended to be a major tourist attraction in the area. The Village was designed to reflect the cultural diversity of the community in Shepparton and it was, from its inception, intended to include an Aboriginal Keeping Place. The local Aboriginal communities were approached and plans submitted to the Aboriginal Arts Board of the Australia Council who approved the plans and met with representatives of the local Aboriginal population, the City Council and the International Village Committee. As a result of these discussions, a local Aboriginal cultural organisation, the Shepparton Aboriginal Arts Council Co-operative Limited, was established in 1974 to administer funds, acquire cultural material and liaise with the Village planners.

The Keeping Place received an initial grant of A$20,000 from the Aboriginal

Figure 5.5 Interior of the Aboriginal Keeping Place at Shepparton, Victoria, Australia

Source: Photo by M. Simpson, 1993

123

Arts Board in order to cover the costs of establishing the organisation, acquiring cultural material and for the design of the Keeping Place. They also received an ongoing annual grant of A$15,000 for administration and educational activities. The Aboriginal Arts Board subsequently acquired a substantial collection of Aboriginal artefacts and art works to be displayed in the Keeping Place. Owner-ship was transferred to the Shepparton Aboriginal Arts Council and a perpetual trust formed in order to ensure the preservation of the collection for the benefit of Aboriginal peoples in the future. A$170,000 was received from the govern-ment of Victoria and the balance from federal government to meet the estimated A$400,000 construction costs. The City Council provided A$70,000 allocated from a state lottery and a landscaped site within the International Village. The round building, designed by architect Professor Frederick Romberg, contained four large dioramas of the Goulbourn River area and additional displays of weapons, tools, baskets and other domestic items (Edwards, 1980: 11–15).

The aims of the Keeping Place were to provide facilities for the benefit of the Aboriginal community and to provide a vehicle for education about Aboriginal culture to non-Aboriginal people. It was envisaged that, through a range of activities, it would fulfil the role of interpretation to the general public. The collections in the Keeping Place would provide a focus of Aboriginal cultural identity and engender a sense of pride in their heritage. They would consist of a representative collection of Aboriginal arts and material culture and, more specifically, material relevant to the Aboriginal people of the Goulburn and Murray Rivers region and other areas of Victoria. These would be supplement-ed by occasional temporary exhibitions of material representing other tribal groups which would illustrate the diversity of Aboriginal peoples. Additional interpretive activities would consist of demonstrations by Aboriginal peoples of their dance, music and artistic skills and a resource centre would enable Aboriginal peoples to provide educational activities to all sectors of the educa-tional system (Edwards, 1980). In its first few years of opening, Shepparton Keeping Place proved to be very popular attracting an average of 50,000 visitors annually (Atkinson, 1985: 9), no doubt benefiting from its location within a more extensive tourist site. However, its proximity to the other buildings within the International Village may also be to its detriment, certainly as regards interpretation.

The International Village provides a series of national displays spread over a large, sixty-acre site. The buildings are usually quite small and their displays outdated and limited in diversity of techniques, resulting in static displays with limited attraction and educational value. The buildings are designed to incor-porate the most familiar aspects of architecture associated with each country (the Dutch windmill, the Chinese pavilion) and contain small displays of the most typical items associated with each country (such as traditional Dutch costumes and photographs of windmills). The quality of the displays and the buildings is variable and, in some, little concession is given to either quality of the artefacts or the interpretation; as such these cameos of ethnic life are likely to reinforce stereotypes. Like the worst of the community museums showing immigrant origins, they dwell on the past and highlight the most renowned

Figure 5.6 The Chinese garden and pavilion with the Dutch windmill in the backgroud, Shepparton International Village, Australia

Source: Photo by M. Simpson, 1993

125

aspects of a culture and, as a result, are sentimental and nostalgic in the extreme.

One of the most successful Aboriginal museums, in commercial and educational terms, is Brambuk Living Cultural Centre near *Budja Budja* (Hall's Gap) in the *Gariwerd*, or Grampian region of Victoria. Brambuk is named after the Bram brothers, two legendary figures believed to be responsible for the creation and naming of many of the landscape features in the region. Opened in December 1990, Brambuk is managed by a committee representing several Aboriginal organisations in the region under the umbrella of Brambuk Incorporated. The planning of the centre involved five communities who traditionally had used the Grampians as a spiritual base: the Kerrup-jmara, the Lake Condah people; the Gunditjmara (Dhauwurd Wurrung) from the co-operative in Warrnambool; the Framlingham Aboriginal community; the Goolum-Goolum from the Dimbula–Ebenezer–Horsham areas; and the Wergaia Jardwadjali.

The idea for Brambuk was conceived in the 1970s as a means of responding to the tourist interest in Aboriginal culture with some sort of museum or cultural centre run by Aboriginal people. Capital costs came from funding made available by the Victoria state government in order to promote the international tourist potential of the south western region of Victoria. From the outset, the Aboriginal people involved insisted upon total control over the project, including the design, location, and the function, and perceived it as substantially different from a museum. Geoff Clark, Chairman of the Framlingham Aboriginal Land Trust, described the concepts which the Aboriginal community wished to develop:

> We were familiar with the role of museums as they currently stood, and the way in which they interpreted Aboriginal culture as a dead culture, an ancient culture, in fact as something which needs to be protected rather than be maintained. We believed that, through the design of the building and its actual functions, we could achieve something closer to a display of living culture rather than a stagnant one that needs to be preserved. We wanted to include the political aspirations of people as well, because too often the image of Aboriginal people overseas is one of the Noble Savage standing on one leg with his spear, and 'you've got some nice dot paintings or some art work, and you can play your didgeridoo'. The image of what constitutes an indigenous person in this country needs to be changed, so hopefully Brambuk attempts to do all that and create understanding of the true history.
>
> (Clark, 1993)

The centre consists of a permanent exhibition space, a shop, the Brambuk café and Gugidjela restaurant, and a theatre. Outside, there is a ceremonial ground which is used for demonstrations of music, dancing and cooking, while the grounds around the building have been planted with native plants. The exhibition provides 'a journey through time'. An introductory audio-visual presentation describes how the people, the plants and animals were created by the legendary creator, Bunjil, who was also believed to have created the tools and weapons the people used for hunting and gathering food, and the religion and laws by which they lived. Inside, the small gallery begins with an area devoted to traditional

Aboriginal life prior to European colonisation, particularly the hunting and gathering of plants and animals and their uses as food and medicine. It then proceeds to describe the processes of colonisation through video, photos, and documents. It highlights the massacres of Aboriginal people and gives an insight into some aspects of the assimilation process, the establishment of missions, and the removal of children from their Aboriginal parents.

The first section, devoted to the Aboriginal uses of flora and fauna, includes photographs, as well as artefacts such as boomerangs, digging sticks and baskets. Text panels describe the wide range of uses to which the raw materials were put. For example, kangaroos and wallabies provided meat; skins, used to make cloaks and rugs; sinew, which was dried and used as string or sewing thread; and bones, from which tools such as needles and fishing hooks were carved. From the grass tree, they obtained seeds which were crushed and ground to make flour, while the stem was used as a fire-stick, and the resin or sap provided an adhesive strong enough to attach a stone spearhead to a wooden shaft.

One of the most dramatic parts of the exhibition is the section highlighting the deaths of Aboriginal peoples following the arrival of European settlers in the Western Victorian region. A 'forest' of poles in a dimly lit corner of the gallery creates an impression of woodland. White text panels are pinned to the wooden poles like public notices pinned to trees. On each is a quotation taken from the journals of white settlers and travellers in the period 1836 to 1843 describing the killing of Aboriginal peoples as part of the efforts employed by some whites to obtain land for themselves and exterminate the Aboriginal population.

Following this are sections examining the establishment of missions, and the government assimilation policy, in which the text states: 'We became the innocent victims of an attempt to bring about cultural genocide.' It also highlights the bitter irony of Aboriginal (or Koori) servicemen's involvement in the Second World War: on their return all servicemen were promised land under the Soldier Settlement Scheme. 'Sadly the Koori soldiers were excluded from this. Even the very place they called home, the land around the Mission sites, was divided up and given to non-Kooris.'

The exhibition has drawn some criticism from visitors who are unaware of the more unpalatable aspects of Australian history and disbelieve what they read. As Geoff Clark (1993) explained: 'It's very difficult in this situation because we're walking a fine line between exposing the real history of this country and trying to please the taste buds, I suppose, or the curiosities of tourists, which is very difficult when you are trying to tell a history for its brutality'. Clark believes it is necessary to present an accurate, but balanced interpretation of history which will create awareness amongst visitors 'as opposed to making the guilt factor, or some of the other feelings that non-Aborigines might feel, and find themselves justifying, or having to rethink in terms of their perspective on how the place was settled or colonised.' He feels that many of the things they were saying in Brambuk have been reinforced by the Mabo decision, particularly the court's repudiation of the concept of *terra nullius* and the acknowledgement of Aboriginal resistance to white encroachment upon their lands.

The centre is not currently run purely as a commercial enterprise but as an educational centre. Clark believes that the centre is very important as a first point of contact for the many school children and international visitors who visit each year, many of whom are largely ignorant about Aboriginal people and culture, and the continuation and interaction of traditional life with modern-day society. He regards the education of the public as the primary function of Brambuk and believes that it offers a unique opportunity, 'through a very warm and open atmosphere', for visitors to view the artefacts and creative arts, and engage in various educational activities which provide an insight into traditional Aboriginal culture:

> What the centre attempts to do is provide . . . a holistic view, . . . a place where there is a window into Aboriginal lifestyle, philosophy, thinking, tradition, culture and heritage . . . rather than the stone implements that are normally seen in museums and also the skeletal remains that are sometimes used by museums to depict how our Aboriginal life was. . . . Those are aspects of culture you usually associate with a lost civilisation, with the 'Noble Savage'.

> (Clark, 1993)

Interpretive programmes include the gathering, preparation and tasting of food, and provide examples of traditional methods used prior to European occupation, as well as showing how these same ingredients are being utilised today. In the Brambuk Café visitors can sample bush tucker: the modern presentation of native foods. Traditional ingredients, such as crocodile and kangaroo meat, wattle seed and bunya nuts, are prepared in a modern way to provide dishes such as crocodile and emu sausages, roo burgers, and 'wattlechino' as an alternative to cappuccino. Three evenings a week, as the Gugidjela restaurant, it is open for dinner for which dishes of a more 'cordon bleu' nature are served: *cumbungi djark gadjin cress*, (hearts of reed and water cress), *gadjin yabidj* (garlic yabbies in bush tomato concasse and wild rice), and *midjun quandong* (kangaroo fillets pan-fried with wild peach and bush chutney relish).

Clark believes that the other important function of Brambuk is in teaching young Kooris. 'Aboriginal culture and indigenous cultures world-wide are continually under threat and we would like to use this place for the reintroduction of language, ceremonies, dance exchanges – an exchange place for cultures.' The centre provides an opportunity for Aboriginal people to practise their culture, to demonstrate some of their dances and to market their arts. The shop provides an outlet for good quality, Aboriginal products such as paintings, t-shirts, jewellery, and toiletries. Visiting artists, dance performances and workshops are included in the centre's programme of events.

The administrators are currently considering whether the centre should be upgraded and expanded, or continue as it is. The exhibition is permanent at present: they would like to change it but the cost this would entail means this is not feasible. They operate a motel across the road from Brambuk which they are considering upgrading into a five star motel. They are contemplating upgrading the restaurant and establishing a processing plant for packaging

Koori foods for tourists. Clark explained that they would also like to take over responsibility for the management of rock art sites in the National Park; at present they offer cultural visits to some of them. He hopes 'that the state government would consider releasing back all management considerations for the sites because 80 per cent of rock art in Victoria is in the Grampian ranges' but local resistance has prevented this.

At present, Brambuk is run by a staff of five. Administrative costs, primarily salaries, were supported by the state for the first few years at a declining rate per year and Brambuk will have to become fully commercial and financially viable. A$135,000 dollars per annum are required to run the centre, money which has to be generated by the commercial side of the facility: the shop and restaurant. There is a A$3.00 admission charge redeemable against purchases in the shop or restaurant, intended to encourage visitors to spend money in these areas. While the shop has been very successful the restaurant has been less so, as there is still some resistance from visitors to eating unfamiliar foods such as kangaroo and crocodile. Clark fears that financial pressures will force them to commercialise some of the cultural activities, such as boomerang throwing and dancing, which are at present offered free. He is also concerned that the centre has to charge people to gain access to information he feels it is important to disseminate. He believes that:

> there's a moral obligation by states to provide this sort of facility in order to educate and create awareness, because we do a lot of work with school groups, and yet we're meant to slug [charge] them. People resent being slugged. We think that the benefits of Brambuk as a service far outweigh its function of trying to generate money, but unfortunately we may have to go down that track, the way everything seems to go.
>
> (Clark, 1993)

The first national or state institution devoted to Aboriginal arts and culture opened in Adelaide in South Australia in October 1989. Tandanya, the National Aboriginal Cultural Institute, is managed and controlled by Aboriginal people. 'Tandanya' means literally 'place of the kangaroo' and is the name given by the Kaurna, the Aboriginal people who inhabited the Adelaide plains, to the area on which the modern city of Adelaide now stands. It was once the site of the Red Kangaroo Ceremony linked to the Red Kangaroo Dreaming.

Tandanya was an ambitious project which sought to 'foster the development and preservation of the culture, tradition, heritage, language, mythology, craft, visual and performing arts of fifty traditional Aboriginal groups in South Australia' and provide a programme of temporary exhibitions drawing upon works in other collections throughout Australia (Tandanya, nd). Tandanya provides a venue for exhibitions of Aboriginal arts and crafts, and for performances of traditional and contemporary Aboriginal music, dance and theatre. It also provides facilities for seminars and conferences, and workshops for the production of arts and crafts. It has a cafeteria and a retail shop selling arts, crafts, music, clothing, and other Aboriginal artefacts. Housed in an old power station, the interior has been remodelled to create a vast central exhibition space used to display major exhibitions, and a smaller gallery used mainly for exhibitions of the work of local artists. A performing arts space provides seating for audiences of 160 and is equipped with computerised lighting, video, film and slide projection facilities.

Tandanya serves as a cultural venue for the Aboriginal peoples of the Adelaide region and promotes and presents Aboriginal works in all art forms at a national level. It also has an educational mission seeking to promote and sell Aboriginal art and culture to non-Aboriginal peoples in Adelaide and South Australia, and to become a significant tourist facility attracting visitors from overseas. In the early years of its establishment, it faced severe financial difficulties and was threatened with closure. With debts of A$440,000, it was rescued by the state government and, under new management, the Institute's financial decline was successfully halted.

The Koorie Heritage Trust, based in Melbourne, Victoria, is housed within the Museum of Victoria and is managed and staffed by Aboriginal people who work in association with staff of the Museum. Established in 1985, the Trust collects Aboriginal artefacts of historical and sacred importance from throughout Victoria and displays them at the Keeping Place within the Museum of Victoria, and in Aboriginal Keeping Places in other parts of the state. Its interpretive activities are mainly confined to exhibitions and outreach programmes to schools and other groups, supporting its mission to 'bridge the cultural gap'. The Trust also established an Elders Oral History Program, and has produced postcards and posters; fifty banners on Koorie achievers; and videos examining Koorie bush tucker, the use of medicinal plants, health issues, and sea foods.

Koorie was a major touring exhibition and accompanying book created by the Koorie Heritage Trust in association with the Museum of Victoria, and sponsored by the Victorian Tourism Commission. *Koorie* examined the traditional culture and heritage of the Aboriginal people of south-eastern Australia and contemporary issues facing Aboriginal people today. The exhibition was installed in the Kershaw Hall in the Museum of Victoria where it was located in the main area of the gallery and around the walls of the mezzanine level. In the centre of the room, a ramp zigzagged up to the mezzanine floor like the twisting body of the Rainbow Serpent which features in many Aboriginal stories of the Dreamtime. The exhibition was arranged chronologically beginning with historical information describing the 40,000 year history of the Aboriginal population in Australia, and moving on to describe anthropological data about pre-contact lifestyles, work practices, tools, religious beliefs, community laws, family and kinship, healing and caring, carvers and painters and so on. The visual material in this section consisted of artefacts in showcases and dioramas, supplemented by nineteenth-century drawings and photographs by Europeans documenting their first impressions of the Aboriginal cultures that they encountered.

The next two sections dealt with European contact and its consequences under the general headings of 'contact' and 'survival', and led the visitor up the stairs to the mezzanine floor where the contemporary material was located. In the post-contact and contemporary sections, much of the interpretation utilised documentation and graphics to convey a message which was strongly political in nature. The language was simple and bold, conveying a message which was forceful and unequivocal. The heading *Civil War* introduced a text which described the clash of cultures that followed the arrival of Europeans in Victoria, as Aboriginal people fought to defend their land and their lives against the invasion of settlers.

> People on both sides died violently – Europeans by spear and club, Aborigines by gun and poison. The choice of weapons, combined with starvation and disease, eventually tipped the scales against the Aboriginal resistance fighters.
>
> From an estimated Aboriginal population of 200,000 plus in Victoria in the late 18th century, less than 5,000 – maybe as few as 2,500 – survived the massacres, the poisonings, the starvation and the diseases of the 1820s to 1840s.

A map, entitled 'Massacre Map', showed 'the locations of known killings of Aborigines by Europeans for the eighteen years between 1836 and 1853' and listed dates, locations and brief details of incidents which accounted for the deaths of hundreds of Aboriginal people – thousands more died in undocumented incidents (Koorie Heritage Trust, 1991: 18–20).

A section entitled 'Survival' described the ineffectual attempts of the colonial government to establish a protectorate in the 1830s to safeguard the Aboriginal people, and the later policies of the Victorian government which led to the creation, from the 1860s, of reserves to which Aboriginal people were to be relocated. These were designed to protect Aboriginal people and enable them to be 'civilised' and Christianised by Europeans, compelled to adopt the English language and European domestic practices, modes of dress, and names.

In the contemporary section, the efforts of Aboriginal peoples to resist the processes of acculturation were emphasised, showing that they were not the 'tragic victims' of popular history but have continued the struggle to maintain their cultural identity and their rights from the earliest days of European settlement to the present day. In a section dealing with land rights and sovereignty it stated that 'Aboriginal sovereignty has never been surrendered, and neither European settlement nor the passage of time negates its validity.'

While walking around the gallery, visitors were able to hear the gentle tones of a continuous-loop tape quietly playing the melancholy songs Aboriginal singer-songwriter Archie Roach. His words tell haunting tales of pain and sorrow, of children taken from their parents, of loss of family and identity, of homelessness, of alcohol and drug abuse. The sound track added a poignancy that reinforced and personalised the impact of the factual data presented in the exhibition text.

Like Brambuk, the message of *Koorie* was of survival and a retelling of history which hides nothing but instead exposes the barbaric treatment of Aboriginal peoples and the injustices which were inflicted upon them and which continue to feature strongly in white–Aboriginal relations today. The exhibition medium provides a means of confronting visitors with truths which are frequently expurgated from white histories, exposing facts of which many non-Aboriginal visitors may have little awareness. While the exhibition texts in Brambuk and the *Koorie* exhibition challenge visitors with hard facts and shocking realities, they do so in the non-confrontational environment of the exhibition which enables the visitor to proceed at their own speed, to continue, to halt, or to retreat, as they choose. They enable Aboriginal views to be presented and visitors to read and consider them in an environment which allows for quiet contemplation and the consideration of information which is disturbing, yet heartening, for it tells of the survival and strengthening of a culture almost wiped out. In this way, the exhibition medium provides a powerful means of communication.

Blending old and new

As the potential value of museums and cultural centres is being recognised by Aboriginal people, their adaptation to local situations is being explored. Many of the museums and cultural centres have been established in urban areas. However, Aboriginal communities increasingly recognise the potential of adopting the interpretive role of European museums and, as a result, the visitor-oriented Keeping Place is gradually being adopted in more remote regions where tourism brings in substantial numbers of outsiders. Some of the earliest examples of these were established by Europeans interested in preserving and promoting the Aboriginal artistic heritage.

Over the past twenty-five years, Keeping Places have been established at Yuendumu, Yirrkala, Bathurst Island, and other communities in Western Australia, the Northern Territories, Northern Queensland and northern South Australia. In Maningrida, an arts and craft centre provides a sales outlet for Aboriginal arts, while Djomi Community Museum, a small existing museum, holds a collection which was established by a European craft advisor. This museum is to be up-graded and expanded to provide for tourists as well as the community.

Although many communities clearly need either a Keeping Place or a museum, some are finding that the differing roles of each suit the varied needs of maintaining control and security of secret/sacred material, while enabling tourists and other visitors to learn about the unrestricted aspects of Aboriginal culture. Consequently, an Aboriginal community may well have two museums: a men's museum and a women's museum, as in Yuendumu. Here, the potential of a conventional museum to display and interpret secular material to visitors was also recognised and resulted in a three-stranded Keeping Place/museum managed by Aboriginal and European staff (West, 1981: 12).

In 1995, Warradja Aboriginal Cultural Centre opened in Kakadu National Park. It has been a very popular destination for tourists wishing to learn about Aboriginal culture and visit some of the country's most significant rock art sites and stunning scenery. In conjunction with this, the Keeping Place has been established as a storehouse for secret/sacred objects, important historic artefacts, publications dealing with the region, photographic archives, and other materials which are seen to be important for future generations. The Cultural Centre will enable Aboriginal guides to accompany visitors to selected rock art sites and flood plain areas; provide information about Aboriginal art, culture and technology; and demonstrate various skills such as the collection and preparation of natural foodstuffs, cooking, tool-making, weaving, and so on. It will also enable them to display and sell art works, ensuring that the artist receives a fair price. It is intended that the centre will become the focus for tourist visits and so alleviate some of the problems that tourism places upon the Aboriginal communities themselves and upon the physical safety of rock art sites. Visitor access will be monitored and controlled as appropriate to the cultural concerns of the Aboriginal community and the conservation needs of the rock art sites.

Such developments offer Aboriginal people the opportunity to develop commercial enterprises, bringing employment opportunities and cash into the community. They also enable Aboriginal communities to control the flow of visitors and so safeguard their natural resources and artistic treasures. By combining Keeping Place and museum, the community is able to provide for the differing needs of its own people and visitors. In these instances, the western museum model and the traditional Keeping Place stand side by side to serve the community to the best advantage.

6

Native American museums and cultural centres

'It shall not be called a museum, for we are not a dead people; let it be called the Skeena Treasure House.'

Alfred Douse, High Chief of the Kitwancool Band, Hazelton, British Columbia ('Ksan Association, nd).

Over the 500 years since colonisation of the Americas, many in the immigrant population have reviled and mistreated the native population, subjecting them to gross inequities and attempting to eradicate their cultural practices. At the same time, their material culture has been studied, admired, and collected. The subject of extensive anthropological research and the prey of voracious collectors, American Indians have been unequal partners in a relationship from which they have benefited little. The attention of anthropologists and museums served their own interests, not those of the Indians. In these unequal relationships, benefits travelled one way: *from* the community. Through colonialism, American Indian communities lost lives, lands, and much of their material culture which is now held in museums and private collections around the world. The effects of decades of government assimilation policies and the pressures and influences of contemporary society had threatened the survival of traditional tribal cultures.

As with the African American population, Native Americans in the United States began seeking increased civil rights and greater self-determination. This was marked by the resurgence of interest in traditional cultural practices and a reawakening of cultural identity and pride amongst Native Americans, paralleled by an awakening of political consciousness. This trend can be illustrated by examples dating back to the nineteenth century, such as the Ghost Dance of the Plains Indians and the Longhouse Religion of the Iroquois. The 1960s and 1970s were marked by a series of events which drew national attention in Canada and the United States to the grievances of the native population. There was a growing movement towards cultural revival and self-representation by tribal groups seeking to re-establish and enhance their cultural identity through the preservation and revival of traditional culture, history and art, and to counteract the negative and stereotyped image of the Indian. One manifestation of this self-determination movement was the establishment of Native American museums and cultural centres.

Coinciding with this were changes in government policies towards the native population which encouraged economic self-sufficiency and resulted in changing demographics. In the US, the Indian Civil Rights Act of 1968, the Indian Self-Determination and Education Assistance Act of 1975, and the American Indian Religious Freedom Act of 1978 provided tribal groups with greater control and autonomy. Whereas previous employment opportunities had encouraged moves from reservations to urban areas, changes from industrial to post-industrial work resulted in moves from the industrialised north-east to the south and southwest. Government economic strategies and concerns amongst tribal groups about the possible loss of traditional customs combined to provide the incentive for many to remain on or move back to the reservations. Increasing tourism and interest in Indian cultures offered commercial possibilities. New legislation also made funding available to tribal governments from various federal sources.

Many tribal groups decided that the establishment of a tribal museum or cultural centre would provide them with the means to reinforce the cultural identity of the tribe, particularly for the benefit of the youngsters. In areas popular with tourists, a museum and cultural centre was often seen as a viable commercial proposition which would provide employment and bring money into the economy of the reservation. By this time, US federal policy towards Indians had changed and the Government was keen to support projects which would lead to greater self-sufficiency amongst Native Americans living on reservations. The Federal Government saw museums and cultural centres as part of a larger commercial plan to provide shops, restaurants, hotels and other facilities which would cater for and attract tourists, so increasing the tourist industry to reservations, providing employment for tribal members and a sales outlet for tribal craftspeople.

A few Indian museums existed prior to the Second World War: the Cherokees of North Carolina reportedly had a museum collection as early as 1928 and at least five other Indian museums were established during the 1930s and 1940s (Childs, 1980: 19; Hanson, 1980: 44–51). Some of these, such as the Plains Indian Museum at Browning, Montana (1941), were established and operated by the Office of Indian Affairs of the US Department of the Interior with non-native staff (AAM, 1941). However, as money has been made available in recent decades to build museums and service the tourist trade, many more Native American, Aleut and Inuit communities decided to establish their own museums and cultural centres, and the 1960s and 1970s witnessed a dramatic growth in number which has continued into the 1990s.

A specialist advisory body, the North American Indian Museums Association (NAIMA), was established in 1978 to support the work of Indian museums throughout North America and to assist in their further development including resources, collections, marketing, research and interpretive programmes. The preservation and enhancement of traditional culture, history and art were also identified as key functions of the new organisation, including the education of Indian children, and the promotion of public awareness of the cultural diversity existing within the American Indian population (NAIMA, 1980; Brascoupé, 1981: 5). By the early 1980s there were over 100 museums in North America operated by Native Americans (Brascoupé, 1981) and in 1994 the Smithsonian Institution's American Indian Museum Studies Program listed over 200 (Smithsonian Institution, 1994). According to Article III of the North American Indian Museum Association by-laws (NAIMA, 1980):

> An Indian museum is defined as an established non-profit institution essentially educational or aesthetic in purpose, with professional staff, that provides exhibits, research, or programs in North American Indian subjects. In addition, the institution must meet the following requirements: 1. A majority of either, the Board of Directors or the staff members, must be North American Indian, Eskimos, Aleuts, Inuit or Métis. 2. The institution must serve a local Indian population.

Most of the earlier types of Native American museums were established primarily as commercial enterprises to exploit the tourist industry and the growing public interest in Indian cultures, so creating jobs and income in many sectors of the tourist market, and encouraging Native Americans to remain in their communities. In addition, they were percieved as a means by which Native Americans could counteract the inaccurate and negative images of Indian peoples. They ranged from small ventures (family-run concerns on reservations, community-run museums and cultural centres, and small tourist-oriented 'museums' and craft shops attached to hotels and restaurants) to multi-million dollar establishments with a range of activities: museum, cultural centre, library, archive and educational establishment (Hitchcock, 1976; Doxtator, 1985). Others were established or have evolved as facilities which place greater emphasis upon community service.

George P. Horse Capture (1981), curator of the Plains Indian Museum at the Buffalo Bill Historical Center, describes how the need for tribal museums has arisen:

> Traditionally Indian groups had no need for museums because the culture was self-perpetuating. For untold centuries they lived with their material culture and preserved knowledge of it by the oral tradition. There was no need to preserve everyday items to remind people of the past because essential change was slow enough for people to adjust and live comfortably within. Within a very brief period, however, the Indian ways were disrupted critically. The land, the religion, the material culture almost disappeared from the earth. We now are engaged in the long struggle to regain some of the former glory and traditions. To do so successfully, we must adapt some of the white man's ways and methods, but do this in such a way that we revive and preserve our 'Indianness'.

Museums can assist in the reaffirmation of cultural identity by providing a means of preserving elements of culture including artefacts, language, and skills. They can also provide a venue for community education and activities thus ensuring the perpetuation of cultural traditions to younger members of the tribe. The tribal museum provides a venue in which Indian people can take control of representation of their culture to others. Through museum exhibitions, performances, demonstrations, publications and so on, they are able to provide their own interpretation of their history, culture and art; to present their religious beliefs and world views; to tell their story. Thus, 'a vital contribution Native American museums can make to their communities is the fostering of group pride, intercultural understanding and positive self-image. These museums serve an important psychological need and provide stability and security' (Hanson, 1980: 47).

Native Americans are in a unique position within US federal funding policy. Under treaty agreements and subsequent government acts, federal funding provides much of the financial framework for education, medical and social services, housing and law enforcement provision on reservations. Preservation of 'Indianness' therefore ensures that the government still recognises tribal status and the treaty obligations. It also helps to alleviate some of the destructive effects of attempts to assimilate Indians into Anglo-American culture (Biddle, 1977; Hill, 1977). Hence, tribal museums serve important political roles as well as social.

In 1967, the All Indian Pueblo Council had the idea for a museum 'to express the Indian Pueblo Culture and the traditions of our people, to promote understanding of the Pueblo Culture and to perpetuate this culture' (Suina, 1979: 6). With the aid of a $1.6 million grant from the Economic Development Administration, and $50,000 raised by the efforts of the Friends and employees, the Indian Pueblo Cultural Center in Albuquerque, New Mexico, was built and opened in 1976. The design of the building was based upon the multi-storey, semi-circular structure of Pueblo Bonito, one of the largest Pueblo buildings, constructed around the eleventh century AD. The Cultural Center houses a permanent exhibition of Pueblo cultural material, much of it collected from members of the community:

> Through these items we are telling our story, the Pueblo story as told by the elders. This is our story, and we tell it the way that the old folks told it to us from our emergence up to the present time. All the Pueblo activities are centred around the Indian Pueblo Cultural Center, so you get to share what is in the past, what is in the making, and what plans and dreams we have for the future.
>
> (Suina, 1979: 7)

The activities of the centre include tours for visitors and school groups, dance programmes, lectures, films, and a mural programme. The centre is able to cover its running costs and offer this range of activities with the help of the friends of the centre and because it has a strong marketing approach. The friends raised $20,000 for the mural programme and volunteers man the reception desk, saving a great deal on staffing. There is an Indian restaurant serving authentic Indian food. Office space is available for rent to local businesses. There is also a profit-making arm which provides income for the centre. Indian Pueblo Marketing Incorporated is a marketing outlet for Indian arts and crafts produced on the reservation. It runs a gift shop and provides a wholesale and retail service, plus injecting over $500,000 into the economy of the reservation.

The Oconaluftee Indian Village and Museum of the Cherokee Indian in Cherokee, North Carolina, and the Cherokee Heritage Center in Tahlequah, Oklahoma, provide examples of successful enterprises established with the intention of creating employment opportunities and developing the commercial potential offered by tourism in areas where unemployment on the reservations is high. At the same time, the interpretation of Cherokee history and culture are fundamental to their operations.

The history of the Cherokee nation provides a dramatic story of colonisation, cultural development and betrayal. The people of the Cherokee Nation lived in the southeastern United States, in the states of Georgia, Tennessee, North and South Carolina, and parts of Kentucky and Alabama. Following the arrival of the Europeans, the Cherokee adopted many aspects of European culture and by 1828 they had a school, a church, a bible translated into Cherokee, and a newspaper written in Cherokee and English, the first newspaper written in an Indian language. Despite this, in the 1830s, thousands of Cherokee were forced off their tribal lands and relocated far to the west, with many dying on the 1,200 mile journey that they were compelled to undertake.

During the late eighteenth and early nineteenth centuries, land became scarce as the population of American settlers grew in the eastern regions of the United States. There was increasing pressure upon President Andrew Jackson to force the Indians of the eastern states to move westward to make room for American settlers and, in 1830, he authorised the Indian Removal Act which called for the relocation of the tribes from the east to regions west of the Mississippi. Then, in the 1830s, gold was discovered on Cherokee land in Georgia and, despite opposition to the proposed removal of the Cherokee, a treaty was signed in 1835 by some of the Cherokee leaders who represented only a minority of the tribe. The Treaty of New Echota relinquished all the Cherokee land lying to the east of the Mississippi and gave them, in exchange, land in Indian Territory or, as it is known now, Oklahoma; plus a large sum of money, livestock, tools and other provisions. Approximately 2,000 Cherokee agreed to go to Indian Territory but the remainder, led by Chief John Ross, were determined to stay.

In 1838, the US government began rounding up the remaining Cherokee population for their forced removal to Indian territory. Between June 1838 and March 1839, 14–15,000 Cherokee were rounded up at bayonet-point and kept in stockades before being forced to march 1,200 miles through Tennessee, Kentucky, Illinois, Missouri and Arkansas. Men, women and children were forced to negotiate the rough terrain enduring harsh weather conditions. With inadequate food and clothing, approximately 4,000 died from exposure, malnutrition or disease. This harrowing journey became known as the 'Trail of Tears'. Those who had not been rounded up, approximately 1,000, remained hidden in the mountains until they were granted a reprieve and allowed to stay. They became known as the Eastern Band of Cherokee while those who survived the forced march became known as the Cherokee Nation of Oklahoma.

Today, the town of Cherokee in North Carolina is a major tourist attraction in the area, not far from the Blue Ridge Parkway, which leads into the Smoky Mountain National Park. Tourists crowd the area in summer, leaving the town quiet in winter. One of the major attractions in Cherokee is the outdoor drama 'Unto These Hills' written by Kermit Hunter, which recounts the history of the removal of the Cherokee from their homelands and the tragedy of the 'Trail of Tears'. In a 2,900-seat outdoor theatre, constructed on a hillside above the town, a cast of 130 gives 60 performances during the summer months. The drama has been immensely successful, having been operating since 1950, and it now attracts audiences of approximately 90–100,000 per annum (Douthit, 1995). Initiated in the post-war years by the Western North Carolina Associ- ated Communities (WNCAC), a regional organisation of eleven counties, the project was envisioned as a means of developing the tourist potential of the area and generating employment and income for the Cherokee and others living in the region. The WNCAC then formed a non-profit organisation, the Cherokee Historical Trust, in 1948 to produce the show. The Cherokee Historical Trust, although not a tribal organisation, has a mixed membership of non-Indians and those on the tribal roll. Over the years, it has played an important role in the Cherokee community, providing educational scholarships, art prizes and grants, and, through its own commercial activities, has contributed greatly to the increased prosperity of the area.

The drama proved to be a great success, attracting over 107,000 people during the first season, and repaying the debts incurred in constructing the theatre and staging the performance; in addition there was a profit of $70,000 (Connor, 1982: 26). The success of 'Unto These Hills' enabled the Cherokee Historical Association to proceed with additional projects that they had planned. The first of these was the construction of a replica eighteenth-century Cherokee Indian village located in a woodland setting on the mountainside above the town of Cherokee. Oconaluftee, as it was called, depicts life in the late eighteenth century. In order to discover the archaeological data that would be required to construct an authentic village, the Cherokee Historical Association founded the Tsali Institute of Cherokee Research to undertake scientific study into Chero- kee history and liaise with other relevant organisations such as universities. The Association funded excavations by archaeologists from the Universities of North Carolina, Tennessee, and Georgia (Connor, 1982: 29) and gathered data for the planning of the village and its contents. Excavated artefacts were later to form the basis of a significant collection of prehistoric and historic material in the collections of the Museum of the Cherokee Indian, while replicas were made for use in Oconaluftee Indian Village, which opened in 1952. Here visi- tors can see costumed guides and demonstrators engaged in various activities such as pottery making, basketry, finger weaving, canoe building, flint chipping, and using a blow gun. The village has continued to be immensely popular with the summer tourists and attracts around 150,000 per year.

The Cherokee Historical Association had planned for several years to establish a Cherokee Museum and in 1952, it was agreed to purchase an important collection of artefacts representing the Cherokee and other tribes of the

Figure 6.1   Arrow-head showcases in the Museum of the Cherokee Indian, North Carolina. The shape echos that of the arrowheads and points which feature in the section dealing with the early history of the region.

Source: Photo courtesy of the Museum of the Cherokee Indian in Cherokee, North Carolina

Figure 6.2 Display relating to the invention of the Cherokee syllabary by Sequoyah, in 1821,
Museum of the Cherokee Indian, North Carolina

Source: Photo by M. Simpson, 1995, with permission of Museum of the Cherokee Indian

southeastern United States. The collection had been purchased by Samuel Beck in 1945 and three years later, he opened the Museum of the Cherokee Indian in the Oconaluftee Inn, a log building in Cherokee. After purchase by the Cherokee Historical Association, the Museum remained in that location until 1958 when the building was destroyed by fire; fortunately, the collection had been in storage over the winter and so was undamaged. The following summer the Museum reopened in a building owned by the Cherokee Historical Association, but larger facilities were required and fundraising began for the purchase of a suitable piece of land and the cost of building a purpose-built, fire-proof building. A large grant of $600,000 was received from the Economic Development Association with additional substantial grants from the Cherokee Historical Association, the State of North Carolina and various foundations (King, 1976). The plans for the new museum included provision for training so that management of the Museum could be undertaken by Cherokee staff. The Museum now operates separately from the Cherokee Historical Association and is owned by the Cherokee tribe from whom it is leased. It is administered by the Museum Corporation, a fifteen-member board, the majority of whom are enrolled tribal members.

Located in the centre of the town, the Museum of the Cherokee Indian tells the story of the prehistory of the Cherokee tribe and recounts the events following European settlement. Visitors can listen to recordings of Cherokee myths and examine colourful illuminated glass illustrations of the stories. Archaeological materials are utilised in displays which chart the development of the Indian population in the southern Appalachian region from the Pleistocene period. The shape of the arrowheads and flints so prevalent in these displays is echoed in the design of the showcases which display weapons and tools of the post-contact period; nearby panels describe the acculturation process and recount the events of the Civil War.

A large wall panel shows Sequoyah, one of the most famous figures in Cherokee history. Unable to read or write English, he was, nevertheless, fascinated by the ability of Europeans to record words in written form. After twelve years of work, Sequoya developed a Cherokee syllabary which was easily learned by the Cherokee enabling the widespread development of literacy amongst the tribe. In 1825, a translation of the New Testament was completed and in 1928 the first Indian newspaper, the *Cherokee Phoenix*, was established. The panel shows the 86 letters which form the syllabary representing the 86 syllables which Sequoya identified in Cherokee speech. Audio-visual equipment enables visitors to hear the sounds of the Cherokee language, and nearby displays contain examples of books and newspapers written in Cherokee.

The story of the 'Trail of Tears' is shown in a series of audio-visual booths where visitors can listen to the tale of betrayal and observe the reduction of Indian lands shown on maps using fibre-optics to chart routes and define areas. Finally visitors can examine photographs of the Cherokee in earlier decades, view a display of contemporary arts and crafts, and watch a short presentation in the auditorium showing contemporary Cherokee life. The latter provides 'a glimpse of the present-day Cherokee community seldom seen by the visiting public'.

Figure 6.3 Shop front, Cherokee town, North Carolina. The mélange of imagery used by the retail outlets, hotels and restaurants in Cherokee may appeal to the tourists, but they reflect nothing of Cherokee culture.

Source: Photo by M. Simpson, 1995

Following the success of the drama 'Unto These Hills' and the other projects developed by the Cherokee Historical Association in North Carolina, and impressed by the economic development of the growing tourism which it attracted to the Cherokee area, the Cherokee Nation of Oklahoma decided to develop a similar project (CNHS, 1976). In 1963, the Cherokee National Historical Society was formed with the aim of preserving and interpreting the story of the Cherokee tribe, and developing tourism in order to generate income and create employment in the area. The Society proposed to create an outdoor historical drama, similar to that in Cherokee, North Carolina; an authentic re-creation of a seventeenth-century Cherokee village; and a Cherokee Cultural Center, incorporating a museum, archives and library. Funding was obtained from the Cherokee Nation, the Cherokee Foundation, Oklahoma State, the Economic Development Administration, and various private companies and individuals.

Tsa-La-Gi, the Cherokee Heritage Center, has been constructed on the site of the old Cherokee Female Seminary, which opened in Tahlequah in 1851, but was destroyed by fire in 1889 and relocated to the north of Tahlequah. Located in woodland, a site was cleared amongst the trees to enable construction of the Ancient Village. A three-month training programme was established in co-operation with the Bureau of Indian Affairs and North-eastern State College to provide training for the Cherokee who would act as guides and demonstrators. The village opened in June 1967 and employs around 35 to 40 Cherokee each year who demonstrate to visitors the life of the Cherokee at the time of European contact in 1650. Visitors to *Tsa-La-Gi* are guided round the village by a costumed interpreter who describes the uses of the different buildings. At each stop, demonstrators can be seen performing some activity: food preparation, pottery, shaping arrowheads, and soaking fibres in the stream for weaving baskets. The following year, a 1,800-seat outdoor theatre opened at *Tsa-La-Gi* showing the 'Trail of Tears' drama also written by Kermit Hunter, the author of 'Unto These Hills' (CNHS, 1976). The drama continues to attract visitors and is performed six times a week with a cast and crew of 70.

The Cherokee National Museum opened early in 1974 and, in the grounds around it, a Cherokee arboretum has been developed with paths and markers identifying the flora in the area. Since then, the Cherokee National Historical Society has also opened Adams Corner Rural Village next to the Museum, showing life in the Cherokee Nation in the period 1870–90, and the two out-door villages provide an illustration of the dramatic changes in lifestyle that the Cherokee underwent following European contact. Entrance to Adams Corner Rural Village is included in the price of the ticket for the Museum and is self-guided. Here, costumed staff are present in one of the houses and the shop, but visitors are free to stroll at their leisure. The Historical Society provides educational facilities for Cherokee and non-Cherokee visitors and offers a range of activities: a history exhibition in the Museum, drama performances, the 'living history' of the villages, art exhibitions, education programmes for schools, workshops, lectures, and access to the research collections.

145

Figure 6.4 The Ancient Village at *Tsa-La-Gi*, the Cherokee Heritage Center in Oklahoma, where Cherokee guides and demonstrators show visitors what life was like in a Cherokee village in 1650

Source: Photo by M. Simpson, 1995

Figure 6.5 Adams Corner Rural Village showing a Cherokee community in the period 1870—1890, *Tsa-La-Gi*, Cherokee Heritage Center, Oklahoma

Source: Photo by M. Simpson, 1995

The displays in both the Museum of the Cherokee Indian and the Cherokee National Museum are now more than twenty years old and their current directors are preparing plans for new displays with substantial funding from the National Park Service (NPS). Ken Blankenship, director of the Museum of the Cherokee Indian in Cherokee, North Carolina, is keen that the new exhibition should emphasise contemporary life for the Cherokee, and also the history of Cherokee assimilation which, since the nineteenth century, has meant that the Cherokee have lived in homes very similar to those of their white neighbours. He has found that many visitors still carry images of Indians in feather headdresses and tipis and do not realise that most of the people around them in Cherokee are Indians (Blankenship, 1995).

Ironically, while the Museum attempts to educate visitors about Cherokee history and culture by providing an authentic and factual account of their life and customs, outside the Museum the town is full of every conceivable stereotype of American Indians representing tribal groups from all across the North American continent. Hotels, restaurants, shops and carparks bristle with model totem poles and tipis – in the windows, outside the doors, on the roofs. The shops are full of tomahawks, war-bonnets, fringed vests, and moccasins; Cherokees in full Plains Indian costume, complete with war bonnets, stand outside Plains Indian tipis waiting to receive tips in return for posing for the cameras of undiscerning tourists who probably know little of the true nature of the Cherokee, past or present. The traditional costume of the Cherokee is not as dramatic and colourful as that of the Plains Indian, and does not attract the tourists as much. Here, harsh commercial reality has forced the Cherokee themselves to re-create an image of 'Indianness' which conforms to many people's notions of the American Indian, but one which bears more relationship to Hollywood than it does to the Cherokee of North Carolina. The Museum of the Cherokee Indian faces a difficult task in trying to counteract the kitsch and inaccurate imagery that fills the streets of Cherokee and the media.

Ken Blankenship and two other Native American curators, Duane King, the Museum's first director, and Jim Volkert, a curator at the Burke Museum in Washington, have planned an exhibition concept which, at the time of writing, is still in draft form. The theme for the exhibit will be 'a step back in time' and will begin with the present and take visitors back to the pre-contact period through a series of life-sized dioramas. The exhibit concept (Blankenship, Volkert and King, 1993) suggests beginning with a short video presentation describing Cherokee beliefs; then a video sequence showing a Cherokee woman inviting visitors into her home. This is a 1990s HUD (Housing and Urban Development) home with TV and other electrical appliances, and a view of a car in the carport outside.

The next exhibit area will show the interior and furnishings of a 1945 log cabin to demonstrate the developments in housing and living standards over the past 50 years. Information pertaining to the transition period will provide data concerning population growth, political developments, economics of the region and so forth. The removal period, the 1830s, will be dealt with using a diorama showing a Council meeting, the exterior of a Cherokee cabin, part of a stockade where the Cherokee were held prior to removal, a campsite on the 'Trail of Tears', and a cave that was used by some of those who resisted relocation. The exhibition will conclude with an outdoor exhibit of a pre-contact settlement. With this reversal of the usual time-sequence, it is hoped to counteract the impression of Indian cultures frozen in a time past.

Until recently, the story of the Cherokee Nation and the 'Trail of Tears' was told in these two museums but received little prominence elsewhere. Uncomfortable though it may be to remember such events, they should not be forgotten. Legislation, in the form of the National Trails System Act of 1968, amended in 1994, charged the National Park Service with responsibility 'to preserve and interpret the cultural heritage of Native American tribes or groups'. The NPS now proposes the development of interpretive activities and historic sites at locations along the 'Trail of Tears' National Historic Trail, the route of that terrible journey from Cherokee to Oklahoma, to give this tragic story the attention it deserves in the interpretation of America's history. In 1995, the National Park Service allocated $1.2 million to the Museum of the Cherokee Indian and the Cherokee Heritage Center for the planning, design and production of exhibitions related to the 'Trail of Tears' (NPS, 1995). The two museums will be important sites marking the start and end of the 'Trail of Tears' and providing a historic overview of events from the Cherokee perspective. This will doubtless give considerable additional publicity to the Museums and lead to an increase in visitors. These operations show all the signs of continued growth and expansion.

Despite there being a number of possible sources of funding for tribal museums and cultural centres, financial assistance is not easy to obtain. Many tribal communities wishing to establish museums and cultural centres struggle for years to raise the capital costs of building and equipping a centre, then continue to struggle to meet the overhead costs. Individual tribal groups or bands have been very determined and resourceful in raising the additional funds required through sponsorship, private donations and commercial activities.

Further to the north, in British Columbia, Canada, 'Ksan Historic Indian Village Museum is the reconstruction of a Gitksan Indian village. It was established by the Gitksan Indians who live in an inland location beside the Skeena River. The village consists of six houses built in the style of the traditional communal houses. Three of these are display buildings, one is a shop, another a carving school, and the sixth houses the NorthWestern National Exhibition Center and Museum. In a clearing just outside the town of Hazelton and on the edge of the Gitanmaax Indian Reserve, it sits beside the waters of the Skeena and Bulkley Rivers, on the site of the old Gitanmaax village, facing the magnificent Rocher Deboule mountain range. In this setting the Gitksan Indian people interpret their history and their arts to visitors as well as providing a training centre and sales outlet for artists.

Visitors are guided through the first three buildings starting with 'The Frog House of the Distant Past' which presents the life of the Gitksan in pre-European times using artefacts and life-sized models. The interior has been arranged to some extent as the interior of a house would have been. Around the central fireplace are cooking pots and utensils including an enormous wooden feast bowl carved with the frog design. The sleeping platforms around the walls are laid out with various items of equipment used in hunting, fishing, gathering, and domestic chores. Life-sized models show figures in various scenes: a man gambling, a woman sewing a moosehide robe; a chief occupying the seat reserved exclusively for him; and a shaman or *halyte* with a variety of curing aids.

The next building, 'The Wolf House of Feasts', shows aspects of life after the arrival of European traders. The interior has been arranged to convey the formalities of a potlatch, with a chief's seat, coppers, a 'talking stick' or speaker's staff, and the figure of Wegyet, a mannequin used in the 'Ksan dancers' performances. Trade goods such as muskets, blankets, iron pots, and knives are laid out as part of the goods to be distributed at the potlatch. The house is also used as the venue for the weekly performances of Gitksan Ceremonial Dancing which take place during the summer. The third building is 'The Fireweed House of Masks and Robes', the former Skeena Treasure House, which houses a collection of Gitksan artifacts.

The House of Wood Carving/Carving House of all Times is the training centre for young carvers, who are registered for courses with the Kitanmax School of Northwest Coast Indian Art to receive instruction in Gitksan arts and crafts using traditional forms of designs in new and innovative ways. 'The Today House of the Arts' provides a sales point for hundreds of items made by Gitksan artists incorporating old and new techniques including carved masks, head pieces, bowls, ladles, plaques and totem poles; gold, silver and copper jewellery, usually engraved with traditional designs; silkscreened fabrics; and appliquéd button blankets. Beside the river are three smaller structures: a smoke house, used to smoke meat, fish and berries; a food store; and a burial house reflecting the modern practice of burial replacing the traditional cremation practices.

The sixth building is the NorthWestern National Exhibition Centre and Museum which houses a small permanent gallery containing masks, button blankets and other artefacts, and a temporary gallery in which touring exhibitions are displayed. During 1993 the varied programme included *Eulachon: A Fish To Cure Humanity*, organised by the University of British Columbia Museum of Anthropology, which described the economic and cultural importance of this tiny fish to the coastal peoples; *Arlon Gislason – Jazz Pictures*, 'an exhibition of photographic improvisations'; and *The Wonder of Wood*, on loan from the Manitoba Museum of Man and Nature. Although there is no education officer, visiting school groups can obtain educational leaflets on topics such as the potlatch, Gitksan Indians, plank houses, totem poles, Indian fishing techniques, and rattles.

'Ksan Historic Indian Village opened in 1970 replacing the small Skeena House of Treasures which had been operating as a museum for the previous ten years, part of the efforts of the Gitksan people to see their cultural and artistic traditions revived. As in other parts of the North American continent, the settlement

Figure 6.6 'Ksan Historic Indian Village Museum is the reconstruction of a Gitksan Indian village. 'Ksan, near Hazelton, British Columbia, Canada

Source: Photo by M. Simpson, 1993

151

of the Europeans in the area during the nineteenth century had brought about many changes which almost destroyed the Indians' traditional culture.

The effects of the fur trade and the establishment of the logging industry and the fish canning factories vastly changed the social and economic life of the Indian people throughout British Columbia. Missionaries, in their efforts to convert the Indians to Christianity, and government officials, keen to see an end to the economic and cultural independence of the Indians, attempted to put an end to the traditional customs and beliefs: totem poles were cut down and ceremonial regalia burned or confiscated. The people lost their lands and were confined to reservations, becoming dependent upon European goods and foods. In 1894, the Canadian government outlawed the potlatch, the ceremony which was at the heart of the structure and operation of the Indians' culture: ceremonies could only be carried out occasionally and in great secrecy. All of these factors combined to result in the near-destruction of both the economy and the culture, including the arts, for they resulted from and were dependent upon the continuation of the economic structure and cultural traditions that the Indians had known before the arrival of the Europeans.

Following the banning of the potlatch, many fine examples of artefacts were sold to museums and private collectors. However, many did remain and gradually some of the Gitksan people began to consider the idea of establishing a museum in order to protect those they had retained. Initial planning began in 1950 but, while much research and planning was carried out, there was little success with obtaining financial support for the project. However, the Provincial Government announced that funds would be made available for suitable projects as part of the Centennial celebration in 1958. The Skeena Treasure House Association was formed to organise the project and government approval and funding for the scheme were obtained. The museum was finally completed in 1960 and opened with a fine collection of artefacts on display.

In 1951, the legal ban on potlatches was rescinded and many hoped that the ceremonies of the nineteenth century would be practised once again but, after more than 60 years, few people with the necessary knowledge were alive. The same problem existed regarding the old skills of carving, now in demand once again, this time from non-Indians. The Treasure House Association realised that there was a need for an arts training and development programme so that the traditional arts could be taught and presented. So the idea was formed for 'Ksan Historic Indian Village which would be an education centre and a performance and exhibition centre for the revival of the arts.

After years of planning there had been no success in obtaining finance for the project, then a large sawmill, a major employer in the area, closed down leaving many unemployed and the economy of the area depressed. The new Treasure House Association applied to the Federal Government for grants under the Agricultural and Rural Development Act. The application was accepted and the Treasure House Association was allocated two-thirds of the funding from the Federal and Provincial Governments. The remaining $33,333 was raised by the Association from its own resources, from cash grants and donations.

Over the next two years the buildings were constructed and 'Ksan Historic Indian Village was opened on 12 August 1970 ('Ksan Association, nd).

When the original museum building was being constructed, Alfred Douse, one of those most actively involved in the project, was asked to think of a name for it. His reply, 'It shall not be called a museum, for we are not a dead people; let it be called the Skeena Treasure House', sums up the philosophy which lies behind the establishment and running of the 'Ksan Historic Indian Village. It is a centre for the living arts, a centre in which history lives. The collections are used as an educational resource by Indians and non-Indians, and play an active role in the revival and development of the economic, cultural and artistic life of the Gitksan people.

It is clear from this example that one of the main functions of the museum for the Gitksan is the re-establishment or preservation of the cultural identity of the Gitksan people and the teaching of traditional skills, values and knowledge to the younger generation. The practice and production of the arts, as an important element of cultural expression, is a central activity in the attainment of those objectives. For North American Indian groups, the proposal to establish a museum can also be an essential element of the fight for the return of cultural property, sometimes being a prerequisite of a successful repatriation claim. Government agencies and mainstream museums which have negotiated loans or repatriation agreements for religious artefacts have sometimes laid down the condition that tribal groups must be able to provide suitable storage and display facilities which ensure that the objects are secure and correctly conserved. In some cases this has been a further motivating factor for the establishment of a museum by those tribes wishing to once again hold and use the sacred objects of their ancestors. Such was the case with the establishment of two other tribal museums in British Columbia.

U'mista Cultural Centre in Alert Bay on Cormorant Island, and the Kwagiulth Museum in Cape Mudge, on Quadra Island, were both established as part of the conditions laid down for the return of the Cranmer Potlatch Collection. This important collection of artefacts had been confiscated in 1922, and had since then been in the collections of the Canadian Museum of Civilisation in Hull, the Royal Ontario Museum in Toronto, and the Museum of the American Indian/Heye Foundation in New York City. Both tribal museums initially received federal funding including grants from the Federal Government's Museum Assistance Programmes and the Department of Indian Affairs, and also received financial assistance from the British Columbia First Citizens Fund. These grants enabled the Potlatch Collection to be returned and preserved in museum conditions within the communities from which they originated.

The potlatch, an elaborate status ceremony involving the gifting of large quantities of goods, was an important socio-economic practice amongst the tribes of the Northwest Coast. It was banned in 1884 when the Canadian Government passed the Potlatch Law, an amendment to the Indian Act (1880). In December 1921, Dan Cranmer of the Nimkish band of the Kwakwaka'wakw (formerly referred to as Kwagiulth or Kwakiutl) gave a huge potlatch on Village Island

153

near Alert Bay. He gave away $10,000 worth of goods including canoes, gas boats, pool tables, bedsteads, bureaux, oak trunks, gas lights, gramophones, violins, guitars, washtubs, sewing machines, clothing, blankets, sacks of flour, and cash (Shein, 1987: 79; Cole and Chailkin, 1990).

The Indian Agent, William Halliday, received information about the potlatch and some of the participants were arrested. Over the next few months, over 50 men and women were charged but were offered the opportunity to avoid imprisonment if they signed an agreement never again to participate in a potlatch, to try to dissuade others from doing so, and to assist the authorities in ensuring that the Potlatch Law was not violated. The agreement also included a paragraph stating that:

> in token of our good faith in this our agreement we voluntarily surrender to the Department of Indian Affairs through its representative the Indian Agent all our potlatch paraphernalia to wit:- coppers, dancing masks and costumes, head dresses and other articles used solely for potlatch purposes.
>
> (Sewid-Smith, 1979: 35)

Many of those involved assented and signed the agreement in order to avoid imprisonment and further prosecutions. Of those charged, twenty-two were imprisoned for two months, four second offenders were given prison sentences of six months but were paroled, twenty-three received suspended sentences, and the remainder were acquitted or had their cases dismissed (Halliday in Sewid-Smith, 1979: 38–9, 44; Cole and Chaikin, 1990: 120–3). Several hundred ceremonial items were surrendered to Halliday including coppers, masks, rattles, whistles, and other dance paraphernalia.

The Department of Indian Affairs paid token compensation of $1,495 for the potlatch collection, excluding the coppers, while estimates place the actual value at many thousands of dollars and Halliday described it as 'a very valuable and very rare collection . . . should command good prices for museum purposes' (Halliday in Sewid-Smith, 1979: 39). The coppers alone were estimated by their owners to be worth over $35,000 (U'mista, nd) with owners placing individual values upon them of between $245 and $10,500 (Sewid-Smith, 1979: 39). Halliday believed that they 'in some instances have a large fictitious value' (U'mista, nd: 36), and, in a letter to Duncan C. Scott, Deputy Superintendent Indian Affairs, Halliday noted that 'No museum collector would ever pay anything like what the Indians consider the face value of these coppers'. He did acknowledge, however, that 'financial loss must inevitably result to the owner of these coppers' (ibid.: 39).

Halliday estimated that there was at least 300 cubic feet of potlatch material which he was instructed by the Department of Indian Affairs to ship to the Victoria Memorial Museum in Ottawa (later the National Museum of Man and now the Canadian Museum of Civilisation). He stored the ceremonial masks, rattles, whistles, and coppers, first in his shed and then in the parish hall, prior to its shipment to Ottawa. During this time he sold 33 items to George Heye for the Museum of the American Indian/Heye Foundation in New York City for a sum of $291.00. Halliday was reprimanded for conducting this transaction without authorisation, so allowing the items to be taken to the US rather than remaining in a Canadian museum (Sewid-Smith, 1979: 74–5). The remainder of the collection was shipped to Ottawa in seventeen crates and distributed between the Victoria Memorial Museum and the Royal Ontario Museum (ROM) in Toronto. A small number of objects also passed to the personal collection of the Superintendent General of Indian Affairs, Duncan Campbell Scott (Carpenter, 1981; U'mista, nd; Webster, 1988: 43).

Efforts to obtain the return of the potlatch collection began almost immediately after their confiscation and continued for more than twenty-five years. In the 1970s, the Kwakwaka'wakw renewed their efforts to secure return of the collection and, in 1974, they finally succeeded in securing agreement from the board of trustees of the National Museums of Canada for the return of the collection held in the National Museum of Man (NMM). The Museum insisted upon the collection being held in trust by tribal societies on behalf of the families who had surrendered the items in 1922. They also specified that the items could not be sold and were to be accommodated in conditions which met museum standards. Initially, it was proposed that one museum would be established to house the collection but this was not acceptable to the bands which were located in a number of villages along the coast of Vancouver Island and on small islands in the Queen Charlotte and Georgia Straits. Instead, it was decided to build two museums: one at Alert Bay on Cormorant Island, from where Dan Cranmer of the Nimpkish band came; and the other at Cape Mudge on Quadra Island, where Billy Assu, who assisted with the potlatch, was Chief of the Lekwiltok. The return of the collection from the National Museum of Man progressed smoothly and the Kwagiulth Museum at Cape Mudge opened in 1979 and U'mista Cultural Centre in 1980. However, negotiations with the Royal Ontario Museum were more difficult and it was not until 1987 that the Kwakwaka'wakw people succeeded in obtaining the repatriation of the ROM potlatch collection.

In the past, the word *u'mista* was used to describe the return of people captured by raiding parties (Shein, 1987: 77), and its use today as the name of the museum established at Alert Bay refers to the return of the potlatch collection which now forms the central focus of the exhibitions at U'mista Cultural Centre. The modern museum building of U'mista has been built adjoining the community's Big House, the traditional cedar plank building used for ceremonies and other community events. Inside, the potlatch collection has been arranged on the wooden platforms around the outer walls, while the new building houses another display gallery, the shop, curatorial offices and stores.

Central to the creation and function of the museum is the history of the prohibition of the potlatch; the confiscation and return, many years later, of the Cranmer potlatch collection; and the continuing potlatch tradition in modern form. In the display of the potlatch collection, references to the arrests and the confiscation of the regalia feature prominently, telling a story of tribal loss and of repatriation. The views and feelings of the individuals involved are illuminated through letters, reports, petitions, newspaper articles and other documentation, which vividly carry their message to us across the intervening years. Halliday's zealous actions in enforcing the Potlatch Law are explained by his view of the potlatch as 'the great stumbling block in the way of progress'. His view of the pervasive and damaging nature of the potlatch is clearly articulated in his words of 31 May 1913, when he stated that

> The potlatch has great hold over the whole people and in this respect the Kwawkewlths rank first. Until the potlatch is eliminated, there is not much chance of any great progress, as the potlatch takes so much of their time and so many hours are spent at it in laziness and idling that it does not produce energy and ability.
>
> (cited on U'mista label text)

In addition to this storyline, there is a second theme evident in the display, one which is less obvious to those unfamiliar with the potlatch, for the artefacts themselves are not individually labelled or identified. Visitors are encouraged to enter the Big House from the right as would dancers in a potlatch, and the objects are arranged in an anti-clockwise direction in the order in which they would appear in a traditional potlatch ceremony. They are positioned on wooden platforms around the walls, where the audience would sit when attending a potlatch, with no glass but sometimes lengthy texts documenting their history as a collection once lost, now returned to the community. The message of the display is overtly political, attesting to past wrongs and injustices.

Visitors to U'mista may well find themselves sharing the Big House with children from the tribal school practising traditional Kwakwaka'wakw dances and songs; for, as well as housing the potlatch collection, the Big House functions as a venue for practice sessions by children from the tribal school, and for performances by them and other artists. It also provides a venue for potlatches and other ceremonies, for potlatches are once again being held as they were in the past. In 1951 the Canadian Government revised the Indian Act and section 149 was omitted; since then, potlatches have once again been held without fear of persecution and prosecution.

U'mista has developed into a strongly community-based museum which seeks to preserve and exhibit artefacts of value to the Kwakwala-speaking people and to recover artefacts and records held in the collections of other institutions or by individuals. It promotes cultural and artistic activities such as carving, dancing, and ceremonials, and collects, records and teaches the history and language of the Kwakwaka'wakw. Its staff also undertake activities designed to disseminate information to a wider population in Canada and overseas. The story of the prohibition of the potlatch and the subsequent confiscation of the potlatch collection has been documented in an award-winning film: *Potlatch: A Strict Law Bids Us Dance* (1975), while the effects of the prohibition upon the Kwakwaka'wakw people, and their fight to bring the potlatch collection home is told in *Box of Treasures* (1983). These films, and the efforts of Gloria Cranmer Webster, Dan Cranmer's daughter and the former curator of U'mista, have been indispensable in bringing the issues and the work of U'mista Cultural Centre to the attention of museum curators, anthropologists and others, at an international level.

In almost total contrast to U'mista, the Kwagiulth Museum at Cape Mudge looks little further than the Kwakwaka'wakw community and has a more localised profile. The Kwagiulth Museum opened with a traditional cedar bark ceremony on Friday 29 June 1979, in an event which was attended by hundreds of people (Fuoco, 1979). A potlatch had been held the previous day to dedicate a new 29-foot totem pole which now stands in front of the museum. It was erected in memory of Chief Billy Assu, one of those charged following the 1921 Cranmer potlatch. Like U'mista, the Nuyumbalees Society, which operates the Museum, has, however, taken steps to inform the public of the circumstances surrounding the loss and return of the potlatch collection, though this is less evident in the displays.

In 1979, the Nuyumbalees Society published a book documenting the prosecutions which was edited by Daisy Sewid-Smith, whose grandmother, Agnes Alfred, was one of those arrested for participation in the Village Island potlatch. It includes correspondence sent and received by Halliday, dealing with these and other cases and with the disposal of the potlatch collection. Also included are the accounts of several of those brought to trial. Echoing the progress of a court case, the evidence is presented in sections headed 'The Charge', 'The Prosecution', 'The Defense', 'The Summation' and in the final sentence the reader is asked 'to decide after reading the facts, was it Prosecution or was it Persecution?' (Sewid-Smith, 1979: 87).

Inside the museum, the potlatch items are displayed in showcases in a bright room, modern in decoration; but here they are arranged in groups according to their ownership. An introductory text informs visitors that:

> all the masks and regalia, the histories of their acquisition and the songs and dances associated with them are owned as property by individual families. Only a limited number of families amongst the Kwakwaka'wakw are acknowledged as having the hereditary right to this wealth conveyed to them by illustrious ancestors. Family right to the possession of these treasures is asserted at the potlatch gathering.

Here the contextualisation of the artefacts in their social and functional roles is the main theme of the accompanying labels and text. Ownership is clearly stated with a brief reference to the artefact's function and associated ceremony or dance. For example a collection of four objects was labelled 'Owned by Jimmy Bell. 1. Rattle used in Kwekwe dance; 2. Face mask used in Hamatsa ceremony; 3. Hamatsa head ring; 4. Grizzly bear Mask.' The story of the loss and return of the regalia is not prominent, rather it is the family ownership rights which are most clearly asserted.

Another museum established in the Northwest Coast region illustrates the results of collaboration between a tribal group and a university over the discovery of tribal heritage material. An important archaeological site was discovered by the Ozette Archaeological Project on land belonging to the

Makah Indian Tribe. In 1970, tidal erosion at a coastal site at Ozette exposed 500-year-old homes which had been preserved in a mudslide. The Makah people were concerned about allowing the continuation of work that would result in further disturbance of the site, yet they were also interested to find out more about their history. The Makah Tribal Council and staff of Washington State University forged an agreement enabling the work to proceed in a fashion that would be sensitive to tribal beliefs, would ensure tribal involvement in the decision-making process and guarantee that the material excavated would remain in the possession of the tribe. In order to ensure this, the tribe and the University worked in partnership to seek funding for the establishment of a tribal museum, successfully receiving grants from the National Endowment for the Arts, The National Endowment for the Humanities, the Environmental Protection Agency, and the Crown Zellarbach Foundation. The Makah Cultural and Research Center opened on 2 June 1979 (NARF, 1979: 21).

One of the newest tribal museums is the Ak-Chin Him Dak Indian Community Ecomuseum in Arizona which originated in a manner not dissimilar to the situation of the Makah Museum. The Ak-Chin museum project arose almost by accident resulting from the finds made during archaeological work undertaken as a result of the excavation of an irrigation system. The Ak-Chin Indian community lives in the hot, arid Sonora Desert of Arizona and relies upon water to sustain their livelihood. About 500 descendants of the Tohono O'odham and Akimel O'odham, or Papago and Pima Indians, live on the 21,840 acre reservation. Leases of reservation lands to non-Indian farmers and employment as farm labourers brought little income to the community and in 1962 the Ak-Chin Community Farms Enterprise was established. By 1964 they were farming 4,900 acres with profits in excess of $21,000 and, by the mid-1970s, the figure passed $1,000,000 (Ak-Chin, 1987; Fuller, 1992: 335).

During the 1970s, there was a tremendous growth in the populations of Phoenix and Tucson with resultant demands for green lawns and golf courses, and for swimming pools and spas. Water consumption rocketed, the water table lowered, and this began to affect the water in the remaining wells on the Ak-Chin reservation. According to the terms of the 1908 Supreme Court Winters doctrine, the federal government must supply enough water for Indians to irrigate their land; however, the government had failed to protect the water resources of the Ak-Chin community and, after ten years of protracted negotiations, the Ak-Chin Council and government agencies agreed a water settlement which would provide the reservation with a permanent water supply from the Central Arizona Project (CAP), a 3.5 billion dollar network of canals which pumps water from the Colorado River to Tucson in southern Arizona. A spur was built to bring water to the reservation and this enabled the Ak-Chin to triple the acreage that they farmed, growing crops such as cotton, small grains, and alfalfa. The increased production and employment opportunities resulted in a drop in unemployment from 38 per cent to 4 per cent and turned Ak-Chin into a self-sufficient farming community (Carrier, 1991: 28).

When the water settlement was awarded to them, the Ak-Chin had to build irrigation canals to carry water to the fields, and level, ditch and clear 16,000 acres of farmable land. Archaeological work, which had been started in the mid-1970s, had to be completed prior to the installation of the irrigation system. Archaeologists discovered more than 300 pit houses and removed twenty-one skeletons and 700 boxes of material: pottery, stone tools and shell jewellery. Archaeological research provided evidence of 15,000 years of continuous occupation, refuting previous theories concerning Ak-Chin history. The federal government took control of the material, including twenty-three human remains, and placed it in storage. The tribe requested the return of the material but, although the skeletal material was returned to them for reburial, the artefacts would only be return if the tribe could provide suitable storage facilities and trained staff to care for them.

The need for a depository for the archaeological material combined with tribal concerns about the erosion of traditional cultural practices and knowledge, and a desire to preserve and communicate to younger tribal members aspects of Ak-Chin heritage which no longer featured in daily life. The agricultural success of the community, which ensured its future prosperity and improved social conditions, changed the economic and educational structure of the community and jeopardised the survival of cultural traditions (Fuller, 1992: 336–7). The development of the museum was perceived as a means of exploring the history of the Ak-Chin and ensuring that knowledge of traditional culture was not lost, while ensuring that the Ak-Chin retained control over the archaeological material of their ancestors. A grant providing financial support for the planning of the museum was received from the Administration for Native Americans (Department of Health and Human Services) and further funds were received from the Bureau of Reclamation under the Reclamation Small Loans Act for archaeological data recovery and public education (Parker, 1990: 134).

In October 1987, tribal representatives approached Nancy Fuller, who was the Research Program Manager in the Office of Museum Programs at the Smithsonian Institution, Washington, DC. Fuller was responsible for providing advisory services to community museums, and together, Fuller and tribal representatives established a programme of planning and research in order to identify the nature of the museum, its functions and requirements (Fuller, 1991a; 1992). They travelled across North America and to Mexico making links with people in community museums, discussing their experiences and formulating plans for their own. It was ultimately decided to adopt the concept of the ecomuseum, which expands the ideas and functions of the museum to sites and to social relationships within the community. As stated in the Ak-Chin Ecomuseum leaflet:

> The museum is not confined to the building but reacts and interacts with all functions and activities of the land and its peoples and encourages their participation. The goal of the Ak-Chin Ecomuseum is to promote the sharing of the past, the present and the future to increase the awareness and perceptions of all members of the community to their evolving environment.

The existing tribal records were surveyed and a tribal records management programme was established to ensure the preservation of appropriate documents from various departments of the reservation: fire, police, health, etc. Temporary exhibitions were presented in a room in the community centre. Six tribal members undertook training at Central Arizona College to enable them to operate the museum. A tailor-made, two-year Associate of Arts degree included English, history, science, and museum and archives training, and also involved work experience in existing museums. As the college was 60 miles away, they arranged for a tutor to go to the reservation for some classes, such as English and maths; and other members of the community were able to attend too, so satisfying some of the educational requirements of the reservation community. Botany class involved studying desert plants of Arizona and students undertook field trips to different areas to see plants in their natural habitats. The college class was invited to the reservation for a teaching session in the two rooms being used for the museum planning project, and the Ak-Chin students prepared a small exhibit *What the desert has given us*. They took the other students round the reservation showing them plants and explained how the Ak-Chin people used them traditionally for making baskets, food and medicines. In this way they brought a Native American perspective into the botany class (Fuller, 1991b).

In June 1991, Ak-Chin community opened a museum building which, as a purpose-built structure, incorporated all the facilities that were required for the successful acquisition, processing, display and storage of artefacts and archives, and also provided space for educational and community activities. Members of the community have been involved in collecting photographs, documents, artefacts, and other materials that reflected the recent history of the Ak-Chin people. Archaeological material was documented, classified and stored. Learning oral history recording techniques and photographic methods has enabled interested individuals to become involved in documentation. Classes in basketmaking enable those with the knowledge of plant collecting and preparation to teach others to take natural plant materials and turn them into baskets with beautiful patterns. Language classes ensure that the native language of the Ak-Chin will not die out. Around the building a garden of native plants is being established which will include plants used for clothing, food and medicinal purposes; and a ramada and 'sandwich' house made from cactus ribs and mesquite posts showing the construction techniques used in the nineteenth century (Peters, 1993).

Ak-Chin is first and foremost a facility which provides preservation facilities for material culture and traditions and is designed to pass on traditional skills and knowledge to future generations of the tribe. It is an active place providing educational facilities within the tribal group and a means of communicating the role of agriculture in the economic and cultural development of the Ak-Chin people. The museum that has been developed is typical of the more recent concerns within tribal museum development to provide for the cultural needs of the tribal community rather than providing a tourist facility. However, like U'mista and 'Ksan, although it is essentially oriented towards the needs of the tribal community and driven by a desire to ensure the continuity of cultural traditions, the Ak-Chin will endeavour to develop the tourism potential and so generate additional income, and will also seek to inform non-Indian people about their history and culture.

The Ned Hatathli Cultural Center Museum on the Navajo reservation shares this community focus, but provides almost no tourist function and is quite different from those so far discussed. It combines traditional museological inter-pretation and display methods with labelless displays reliant upon visual interpretation and oral history traditions central to Navajo culture.

The Ned Hatathli Cultural Center Museum is a part of Navajo Community College in Tsaile, Arizona, the first tribal college in the United States, opened in 1969 at Many Farms, 35 miles from Tsaile in a Bureau of Indian Affairs boarding school. Initially receiving money from the Federal Office of Econom-ic Opportunity, the Navajo Tribe, and private sources, the founders of the college successfully sought congressional support for federal funding. This resulted in the Navajo Community College Act of 1971, and the Tribally Con-trolled Community College Assistance Act of 1978 which authorised funding for other tribal colleges (Ambler, 1991: 22). Prior to this, Native American youngsters seeking further education had to leave the reservation in order to attend college. Due to strong family and cultural ties, few would do this, and amongst those who did enrol there was a high drop-out rate. The establishment of tribal colleges enabled Indian tribes to direct the education of their young people, providing programmes of study that integrated the courses to be found in other college curricula with courses which reflected tribal culture and values. At Navajo Community College, Navajo leaders and educators have established a syllabus combining regular courses with courses in Navajo language, history, culture, arts and crafts, religious teachings, and ceremonials, endorsed by the Navajo Medicine Man Association. They also wanted to establish a museum where cultural and religious artefacts would be housed and used for educational purposes within the college.

Navajo Community College's Tsaile campus was opened in 1974 and, two years later, work was completed on the Ned Hatathli Cultural Center, named after Dr Ned A. Hatathli, a Navajo educator who worked toward the establishment of the college and was the second president before dying in office in 1972. The museum, which is part of the College's Centre for Dineh Studies, is housed within the Cultural Center along with administrative offices and classrooms. The Cultural Center combines traditional architecture with the highly modern. It is a five-storied, eight-sided, smoked glass building which echoes the shape of a Navajo hogan, the traditional form of housing and also the place in which traditional ceremonies were performed. A hogan on the campus maintains that age-old practice, providing a venue for lectures, conferences, and graduation ceremonies, and students can also sponsor traditional ceremonies within it.

The museum operates on a low budget, receiving $38,000 from the college, an NEH grant for installation of the exhibits, plus some additional grants from corporations and foundations. Maintenance, lighting and equipment are part of the main college overheads. There are two full-time staff, supplemented by the efforts of work studies students, debt liquidation students who owe money to

161

the college, and, in summer, participants of the tribal work programme. This is a programme for students that provides state, federal and tribal funds to different chapters on the reservations, enabling students to undertake employment in public places such as hospitals, schools, chapter houses, and the museum. When planning exhibitions, the curator, Harry Walters, researches and writes the text, designs the layout and presentation, and produces scale models of both floors, showing the planned exhibitions. College students assist with the installation and Navajo carpenters, who are employed locally on contract work for nine to ten months of the year, are hired on a temporary basis to build display cases and partition panels.

The collections are small, mostly contemporary, but including some weaving and jewellery from the late nineteenth century, with some additional exhibits borrowed from other museums. The museum has no funding for acquisitions, but does have a collections policy which incorporates the acceptance of donations of any Native American material, although most is Navajo. There are two main galleries, plus a temporary exhibitions gallery. The two main galleries are octagonal in shape with central octagonal exhibition areas which face an octagonal seating area in the very centre of the room.

The lower gallery is devoted to Navajo history which provides both the Navajo and non-Navajo interpretations of the origins of the Navajo people. The central, octagonal exhibit area is titled *Navajo Oral History*. On either side of the entrance to this section are murals: one showing a young Navajo woman, the other an elderly Navajo man. Set into the inner faces of the four display units are small dioramas depicting scenes from the Navajo Creation story. These are displayed without labels reflecting the Navajo tradition of oral history and the primary function of the museum: the education of young Navajo people in the history and culture of their people. For these students written words are unnecessary, for the oral tradition is a part of their past and a part of their present education, the Creation story a familiar and relevant part of their lives.

In the outer area, a series of five posters by Rudi Begay chart the history of the Navajo people in the Southwest from AD1400 to the present. The periods between 1600 and 1940 are referred to as times of 'expansion and change'. Included is the 'Long Walk' of 1864 when several thousand Navajos were forced by the US army, led by Colonel Christopher 'Kit' Carson, to walk over 300 miles to Fort Sumner (Bosque Redondo) on the Rio Pecos in New Mexico, where they remained in appalling conditions for four years. The final period from 1940 is headed 'expansion and progress' marking the re-strengthening of Navajo culture over recent decades. There is a panel displaying twenty-one black and white photographs of Navajo leaders, and four further photographs of Navajo people taken during the first decades of the century. The remaining area of the gallery contains a number of reproductions of sand-paintings and a petroglyph depiction of a male *yei* from the Coyote Way ceremony. Throughout the outer gallery area, labels are used to identify artefacts, photographs and graphics, a practice continued in the upper gallery. Here, the exhibits relate to the archaeology of the Southwest and the ancient Hohokam, Mogollon and Anasazi peoples who inhabited the region until around AD1400. The exhibits consist of a number of pieces of pottery, mainly Anasazi, an artistic tradition which continues to this day amongst the Pueblo Indians, the present-day descendants of the Anasazi.

The museum is a blend of Navajo and non-Navajo historical interpretation and also a blend of Navajo and non-Navajo communication methods. It serves a predominantly Navajo audience (80–90 per cent), but is also accessible to the general public. According to Walters the exhibitions and museum operations cater for the needs of the Navajo audience although non-Navajo visitors are welcome; but without any previous knowledge of the Navajo concepts of Creation, a non-Navajo would gain little understanding from the dioramas. Their meaning is imbedded in culturally coded imagery inaccessible, on all but the most superficial level, to the uninformed outsider.

The museum is used by staff and students of the college as part of classes in Navajo history and culture, religious education, and visual and performing arts. It provides a venue for singing and dancing classes and for demonstrations and lessons in basketry, pottery, moccasin-making, and weaving. The college also proposes to establish a Medicine Man Training Program with the assistance of the tribe's Economic Development Program. In former times medicine men had apprentices, usually a relative – son, son-in-law, nephew – who undertook the training process which started when they were still children and lasted for many years. Nowadays, young men have other regular employment commitments and find it difficult to devote the time required to the demands of apprenticeship. The college programme would be open to those who had already been apprenticed for some time and would offer a scholarship or stipend to cover basic living expenses.

The museum has one of the largest collections of Navajo medicine bundles, the results of a successful campaign to repatriate Navajo religious paraphernalia. It is not the policy of the museum to acquire medicine bundles in order to simply build up the collection, but to enable the bundles to be used in Navajo ceremonies, for they are still used as a means of healthcare today. To this end, the museum operates a lending system enabling medicine men to borrow medicine bundles for the duration of ceremonies or the season and then return them to the museum. In Navajo tradition they are powerful, religious objects which, in the hands of qualified men and women, are effective instruments for healing. However, expectant mothers are not allowed to handle or view medicine bundles in case it causes harm to the unborn babies. Furthermore, abuse of the medicine bundles can have serious repercussions for the Navajo nation. The medicine bundles are, therefore, not exhibited; nor are they handled by students, only by Walters and elders of the Center for Dineh Studies (Walters, 1991). The medicine bundles, Walters explained, are living things which should not be kept locked up as they need to breathe. In early spring when the vegetation starts growing, they are opened, then a blessing is performed in the autumn at the harvest. When they are used in ceremonies, the medicine bundles are restored and regenerated; their continued use is, therefore, a part of their necessary conservation as well as facilitating the continuation of Navajo traditional practices (ibid.).

163

Another interesting college museum is located in the grounds of Bacone College, in Muskogee, Oklahoma. Since its foundation, the College's mission has been to provide educational opportunities for Native American students (Bacone, nd.a). Originally founded as the Indian University in Tahlequah in 1880, it was the dream of a New Yorker, Almon C. Bacone, who became a teacher at the Cherokee male seminary in Tahlequah. With support from the American Baptist Home Mission Board, 160 acres of land donated by the Muskogee (Creek) Tribal Council, and a $10,000 donation from the Rockefeller family, the educational institution was re-located to its present site on the edge of Muskogee. Its name was changed to Bacone College in 1910 in honour of Almon Bacone and it continues to be supported by the American Baptist Churches, USA (Bacone, nd.b; McDermott, 1995). Since 1959 the college has been open to students from all races and religions; today the student population is multicultural in composition and includes a number of students from overseas, but Native American students originating from all over the Americas continue to form a large percentage.

The museum, known as Ataloa Art Lodge, is named after a former staff member, Mary Stone McLendon, who was a descendant of the last chief of the Chickasaw nation; her Indian name was Ataloa, or Little Song. From 1927 until 1935 she taught English and philosophy at Bacone College and collected Indian art and artefacts to be used as a teaching collection with students (Bacone, nd.a). Through the effects of the acculturation process, many traditional Native American craft skills had been lost and Mary McLendon was an active promoter of the traditional skills. During the 1930s, there was a revival of interest in Indian arts. The College offered art classes which included drawing and sculpture, as well as traditional Indian arts and crafts such as rug weaving, basket weaving, pottery, beadwork, and silversmithing, and even taught students how to chip flint and make arrow heads (McKinney, 1995). The students were encouraged to refer to the collection in order to learn traditional techniques and patterns.

Mary McLendon dreamed of establishing an Indian Museum; she worked hard to raise funds for the college and to establish a permanent facility for her growing collection. On 2 December 1932, a building was completed and dedicated as the Art Lodge to serve both as additional classroom space and as a storage and display facility for the collection. The building was constructed largely through the efforts of students; at that time, the college offered vocational training for Native American students designed to enable them to assimilate into modern American society. Much of the brick work and electrical work was completed under staff supervision by students in the vocational programme. The college had its own sawmill on campus and most of the furniture in the lodge was also built by the students. Mary Stone McLendon died in 1967, and in her memory the name of the Art Lodge was changed to Ataloa Lodge (Bacone, nd. a; McKinney, 1995).

Although Ataloa Lodge opened as a museum in 1967, initially it was only open at special request and when someone was available to unlock it and to show visitors around. Then, in 1989, Tom McKinney was employed in the role of

Figure 6.7 Ataloa Art Lodge, Bacone College Campus, Muskogee, Oklahoma

Source: Photo by M. Simpson, 1995

165

Museum Co-ordinator. Although only employed part-time, McKinney has been able to ensure that the museum is open full-time through the assistance of volunteers and students gaining work experience.

The lodge sits, surrounded by lawns, close to the Memorial Chapel on Bacone College campus. Inside the lodge, the upper floor accommodates office and storage space while the ground floor has a shop and three rooms of displays. The spacious main room, overlooked by a wooden gallery from the floor above, looks almost like a commodious hunting lodge, with a huge stone fireplace at one end, Navajo and Pueblo rugs hanging from the walls and the rafters, and two massive couches facing each other in the centre. Adding to the domestic feel of the room are table showcases with rugs draped over them to protect the light-sensitive items inside, and benches on either side enabling visitors to sit and study the fine beadwork and stitchery. At the other end of the room stands a vertical showcase with a collection of more than one hundred kachinas, most of them made in the last 40 years, but some over 100 years old. To one side is a case containing more than twenty pieces of black-on-black pottery by the San Ildefonso potter Maria Martinez, and by her husband and sister. Each piece is signed by the maker and, according to McKinney, this represents one of the largest individual collections of Martinez work anywhere. A couple of pieces were brought by Maria Martinez herself when she visited the College; the others were given as gifts by her children who were students of the college.

One of the most poignant items in the Ataloa Art Lodge collection is a tiny baby's bonnet made from buckskin heavily beaded with designs which include the American flag. The bonnet belonged to a six-month old baby girl, Zintkala Nuni, or Lost Bird, one of the few survivors of the massacre of 300 Minneconjou Sioux by the US 7th Cavalry at Wounded Knee on 29 December 1890. Four days after the massacre, a Dakota physician led a rescue party to look for survivors and discovered a handful of infants who had survived despite their mothers being killed (Flood, 1995). Lost Bird was adopted by Brigadier General Leonard Colby. According to her biographer, Renée Sansom Flood, she led an unhappy life, removed from her Sioux culture and raised in a non-Indian environment, subjected to abuse and racial prejudice; she died at the age of 29. In July of 1991, Lost Bird's coffin was exhumed from its burial place in California and her remains were returned to South Dakota and buried near the mass grave of those who died in the massacre of Wounded Knee (ibid.: 300–9).

Unlike many other Native American museums, Ataloa Art Lodge holds collections representing many Indian peoples from across the Americas. Now numbering in excess of 20,000 items, the collection is far more than the lodge can accommodate and larger premises, with improved fire and security systems, are required. The museum is completely funded through the college but they intend to establish a board of directors for the museum and seek financial assistance through grants and other sources. The budget covers the care and maintenance of the building, salaries and other overheads. There is no purchasing budget; indeed the museum has never purchased any artefacts, nor are any on loan; the entire collection has been donated, mainly through individual gifts by students and their families, by college trustees and others closely associated with Bacone College.

Over the years, the collection has continued to provide an important resource for the college's art and design students, a number of whom have established reputations, including Dick West, the Cheyenne painter. The arts programme is intended to contribute to the revival of many of the ancient crafts of the Native American people so that students can keep in touch with their traditional past as well as being prepared for, and moving on into, the future. The traditional skills have also enabled students to find summer employment working as costumed demonstrators in some of the open-air museums such as the ancient village at *Tsa-La-Gi*, in nearby Tahlequah.

Rug weaving, basket weaving, pottery, beadwork classes, and silversmithing are still taught, and also bronze-casting and woodcarving. Students visit the museum throughout the year to get ideas for art projects, such as paintings or beadwork, and the collection is also used in humanities classes studying the art, music and musical instruments of the past and trying to revive the same processes in the present. Other areas of the curriculum have also been designed to encourage Native American students to be proud of their heritage, with classes in traditional Indian dancing and singing, traditional languages, Indian religions and tribal government (McKinney, 1995). In addition to its educational role within the college, the museum offers tours for school groups from the surrounding communities. Using items which are duplicated in the collection, and modern, less valuable examples, children are given the opportunity to handle some artefacts, to feel their texture, and weight, and see how they were constructed.

McKinney has been actively promoting the museum to try to create greater awareness of it in the local community and has been working with people in the chamber of commerce and those involved in tourism to generate greater usage by visitors and others, and hopefully to attract further financial support. According to McKinney 'we are trying to make it a focal point so that the community can be as proud of us as the school has been for quite some time'.

The National Museum of the American Indian, USA

While the interpretation of American Indian cultures has been a major focus of ethnographic work in North American museums, there has been no national institution in either Canada or the United States devoted exclusively to the interpretation of native cultures in North America. This is particularly surprising with regard to the USA, given the size and scope of the Smithsonian Institution's collections and its range of museums, numbering fourteen.

Finally, a National Museum has been established which will be devoted exclusively to the history and culture of the indigenous peoples of the Americas.

On 28 November 1989, President Bush signed the National Museum of the American Indian Act, enabling plans to proceed for the establishment of a museum which would be 'a living memorial to Native Americans and their traditions' (US Govt., 1989). Dr Richard West, a distinguished Cheyenne lawyer, was appointed Director of the National Museum of the American Indian (NMAI) and is overseeing the development of this long-awaited, prestigious museum.

Once completed, it will give due status to the history and culture of the Native American population and will take its place alongside other national museums on the Mall in Washington, DC between the National Air and Space Museum and the US Capitol. A second site has been developed in New York City, built upon the collections of the Smithsonian Institution and those of the Museum of the American Indian, Heye Foundation, which consists of 'more than 1,000,000 art objects and artefacts and a library of 40,000 volumes relating to the archaeology, ethnology, and history of Native American peoples' (US Govt., 1989). A third facility, a cultural resource centre, will be constructed at Suitland in Maryland, and will house the reserve collections and support services such as conservation.

Although this is not a community-run museum but a federally-funded national institution, it will, like tribal museums, have a strong community focus in terms of planning and implementation, research and interpretation, which will be reflected in exhibitions, public programmes, outreach activities, and many other aspects of its work. Native American views have been sought at all stages of the planning process beginning with a series of meetings held across North America involving Smithsonian Institution staff, academics, artists, educators, and others, Indian and non-Indian. Advisory boards have been established to contribute to all areas of the Museum's work and exhibitions have involved many non-curatorial selectors and interpreters.

The New York site opened in November 1994, after the collections of the Museum of the American Indian, Heye Foundation, were transferred from their former inadequate, overcrowded location in Upper Manhattan, to the old United States Custom House in Lower Manhattan. The exterior of the building provides an interesting juxtaposition of images: the grandeur of the neo-classical architecture is highly symbolic of western imperialism while, to the left of the steps, a sculpture by Daniel Chester French entitled 'North America', shows 'America' sitting on a throne. An American Indian with war-bonnet is shown peering over her right shoulder as if seeking her protection, while her left hand rests protectively on the shoulder of a black man; all three gaze ahead as if looking towards a future offering hope and security under the 'civilising' influence of white America. Other elements of the composition allude to the native population: on her lap she carries a sheaf of corn, one of the contributions native cultures made to European agriculture; a piece of broken pottery and a buffalo skull are suggestive of the 'dying' race; while an eagle, which is sacred to many Indian tribes, is an image that was appropriated as a symbol of the power of the American nation. Above the steps, a banner carrying the face of a Native American suggests that, at last, Native Americans have gained access to this bastion of American imperial power – to take their rightful place in the modern American nation and to take control over their heritage and its interpretation within the walls of this grand building.

The inaugural exhibitions clearly demonstrated the NMAI's philosophy of participation by native peoples and its intention to be at the forefront of cultural interpretation, with an emphasis upon the use of native voices reflecting native values. This was clearly articulated in *All Roads Are Good: Native Voices on Life and Culture*, an exhibition of over 1,000 items chosen from the Museum's collections by twenty-three Indian selectors, from a variety of disciplines and all parts of the American continent. Labels and videos provided the selectors' views of the objects, their functions and significance, to Indian culture and to themselves as individuals. The personalised element is also apparent in the permanent exhibition, *Creation's Journey*, which presents masterworks from the Museum's collections with the words of native peoples describing the relevance of objects to them, and contrasts this with interpretations provided by art historians and anthropologists. It is an interesting technique which illustrates well the different ways in which an object may be viewed and understood.

In addition to exhibitions and other aspects of the work of collecting, preserving, researching and disseminating information about the collections, the National Museum of the American Indian is forging links with tribal museums, native organisations and individuals throughout the Americas. This strategy has been called 'the fourth museum' and will extend the Museum's work beyond the three facilities in New York, Virginia and Maryland, into communities across the country and throughout the continent.

Staff working in tribal museums will be able to seek advice and assistance from the National Museum. The National Museum of the American Indian Act established a Tribal Museum Endowment Fund to provide grants enabling Indian organizations to undertake repairs or renovations of exhibition areas and so enable them to exhibit artefacts loaned from the Smithsonian Institution collections and other sources. It will also ensure that strong links are forged between the National Museum of the American Indian and tribal museums and cultural centres, and create opportunities for smaller institutions to hold and display items from the largest Native American collection in the world. This will help to counteract the difficulties many individuals face in reaching Washington or New York and will ensure that distant or isolated communities will also have access to the collections and exhibitions of the National Museum of the American Indian.

This intention to reach out to all native peoples is seen as being an essential element of the concept of the new National Museum of the American Indian which aims to address audience needs on a national level and ensure that all Native American communities can share a sense of ownership in this important institution.

Part 3
Human remains and cultural property
The politics of control

'It is well-known that some museums indulged in practices that morally could never be condoned and today would certainly not be undertaken.'
(Council of Australian Museum Associations in *Previous Possessions, New Obligations: Policies for Museums in Australia and Aboriginal and Torres Strait Islander Peoples*)
(CAMA, 1993b: 3–4)

One of the most difficult issues seeking resolution by museums in the post-colonial era is that of repatriation. Emerging nations and indigenous peoples in western nations are calling for their cultural treasures and the remains of their ancestors to be removed from display and many are demanding their return. As their demands continue to grow in frequency and volume, their voices are being heard and effecting change, bringing the debate firmly into the public and political arena and forcing professional bodies to address the issues. As a result, curatorial staff are re-examining museological practices and the legitimacy of their possession of materials which previously were held and displayed without question as to property rights, authority or wishes of those from whom they were taken. They are having to address questions of ownership, care, display, and interpretation. Many museums have been removing human remains from public display and some are also entering into dialogue to activate the process of repatriation and reburial by the descendants or those with a cultural affiliation.

This has become one of the most contentious and difficult areas of museum management in recent years and has divided the profession between those who support such returns and those who are opposed to the disposition of any part of the collections. The issues are intensely complex and highly emotive. They represent a clash between two opposing philosophies: on one hand, western scientific views and philosophy value preservation for the future and justify the acquisition of knowledge for the benefit of all mankind; and on the other, indigenous views assert that knowledge and access to artefacts may be limited, determined only by rights, status and initiation. Opinions vary greatly about appropriate actions to be taken and many solutions to repatriation requests have been attempted. The following chapters will provide evidence of the conflicting views and the negotiations undertaken by indigenous peoples, anthropologists, museum curators and professional organisations as they struggle to find solutions to the repatriation question.

7

Bones of contention

Human remains in museum collections

'Desecrate a white grave and you get jail. Desecrate an Indian grave and you get a PhD.'

(Walter R. Echo-Hawk, Senior Staff Attorney for the Native American Rights Fund, (cited in Arnold, 1990: 28)

In most cultures, the remains of the dead are treated with respect and the bodies are buried, cremated, or otherwise disposed of, with ceremony and respect. In many cultures burial grounds remain potent memorials and sanctified sites for many generations. The continued well-being and approval of the deceased is sometimes believed to be essential for the well-being of the living, and desecration of burial sites may disturb the spirits of the deceased. Disturbance of the dead is offensive to religious beliefs and, in times of war, grave desecration is often used as a means of demoralising a population. Yet western museums house the skeletal remains of hundreds of thousands of peoples, not only from ancient cultures but also from the nineteenth and twentieth centuries.

Shrunken heads, Egyptian mummies, and other skeletal remains have, for centuries, been on public display in museums around the world. Such items were collected to provide specimens for anatomists, archaeologists, anthropologists and other researchers into the lives and deaths of peoples of other cultures and other times, and to satisfy the curiosity and fascination of the general public. Murray wrote in 1904: 'A collection of human skulls is one of the features of a modern anthropological museum.' In his book *Museums, Their History and Their Use*, vol. 1, David Murray described some of the exhibits to be seen in European museums during the sixteenth to eighteenth centuries:

> The object in view was to create surprise rather than to afford instruction. For example, the anatomical collection at Dresden was arranged like a pleasure garden. Skeletons were interwoven with branches of trees to form vistas. Anatomical subjects were difficult to come by, and, when they were got, the most was made of them. At Leyden they had the skeleton of an ass upon which sat a woman that killed her daughter; the skeleton of a man, sitting upon an ox, executed for stealing cattle; a young thief hanged, being the Bridegroom whose Bride stood under the gallows, very curiously set up in his ligaments by P.S.V. Wiel the Younger.

(Murray, 1904: 208–9).

Prior to the establishment of formal classification systems, early museum collections contained such oddities as 'unicorns and alligators, /Elks, mermaids, mummies, witches, satyrs, /And twenty other stranger matters,' (cited in Crook, 1972: 63). In order to excite curiosity and so attract more visitors, museums used to fabricate weird and wonderful creatures such as the basilisk, a legendary dragon (Murray, 1904: 203–4). In the early twentieth century, the Horniman Museum in London displayed a fake merman, which supposedly had been caught in the net of a Japanese fisherman. Mr Jonathan Parker, curator of the Ashmolean Museum in Oxford, said in 1871: 'I do not wish to exclude curiosities from it; they attract people, and when they are brought hither by curiosity, they may stop to learn something better; they may want to know something of the history of the curiosities they have come to see' (Murray, 1904: 204).

Such items have long proved a draw for the general public and displays of human remains continue to excite the imaginations of both children and adults. The Pitt Rivers Museum in Oxford has a 'top-ten' list of favourite exhibits amongst its young visitors, of which the shrunken head is firm favourite. Following a primary school visit to the University of Aberdeen's Marischal Museum, a young visitor wrote an appreciative letter in which she described things which had particularly interested her: 'My favorit room was the WORLD ROOM, because it was so bright I just wanted to look around – the things I liked best were the mummified man, I liked him because you only usually see pots and tools that are years and 1000's of years old but a human it just amazed me. Same with the <u>pickled foot</u>. I knew about bandajing up their feet befor I went but I had never seen one' (sic).

We no longer see in museum displays the sort of vistas and scenes created in the Dresden and Leyden museums in centuries past. However, even today open burial sites and displays of human remains portraying cultural evolution, mortuary practices and head-hunting are still common. Many people feel shocked when they become aware of the nature of some of the human material that museums hold: the amputated penis of an Aboriginal Australian was reported to have been repatriated from a British museum in 1990 (Cledhill, 1990) and stuffed bushman in the Museo Darder in Banyoles, Spain, caused a storm of protest and a threatened African boycott of the Olympic Games in 1992 (Hooper, 1992; Jaume *et al.*, 1992).

The acquisition of human remains

In the stores of thousands of museums in Europe, North America, Australia and New Zealand millions of items of skeletal remains are held in the collections. These include the remains of those who lived as recently as the late nineteenth and early twentieth centuries, the results of collecting activities for scientific and medical studies of the indigenous peoples of the Americas, the Pacific, Africa and Asia. In the United States, a Congressional Budget Office report suggested that federal museums and agencies possessed the skeletal remains of 200,000 Native Americans (cited in Metz, 1993) while other estimates suggest that between 300,000 and 2.5 million Indian skeletons are held in museums and private collections (Echo-Hawk and Echo-Hawk, 1991: 67; Moore, 1994: 201; Rodgers, 1994). In 1987, Robert McCormick Adams, Secretary of the Smithsonian Institution, stated that:

> of some 34,000 specimens . . . approximately 42.5% (14,523) of the specimens are the remains of North American Indians, most of which date from the pre-historic periods. Those of Eskimo, Aleut, and Koniag populations account for another 11.9% (4,061); Blacks, 5.1% (1,744); Whites, 20% (6,829); and all others, 20.6% (7,033).

Adams asserted that almost all had been acquired either through approved archaeological excavations or as the results of salvage operations following erosion or construction work (Adams, 1987b: 14).

However, some of the specimens in the collection of the Smithsonian Institution were dug up from fresh graves or removed from the battlefields in the nineteenth century. This followed a request in 1862, issued by the US Army Surgeon George Otis, the first curator of the US Army Medical Museum, for Army surgeons to collect human body parts so that research could be conducted into 'the characteristics of impact trauma and infectious diseases and the means by which to treat them'. Over the next 38 years, the Army Medical Museum collected specimens from white, black and Indian populations, including the bones of approximately 3,000 Civil War soldiers. In September 1868, an order was issued by the Surgeon General requesting medical staff to collect specimens for inclusion in the Army Medical Museum's growing craniological collection: 'The chief purpose had in view in forming this collection is to aid in the progress of anthropological science by obtaining measurements of a large number of skulls of aboriginal races of North America.' Those 'stationed in the Indian country or in the vicinity of ancient burial mounds or cemeteries in the Mississippi Valley or the Atlantic region' were considered to have 'peculiar facilities for promoting this undertaking' (cited in Echo-Hawk, 1988: 12).

Specimens were sent for research to the US Army Medical Museum in Washington, DC, which was established in 1862, and were later added to with the transfer of Native American human remains from the Smithsonian Institution collection (Makseyn-Kelley, 1994). Around the turn of the century 4,000 specimens were transferred from the Army Medical Museum to the Smithsonian Institution and, according to Adams, it is on these that most of the contention centres. Nearly 3,400 of these are pre-historic in origin, while the remaining 600 were identified by tribe, although at that time the Smithsonian Institution's documentation only supported 270 of those (Adams, 1987b: 14).

The methods of acquisition of human remains and the reasons for their collection anger indigenous peoples and others who feel that they are evidence of colonial and racist attitudes, reminders of nineteenth-century European attempts to prove the superiority of the white race over others. Bob Weatherall, of the Foundation for Aboriginal and Islander Research Action (FAIRA), claims that 'most of these people were robbed from graves or hunted down or murdered by the so-called great men of science in the eighteenth and nineteenth centuries' (cited in Small, 1990). Collecting activities, even in the nineteenth and early twentieth centuries, were undertaken without regard for the spiritual beliefs of relatives or descendants, and their permission was not deemed necessary. Walter R. Echo-Hawk, in his testimony to the Senate Select Committee on Indian Affairs (1988: 11–12) argued that:

> Humanity has always buried its dead with varying degrees of religion, ritual, reverence, and respect. Sanctity of the dead and their final resting place are *not* the exception to the rule. . . . On the contrary these values are deeply ingrained in Western civilization and social mores. . . . Because these same fundamental values are deeply held by Native Americans, past and present, injury to those values caused by the withholding of Native dead must surely be self-evident to any informed observers. Yet somehow these real feelings of Native people have simply been ignored and disregarded as federal, state and private parties have worked historically and presently to disturb and remove as many Indian burials as possible.

In his testimony, Nelson Wallulatum, religious leader and chief of the Wasco Tribe, pointed out that 'Some of the remains that we are talking about are less than 100 years old. You can imagine your dismay if Thomas Jefferson's bones were removed from his grave and displayed on a museum shelf. You would even feel more strongly if he were your great grand-father' (1987: 1).

History is full of illustrations of the gruesome methods and zealous collecting of those who sought bodies and skeletal remains for their own research work or for sale to researchers (Hinsley, 1981; Fforde, 1992; Cole, 1985). Professional interests which demanded the acquisition of human skeletons and crania condoned the exhumation of graves, the removal of bodies from battlefields, the theft of bodies from mortuaries, graves, burial caves and other mortuary sites. As Douglas Cole wrote in *Captured Heritage*, 'few collectors were above a little stealing and skulls and skeletons, highly regarded by museums in the nineteenth century, could scarcely be obtained in any other way' (Cole, 1985: 307). The bodies of individuals who held some significant position or displayed notable physical features were especially sought after. The Tasmanian Aboriginal, William Lanne, commonly known as King Billy, died in 1869 and was believed to be the last male Tasmanian Aboriginal. Fforde (1992: 63–9) has described the theft and deceit which surrounded the acquisition of his remains and the final, bloody degradation to which his body was subjected. Charles Byrne, 'the Irish Giant', who died in 1783, had requested that his body be buried at sea in order to avoid having it fall into the hands of the anatomists; yet his skeleton is today in the collection of the Hunterian Museum in the Royal College of Surgeons in London, England (Fforde, 1992: 22).

Non-European peoples were of particular interest to nineteenth-century researchers seeking evidence of cultural evolution and theories of racial variation. No respect was shown to the dead and little thought was given to the families or the descendants of those whose remains were obtained, often by theft and deception. Andreas Reischek collected artefacts and human remains in New Zealand in the 1880s for European museums, and has recounted how he stole some Maori mummies:

> The undertaking was a dangerous one, for discovery might have cost me my life. In the night I had the mummies removed from the spot and then well hidden; during the next night they were carried still farther away, and so on, until they had been brought safely over the boundaries of Maori land. But even then I kept them cautiously hidden from sight right up to the time of my departure from New Zealand. Now both of these ancestors of the Maori adorn the ethnographical collection of the Imperial Natural History Museum at Vienna.
>
> (Cited in Fforde, 1992: 3–4)

Ken Harper, in his book *Give Me My Father's Body*, recounts the deception surrounding the death and fake funeral of Qisuk, a Polar Eskimo, one of six who, in 1897, had been taken by Robert Peary, the Arctic explorer, from their homeland in Smith Sound to the American Museum of Natural History in New York. The polar Eskimos were intended to 'provide an interesting ethnological and anthropological study' and to be exhibited as a means of raising funds for future expeditions (Harper, 1989: 33). Five of the group died within months of their arrival in New York and a fake funeral was arranged for one of them, Qisuk, in order to deceive his young son, Minik, into believing that he had been buried. In fact, the body had been taken to the College of Physicians and Surgeons for autopsy, and the brain kept there in preserving fluid while the bones were cleaned for display and sent to the American Museum of Natural History (Harper, 1986; Roth, 1992b).

Even worse was the collection of mementoes made from human body parts. While trophy-gathering practices such as scalping and head-hunting have long been regarded by Europeans as the barbaric practices of savage peoples, the gathering of body parts as trophies, along with weapons, clothing, and jewellery, was not uncommon amongst European and American settlers and military personnel (Forbes, 1964: 46–7; Flood, 1995: 51–4) and was even indulged in by some researchers (Fforde, 1992: 67). Examples of such items have found their way into some museum collections; however, contemporary attitudes are such that some of the more repulsive items cease to be displayed. Noting that 'over the years, ethnographic collections have been edited to exclude items shocking to contemporary sensibilities, such as the "scalps, fingers, and men's, women's and children's privates", Susan Hiller asks 'at what point do [such items] disappear from history?' (Hiller, 1992: 188). Their removal, while demonstrating changing attitudes and greater sensitivity towards the public display of gruesome mementoes, also serves to remove such items of unsavoury history from the public consciousness and the actions of their collectors from the public conscience. While such histories should be told, display is not always the most appropriate method: one would not wish, for example, to see the remains of Jewish holocaust victims of Auschwitz or Belsen displayed for all to see, as they were found in the gas chambers and incinerators. More subtle means must be used.

Cases such as those cited here demonstrate that there are significant portions of collections which must be considered to have been unethically collected and illegally held, for can skeletal material obtained under these circumstances, by members of one culture which has dominated and disempowered another, ever be regarded as ethical or legal? If colonial practices are not to be perpetuated, the future of these collections must be decided upon in consultation with, and with the agreement of, those of lineal descent or cultural affiliation.

Mounting opposition

While human remains may continue to excite the imagination of some visitors, continued archaeological excavation, and the display and retention of such material in museum collections, has over the past twenty-five years been attracting increasing criticism from some indigenous peoples, particularly Native Americans and Aboriginal Australians, and numerous court actions have been brought in attempts to secure repatriation and reburial (Ubelaker and Grant, 1989; WCIP 1990; Trope and Echo-Hawk, 1992).

The practice of publicly displaying human remains demonstrates a total disregard for the rights and concerns of peoples of other cultures, particularly non-western and fourth world peoples: those who previously were subjected to the political control of European nations. Subjected to repression and cultural domination under colonial administration, their religious beliefs have been disregarded by researchers and collectors excavating burial sites in their search for human remains and cultural artefacts. Such collections continue to provide research material for archaeologists, physical anthropologists and others, but are increasingly the subject of political representations by indigenous peoples. Egyptian mummies, Maori shrunken heads, early Native American burials and so forth have become the subject of vociferous international debate concerning their removal from display and possible repatriation and reburial. President Sadat of Egypt called for the reburial of the many Egyptian mummies on display in museums throughout the world, a request which went unanswered (Chamberlin, 1983: 8). In recent years, western museums have been targeted by Native American, Maori, and Australian Aboriginal organisations actively campaigning for the return of their ancestors' bones. Michael Mansell, an Aboriginal lawyer and activist who has campaigned strenuously for the return of human remains, has commented that 'the remains of Aborigines are not "relics" just because white people deem them to be. Like other humans in the world, the remains of our dead are for the families and the people of the deceased to deal with according to our culture' (Mansell, 1993). As a result, attitudes are changing and many museums, more sensitive to the cultural concerns expressed, no longer display certain categories of human remains in public exhibitions.

Collections of human remains fall into three distinct categories. The largest category is that of archaeological collections of skeletal material from many sources and periods of time. These have provided much of the material for research in the fields of paleopathology and osteology, giving evidence of the health and lifestyles of ancient peoples as well as enlightening knowledge of trends affecting more recent cultures.

Secondly, there are collections acquired for research related to evolutionary theories, the study of human development and medical research. These collections tend to be housed in natural history museums and in associated collecting institutions such as medical colleges. Many of the nineteenth-century museum collections of human remains were established in order to provide data for scientific research, particularly in the fields of cultural evolution and phrenology. Many of the contested collections of Australian Aboriginal and Native American remains fall into these first two categories. The third, and smallest group, is that of ethnographic artefacts and 'curiosities' such as Egyptian mummies, Maori tattooed heads, decorated skulls from Melanesia, shrunken heads from South America, Tibetan skull drums, and other miscellaneous items.

Although the wholesale collecting of bodies for research collections may have all but stopped, grave sites have been disinterred by vast numbers of looters seeking relics and grave goods. The looting of graves remains a problem which affects many unregistered burial sites, despite national and international laws designed to prevent the sale of material illegally acquired. It is also a problem which affects registered burial sites such as military cemeteries from which buttons, buckles and medals are sought by unscrupulous collectors, as attested by the recent desecration and robbing of graves of the South Wales Borderers in South Africa and the graves of Civil War dead in the USA (Fforde, 1992: 21).

Evidence also suggests that human remains found in archaeological excavations often receive differing treatment according to their ethnic origins. While the remains of Native Americans, Australian Aboriginal peoples, and other indigenous peoples have been held in long-term collections as materials for archaeological and scientific research, archaeological remains of European origin have usually been reburied with appropriate religious ceremonies.

In the United States, the recently-discovered remains of American military personnel killed during the nineteenth century are buried in national cemeteries with full military honours. In 1987, the remains of 28 American soldiers killed during the War of 1812 were discovered in unmarked graves on Snake Hill near the site of Old Fort Erie, Ontario, in Canada. They were returned to the US authorities for military burial and interred in the Bath National Cemetery on 30 June 1988. This action reflects the US government's policy to return home and bury the remains of American servicemen killed overseas. 'It's the homecoming that counts, honoring the nation's war dead, even after nearly two centuries in a forgotten grave' (John Arden-Hopkins, 1988). Despite this national policy, Native American war dead were not granted the same honour and respect. Prior to the passage of US Public Law 101–601, the Native American Graves Protection and Repatriation Act, in 1990 the remains of Indians, perhaps killed in the same battles as the US servicemen, were likely to end up in academic collections.

179

This discrepancy is partly explained by the distinctions which were made under US law between marked and unmarked graves. The marked graves, the majority of which contained the remains of those of European ancestry, have tended to be accorded greater legal protection. However, Martin Sullivan, Director of the Heard Museum, points out that the remains of whites found in unmarked graves may also be subjected to scientific study, as happened while he was director of the New York State Museum: 'White remains were disinterred from an unmarked site at a nineteenth-century paupers' farm where an excavation was underway to construct new public buildings. Those remains were analyzed by physical anthropologists and were reburied at the conclusion of their study' (Sullivan, 1993).

Two Indian writers, Walter and Roger Echo-Hawk have pointed out that, until recently, criminal statutes in the United States strictly prohibited grave desecration, grave robbing, and mutilation of the dead, but were not applied in protection of Indian dead:

> Instead, the laws and social policy, to the extent that they affect Native dead, do not treat this class of decedents as human, but rather define them as 'non-renewable archaeological resources' to be treated like dinosaurs or snails, 'federal property' to be used as chattels in the academic market-place, 'pathological specimens' to be studied by those interested in racial biology, or simple 'trophies or booty' to enrich private collectors. The huge collections of dead Indians are compelling testimony that Indians have been singled out for markedly disparate treatment
>
> (Echo-Hawk and Echo-Hawk, 1991: 68)

This differentiation was highlighted in the United States in the 1970s, when a series of incidents drew attention to Indian concerns about the excavation of human remains and the differential treatment that Indian remains received. The issue came to public attention following the disruption of an archaeological dig outside Minneapolis-St. Paul by members of the American Indian Movement in 1971 (Grimes, 1990: 241, Zimmerman, 1994b: 213). Of particular significance was an incident which involved the discovery of an Indian skeleton on the edge of a white pioneer cemetery which had to be relocated due to the construction of a highway. While the white remains were reburied after exhumation, the Indian remains were removed by the State Archaeologist to have studies carried out. However, Running Moccasins (Maria Pearson), a Yankton Sioux, challenged the differential treatment, took the matter up with the Governor of Iowa, and refused to give up the fight. Eventually a court decision determined that the remains would be reburied and Pearson's actions led to a change in Iowa state law in 1976, the first state to pass laws protecting Indian burial sites. This was the first of many such battles waged by Native Americans against the exhumation and study of Indian remains and, in the years to follow, other states passed similar laws as Indian groups continued their protests (Deloria, 1973: 32–3; Zimmerman, 1994a: 61).

In 1976, members of the Union of Ontario Indians placed an archaeologist from the Royal Ontario Museum under citizen's arrest while engaged in the excavation of a seventeenth-century Neutral Indian graveyard which was on a site marked for construction. The Union of Ontario Indians claimed that the archaeologist's actions were in contravention of the Ontario Cemeteries Act; and they also charged that the archaeologist was offering an indignity to human remains (Tivy, 1993: 26). The following year, a burial site at Grimsby, Ontario, in Canada was the subject of some controversy including a sit-in at the Royal Ontario Museum. In 1985 the American Indians Against Desecration (AIAD) sparked off a debate between scholars and Indians when they approached the American Anthropological Association in Washington D.C. with the request that uninvited excavation of Indian burial sites should cease and mortuary remains be returned for reburial from collections (Grimes, 1990: 241).

However, legislation designed to protect Indian burial sites has not always been effective; likewise earlier legislation, which was introduced as part of federal efforts at cultural resource management, failed to provide protection for burial sites and, in fact, hastened the excavation of sites and established the concept of federal ownership of archaeological resources, including human remains (Moore, 1994: 201–10). The Archaeological Resources Protection Act of 1979 made the excavation, removal and trafficking of artefacts from federally owned or administered land, punishable by up to five years in prison and $250,000 in fines; but between then and 1990, only 58 cases had been prosecuted. Of these only eleven resulted in a prison sentence, and the longest of these was just six months (Sugarman, 1992: 82). This failure to apply the law to looters of Indian graves has caused Walter Echo-Hawk, Senior Staff Attorney for the Native American Rights Fund to remark: 'Desecrate a white grave and you get jail. Desecrate an Indian grave and you get a PhD' (cited in Arnold, 1990: 28).

In Britain, while British museum collections contain the remains of Aboriginal Australians who died in the nineteenth century, human remains excavated by archaeologists from British sites may well be reburied after research with a ceremony appropriate to the faith of the deceased. In 1990, the remains of 40 Romans, excavated following their discovery on a construction site in Shepton Mallet in Somerset, were given a Christian burial (Frampton, 1994: 24–5). Restoration work on Christ Church in Spitalfields in London, necessitated the clearing of burials in the crypt. The remains of 968 individuals were exhumed, the majority of Huguenot descent. In 387 cases, the name and age at death were known (Molleson *et al.*, 1993: 206). Dating from 1729 to 1852, these remains proved very valuable providing provenanced and closely dated material for anthropological studies concerning health in relation to age, occupation, and diet. They also provided evidence of funerary practices, artefacts and clothing, increasing knowledge of the sexton's role and the undertaking industry during the eighteenth and nineteenth centuries. Following research, the remains were cremated and the ashes returned to the church for reburial.

Over 500 graves were unearthed in a twelfth-century Jewish cemetery being bulldozed to make way for a supermarket carpark in York, England. Human biologists at York University began research work on the remains but, after

181

complaints from the Chief Rabbi, the research was stopped and the remains were reburied (Hubert, 1994: 133).

When the sixteenth-century warship the *Mary Rose* was raised from the seabed off the coast of southern England in 1982, the remains of nearly 200 sailors were recovered. One of these was given a Christian burial following a combined Roman Catholic and Church of England service in Portsmouth Cathedral on 19 July 1984. This ceremony was a symbolic gesture of respect to the dead, but the remains of the other sailors remain in the care of the Mary Rose Trust. Initial paleopathological studies were conducted on the remains and a skeletal report produced. The remains are now held in a secure storage facility with close monitoring of environmental conditions and access restricted. Over the next few years the Trust will be conducting research into methods of reburial on the seabed in the hope of identifying a method which will enable the remains to be subjected to further research in the future when technological advancements will present opportunities for the acquisition of data not possible at present (Hildred, 1995).

Displays of human remains

However, opposition to museological practices, which place western values upon dissemination of knowledge and education before the beliefs and sensitivities of descendants or culturally affiliated groups, has led to the current controversy over the continued holding, research and display of human remains. Criticism and debate about the continuing display and retention of human remains in museums has influenced museological practices: Australian museums no longer display Aboriginal remains, and museums in New Zealand have removed the tattooed heads, or *moka mokai*, from display. Likewise, in North America, most Native American human remains have been removed from display. In the United States, circumstances have undergone a dramatic change with the passage of the Native American Graves Protection and Repatriation Act (NAGPRA) in 1990. Under NAGPRA, ownership of Native American material is given in the first instance to lineal descendants; secondly, to the tribe upon whose land the objects or remains were discovered; thirdly, the tribe with the closest cultural affiliation. Excavation and study of such material can only be undertaken with a permit and with appropriate tribal consent.

However, other categories of material, such as Jivaro shrunken heads and Egyptian mummies, continue to be shown widely in western museums, though not without some criticism, demonstrating the continuing inequity in the treatment of the dead of different cultures. Even where museums have responded to current concerns and removed items from display, some may question their motives, especially when there appears to be different treatment accorded to the remains of different cultural origins. Tariq Mehmood, commenting on the practices of museums in Liverpool, noted that the removal of Maori heads from display was:

> not out of respect for the Maori, but the result of criticism. The Museum concluded that the display of these heads was not in 'good taste'.

Obviously as far as British museums are concerned, displaying the dead bodies of Africans from Egypt is still in 'good taste'.

(Mehmood, 1990: 27).

Regarding the justification that such displays have scientific value, Mehmood sees the discovery of such material as 'part of the process of the conquest and control of Africa and other peoples' lands by Europeans' and is critical of a practice in which human remains 'were dug up out of their ancestral graves, transported thousands of miles and put into glass cages of so-called civilised people'.

In the United States, the most graphic illustrations of the recent offensive treatment of human remains in museum displays, was illustrated by the public display of open burial sites which, until recently, were scattered across the country; most of these have closed in recent years as public opinion has increasingly opposed their continued display. This change in attitude has been largely brought about by the efforts of Native American pressure groups such as American Indians Against Desecration (AIAD) who waged protests against such sites. In November 1990, this opposition forced the closure of one of the last open burial sites in the United States, Dickson Mounds, near Lewiston in Illinois. The site was discovered in 1927 by an amateur archaeologist, Dr Don F. Dickson, a local chiropractor. He preserved the site, conducted tours and gave lectures, then in 1945 he sold the site to the State of Illinois. One of the last open burial sites in the United States, it is believed to contain between 1,000 and 3,000 graves of which 237 have been excavated, exposing skeletons along with pottery, jewellery, tools and weapons. Research on the bones has exposed evidence of health problems caused by diet following the introduction of an agricultural life-style amongst the Pre-Mississippian and Mississippian cultures which inhabited the Illinois River valley between 600 and 1,000 years ago (Goodman and Armelagos, 1985). In the early 1970s, a new $2.5 million Dickson Mounds Museum was opened in order to house and display the 234 open graves. However, Native Americans were increasingly protesting the display of human remains; open grave sites such as this became the subject of heated debate. In 1989, the Dickson Mounds exhibit was cited as an example of unacceptable museum practice at a meeting of the World Archaeological Congress. Other open burial sites had already closed and, it became clear to the museum staff that Dickson Mounds should also close.

Governor Jim Thompson accepted the recommendation of the Museum staff; however, a leak to the newspaper resulted in a public outcry. Many local people were opposed to the closure of the site which was a popular local tourist attraction and, therefore, of some importance to the economy of the local area. Frank Hummel, a resident opposed to the closing of the burial site display, wrote to the Peoria newspaper:

> We who live in this area have love and respect for these ancestors of the American Indian living today. We visit the burial site with the same reverence that we have when we visit the remains of our relatives, friends and neighbors. . . . When I gaze upon the remains, I try to visualize which ones made the different artifacts which I possess.

(Quoted in Smith, W., 1990)

Figure 7.1 The exposed graves at the Indian burial site of Dickson Mounds, Illinois. It closed in 1990 following demonstrations during which protestors draped blankets over skeletons and attempted to bury some of the remains.

Source: Photograph courtesy of Illinois State Museum

Of course, when he visits the graves of his relatives, friends and neighbours, it is not to gaze down upon their exposed remains in an open grave, but to stand before a memorial stone. His comments reflect his interest in the artefacts as possessions and reveal his failure to relate to the emotions of the native protesters upon seeing the exposed remains in an open grave, a very different experience from standing in front of a memorial stone which identifies the individual, marks the place of their burial, and tells of their birth and death.

The fate of Dickson Mounds became a key issue in the 1990 campaign to elect a new State Governor and, in the face of massive public opposition to its closure, all three candidates, including Thompson, were ultimately stating that, under their governorship, the site would remain open. However, there were lengthy demonstrations and protests by Native Americans culminating in a dramatic and solemn protest in October 1990 when demonstrators climbed over the railings and draped blankets over several of the skeletons. In another demonstration, protesters attempted to rebury some of the remains. Following election, the new Governor, Jim Edgar, realised that the issue must be resolved. The site was closed, but the proposal that the graves should be entombed in concrete was an unsatisfactory solution for Native American groups who wished the remains to be returned to the earth to complete the normal cycle of life and death (Pridmore, 1992: 18–19).

'The dead are our teachers': the scientific value of human remains

In recent years, human remains have become the subject of strenuous efforts to facilitate repatriation to the cultures of origin; indigenous peoples, particularly Native Americans and Aboriginal Australians, have been mounting campaigns in efforts to obtain the bones of their ancestors. Museums must now address this issue and develop policies for dealing with such requests. They need to discard the assumptions of dominant cultures which have shaped their treatment of the human remains of minority cultures and develop new codes of practice which accept and respect alternative world views and the wishes of indigenous peoples with regard to the treatment of their dead.

Repatriation campaigns are dismissed by some as politically motivated, and individuals such as Michael Mansell and Bob Weatherall have been accused of not representing the views of the Aboriginal community (Stringer, cited in Morison, 1990). Mansell, however, in an open letter concerning the negotiations which were currently being conducted with the Pitt Rivers Museum in Oxford in 1990, named nine Aboriginal organisations as just a few of those which supported the efforts to repatriate ancestral remains. Furthermore, Mansell and Weatherall's visits to museums in Europe have been financially supported by the Aboriginal and Torres Strait Islander Commission (ATSIC), a statutory authority which was established to represent Aboriginal and Torres Strait Islander interests. ATSIC's responsibilities include 'the provision of policy advice to the Commonwealth Government' and 'the administration of services and programmes for Aboriginal and Torres Strait Islander communities' (ATSIC, 1993a: 2). The determination of indigenous peoples to succeed in their repatriation demands stems from centuries of subjugation, abuse and genocide. As a result, repatriation has indeed taken on political overtones, but understandably and justifiably so: the domination of one culture over another is in itself a highly political action, and the appropriate treatment of the dead is a highly sensitive matter.

The repatriation issue has become one which museums cannot ignore, yet there is no easy solution. Blanket policies which attempt to cover all institutions and eventualities are both undesirable and unviable, for the issues are too complex to allow such a simplistic approach to work satisfactorily in all cases. Attitudes towards the display of human remains vary from culture to culture and it is the clash of these differing attitudes which lies at the heart of the problem of human remains in collections.

Human remains continue to be regarded as a valuable component of the interpretive process to be used in displays which are intended to inform visitors about beliefs and practices concerning death and burial. As such, it is argued that they have great educational value. They can also be used to broaden public attitudes towards subject-matter about which many people have misconceptions. The Muzium Negara, in Kuala Lumpur, presented an exhibition *The Head and Skull in Human Culture and History* (1991) which included shrunken heads, trophy skulls, and medical specimens, covering many aspects of cultural beliefs and practices concerning the head: phrenology, trephination, head-hunting, and related objects such as costumes, tools and weapons. Also included was skull imagery in every form from seventeenth-century Dutch paintings to a twentieth-century heavy-metal record sleeve (Balasegaram, 1990). Although the subject matter was somewhat controversial, the museum's director-general, Datuk Shahrum Yub, felt that the subject needed to be discussed: 'Head-hunting is seen as a dark period of world history. I'm hoping that this exhibition will help people understand it and broaden their outlook' (cited in Balasegaram, 1990).

An exhibition about head-hunting practices in Papua New Guinea was presented by Liverpool Museum in an effort to provide a reasoned and informed portrayal of the social context of head-hunting, and thus give visitors a better understanding of what many may see as nothing more than a savage and bloodthirsty sport. The display cases contained all the paraphernalia of headhunting including weapons and tools, plus *gope* figures, and skulls presented as human offerings to the *gope* as part of initiation ceremonies. However, the exhibition content was not clearly placed in a time context, giving the impression that such head-hunting practices continue to this day. The only reference to time was in the text introducing one of the four areas being examined: 'The vast swampland of southwest New Guinea is inhabited by the Asmat, formerly great headhunters and cannibals'. In addition, the text included quotations using emotive language which tended to sensationalise and highlight the aspects most likely to excite the imagination and reinforce preconceived notions. References to 'orgiastic fertility ceremonies' and 'cannibal feasts' can do little to counteract the stereotypical impressions that the exhibition was intended to address.

Exhibitions which show human remains which were traditionally utilised in public displays, such as the display of trophy skulls in Papua New Guinea, have not tended to be the subject of requests for removal or repatriation. However, displays showing mortuary practices in different cultures and in different time periods have been widely used in museums, and have invariably included human remains. Such displays are intended to provide greater insight into the funerary rites of the cultures concerned, their belief systems, and factors relating to cause of death. In most cases, those bodies were originally disposed of with respect and ceremony, and with the intention that the burial would provide a final resting place for the remains of the deceased. It is displays of such material, and their continued presence in museums and other research collections, which have tended to attract greatest protest.

The efforts of indigenous groups in Australia and North America provide continuing evidence of the intensity of feeling and the extent of opposition to displays and the continued holding of collections of human remains. However, in contrast to this, Anita Herle, curator of anthropology at Cambridge University Museum of Archaeology and Anthropology, found that the Naga people with whom she worked on a project were not at all concerned about the use of human remains in displays, feeling that it was a natural part of their culture. Clearly, attitudes towards displays of human remains vary from culture to culture and repatriation is not a universal issue.

The value of material for scientific research continues to be one of the major arguments for retaining human remains: forensic scientists, archaeologists, physical anthropologists and others, argue that their value for scientific research, particularly medical, far outweighs the cultural considerations. Researchers argue that the study of human remains provides increased understanding of past cultures, and valuable information of importance to contemporary societies through research activities in fields such as epidemiology and paleopathology. Reflecting this perspective, '*Mortui Viventes Docent*' or 'The dead are our teachers', is the motto of the Paleopathology Association (Paleopathology Association, 1986).

However, indigenous campaigners may find it hard to accept the continued retention of human remains buried in an institution's reserve collections with no evidence of continuing, relevant research. Opponents of repatriation argue that the possibilities offered by improved research methodologies, such as dating, DNA analysis, and other as yet undiscovered techniques, necessitate the continued holding of skeletal remains for future research of factors such as genetic variation, micro-evolution, and patterns of migration of the world's earliest inhabitants.

An example of this is the return and reburial of the Kow Swamp collection of human remains from southeast Australia. They were found in Pleistocene burials which were excavated in 1968–72 when they were threatened by irrigation work. The bones are 9,000–15,000 years old and are of a different racial type to present-day Aboriginal Australians. The collection would be of tremendous importance to understanding Australian Aboriginal history and also to charting migration patterns in Australia and other parts of the world, but has now been lost to researchers. The Echuca community, now living in the Kow Swamp area, although unrelated to the ancient Aboriginal peoples, had called for the return of the collection in order to provide a mass re-burial. They succeeded in utilising State and Commonwealth legislation to achieve this aim, and in 1990 the Museum of Victoria gave the Kow Swamp collection to the Echuca community.

Don Borthwell, of the Department of Archaeology, University of York, England, is opposed to the repatriation of such collections, and is particularly concerned about the loss of 'priceless prehistoric material'. He argues that 'what this amounts to is that the Aborigines are being allowed to destroy – in their ignorance – an aspect of their own prehistory. And *their* prehistory is a part of *world* prehistory' (Borthwell, 1994). He also suggests that a compromise could be reached by returning archaeological remains to tribal areas for curation in grant-supported museums. John Mulvaney, a senior Australian prehistorian who fought the return of the Kow Swamp collection, emphasises the enormous scientific value of the collection, stating that:

> Their importance for Aboriginal self-knowledge is undoubted, but its global significance may be equally great. As Australia, Europe and the New World were colonized by *Homo sapiens* in what may be a near-synchronous surge across the continents, this was one of the major events of humankind. Such a large group of ancient remains could contribute vital clues to some future resolution of that global quantum leap in intellect and adaptability.
>
> (Mulvaney, 1991: 14)

Mulvaney saw the establishment of a Keeping Place where they could be stored 'under absolute community custodianship' as 'a prudent compromise . . . which kept future options open' and offered to mediate at Echuca (ibid.: 19). He claims, however, that when he, and others seeking to safeguard the future of the Kow Swamp collection, made attempts to discuss the matter with the Echuca community and the Victorian government, they were met with 'a wall of silence' (ibid.: 20).

Borthwell is critical of developments in the USA and Australia contending that 'politicians in the USA and Australia (in particular) have acquiesced rapidly to tribal pressures to return their "ancestors", because a) it kept them friendly with tribal groups b) it cost them nothing and c) diverted tribal concern from more critical factors such as land and mineral reserves' (Borthwell, 1994). Using an analogy to illustrate the research potential of human remains, Dale Idiens, Depute Director (Collections) for the National Museum of Scotland, pointed out that 'one has to remember the role that old bird egg collections – made long before chemicals such as DDT had ever been synthesised – had in proving that organochlorine pesticide residues were seriously damaging the ecosystem'. In years to come collections of human remains may also prove to have profound and unforeseen importance.

In recent years, museums throughout North America, Australia and New

Zealand have been addressing the human remains issue. They have successfully negotiated legislative and procedural agreements and significant developments have been initiated, although ethical and academic debate about repatriation continues. This interest in repatriation is a turn-around from a decade ago when the organisation American Indians Against Desecration (AIAD) invited members of the Society for American Archaeology to a reservation for a meeting, but none responded. Such developments have been the result of changing professional attitudes and resultant initiatives driven by enlightened individuals; but the catalyst for these changes were the pressures exerted by indigenous peoples and their representatives as they became increasingly vocal about their frustrations and anger over the treatment of their dead ancestors and their cultural heritage (Fourmile, 1989c; WCIP; 1990; Echo-Hawk and Echo-Hawk, Hammil and Cruz, 1994; Richardson, 1994). Increasingly, it is recognised that museums have an obligation to inform those peoples of their holdings of skeletal remains and cultural material and accept shared responsibilities for care, preservation, interpretation, and retention or repatriation.

8

Cultural artefacts
A question of ownership

'With all the outreach programs, lectures, exhibits, and other public and educational programs we have accomplished over the years, our museum never could do anything more beneficial than return this sacred object to its tribe . . . What better contribution to a people can a museum provide than to help them survive?'

(George P. Horse Capture, former curator of the Plains Indian Museum of the
Buffalo Bill Historical Center, Cody, Wyoming, 1992)

Equally as complex as the issue of human remains is that of sacred objects and other items of cultural significance which are held in museum collections. The issue is complicated by differing perceptions of the nature of the artefacts, and difficulties in defining terms such as 'sacred objects'; also by the conflict of interests amongst the parties involved which leads to complex definitions of ownership (Fourmile, 1990a; Welsh, 1992: 856–858).

Over recent decades, there have been increasing demands for the return of cultural objects held in museum collections, primarily in Europe, North America, Australia and New Zealand. Repatriation campaigns have brought to the attention of curators and the general public the ethics of the ownership and display of cultural objects. Intensely complex and political, these issues are also debated at government levels. More recently, claims have come particularly from new nations in the former colonial regions, seeking to reaffirm their cultural heritage and establish a sense of national identity. They have also come from the disempowered indigenous peoples of countries such as New Zealand, Australia, the United States and Canada, amongst whom there has been a re-awakening of cultural identity and a determination to preserve and regain control of their cultural heritage. As Fourmile has commented with regard to the colonial repression of her Aboriginal ancestors 'along with the dispossession of our land went the dispossession of our cultural property' (1990a: 57).

The significance attached to objects also changes within a culture, particularly during times of cultural upheaval. Amongst peoples who suffered acculturation under European colonialism and who are now experiencing a period of revival and reappraisal, artefacts may regain their lost meaning and functions and be valued once again for their expression of old values and traditions; or they may acquire new significance which is not without political relevance.

Central to the debate concerning the repatriation of cultural material is the question of ownership, a multifarious and emotive issue. The legal acquisition of material is often quoted as a defence against possible repatriation but this can be difficult to prove when dealing with material gathered in the first decades of this century, or earlier. Furthermore, the colonial ancestry of the collections cannot be omitted from the repatriation debate. While curators and trustees argue that their museum legally acquired the artefacts in the collections, objects which were originally received as gifts or purchased from their original owners may now be subject to argument about their true ownership. The cultural insensitivity of the methods with which many collections were acquired calls into question the legality of the acquisitions.

During the colonial era, vast quantities of cultural material were collected and placed in museums leaving many cultures today with little evidence of their cultural heritage. Some artefacts were purchased or received as gifts but many others were taken as loot during military campaigns and periods of colonial rule, or were confiscated by European missionaries intent on wiping out indigenous religions and replacing them with Christianity. Fourmile (1990a: 58) has observed that 'obviously there are a whole host of circumstances by which museums acquired their collections of our cultural property, but virtually all on a basis which could not be seen as constituting transactions under fair and equal conditions for both parties'.

In many instances, the manner in which items were collected resulted in poor documentation, particularly in the early years of collecting by amateurs in the colonies. This, combined with the inequities of the power relationships between the collector (coloniser) and the traditional owner (colonised), mean that the status and provenance may be difficult to establish or may be perceived differently by opposing parties (Echo-Hawk, 1985; Fourmile, 1990a; Vecsey, 1991; Sullivan, 1992). In *LOOT! Heritage of Plunder* Russell Chamberlin (1983: 8) points out the wider implications of the controversy over the Parthenon (Elgin) Marbles:

> Central to the controversy is the Sultan's right – or otherwise – to dispose of the property of the Greeks, whom the Turks happened to have conquered. If he had such a right, then no national heritage is safe and Germany is entitled to the loot collected by Hitler and Goering. If he did not have such a right, then the contents of a number of museums in Europe – Germany, Britain and France in particular – are being held illicitly.

In the past, items accessioned into a museum's collections have been regarded as the property of the museum if they were acquired legally or in good faith. However, such decisions have been made on the basis of western legal systems and concepts of ownership, with scant regard for indigenous peoples' concepts of individual or communal ownership and rights over objects or knowledge.

Furthermore, it can now be seen that many objects were obtained through unequal power relationships. Some objects were given as tokens of friendship and symbols of trust between peoples of different cultures; such gestures were surely nullified by subsequent events in which the indigenous population was subjugated and forced or misled into complying with inequitable treaties, or those which were later violated or revoked. Even in instances in which items were purchased, there may be little actual evidence of transactions which took place when items were acquired 50, 100, and more, years ago and the circumstances of a transaction may give rise to questions about the ethics, if not the legality, of the sale. They may have been compulsorily 'purchased', or confiscated, thus invalidating any earlier bilateral agreements. Objects may have been purchased from individuals with no right to sell communally owned objects, making the sale illegal under customary law; they may have been purchased at prices which were exploitative and mercenary; or simply purchased from a party lacking adequate legal knowledge or linguistic skill to fully understand the implications of their actions.

A clear example of this latter point can be illustrated by the case of wampum belts held in the collections of the New York State Museum (Fenton, 1971; Sullivan, 1992). Amongst the tribes of the Iroquois confederacy, strings of white and purple shell beads were strung together to create patterned belts which serve as tribal records of treaties, agreements and other significant events. Martin Sullivan, director of the Heard Museum, has described the importance of wampum belts to traditional Iroquois people: 'Their wampum belts are a common heritage as important as documents such as the Declaration of Independence, the Constitution, and the Bill of Rights have become to the citizens of the United States' (Sullivan, 1992: 8).

In 1891, the official Onondaga wampum-keeper sold four important belts to a collector without sanction from the tribal government. When their loss was realised in 1898, the Onondaga sought to recover the belts. Tribal leaders were advised by non-Indians to appoint the New York State Board of Regents as their authorised wampum-keeper in order that the Board could act on their behalf in a lawsuit. Acting on this advice, the Onondaga transferred custody of a number of wampum belts to the Board of Regents. In total about 26 belts were transferred to the Board of Regents and hence to the collections of the New York State Museum, of which they were trustees. The Onondaga failed in their attempt to recover the four belts which had been the subject of the lawsuit and, in 1927, the belts were bequeathed to the State Museum by the widow of the collector. Although the Onondaga repeatedly requested that the Board of Regents return custody of the wampum belts to the Onondaga, it was over 90 years before the tribe regained possession of twelve of their belts. As pointed out by Martin Sullivan, who was director of the New York State Museum and their principal negotiator in the 1989 repatriation of the belts, the Onondaga signers of an 1898 bill of sale 'had very little command of the English language or of Anglo-American legal practices, and were not likely to have given the informed consent to the transaction that modern legal standards would require' (Sullivan, 1992: 12).

Such were the circumstances of colonial relationships that many indigenous populations have lost much of their material culture to collectors and museums;

193

but with the passage of time and the revival of traditional cultures has come the dawning of recognition of the potentially destructive impact of the activities of collectors. Although most of the discussion in this book relates to items collected in the past, looting and the illegal export of cultural property continue to present problems today. Items which are rare, of high quality, or particular significance, command high prices on the art market and destructive collecting activities and the illegal exportation of artefacts continue to decimate the historic artworks and archaeological sites in many countries.

Attempts have been made to introduce international regulations to control and prevent such trafficking. In 1970, UNESCO adopted the Convention on the Means of Prohibiting and Preventing the Illicit Import, Export, and Transfer of Ownership of Cultural Property, which stated that such trafficking was 'one of the main causes of the impoverishment of the cultural heritage of the countries of origin of such property' (UNESCO, 1970: 6). However, this could not be fully effective without changes to national law and in 1984 UNESCO asked UNIDROIT, the International Institute for the Unification of Private Law, to address the issue of private law as it applied to the illicit trade in cultural property. In June 1995, the Diplomatic Conference convened in Rome in which 70 states participated, adopted the UNIDROIT Convention on Stolen or Illegally Exported Cultural Objects (UNIDROIT, 1995). The EC has also attempted to take action: in 1993, the Council of the European Communities issued Directive 93/7/EEC on the return of cultural objects unlawfully removed from the territory of a Member State, which also had to be supported by appropriate legislation in each country (EC, 1993). However, these initiatives can only be effective in countries which support them and none of them can be applied retrospectively.

These efforts have enabled some action to be taken against those attempting to traffic in stolen cultural property, but the demand for ethnographic and archaeological artefacts remains high amongst private collectors and museums. While museums attempt to purchase only artefacts which have been legally obtained, methods can be found to circumvent the law by producing bills of sale, letters or other documents intended to 'prove' legal acquisition. In the United States, Walter and Roger Echo-Hawk have cited several examples of desecration of Indian graves in the United States, including that of the Tunica Treasure case in which an amateur archaeologist tried to sell to the Peabody Museum two-and-a-half tons of grave artefacts looted from 150 Tunica Indian graves. A series of legal moves finally resulted in a court finding the Tunica-Biloxi tribe to be the lawful owners of the artefacts (Echo-Hawk and Echo-Hawk, 1991: 67; Peterson, 1990: 534–5).

In an article describing the activities of looters in the United States, Aaron Sugarman explained how museums could be unwitting accomplices in the illegal handling of looted material. He gave the example of an illegally acquired bowl, purchased for $450 by a collector, lent to a museum which had it appraised at $250,000 and displayed with a plaque in the collector's name. Under US law the collector would receive a substantial tax deduction, as well as respect and status as a philanthropist, if he was to donate the piece to the museum (Sugarman, 1992: 123). Even when investigations show that illegal excavation and trafficking have occurred, the individuals are rarely prosecuted and, on the few occasions when they have been, they have received fines rather than prison sentences, despite the fact that those found guilty could be sentenced to terms of up to five years (Sugarman, 1992).

Sacred objects

Conflicting views about ownership become more emotive and take on a special significance when dealing with sacred objects, particularly those which are believed to have a life force; for certain categories of objects are regarded as inanimate artefacts by curators, but are perceived as animate beings by the peoples who made and used them. To most collectors, curators and visitors to museums, objects such as Zuni *ahayu:da*, Iroquois False Face masks, and Maori *taonga* (treasures), are inanimate objects which vary in significance and status according to each individual's perspective. The private collector may see such items as curiosities or works of art, perhaps rare and financially valuable. To western anthropologists they are of academic interest, providing physical evidence of cultural traditions, religious beliefs and artistic skills. To the museum visitor they may well be of no more than passing interest, curiosities from an exotic culture; but to members of the Maori, Zuni and Iroquois communities they are not only important sacred objects, they are animate, living beings, embodying the spirits and imbued with strong spiritual power.

The issue is further complicated by the concept of communal ownership. Certain types of objects were not owned by any one person and therefore could not rightly be sold. Harry Walters, curator of the Ned A. Hatathli Museum on the Navajo reservation, believes that all Navajo medicine bundles in museum collections have been acquired under questionable circumstances. To the non-Navajo they are ethnographic artefacts, owned by an individual or displayed in public collections. To the Navajo, they have power, they are living entities which are passed on through the generations, and belong to the tribe as a whole: no individual has the right to sell a medicine bundle. The person with the healing skills, the medicine man, has the right to use a bundle and takes on the role of custodian but, nowadays, when a medicine man dies, there is rarely anyone trained to whom it can be passed on. It goes, therefore, to his children but if they do not know how to use it, they may sell it to outsiders from whom there is great demand for such material.

Zuni *ahayu:da*, often referred to as 'war gods', are in a similar category, being communally owned by the Zuni Indian tribe of New Mexico in the United States. *Ahayu:da* have been the subject of an extensive repatriation campaign by the Zuni people during recent years (Hustito, 1991; Ladd, 1991a). By tradition, twin *ahayu:da* were carved each year by leaders of the Deer and Bear Clans in ceremonies which take place at the Winter Solstice, and also to mark the occasion of the initiation of a new Bow Priest. The *ahayu:da* are placed in open shrines on the land surrounding Zuni Pueblo from where they are believed to protect the Zuni people, and to provide stability and harmony in the natural world. They are left in the shrines where they are allowed to decompose naturally in the elements and it was from these shrines that many *ahayu:da* were stolen in past decades (Ladd, 1991a).

Non-Indian looters, finding these shrines, would sell the *ahayu:da* to private collectors and museums, and it is in this way that most of those in museum collections were initially removed from Zuni land. It is equally certain that some were sold by members of the tribe in need of money. However, according to tribal law, sacred objects such as the *ahayu:da* are communally owned by the tribe; therefore no individual had the authority to sell or otherwise dispose of *ahayu:da*. Consequently, in the view of the Zuni people, any *ahayu:da* removed from the shrine was considered to have been stolen, making illegal any past sales or gifts of such objects (Ferguson, 1979; Ferguson and Eriacho, 1990; Ladd, 1991a).

With regard to Australian Aboriginal material John Stanton has acknowledged that

> in the past few Aboriginal groups had the opportunity to refuse the collection of particular objects, etc. While this was not always a one-sided relationship, it mostly was. This inequality made it unnecessary for many early collectors (and some more recent ones too) to concern themselves with ethical issues.
>
> (Stanton, 1982, cited in Fourmile, 1990a: 58)

However, Chris Anderson, an anthropologist and director of the South Australian Museum, challenges the view that Australian Aboriginal peoples were passive victims of colonial encounters who were, as a consequence, stripped of their material culture by anthropologists and other collectors. He sees Aboriginal repatriation efforts as part of an expression of inter-cultural relationships based upon traditional exchange systems in which requests for the return of sacred objects are a method of 'calling in social debts'; in other words, a form of social currency (Anderson, 1990b). In an article entitled 'The economics of sacred art', Anderson explains his belief that the conflict over ownership of museum collections of Aboriginal material culture arises from an inherent misunderstanding by museums of the nature of giving and ownership in Aboriginal culture, in which transactions are not a one way movement of property, but part of an economic system in which property circulated and established rights and obligations (Anderson, 1990b).

Display, storage and care of sacred objects

Objects which traditional owners believe have a life force require particular care and handling. Ronald Grimes points out that within their cultures of origin they are 'either returned to the elements or kept alive with use' and has referred to such items as 'object-beings' (1990: 254). By this token, their transfer to the museum dooms them either to unnatural preservation or cultural neglect.

> When we whites control humidity, install glass to filter out the sun's rays because they fade colors, and encase objects in glass, we in effect deny both life and death to a sacred item. Perhaps we do with our fetishes what we do with our corpses: preserve them so we can ignore them.
>
> (Grimes, 1990: 254)

Increasingly, however, museum staff are recognising and showing sensitivity to indigenous views. In museums in New Zealand, awareness of Maori beliefs regarding their *taonga* has led to greater respect being shown by *Pakeha* (non-Maori) curatorial staff. Pieces of greenery, the foliage of trees, are placed in front of, or on, Maori *taonga* in museum displays, put there as offerings by Maori staff or, in their absence, by *Pakeha* staff. To the Maori, *taonga* are imbued by the artist with *ihi* and *wana* (power and authority), and also with *wehi* (fear) (Mead, 1985: 23). In some museums one might also find a bowl of water at the entrance to the gallery or the stores where Maori *taonga* are located, available for those who wish to use it to sprinkle water on themselves, after coming into close contact with the strong spiritual forces of the *taonga*.

When 174 pieces of Maori art were selected for *Te Maori: Maori Art from New Zealand Collections*, a major exhibition which toured the United States in 1986–8, it was the first time that most of the *taonga* had left New Zealand. For the Maori, for whom the *taonga* are the ancestors, it was a time of great concern for the well-being of the *taonga* but also an opportunity for American audiences to appreciate the power and beauty of the objects and gain some insight into Maori culture. Throughout the planning and touring of the exhibition, great concern was shown for the objects; concern which went far beyond the normal considerations of museums staff and extended to the spiritual well-being of the *taonga*. The exhibition processes were accompanied by ceremonies blessing the *taonga* and the exhibition opened at each venue with dawn ceremonies performed by Maori elders and *hakas* performed by a cultural group. Many of the non-Maori who were involved in handling the exhibition were deeply affected by their experiences, as has been recorded by Carol O'Biso, the American registrar who dealt with the documentation, packing and transportation of the exhibition and who accompanied the *taonga* throughout the duration of its overseas tour (O'Biso, 1987).

The Zuni Indians regard their *ahayu:da* with equal reverence, believing them to be living beings, and talk about the creation of the wooden *ahayu:da*, Masewi and Oyoyewi, as they would the physical development of a human (Blair, 1979a: 14). Through prayers and instructions by Zuni religious leaders, the war gods learn their role and duties before being placed in shrines where they can be visited by any Zuni wishing to give offerings and seek blessings (Ferguson and Eriacho, 1990: 7). The *ahayu:da* are believed to act as guardians to protect the Zuni from harm, and bring harmony, prosperity and essential rain to the world. Their removal from the Zuni Pueblo is believed to have caused many of the disasters and violent occurrences in the world, such as wars, fires, earth-

197

quakes, volcanoes and floods. War gods which are held in museum collections are beyond the control of the religious leaders and their destructive powers are unleashed. For the Zuni it is therefore imperative that the *ahayu:da* are returned to the shrines in order to ensure the future safety of the Zuni people and their world (Ferguson, 1979; Childs, 1980: 5–6; Ladd, 1991a).

According to cultural traditions, such objects require special care and are often subject to restrictions of access; but in its new cultural location, the object takes on new meaning. Removed from its culture of origin, the Zuni *ahayu:da*, for example, is no longer seen as an animate being or a spiritual power, but becomes a museum artefact, an example of Zuni artistry, an art object, something considered by the non-Zuni curator to be of value to all humanity and therefore worthy of preservation for future generations. While the *ahayu:da* could, until recently, be viewed in museum displays, the Zuni wanted nothing less than to see them returned to their rightful place on Zuni Pueblo land. Believing that 'the war gods had no business in any museum collection', Peter Welsh, Director of Research and Chief Curator at the Heard Museum, asks:

> if the *ahayu:da* is the possession of all humanity then do we care that it is back at Zuni? We shouldn't. We should feel that all humanity is benefiting from the *ahayu:da* being in its place; but somehow the statement that it benefits all humanity doesn't quite mean that it can be anywhere.
>
> (Welsh, 1993)

In the face of demands for repatriation, some curators argue that museums are providing proper care and storage for the preservation of artefacts which otherwise would not survive. Yet, while preservation is a part of the museum's function, it has to be accepted now that some objects which are repatriated may ultimately be destroyed, or returned to the elements, as are the *ahayu:da*, because that is their intended fate. The war gods are believed to protect the Zuni people and the world and are placed in open shrines on the land surrounding Zuni Pueblo where they are exposed to the elements. The *ahayu:da* in museum collections, if returned to the Zuni, will be placed in shrines to decompose naturally, as was intended. However, Edmund Ladd, a Zuni elder and curator of ethnology at the Museum of Indian Arts and Culture in Santa Fe, New Mexico, views the situation through the eyes of a museum curator as well as those of a Zuni elder and accepts that *ahayu:da* which remain in museum stores, despite careful storage and conservation treatment, will decay anyway over time, so fulfilling their intended fate, albeit more slowly than normal (Ladd, 1991b).

Another factor often quoted in opposition to repatriation is the alleged inability of indigenous peoples to preserve material culture in adequate conditions, and repatriation is often contingent upon repatriated material being returned to storage and/or display conditions that will ensure its safety and preservation in conditions comparable to those of a mainstream museum. Clearly this is an issue with regard to objects from poorer nations in which climatic conditions may pose a serious threat unless appropriate – and expensive – facilities are provided. This is a matter which has been debated by ICOM and UNESCO and clearly cases would have to be considered individually in this regard.

The requirement that suitable storage facilities are provided for repatriated materials has been a motivating factor in the establishment of some museums and community centres by indigenous peoples in North America. One of the most notable instances of this is the return of the Cranmer potlatch collection to the Kwakwaka'wakw (formerly referred to as Kwakiutl or Kwagiulth) people of the Northwest Coast. This resulted in the creation of the Kwagiulth Museum and Cultural Centre at Cape Mudge on Quadra Island, and U'mista Cultural Centre at Alert Bay on Cormorant Island, both off the east coast of Vancouver Island (see Chapter 6).

An increasing number of indigenous communities are seeking repatriation to appropriate facilities in order to regain control of their material culture and communicate their cultural heritage to the general public. Ray Gonyea, curator of the Eiteljorg Museum of American Indian and Western Art, in Indianapolis, and a member of the Onondaga nation, maintains that the growing number of American Indian museum professionals and tribal museums will ensure that Native Americans have the skills and facilities to preserve objects that are repatriated to native communities: 'We have our own museums and we know how to properly care for objects to preserve them according to accepted museum standards' (1993: 6). He has also asserted that, historically, tribal peoples were not incapable of preserving artefacts themselves: 'Our reverence, respect, and awareness of the spiritual power inherent in the objects will ensure that the objects survive – that is how the objects survived to be collected by museums in the first place' (ibid.: 7).

The wampum belts of the League of the Iroquois provide an excellent example of this. The wampum belts consist of strings of purple and white clamshell beads which provide a historical record of major events in the tribal histories of the members of the Iroquois confederacy and are considered to be the property of the Iroquois nations rather than any individual (Hill, 1977; Blair, 1979a; Childs, 1980; Sullivan, 1992). The wampum belts were made by members of the Onondaga tribe, one of the six allied tribes of the League of the Iroquois, some as early as the late sixteenth century. The Onondaga hold the position of wampum-keepers on behalf of all the tribes of the League of Iroquois. Some of the wampum repatriated in recent years from the New York State Museum were made in the late sixteenth century but survived intact, and in use, for over four hundred years prior to their transfer to museum collections in the late nineteenth century. Gonyea (1993: 7) cautions, however, that:

> the museum community must realize that sacred objects are of even greater value to Native Americans than they are to museum professionals . . . returned sacred objects will be used. That is how they fulfill their intended purpose in the Native American community to which they belong.

The wampum, once more in the care of the Onondaga, are now kept in a bank vault but withdrawn for use on ceremonial occasions: for almost 100 years prior to their return in 1989, the Iroquois had been forced to use ceramic and plastic replicas.

Ironically, while repatriation agreements may be dependent upon the provision of adequate storage and care for the return of artefacts, the storage facilities in many mainstream museums are often shamefully inadequate. Out of the public eye, the proper storage and conservation of the reserve collections is often woefully underfunded, resulting in storage facilities which pay little concession to basic conservation requirements and none at all to the cultural sensitivities and beliefs of the spiritual owners. Even in museums which do take good care of the physical well-being of artefacts in terms of providing a secure, climatically-controlled storage space, other aspects of an artefact's care may not be catered for due to the differences in perceptions of its meaning and status. Pat Lefthand, a Kootenai medicine man, is critical of some of the storage arrangements that he has seen in museums:

> I see a lot of things that are just sitting on tables, being tossed around, that to my people are sacred. The very people who are scientists haven't the foggiest idea what they are handling, and yet they won't go back to the tribes to find out what it is, how those things should be handled. And when the tribes ask for those things back, they say 'no, you don't have the proper facilities to take care of them.' This is how they are treating our sacred objects.
>
> (cited in Parker, 1990: 43)

When he took up his post as curator of Maori collections at the Museum of New Zealand, Arapata Hakiwai found that the storage of the Maori artefacts was overcrowded and, at times, inappropriate to Maori belief. He has been working to install facilities which enable Maori *taonga* to be stored in a more culturally appropriate manner. Houseboards, for example, were previously stored flat but are now placed in an upright position as befits the status and needs of the ancestors. Outside the stores, a bowl of water is available for staff and visitors to cleanse themselves after contact with the powerful forces of the *taonga*.

The power inherent is some sacred objects is believed to be so great that if they are mishandled or abused, it can cause harm to the community or to those handling them; such is the case with Maori *taonga*, Zuni *ahayu:da*, Navajo medicine bundles or *jish*, and many other types of sacred objects. In museum collections, such objects, removed from their proper cultural context and ceremonial care, are believed to present danger to staff handling them. Conscious of these beliefs, some museum personnel respect such warnings. David Finster, of the Robert H. Lowie Museum in Berkeley, California, took precautions when handling the Blackfoot Blue Thunder bundle in the Museum's collection:

> I made use of sweetgrass smoke and rubbing myself with sage before and after handling the bundle, and treated it with proper respect insofar as I knew how. I also used sweetgrass smoke . . . to purify it after it had been examined. I could not follow the rituals associated with unwrapping it, even had I known them in detail, as it was stored unwrapped.
>
> (Finster, 1975: 47)

Figure 8.1 Bowl of water for ritual washing, Rotorua Museum of Art and History *Te Whare Taonga a Te Arawa* in New Zealand. The bowl of water is placed outside the entrance to the Maori galleries to enable visitors to conduct ritual washing after their close contact with the powerful *taonga.*

Source: Photo by M. Simpson. With permission of Rotorua Museum of Art and History *Te Whare Taonga a Te Arawa*

When the Field Museum invited Hopi elders to visit the Museum in order to peruse the collections of Hopi material, the elders warned them that it was dangerous for pregnant women to work with kachinas. According to Jonathan Haas, vice president of collections and research, that advice is passed on to female staff members involved in working with the collection. In fact, at the time of the elders' visit, Haas' own wife, an anthropologist working actively with the collection, was pregnant and chose to heed the advice of the elders (Haas, 1991).

Zuni *ahayu:da*, as already discussed, are believed to have a life force and possess great power. The University of Pennsylvania Museum of Archaeology and Anthropology has had a Zuni *ahayu:da* in its collections since 1902. Rebecca Buck, the registrar, found the *ahayu:da* in her office upon taking up her new appointment. Never having encountered one before, she was unaware of what it was, but later read an article about the Zuni repatriation campaign in which the *ahayu:da* were illustrated. Realising with what she had been sharing her office, she carefully wrapped the war god up and laid it in a drawer in the stores. In November 1990, following repatriation negotiations, the *ahayu:da* was handed back to a Zuni delegation: Perry Tsadiasi, a Zuni Bow Priest, accompanied by Barton Martza, Head Councilman of the Zuni Tribe, and anthropologist T. J. Ferguson. They were horrified to discover that the war god had been wrapped and laid flat, for in this condition it was unable to breath: in their view, the curator's solicitous and thoughtful actions had placed her in great danger from the power of the *ahayu:da*. The Bow Priest felt that the war god must have looked favourably upon her and this accounted for her well-being despite the inappropriate storage position.

In Navajo tradition, medicine bundles should not be exhibited. In the hands of qualified men and women, they are believed to be powerful tools for healing, but expectant mothers are not allowed to handle or view medicine bundles as to do so can bring harm to unborn babies. For this reason, the medicine bundles in the Ned Hatathli Museum of Navajo Community College are not on exhibition and are not handled by students, only by the director, Harry Walters, and elders of the Centre for Dineh Studies (Walters, 1991).

While western societies encourage open display and the transmission of knowledge, it is quite common in traditional societies for sacred objects to have restrictions regarding who may see them and when. Likewise, the transmission of knowledge may be restricted to those with ownership or other recognised rights. To have sacred objects on open display in a public museum, or even on view in a store room, is therefore a gross infringement of the traditional, religious ordinances, reflecting a total disregard for the religious beliefs of the traditional owners. Pete Jemison, a Seneca, has remarked that

> The concept in the white world is that 'everyone's culture is everyone else's.' That's not really our concept. Our concept is there were certain things given to us that we have to take care of and that you are either part of it or you are not a part of it.
>
> (cited in Parker, 1990: 37)

In the Field Museum in Chicago, False Face masks have been removed from the display *Ritual activities of the Iroquois*, while show-cases, which used to house Hopi sacred masks and re-creations of ceremonial shrines, have also been removed. In both instances this has been at the request of tribal elders who felt that it was improper for ceremonial and sacred objects to be on public display. A sign informs visitors of the reasons for the removal of the displays and also explains that the museum has a policy of inviting the elders to examine the collections and assist with the development of new exhibitions which will be 'more accurate and more sensitive to the cultures they portray'.

In other instances, objections to displays have been made because of the likelihood that the restricted materials will be seen by certain groups such as women, children, or other uninitiated people to whom they are forbidden. In such cases, the location of the museum in relation to an object's culture of origin may be an important factor. The Museum of New Mexico is located in Santa Fe, New Mexico, in close proximity to the Rio Grande pueblos and so must be particularly sensitive and responsive to such restrictions on access amongst the Pueblo peoples, restrictions which vary between the Pueblo groups. The Santa Domingo and the San Felipe Pueblos do not allow women to look at the kachinas. A Shalako kachina figure, in the Museum of International Folk Art, was removed from display because all parts of it were fully visible to uninitiated children visiting from the nearby pueblos (Ladd, 1991a). Peter Welsh, Chief Curator of the Heard Museum in Phoenix emphasises that 'the Heard Museum should not become an agent of premature initiation for any of the numerous Hopi children who visit the museum' (Welsh, 1992: 860). To ensure this, the information provided to visitors is very carefully selected to ensure that it respects the sensitive nature of certain types of material; for example, 'disembodied parts of kachinas – such as masks' are not displayed.

Even reproductions or illustrations of sacred objects can be problematic: at the Indian Pueblo Cultural Center in Albuquerque, a mural of a Shalako was obliterated after complaints from some of the people from the Rio Grande pueblos who objected to the public display of an illustration of a religious ceremony (Ladd, 1991a). When the Museum of New Mexico was visited by a party of Zuni tribal councillors and religious leaders to examine the collection and advise upon the sensitivity of certain items and their curatorial requirements, a number of items were declared sensitive and selected for repatriation. These included replica masks which had been made by non-Zunis using cardboard and painted feathers. Asked why they had requested the repatriation of replica materials, Governor Robert E. Lewis, in a written reply on behalf of the religious council, stated that the power and information in the objects should not be revealed to uninitiated people and their display in a museum would cause confusion and concern to young Zuni people. Despite being replicas, it was their belief that:

> they were made by people with access to prayers and that they were therefore real in many ways that you may not recognize. What you consider a replica is a more fundamental reality to us and a spiritual concern. . . . Information

is power and the replicas embody power or information that belong to the Zuni people which should not be revealed to uninitiated people.

(Cited in Becker, 1991: 8)

Responding to such beliefs, many museums are now adopting the practice of creating separate storage areas for sacred objects so that access can be restricted to those who are initiated or otherwise permitted to view the material. In the USA, the Museum of New Mexico and the Buffalo Bill Historical Museum at Cody, in Wyoming, have successfully created separate storage areas. The Field Museum in Chicago had proposed to create a separate storage area for sacred objects but found their plans were opposed by Native American advisers who were concerned about the concentration of power which would result from all the sacred materials being stored together. They also objected to the proposal to separate sacred material from other material of the same culture, and the possibility of contact with sacred objects from other cultural groups. On the basis of these comments the proposals were abandoned.

In Australia, similar initiatives have been developed to cater for the cultural requirements concerning Aboriginal secret/sacred material. Most major Australian museums now hold secret/sacred material in a separate storage area, with access restricted to specified curatorial staff and to those members of the relevant Aboriginal community who have the right to view such material. In the Australian Museum in Sydney, all the secret/sacred objects have been removed from the main storage areas and placed in a separate secret/sacred store, where they are arranged according to community, and men's and women's materials kept apart from each other. The material is hidden from view in cabinets or on covered shelves so that if a person authorised to view material from their community enters the store, they do not accidentally see objects from another community. This does present some difficulties when categorising material that is not fully documented. If a curator suspects that material is secret/sacred, but the records do not provide details of associations and rights, the artefact or its photograph cannot simply be shown to an elder for identification and advice, for Aboriginal beliefs concerning secrecy are so strong that inappropriate viewing of secret/sacred material can result in illness or even death (Taylor, 1993).

Ownership of sacred objects

In New Zealand, museums have custodianship of Maori *taonga*, but the Maori retain spiritual ownership. In Australia, the Aboriginal and Torres Strait Islander Heritage (Interim Protection) Act of 1984 (amended by the Aboriginal and Torres Strait Islander Heritage (Interim Protection) Amendment Act of 1986), acknowledges 'the need to accord appropriate status to Aboriginal and Torres Strait Islander elders and communities in their role of protecting the continuity of the culture and heritage of the Aboriginal and Torres Strait Islander people.' The Council of Australian Museum Associations (now Museums Australia) commented in their 1993 policy document that, while legally acquired material is in the ownership of museums, underlying the principles of the CAMA policy document is 'the recognition of the inherent interests of

Aboriginal and Torres Strait Islander peoples in the care and control, spiritual and practical, of their cultural property' (1993b: 1).

Furthermore, it is CAMA policy that 'custodianship of secret/sacred material is vested in those people – the traditional custodians or their descendants – who have rights in and responsibilities for it under Aboriginal and Torres Strait Islander customary law' and 'secret/sacred material may be retained by a museum as custodian if requested by the traditional custodians' (ibid.: 13). Consequently one of the principles articulated in the document is that 'Aboriginal and Torres Strait Islander involvement in management of collections and information, and their use in the public programs and communication of museums, including exhibitions, education and publications, is essential' (ibid.: 9).

Consultation with communities as to the custodial arrangements for collections has led to the development of agreements between museums and communities in which the museums recognise the ownership rights of the Aboriginal or Torres Strait Islander community, but at the request or agreement of the community, retain custody and care of collections. Alternatively, artefacts may be returned to the custody of the community to be preserved in a community Keeping Place. The Aboriginal and Torres Strait Islander Commission (ATSIC) and the Australian Aboriginal Affairs Council (AAAC) have made a commitment to support efforts to establish and maintain Keeping Places and museums to fulfil this role and enable communities to develop display facilities if they so wish.

Federal legislation in the United States has resulted in significant changes in the ownership and status of certain categories of Native American material. After years of lobbying, the United States Congress passed the Native American Graves Protection and Repatriation Act (NAGPRA) in November 1990 (US Govt., 1990). This bill gives protection to Indian burial sites and required all federally funded museums to prepare inventories of Native American and Hawaiian human remains and associated funerary objects, which were to be completed by 16 November 1995. In addition, they were to prepare written summaries of unassociated funerary objects, sacred objects and objects of cultural patrimony, to be completed by 16 November 1993. This process was to be undertaken with consultation between the museums, federal agencies and appropriate Native American groups. Museums are required to make this information available to Native American or Hawaiian tribes or organisations, and to provide access 'to records, catalogues, relevant studies or other pertinent data for the limited purposes of determining the geographic origin, cultural affiliation, and basic facts surrounding acquisition and accession of Native American objects subject to this section' (US Govt. 1990). Where cultural affiliation is proven or satisfactorily indicated, human remains and artefacts, covered by the definitions of the act and with the appropriate ownership rights proven, are then to be returned to lineal descendants or to affiliated tribes, if requested to do so.

While the Smithsonian Institution was not bound by the NAGPRA legislation, the National Museum of the American Indian Act (1989) had previously established similar principles regarding the inventory, identification and return of Indian human remains and funerary objects in the Smithsonian Institution's holdings. The policy of the new National Museum of the American Indian (NMAI) now exceeds the legal requirements stipulated by NAGPRA, stating that

> All Native American materials that have been duly identified for repatriation, including human remains, funerary materials, ceremonial and religious materials, and communally owned property, together with all culturally specific information, must be treated as the sole property of the affected Native American culturally affiliated group and with the utmost respect by scholars and interpreters of those cultures, whether in collections research, scientific study, exhibitions, publications, or educational programs.
>
> (NMAI, 1992: 1)

Furthermore, it recognises that certain categories of material, being communally owned, 'could not have been legally alienated, transferred, or conveyed by any individual Native American, [therefore] the Museum's claim to it is invalid, and such items will be repatriated upon request' (NMAI, 1992: 12).

In contrast, there appear to be no government policies or guidelines in Britain with regard to repatriation which is, according to the Department of National Heritage, 'entirely a matter for the institutions in whose collections the items are held, since they are independent of Government and are free to decide what to do with their own property' (O'Mara, 1993). It is significant that the ownership of contested material is seen here to be entirely that of the museum; the question of ownership rights of indigenous peoples is not addressed (see epilogue).

The ownership debate applies not just to artefacts but also to knowledge, and issues of intellectual copyright are increasingly affecting practices in museums and being applied to ethnographic material and associated information. In Australia, the Council of Australian Museum Associations emphasised in its policy document that Aboriginal and Torres Strait Islander peoples have 'primary rights' with regard to their cultural heritage. 'They own their intangible cultural property, the meaning of the items expressed through the design, the dance, the song, the stories' (CAMA, 1993b: 1). The Aboriginal and Torres Strait Islander Commission (ATSIC) is seeking to develop policies which also recognise ownership rights in intellectual property: 'the knowledge, stories, histories, performances, traditions, designs and rituals associated with cultural objects', arguing that this would 'recognise the multi-dimensional aspects of objects, not merely as physical things, devoid of context or content, but as manifestations of living, dynamic cultures'. They recognise, however, that such policies would have 'huge implications for anthropological, archaeological and historical research – that is, records such as archives, manuscripts, diaries, notebooks, photographs and similar materials' (ATSIC, 1993a: 11).

Similar issues are being addressed in Canada. Where interpretation would involve the transmission of traditional Indian stories with ownership rights held by individuals or groups, some museums no longer interpret certain objects or else restrict the interpretation. Previously, such stories would have been used on interpretive labels, in storytelling sessions, in teachers' packs and other forms of public output, but museums now recognise that they do not have an automatic right to use such material. Such examples demonstrate the level of understanding required to curate materials in an appropriate and sensitive manner.

The matter of property rights has become a major issue for indigenous peoples and, in June 1993, the Nine Tribes of Mataatua in the Bay of Plenty region of Aotearoa New Zealand convened the *First International Conference on the Cultural and Intellectual Property Rights of Indigenous Peoples*. The conference examined issues associated with indigenous knowledge and cultural resource management in areas such as arts and crafts and biodiversity, and resulted in the production of the Mataatua Declaration on Cultural and Intellectual Property Right of Indigenous Peoples and the establishment of the International Mataatua Declaration Association (IMDA) to promote implementation of the Declaration (O'Keefe, 1995: 382–7).

Sacred objects and religious freedom

Many native people argue that the retention of sacred objects in museum collections is a violation of tribal peoples' customs and an infringement of their rights to freedom of religious practice. During its consideration of a bill to establish a National Museum of the American Indian, the US Select Committee on Indian Affairs heard testimony from many individuals and organisations representing museum and tribal interests. In reference to the collections of the Museum of the American Indian, Heye Foundation, which were to be transferred to the new National Museum of the American Indian, Oren R. Lyons (1987: 1), Faithkeeper of the Onondaga Nation, Fire Keepers of the Haudenosaunee (Six Nations Iroquois Confederacy) claimed that 'the possession and display of the [Haudenosaunee] Medicine Masks violates the Human Rights of our people, and the group rights of those Medicine Societies and the people that they serve'. He also argued that the retention of wampum belts was 'a violation of the human rights of the Council of Chief of the Haudenosaunee'. In their campaign to have the wampum belts returned to the custody of the tribe, the Onondaga argued that the belts were required for religious purposes.

One of the complexities in debates concerning the repatriation of sacred objects is the difficulty of defining 'sacred'. When the Zunis took legal action to gain the return of the *ahayu:da* in the collection of the Denver Art Museum, they used a definition of sacred objects which emphasised the continuity of religious practice and the communal nature of the ownership of such items.

> For American Indians, Eskimos, Aleuts and Native Hawaiians, native sacred objects are those objects which were created for a specific ritual or spiritual purpose, that are currently a vital part of an ongoing religion and have continuing religious significance or are of important significance in the practice of a native religious rite. Such objects would be communally owned, made for the spiritual use and benefit of a community or tribe as a whole.
>
> (Davies, 1979: 136)

In the United States, despite the First Amendment of the Constitution which established religious freedom as a fundamental right of all Americans, Native Americans have suffered religious suppression ever since the first Europeans began to colonise the American continent. Initially, this was the result of attempts to acculturate and Christianise the Indian population, and assimilate them into Anglo-American culture. In recent decades many repressive actions have been the result of ignorance, commercialism and bureaucratic intransigence. Native Americans have had access to sacred sites denied them, sometimes bringing them into conflict with government agencies or private landowners over access and use of the sites. Religious dances and other ritual gatherings have been banned, and ritual activities or sweats forbidden to those residing in institutions such as prisons and schools. The movement of sacred plants and animals across state borders has been prohibited and criminal charges brought against those transporting or using peyote, a hallucinogenic narcotic; hunting out of season; or killing protected species in order to obtain sacred materials such as eagle feathers (NARF, 1979). Indian remains have been disinterred and these, and sacred objects required for religious ceremonies, have been held and displayed in museum collections.

The need to address these issues led to the passage of the American Indian Religious Freedom Act (AIRFA) through Congress in 1978, a law designed to enable Indians to practice their religion freely.

> Henceforth it shall be the policy of the United States to protect and preserve for American Indians their inherent right of freedom to believe, express, and exercise the traditional religions of the American Indian, Eskimo, Aleut, and Native Hawaiians, including but not limited to access to sites, use and possession of sacred objects, and the freedom to worship through ceremonials and traditional rites.
>
> (US Govt., 1978a)

The 1979 Archaeological Resources Protection Act (ARPA) was intended to provide further protection of Indian cultural heritage by legislating against looting and unauthorised excavation of archaeological sites, burial sites and so forth, yet it reinforced the concept of federal ownership of burial sites and their contents (Moore, 1994: 204–6).

Following the passage of the American Indian Religious Freedom Act through Congress in 1978, a task force was established to report to Congress the results of evaluation conducted in consultation with Native American traditional religious leaders to identify the necessary administrative and legislative changes to protect and preserve the religious rights of native communities across North America. Their report was submitted to Congress in August 1979 and their recommendations were followed up by a survey, initiated by the Institute of Museum Services (IMS-DHEW), which funds private museums and institutions.

The task force report identified several problems in relation to museums including the display of human remains, inappropriate possession and display of sacred objects, the possession of stolen sacred material, and demands for repatriation. The report also stated that 'most sacred objects were stolen from their original native owners. In other cases, religious property was converted and sold by Native people who did not have ownership or title to the sacred object' (NARF, 1979: 20, cited in Echo-Hawk, 1985: 77).

The report made several recommendations with regard to administrative procedures in federally funded museums when dealing with Native American, Aleut, Inuit, or Native Hawaiian sacred material. Firstly they stated that, when offered sacred material of current religious significance for purchase or donation, the museums should refuse to acquire the objects and should inform the tribal and religious leaders of the object's presence on the market. Secondly, the report recommended that museums should return sacred objects required for current religious practice, which were removed from the tribe at a time when they were in use for religious purposes and were removed in a fashion contrary to the 'standards of disposition then prevailing in that community'. It was also recommended that museums should liaise with religious leaders over the storage, handling, conservation, display and labelling of sacred objects, and should enable religious leaders to perform periodic ritual treatment (NARF, 1979; cited in Echo-Hawk, 1985: 81).

The survey, conducted by members of the Native American Rights Fund, examined the legality of claims to artefacts, methods of resolution of conflicting claims, and attempted to ascertain the quantity of material in American museums which might be claimed by Native American religious leaders. The definition of sacred objects used by the task force had similar emphases to that used by the Zuni:

> 1. Sacred objects which serve a continuing religious function, for example, objects whose presence serves as a guard or protection for land; 2. Sacred objects whose proper disposition according to tribal customary law was disturbed, for example, sun dance offerings, which are properly supposed to be allowed to disintegrate; 3. Sacred objects which were illegally 'converted' under tribal customary law, for example, some pipe bundles are not to be transferred outside of the family, group or tribe.
>
> (NARF, 1979: 19–21)

The results of the survey suggested that only a small percentage of museum holdings would fall into this category and so might potentially be claimed by tribal religious leaders.

While the American Indian Religious Freedom Act should have been a landmark in US legislation concerning Native American heritage, it was not effective in bringing about major changes in museological practices and has frequently been referred to as 'the law with no teeth' (Vecsey, 1991). Further legislation relating specifically to museums was required and in 1990 Congress passed the Native American Graves Protection and Repatriation Act (NAGPRA) which may open the way for major changes in the future. In other countries new developments have also been occurring, though without the pressures of government legislation.

Access to sacred objects

The AIRFA report recommended that museums should liaise with religious leaders over the storage, handling, conservation, display and labelling of Indian, Eskimo (Inuit), Aleut and Hawaiian sacred objects, and should enable religious leaders to perform periodic ritual treatment (NARF, 1979: 23). Such practices had been introduced in a number of museums, even before the passage of the American Indian Religious Freedom Act, but developments were limited to a small number of museums and depended upon the enlightened thinking of individual curators and directors.

During the 1970s and 1980s, as awareness grew of the need to address the needs of different cultural groups, various strategies were introduced. Such developments were not confined to museums in North America, but were being implemented also in Australia where Aboriginal activists were drawing attention to indigenous concerns regarding religious practices and objects. Participants of the UNESCO regional seminar *Preserving Indigenous Cultures: A New Role for Museums*, held in Adelaide, Australia in 1978, recognised that cultural leaders should have ownership and control of sacred material, and should have active involvement in decisions concerning their preservation, conservation, and location. They also recommended that, in situations where cultural traditions are no longer practised, museums should enable traditional leaders to have access to cultural material in the collections so that it could be used for education and the development of group identity. They emphasised that museums should assist in this process while noting that 'the teaching of traditional law and the sacred aspects which relate to it should always remain the responsibility of practising traditional elders' (Edwards and Stewart, 1980: 13). Recognising the continuing significance of religious artefacts and the need for certain categories of artefacts to be cared for ritually, even when in a museum collection, museum staff in some museums in Australia and North America have been making their collections more accessible to communities or groups who wish to view them, draw upon them as a resource, or gain access to items of cultural significance for the performance of ceremonies.

In certain Native American cultures, the spiritual care of sacred objects requires periodic offerings of materials such as cornmeal, tobacco or cedar. As a result of discussions with members of the Hopi tribe, the Heard Museum in Phoenix, Arizona, always has cornmeal available. Initiated Hopi people periodically pay unscheduled visits to the kachinas in the Museum and may wish to leave cornmeal as an offering for the kachinas, a practice which could have implications for the conservation of the collections. As a result, the Museum now makes available to Hopi visitors cornmeal which has not been fumigated, but has been frozen to remove any active insect infestation. As part of its endeavours to be proactive in addressing issues relating to potentially sensitive items, the Field Museum in Chicago invited Hopi elders to examine the Museum's collections of Hopi material. The elders visited the Southwestern Hall scattering cornmeal offerings throughout, and also asked if they could 'feed' the kachinas in the gallery and in the reserve collections. Although the location of the Hopi material on the mezzanine floor of the stores presented the museum staff with something of a problem, they consented to the wishes of the elders and covered the items beneath to ensure that the collections were not liberally sprinkled with cornmeal. At the request of the elders, they also removed the kachinas from the display cases and placed them on the floor facing west so that they could be fed. Kachinas in the reserve collections were removed from the plastic bags in which they were being stored because, according to the elders, they could not breathe inside the bags.

Museums are also endeavouring to make religious artefacts available for use in ceremonies outside the museum. In Maori communities in New Zealand, death is marked by a *tangihanga* or death ritual. During three days of mourning ceremonies relatives, friends, and other mourners will visit the meeting house to pay their respects to the deceased. Photographs of close relatives are displayed around the coffin and, during the *tangihanga* of an important person, greenstone artefacts and treasured traditional weapons, such as clubs or *patu*, are also placed around the deceased (Mead, 1985: 98). According to tradition, these items would have been passed down within a family as heirlooms, but many such artefacts are now to be found in museum collections. Some museums hold such heirlooms in safe-keeping on behalf of the family (Horwood, 1995). Upon the death of a descendant, museums may lend the significant artefacts to the family so that they can be placed beside the body of the deceased while the funeral ceremony takes place, then removed prior to burial and returned to the museum.

Similar arrangements are not uncommon in North American museums. Glenbow Museum in Calgary has a policy which enables religious objects to be lent to communities who require them for the continuation of traditional ceremonial practices. A sacred medicine pipe bundle has been returned on loan to the Blood Nation who have invited museum staff to attend and participate in ceremonies in order to achieve fuller understanding of Blood culture. The Museum has also returned on loan a rattle to Black Bear Chief and Council in Saskatchewan 'to assist in cultural renewal' (AFN and CMA, 1992: 17).

On several occasions, the Provincial Museum of Alberta has lent a *natoas* bundle to the Blackfoot community for use in Sundance ceremonies (McCormack, 1991). The *natoas* is a very important type of Blackfoot bundle which is used in Sundance ceremonies (Wissler, 1911; 1918). It is made from a variety of materials including a sacred headdress, a bag of badger skin for the sacred headdress, a digging stick, a rawhide case, a shawl, and other items (Wissler, 1911: 209–10). Blackfoot religious ceremonies had declined during the 1930s and 1940s and the last Sundance on the Peigan reserve was held in 1949. By selling their bundles to the Provincial Museum, many ceremonial owners believed that the powerful bundles would be safeguarded. The Museum's *natoas* bundle was purchased from its ceremonial owner, Joe Crowshoe of the Peigan band, in 1969. Joe Crowshoe sold the bundle to the Museum but retained ceremonial ownership with its associated rights to sing songs and perform ceremonies.

211

During the 1970s and 1980s, there was a resurgence of interest in traditional cultural practices and, in 1977, the Museum agreed to lend the bundle to the Crowshoes for use in a Sundance ceremony. The bundle was borrowed again on several occasions in the following years for use in Sundance ceremonies which took place on various Blackfoot reserves and it became evident that a more permanent solution was required (McCormack, 1991).

While the Museum staff were unwilling to return the bundle permanently to its ceremonial owners, they encouraged the Crowshoes to reconstitute it. As much of the knowledge of how to make a bundle had been lost, the original bundle in the collection of the museum had to be studied closely. The production of the new bundle involved the manufacture of certain items by the Crowshoes while other items were lent by the Museum, and each item was subjected to ceremonial treatment. The Provincial Museum contracted the Crowshoes' son to document the process of making the new bundle and to make a record of the accompanying ceremonies and rituals and, after completion in 1987, the reconstituted bundle was used in a successful Sundance ceremony. The original bundle was borrowed once more, in 1990, so that ceremonies could be conducted which would invest the reconstituted bundle with spiritual power (ibid.: 1991). Patricia McCormack, the curator of ethnology during this time, has noted that the reconstitution of bundles was not a new concept but one which had been documented in the past. She viewed the process of bundle reconstitution as a way in which the museum and the community could co-operate, and the Museum's collections be used to assist in the process of cultural and ceremonial revival amongst the Blackfoot (ibid.: 4–5). However, there are those who would prefer to have the original bundle returned, as they believe that the spiritual power of a bundle cannot be transferred through reconstitution (Berry, 1995).

In recent years, Navajo medicine bundles, or *jish*, have also been returned by some museums for use in ceremonials. The collections of the Wheelwright Museum of the American Indian (formerly the Museum of Navajo Ceremonial Art) in Santa Fe include a large number of ceremonial objects given by Hosteen Klah, a Navajo medicine man, to Mary Cabot Wheelwright in 1937. Mary Wheelwright, a Bostonian aristocrat who became fascinated with Navajo philosophy and culture, persuaded Klah to share his knowledge of Navajo ceremonial practices with her. Klah himself was anxious to ensure that his ceremonial equipment and knowledge were preserved for future use and study, and so, over a fifteen-year period during the 1920s and 1930s, Klah and Wheelwright worked together to collect accounts of Navajo ceremonies and document the associated myths, songs, sandpaintings and ritual paraphernalia. Wheelwright also collected Navajo basketry, jewellery and textiles and later recorded a large number of Navajo song-texts. In the 1930s she built a museum to house the important collection of Navajo religious material which she had accumulated and Klah, who was closely involved with the founding of the Museum, also left his collection of ritual paraphernalia to the Museum (McGreevy, 1987a,b).

In 1977, the Wheelwright Museum transferred eleven sacred medicine bundles to the Ned Hatathli Cultural Center at Navajo Community College in Tsaile,

Arizona (Blair, 1979a: 18; NARF, 1979: 21; Childs, 1980; Frisbie, 1987: 341–3). Some of the materials had deteriorated to such an extent that they could no longer be used for ceremonial purposes and they were disposed of ceremonially by medicine men. The remaining eight bundles were found to require material and ceremonial restoration, a process taking several years. These are now lent, under the supervision of the Ned Hatathli Museum and the College's Navajo Indian Studies Department, to members of the Navajo Medicine Men's Association who will make use of them in traditional ceremonies. The medicine bundles are on loan for ceremonies during the practitioner's life and can then be loaned to their apprentice, if there is one, or to another suitably qualified person, but are to be returned to the museum if there is no other suitable person (Frisbie, 1987: 341–3).

According to Harry Walters, director of the Ned Hatathli Museum, the proposals to lend the *jish* have been criticised by individual evaluators of the Institute of Museum Services. However, Walters responds to such criticisms by pointing out that 'We are a Navajo museum and we serve the Navajo public. . . . Medicine bundles are living things. Because of this we do not keep them locked up; they need to breathe. In early spring when the vegetation starts growing, they are opened. Then a blessing is done in the fall at the harvest. When they are used in ceremonies, they are restored and regenerated (Walters, 1991).

In Sydney, Australia, the Australian Museum allows appropriate individuals into the secret/sacred stores in order to perform ceremonies and also lends ceremonial items back to Aboriginal communities when they are required for ceremonial purposes. Paul Tacon, the Scientific Officer in the Division of Anthropology, feels that this arrangement is important as it serves a dual function: the utilisation of the object in the ceremony strengthens the object and helps to maintain its power, while its use in a particular ceremony is necessary to strengthen the power knowledge of the initiates. The Museum's policy also allows for other types of objects to be lent to the community if, for example, they are required for display in a community-based exhibition or project. Sometimes the community has an adequate budget to cover the costs of accompanied transportation but, if the community-based project is operating under a very limited grant, the museum may assist by absorbing the costs into their own budgets through the use of outside grants or commercialisation funds (Tacon, 1993).

An interesting example of the sensitive handling of sacred materials is also provided by a recent project at the Cambridge University Museum of Archaeology and Anthropology (CUMAA) in England. In 1993, CUMAA funded the collection of Tamu shamanistic material by Yarjung Kromchhain Tamu (Gurung), a practising Pachyu shaman from Nepal. The collection of 50 items that he gathered for the Museum included costumes and ritual objects, some of which had been used by Yarjung and other shamans in healing and mortuary rituals (Herle, 1993: 24). Normal classification, freezing and storage procedures were forsaken, in favour of methods which the shaman and the staff felt were more appropriate to the sacred nature of the objects. All the items were stored together as a collection in a wooden box which was subjected to cleansing and purification rituals by the shaman. Differences in concepts of ownership also played a part in the procedures: Yarjung was concerned that at some future date, a crisis in Nepal could conceivably require the return of some of the most powerful ritual objects and he was anxious to ensure that they would be available to the Tamumai community if needed. In order to accommodate this concern, the Museum staff relaxed their normally strict accessioning procedures and made special arrangements for five of the objects to be placed on deposit, rather than being formally accessioned into the collections (ibid.).

Such initiatives demonstrate a few of the methods being employed in museums to handle sensitive items, and to seek resolution of the conflict that arises from the dual role that is required of religious artefacts held in museum collections. Some groups are satisfied with such developments, content that sacred objects are being stored appropriately, that they are accessible when required, and that the correct procedures are being carried out to ensure their physical preservation and also their spiritual well-being and nutritional sustenance. However, for many, such moves are not enough: they want nothing less than the return of the objects.

9

The repatriation debate
An international issue

'Repatriation has now turned from a conference argument to a federal law. Now, the word repatriation means much more than a legal obligation or a cultural right. Instead it has become an act of human decency.'

(Richard Hill (Tuscarora) in Sackler, Sullivan and Hill, 1992)

Human remains and sacred objects continue to be displayed and stored in museums all over the world and are the subject of on-going repatriation campaigns particularly by Australian Aboriginal, Native American, and African groups; but museums also receive repatriation requests from nations in Europe, Asia, and other parts of the world. In Australia, Michael Mansell, a lawyer with the Aboriginal Legal Service, and Bob Weatherall, of the Foundation for Aboriginal and Torres Strait Islander Research Action (FAIRA), have lobbied museums and visited several overseas in efforts to obtain the repatriation of Aboriginal remains. Native American groups are becoming much more effective in their campaigns. Organisations such as the Native American Rights Fund, the American Indian Movement, and the American Indians Against Desecration, represent tribal groups, liaise with museums, and lobby Congress. They are asking for their cultural treasures and the bones of their ancestors to be accorded the respect and appropriate treatment that one would expect for sacred objects and human remains in one's own society.

This shared concern led to the First International Conference on the Cultural and Intellectual Property Rights of Indigenous Peoples, which was held at Whakatane, New Zealand, in June 1993. The discussions, involving indigenous peoples from many nations, led to the Mataatua Declaration which was passed by the conference delegates. The Declaration included a series of recommendations to states, nations and international agencies concerning human remains and cultural objects held in the collections of museums and other institutions. The recommendations called for all human remains and burial objects of indigenous peoples to be returned to their traditional areas; inventories of any remaining indigenous cultural material to be provided to the traditional owners; and such material to be offered back to the traditional owners (Te Aku Graham, 1995: 33).

Amongst anthropologists, archaeologists, and others who are professionally involved in working with indigenous cultural material and human remains, the views of indigenous peoples have not passed unheard. The Vermillion Accord

(Day, 1989) and the World Archaeological Congress (WAC) First Code of Ethics (WAC, 1990) provide examples of international professional policy guidelines which have influenced other professional and governmental agencies in formulating their own policies and guidelines. The Vermillion Accord was drafted by Professor Michael Day, Chairman of the World Archaeological Congress, and presented at the First Intercongress on Archaeological Ethics and the Treatment of the Dead in Vermillion, South Dakota, USA, in 1989. It acknowledges 'the legitimate concerns of communities for the proper disposition of their ancestors, as well as the legitimate concerns of science and education'. It received the full support of all the anthropologists and indigenous peoples represented at the Intercongress, and was followed by the WAC First Code of Ethics (1990) which states that 'the people related biologically, culturally or spiritually are equals with scholars in the research enterprise'. Policies adopted in the USA, Canada and Australia embody these principles, and the experiences of some museums, which now commonly conduct research in collaboration with indigenous communities, demonstrate the value of such initiatives (Anderson, 1990a,c; Roth, 1991; Ames, 1993; Tacon, 1993).

Repatriation of sacred objects

The last fifteen years have seen the successful conclusion of a number of significant cases of repatriation of cultural material. During the 1970s, the Buffalo and Erie County Historical Society in New York State established a six-member Iroquois advisory team to work with the Museum staff in the planning of exhibitions, and the organisation and presentation of education programmes, in order to address concerns over misrepresentation and inappropriate display materials. They have also worked together to negotiate the repatriation of human remains and sacred objects. The Haudenosaunee, the Six Nations Iroquois Confederacy, submitted formal requests for the return of skeletal remains of their ancestors which were on display in the collections of the Museum. The bones were removed from display and returned to the Tonawanda reservation for reburial. A collection of carved wooden ceremonial masks was also removed from display and the Museum established a programme of lending the masks for short periods of time so that they could once again be used by Haudenosaunee religious leaders. In March 1975, the Buffalo and Erie County Historical Society returned several thousand wampum beads to the Chief's Council at a meeting at the Onondaga Longhouse near Syracuse under a loan agreement which is renewed annually.

A number of museums hold wampum belts of the Iroquois Confederacy in their collections and efforts by the Iroquois to obtain some of these have, in recent years, been successful. Probably the most renowned case concerned the wampum belts held in the collection of New York State Museum. As described in Chapter 8, the Onondaga transferred custody of a number of wampum belts to the New York State Board of Regents in 1898 in the belief that the Board of Regents would be able to assist them in a lawsuit to reclaim four wampum belts which had been sold without tribal authorisation. The Board of Regents believed that the League of the Iroquois was breaking up and that the belts would, as a result, be taken out of the state. They were anxious to ensure that the valuable collection remained in New York State and appointed a representative who persuaded the Onondaga to elect the New York State Board of Regents as wampum-keepers with the authority to take possession of, and care for, all wampums of the Onondaga and Five Nations (Blair, 1979a: 18). In the court case, John Thatcher, Mayor of Albany, who had purchased the belts from the original collector, succeeded in maintaining possession of the belts, which his wife inherited upon his death and in 1927 she donated four of the belts to the State Museum (Hill, 1977: 46; Sullivan, 1992: 10).

The Onondaga initiated a repatriation campaign to have the wampum belts returned to the chiefs living on the Onondaga reservation near Syracuse who claimed their use for religious purposes; a campaign which was to continue for several decades. In 1971, the New York legislature passed an act to return five wampum belts upon two conditions: facsimiles were to be produced and paid for by the Museum, and the Indians were to ensure that the wampum belts were preserved in a sealed, fireproof display case inside an 'approved' facility (Blair, 1979a: 15; Childs, 1980, 13–14). In effect, this required the construction of a tribal museum which the Iroquois were unable to provide (Hill, 1977, 45–46).

The American Anthropological Association's Committee on Anthropological Research in Museums (CARM) expressed concern about the proposed return of the wampum belts on the grounds of the historical importance of the collection. They argued that the Onondaga could not properly claim to require the wampum for religious purposes, as the leader of 'the new religion', the prophet Handsome Lake, was a Seneca and the Seneca chiefs were the principal custodians of the new religion. They pointed out that the collection was worth in the region of quarter of a million dollars and urged that:

> state property should not be legislated away lightly in the illusion of religiosity or as capital in the civil rights movement to an unidentified portion of the aboriginal inhabitants who may not fairly represent the 10,000 descendants of the Iroquois Confederacy now living in New York, or an equal number in Canada.
>
> (Sturtevant *et al.*, 1970)

They also expressed a fear that the return of such cultural treasures might set a precedent 'that would logically require returning Ibo carvings to Nigeria, Asmat art to New Guinea, and the works of Florentine painters to Italy' (ibid.).

The arguments put forward by the five anthropologists succeeded in convincing the Board of Regents that they had legal title to the belts and the negotiations broke down. However, the Onondaga renewed their efforts in the 1980s and were more sympathetically received by members of the Board of Regents and the staff of the New York State Museum. Martin Sullivan, upon taking up the post of director in 1983, was 'startled to find that with the position went the title of *Ho-sen-na-ge-tah*, or wampum-keeper, and that a document dating from 1908 conferred that title in perpetuity on the director of the State Museum and his successors!' (Sullivan, 1992: 10). In the continuing repatriation negotiations, Sullivan was principal negotiator for the State Board of Regents and his recommended course of action was to seek resolution of the issue by concentrating on the future care and use of the wampum belts rather than continuing the discussion over their acquisition which was complicated by conflicting evidence.

Negotiations continued with Chief Irving Powless, the principal negotiator on behalf of the Onondaga, and Ray Gonyea, also of the Onondaga nation, who worked at the Museum as a specialist in Native American culture and a liaison between the Museum and the native peoples of New York State. Late in 1988, agreement was reached for the belts to be returned to the custody of an Onondaga wampum-keeper. The agreement called for the preservation of the belts in their current form using appropriate storage and conservation methods. Once returned they would remain in Onondaga custody forever, but would continue to be accessible for research purposes by qualified scholars. In October 1989, the belts were returned to the Onondaga with a formal ceremony in Albany to mark the signing of the agreement and, a week later, the Onondaga held a day of feasting and celebration to mark the return of the wampum to the reservation. Although several efforts have been made by the Onondaga to establish a tribal museum, they have been unsuccessful and the wampum belts remain in storage in a bank vault in Syracuse, but are regularly removed for educational or ceremonial purposes (Sullivan, 1992: 11–12; Welsh, 1992: 854–5).

A year earlier, in May 1988, the Museum of the American-Indian Heye Foundation, in New York City, returned eleven wampum belts to the Six Nations Iroquois Confederacy of Canada. They were placed in secure storage at the Indian-operated Woodland Cultural Centre in Brantford, Ontario, and were made available to confederacy chiefs on ceremonial occasions (Gonyea, 1993: 7; Tivy, 1993: 28). Since these successful returns, further requests have been made by Iroquois communities and, in October 1995, the Board of Trustees of the National Museum of the American Indian agreed to the return of wampum from their collections to the communities of the Iroquois Confederacy. Other wampum have also been returned from Canadian museums, including a particularly significant example: 'the "circle" wampum that established the authority of the fifty Grand Council chiefs' (Gonyea, 1993: 6).

Another notable repatriation case concerned the return of the Sacred Pole of the Omahas (Roth, 1991; Welsh, 1992). In the late nineteenth century, the pole and other religious items had been given into the care of the Peabody Museum of Archaeology and Ethnology at Harvard University, by the keeper of the pole, Yellow Smoke, who feared that younger members of the tribe would fail to care for them adequately. The Omahas requested the return of the pole in 1988 and, finding records which confirmed that the pole had in fact only been lent to them, the Peabody Museum agreed to return it and other items to the tribe for inclusion in their own museum (Welsh, 1992: 855).

One of the most persistent and successful repatriation campaigns has been that waged by the people of Zuni Pueblo in New Mexico, in their efforts to secure the return of their missing *ahayu:da* or war gods (Ferguson, 1979; Ladd, 1991a; Martza, 1991). In the late 1970s, a Zuni War Chief found an old tin can containing documents dating back to the late nineteenth century (Martza, 1991: 12). From inquiries into the contents of the papers, information came to light which suggested that Arthur G. Clark, the United States Government Surveyor, who had been carrying out survey work at Zuni Pueblo between 1899 and 1901, had removed some war gods from a shrine, and these were now held in the collections of Denver Art Museum (Childs, 1980: 5). The Zuni religious leaders and the tribal council decided to try to regain possession of the war gods and, in 1978, they initiated their repatriation campaign with legal representation by the Native American Rights Fund, and aided by T.J. Ferguson, the tribal archaeologist and director of the Zuni museum archaeology project (Ferguson, 1979).

The negotiations over the return of the *ahayu:da* in Denver Art Museum continued for several months until, in March 1979, the Museum presented the *ahayu:da* to the Pueblo of Zuni. The press release issued at that time stated that

> The board of trustees has been advised by qualified anthropologists and its own staff that in the Zuni religion, as stated by the Zuni leaders, it is true that the war god is a deity and a present, animate object of worship rather than a symbol or art object.
>
> (cited in Chamberlin, 1983: 232)

This was of great significance to museums generally, as it was the first time in museum history that such a distinction had been made. It is also significant that the statement issued by the Museum did not make clear whether the Museum was returning a stolen artefact or making a donation of an item of which it had legal ownership (Childs, 1980: 5–6, 15–16).

In order to identify holdings of *ahayu:da*, the Zuni contacted museums and art galleries throughout North America and requested of each institution that the *ahayu:da* be returned to the Zuni people. Arguing the illegality of *any* sale or other acquisition of the communally-owned *ahayu:da*, and supported by the legislation of the American Indian Religious Freedom Act (1978), the Zuni have met with great success in obtaining *ahayu:da* from museum collections in North America.

In October 1978, an auction in New York was stopped by Federal officials who seized a war god which the Zuni, supported by the Native American Rights Fund, claimed was a religious object communally owned by the Pueblo of Zuni. They succeeded in gaining the support of the US attorneys in New Mexico and New York City citing 18 USC 1163, which states that it is a criminal offence to steal or possess stolen property belonging to an Indian tribal organization. The *ahayu:da* was confiscated by federal officials while the collector who had sent the *ahayu:da* to auction was contacted. An agreement was reached between the tribe and the collector who relinquished his interest in the war god and the *ahayu:da* was returned to the Pueblo of Zuni (Ferguson, 1979: Chamberlin, 1983: 230–2).

In 1988, a similar situation occurred when the Andy Warhol art collection was put up for auction. An *ahayu:da* in the collection was removed from sale and returned to the Zuni people. By 1991, the Zuni Tribe had successfully negotiated for the return of 65 war gods, only having to resort to court action once to obtain the *ahayu:da* from Denver Art Museum. All the *ahayu:da* known to be in museum collections in the United States have been returned to the Zuni and, having achieved such success, they are now beginning negotiations for *ahayu:da* held in museums in Europe and other parts of the world (Ferguson, 1991: 13; Dishta, 1991).

The repatriated *ahayu:da* are back on the Pueblo where they will once more bring harmony and peace to the world. However, although the publicity surrounding the Zuni repatriation campaign has resulted in some individuals and museums informing the Zuni of *ahayu:da* in their possession and offering to return them, it has also resulted in an increase in their scarcity value amongst unscrupulous collectors. Between July and December 1990, two more *ahayu:da* were stolen from the reservation. The *ahayu:da* are now placed in a special reinforced shrine with barbed wire to protect them, a sad reflection of the need for continuing protection against the ever-present threat of theft.

Commenting upon the return of the Zuni war god from Denver Art Museum, Russell Chamberlin's concerns are of the possibility of more far-reaching developments:

> Uneasily one wonders what might be the effect upon the art collections of the world if a Christian were to obtain a similar ruling regarding the prevalence of Christian icons, the Cross in particular, on public but secular display.
>
> (Chamberlin, 1983: 232)

However, Chamberlin's example is fallacious as it fails to take account of the fundamental differences between these two examples. The Christian cross is not only intended for public display but, as a potent symbol of Christianity, has been central to the efforts of the Protestant and Catholic churches to convert to Christianity members of other cultures and faiths throughout the world. On the other hand, the Zuni *ahayu:da* was produced for tribal, ceremonial purposes and was never designed to be seen by outsiders. As Ronald Grimes has stated: 'There is very little in Christianity to contradict the North American ethic of display; free and unrestricted access is of high value. Many native traditions, however, regard the most sacred activities as private: to publicize is to profane' (Grimes, 1990: 256).

Lost heritage

One of the difficulties the Zuni faced initially was identifying collections in which *ahayu:da* were held, and this is a continuing problem for them as they seek *ahayu:da* in museums outside the United States. The same difficulties face other indigenous peoples seeking the locations of holdings of cultural material; indeed, there is very great need for databases or inventories of ethnographic materials to be available for *any* researchers, whether they be anthropologists, museum curators, indigenous communities or interested individuals. A number of inventories have been published; these include: *Polynesian and Micronesian Artefacts in Australia: An Inventory of Major Public Collections*, by Lissant Bolton and Jim Specht under contract to UNESCO (1985); *The National Inventory of Aboriginal Artefacts*, compiled by Betty Meehan and Joan Bonnam and funded by the Council of Australian Museum Directors (1986); Carol Cooper's *Aboriginal and Torres Strait Islander Collections in Overseas Museums* (1989); and the Foreign Ethnographic Collections Research Programme established by the National Museums of Scotland and the Scottish Museums Council, resulting in a document entitled *A Wider World: Collections of Foreign Ethnography in Scotland*, edited by Liz Kwasnik (1994). Clearly, the growing sophistication and widespread use of computer technology, CD-ROMs, the internet and other image and information storage, retrieval and transfer systems, will greatly develop the access to data on an international scale.

As indigenous peoples become more actively involved in research, the compilation and publication of inventories and catalogues of ethnographic collections will prove vitally important. These, and other information sources, will assist in the identification of locations of relevant collections, so enabling indigenous peoples to trace and research their cultural heritage and identify the locations of skeletal remains of their ancestors. However, these publications are produced as general research materials and, while they are available through libraries, they are not directed specifically at the indigenous peoples whose material culture they document. It is therefore unlikely that they would be accessible to, or known of, by anyone other than a serious researcher. Of much greater importance, therefore, are efforts to inform the communities of materials which relate specifically to their culture.

Anthropologists in the Australian Museum in Sydney have developed close working relationships with a number of Aboriginal communities, undertaking community consultation as a natural feature of their work. As a result, they found Aboriginal elders to be satisfied with the current level of care that the objects receive, and happy to see the objects remain in the museum, although some have expressed the desire to see them returned to the community if and when they establish their own Keeping Place. Paul Tacon, a Scientific Officer in the Division of Anthropology, has visited a number of Aboriginal communities in Central and Northern Australia and shown them photographs of the museum, members of staff, the offices, display areas and the main ethnographic stores. He described to them the secret/sacred storage area, the methods used by staff to handle and store the secret/sacred material and explained the restrictions imposed upon access and arrangements made for viewing by authorised individuals. Although some secret/sacred objects have been repatriated, for the most part, they remain in the collections of the Museum with the consent of the Aboriginal communities.

The South Australian Museum in Adelaide has been using photographs in a similar way since 1985 as part of its Custodianship of Sacred Objects Project, designed to apprise Aboriginal peoples about the Museum's collection of restricted material, such as *tjurunga* and sacred boards, and obtain their views concerning the ways in which the Museum might deal with the material, including discussion of the storage arrangements and the possibility of repatriation. The South Australian Museum has also adopted a proactive approach with regard to the repatriation of both sacred objects and human remains. The Custodianship of Sacred Objects Project involved the reorganisation of the storage facilities to create a separate Restricted Collection storage area; the computerisation of all data in the collection; the production of photographs of every item in the Restricted Collection. Groups of senior Aboriginal men have visited the Museum on a number of occasions to view the storage facilities and discuss the restricted material. Chris Anderson, then the curator of anthropology, who has run the project with the assistance of other staff in the Division of Anthropology, undertook a series of field trips to Aboriginal communities in South Australia and the Northern Territory, including Yuendumu, Walungurru, Papunya, Ernabella, Marree, and Oodnadatta using these photographic records to initiate discussions concerning the custodianship of the collections. This consultative process has resulted in approximately 130 secret-sacred objects being returned to the custodianship of these communities (Anderson, 1991b). In 1992, the Museum extended this work to include the human remains collection, employing a curator of physical anthropology to survey and inventory the collection, and initiate consultations with Aboriginal communities with a view to repatriation in appropriate circumstances.

In the USA, prior to the passage of the Native American Graves Protection and Repatriation Act (NAGPRA) in November 1990, the co-operation of museums depended entirely upon the policies of individual museums and the attitudes of individual members of staff. Now staff in all federally funded museums are having to undertake the work stipulated by the Act. While NAGPRA affects federally funded museums and other government agencies, it does not affect private collectors, auction houses, and so on. In May 1991, Sotheby's in New York offered for sale by auction 293 lots of American Indian material at their semi-annual auction of Fine American Indian Art. Amongst these were three sacred masks: one Navajo mask and two Hopi kachina masks – a dance mask worn by the chief kachina, Ahola, and a second worn by the mud head clown kachina, Koyemsi. The masks are used in religious ceremonies and are believed to be the living manifestations of sacred ancestral spirits. Prior to the auction, the Dineh Spiritual and Cultural Society and the Hopi Tribal Council wrote to Sotheby's requesting that the sacred masks be withdrawn from sale, the former stating that 'any sale of sacred paraphernalia of Native Americans is highly disrespectful and a major assault in the destruction of Native American religion' (cited in *Art-Talk*, 1991). Furthermore, the two Hopi masks are believed by Hopi officials to have been amongst 50 or 60 sacred objects stolen from the tribe in 1978.

Despite the letters of protest, Sotheby's proceeded to auction them. The three masks were purchased for US$39,050 by Elizabeth Sackler, who is the daughter of the late Arthur M. Sackler, who accumulated massive private collections of Asian and Middle Eastern art; and the president of the Sackler Foundation, which organises exhibitions of her late father's art collection. She is not herself a collector but had heard about the sale and the objections of the Navajo and Hopi. She was appalled at the prospect of the masks being sold and attended the auction with the sole purpose of purchasing the masks and returning them to the Navajo and Hopi tribes, their rightful owners. She hoped that the gesture she had made would highlight the insensitivity and offensiveness of selling Native American religious artefacts and encourage others to return sacred material, commenting that, 'It is important for museums, the art world, and for collectors to make a distinction between those objects that are sacred (to a living culture) and those that are not' (cited in Brinkley-Rogers, 1991; Wallach, 1991). 'Period examples of Native American ritual objects should not be for trade, purchase or collection' (Sackler, cited in AP, 1991).

Following the auction, she received tremendous support for her actions from native and non-native people. As a result she established AIRORF, the American Indian Ritual Object Repatriation Foundation, in 1991, to assist in the process of seeking and organising repatriation of sacred objects from collections, private or public, to the Indian nations (Sackler, Sullivan and Hill, 1992: 58–61). The foundation provides information about NAGPRA, assists Native people with research into holdings of sacred material in private and public collections, advises and negotiates with Native American tribes and non-native peoples – collectors, foundations, dealers, museums, individuals and corporations – concerning the repatriation, display or publication of native material, and acts as a conduit for the return of religious objects to the tribes. The foundation will provide assistance to museums wishing to identify individuals who can assist them with the authentication of material or escort sacred objects home when repatriation has been agreed. They may also assist in the financing of travel costs for individuals who need to visit museums to participate in the repatriation process. AIRORF is a non-profit organisation; therefore, under US law, those who return sacred objects through AIRORF are eligible for tax relief on such donations. The foundation will also act as a network resource for human remains and grave goods. In addition, the foundation has a commitment to educating people about the importance of ritual objects to the native peoples and does this through lectures, classroom presentations, publications, and the sale of a video 'Life Spirit' (Moore, 1993).

Museum policies and practices

United Kingdom

Museums in the United Kingdom have become the focus of particular criticism concerning their responses to repatriation requests (Bromilow, 1993: 34). Museum authorities and the British government are perceived to be intransigent, obstructive and imperialistic in the matter of repatriation. Following efforts to discuss the repatriation of Aboriginal human remains from the collections of the British Museum, Michael Mansell claims that 'our view clear-ly conflicted with the views of the Natural History Museum in London, and probably the British Government (given their lack of interest)' (Mansell, 1993). Des Griffin, Director of the Australian Museum in Sydney, who has been active in developing the policy of the Council of Australian Museum Associations (CAMA), is highly critical of the repatriation record of museums in Britain:

> I find the attitudes of some of them, particularly the Museum of Mankind, to be unsustainable in 1993. It simply is not good enough that museums in colonising countries – colonial powers – can continue to carry on with attitudes that 'this stuff is there, it is being looked after, it would have been destroyed if they hadn't taken it, but now it is accessible to everybody and therefore it won't be returned.' That is utterly and completely unsustain-able.
>
> (Griffin, 1993)

A survey conducted in 1993–4 suggests, however, that such a reputation is not entirely justified (Simpson, 1994b). Thirty-four museums and other collecting institutions (such as university medical schools and the Royal College of Sur-geons), were asked to complete a questionnaire designed to elicit information about their policies and practices with regard to both display and repatriation of human remains and sacred objects. Six institutions failed to respond while five replied that they preferred not to participate in the survey. Of these, two said that they were precluded by legislation from disposing of any material; two felt that the issue was too important to be addressed via a simple survey; and one noted simply that ' "sacred objects" is such an ill-defined category'. Of the twenty-three respondents, all had human remains in their collections and eighteen indicated that there are human remains on display in the galleries. These are largely in the collections of Egyptology and archaeology.

Although nineteen indicated that they had human remains in the ethnographic collections, it appears that none of them continues to display Native American, Aboriginal and Maori material of human origin. In contrast, many ethno-graphic displays do include objects derived from human tissue and bone that originate from other regions. Many of the objects in question were produced originally for display purposes; others are fabricated artefacts incorporating human remains. These include: a shrunken head from Amazonia, over-modelled skulls from Melanesia, Tibetan skull drums and other religious artefacts, and a carved Mayan leg bone. There is little evidence so far that the continued reten-tion or display of such objects is a matter of concern to the cultures of origin.

Asked if they had removed human remains from display, seventeen respondents confirmed that their museums had. Almost half indicated that this was the result of changes in the attitudes of staff members, one that this had led to a change in official museum policy, and four that it had been the direct result of external pressures. One had consciously omitted human remains from the dis-plays when the gallery was renovated, while another had omitted them purely on design grounds. Six curators also indicated that sacred objects had either been removed from display or excluded from new displays because it was felt to be inappropriate or insensitive to display them. Nine respondents indicated that human remains or sacred objects are given special care; in most cases, this is in the form of separate storage and restricted access. In Saffron Walden Museum, Maori heads are kept separate from other material and have been blessed by a Maori elder. In Bradford Art Galleries and Museums, community consultation preceded the inclusion of Islamic and Sikh sacred artefacts, and ceremonies were conducted when they were installed in exhibitions.

The survey results suggest that curatorial staff are responding to the general climate of change within the profession and the representations made by indigenous peoples. Respondents were asked for their views on the development of policies here and overseas. Several expressed the view that, although in agreement with the need to develop policies concerning the treatment of human remains, they were opposed to any form of blanket policy. A majority, nineteen, expressed support for the development in overseas countries of policies which allow for the repatriation of human remains and sacred objects under certain conditions. Seventeen respondents agreed that museums in Britain should develop similar types of policies. George Bankes (Manchester Museum) commented that 'museums have to relate to the people whose ancestors made the items held by those museums', while Alec Cole (Hancock Museum) believes that 'respect should always be given to the requirements and sensibilities of other cultures'. Pauline Beswick and Julien Parsons (Sheffield City Museum) indicated support for overseas policies 'especially where the material and populations are native to the countries in which the museums are sited' but are opposed to the development of such policies in Britain 'except in very rare cases where objects are well provenanced and their storage genuinely gives concern to a particular community. Otherwise it is wrong to give back large amounts of poorly provenanced material simply because of guilt.'

In most of the museums, the issues of repatriation have been discussed and various policies have been developed. Of the twenty-three museums represented by the respondents, nine have unwritten policies, four of which specifically do *not* relate to the repatriation of sacred objects. Seven have written policies, two of which include the display of sacred objects, and one which also included reference to their repatriation. Several specifically referred to guidelines concerning human remains produced by the Museum Ethnographers' Group and use these as the basis for their own policy development.

The survey results indicate that, contrary to the reputation of British museums abroad, many curators and their institutions are sympathetic to the issues of repatriation and human remains have indeed successfully been repatriated from British museums on a number of occasions in recent years (Simpson, 1994b: 31). However, with the exception of a collection of 304 Aboriginal items returned by Edinburgh University in 1991, most of the repatriation cases pertain to human remains, these being individual items or small groups of items which served no significant purpose in the museum collections in question. Such was the case with material returned by the Kelvingrove, Pitt Rivers, and Exeter Museums. Dr Schuyler Jones commented that five Aboriginal skulls, which were repatriated from Pitt Rivers Museum in 1990, 'were returned on the grounds that they were neither ethnographic nor archaeological and therefore had no place in our collections'.

Major difficulties have arisen when repatriation requests have been addressed to institutions holding larger, more significant research collections such as those held in the Museum of Natural History and the Royal College of Surgeons in London: these institutions have so far refused to hand over contested human remains. Robin Cocks (1993), Keeper of Palaeontology at the Museum of Natural History, did not complete the questionnaire, but in a letter explained that:

> the significance of our human remains collection for scientific research varies immensely and includes past and present disease patterns, the deformation of bones by variety of occupations, ageing patterns and differences and many other such studies. One of the chief reasons for retaining the collection is the unpredictability of future research needs.

If one extends this argument, then all skeletal collections should be retained for future research. However, recent excavations of European peoples often ensure that the research is carried out with speed and the remains are reburied upon completion, as was shown earlier in the examples of the Spitalfields project in London and the Roman site at Shepton Mallet in Somerset.

While recent Australian and US legislative changes now give the indigenous populations ownership rights over the remains of deceased ancestors, in British law there is no right of ownership over human remains. In the United Kingdom, the matter of repatriation has not received formal consideration from the Museums and Galleries Commissioners (MGC) but the Commission considers that 'it is important for museums to be able to respond positively and with sympathy to requests to consider the return of such material' (Longman, 1994). The MGC looks to the Museums Association and other professional bodies to evolve the ethical framework under which UK museums operate and recommends that museums refer to the guidelines produced by the Museum Ethnographers Group. MGC's own standards and policies embody the Museum Association's Code of Practice and use this as the basis for the disposal requirements of the MGC's Registration Scheme for Museums in the UK. Discussions in 1991 resulted in unanimous agreement amongst the MGC Registration Committee that 'restitution to a place or people of origin should be recognised as an acceptable method of disposal. In such cases the normal regulations governing the disposition of deaccessioned material would be waived' (Longman, 1993). Accordingly, the MGC recommends that requests for the repatriation of human remains should be resolved by 'a museum's governing body, acting on the advice of professional museum staff' and allows museums to dispose of human remains by repatriation without first offering them to other museums in the United Kingdom and without the requirement to inform the museum community at large.

As a result of past unsuccessful efforts, Mansell and Griffin are particularly critical of the inflexible responses of national museums in the UK. The trustees of the British Museum have the responsibility for fulfilling their obligations as laid down by the founders of the museum in 1753, enshrined in the:

> fundamental principles from which the Trustees do not think they can in Honor or Conscience depart. 1st. That the collection be preserved intire without the least diminution or separation. 2nd. That the same be kept for the use and benefit of the publick, who may have free access to view and peruse the same, at all stated and convenient seasons agreeably to the Will and intentions of the Testator, and under such restrictions as the Parliament shall think fit.
>
> (cited in Wilson, 1990: 126)

The British Museum and the National Museums of Scotland argue that they are bound by legislation and refer enquirers to the relevant government legislation: the British Museum Act 1963 and the National Heritage (Scotland) Act 1985. The National Museum of Ulster, however, has made available detailed information to Australian Aboriginal groups and other enquirers and returned the sole Maori tattooed head in its collection.

It is not acceptable for museums to disregard alternative cultural values and to claim that legislation prohibits them from deaccessioning material from the collections, thus continuing to follow practices and policies evolved over the past two centuries according to the cultural attitudes of the day and the ethics of a profession which was in its infancy. In recent years, the Conference of Directors of National Museums and Galleries has been examining the issue of repatriation and, apparently, in 1993 or 1994 produced a draft document concerning repatriation, amongst other issues. Indeed, Robin Cocks commented that the Natural History Museum 'subscribes to the policy on human remains agreed by the Conference of Directors of National Museums and Galleries' (Cocks, 1993). Hopeful that this document would demonstrate some flexibility in the light of the changing climate of opinion concerning the repatriation of human remains, I attempted to obtain a copy of the document so that I could include the views of this body in this discussion. My request was met with initial agreement but then refusal on the grounds that the document was unofficial and not for public release. Some institutions have also been less than forthcoming about allowing access to the documentation of their collections of human remains, even to bona fide researchers; such actions are surely contrary to the Code of Ethics of the Museums Association of Great Britain and the spirit of dissemination and education in which our museums are founded.

The repatriation of cultural material has also been requested from the British Museum. Several renowned cases have been outstanding for many years, including that of the Greeks' claim for the return of the Parthenon Marbles, the ongoing debate surrounding the question of Sri Lankan demands for the return of artefacts, and Nigeria's calls for the return of the Benin artefacts taken from Benin City by a British punitive force in 1897. However, the British Museum has returned some items in the past, including a number of Benin bronze plaques, and has also entered into discussions in a number of other cases concerning the lending or repatriation of artefacts. While a significant Benin ivory mask could not be loaned to Nigeria for Festac in 1977 because of the very fragile condition of the mask, in other instances the requesting nations did not proceed with their inquiries despite the expressed willingness of the British Museum to consider the requests (Wilson, 1981: 22).

The issue of the return of cultural property was the subject of a symposium entitled *Lost Heritage*, which was held in London in 1981 and organised by the Africa Centre and the Commonwealth Arts Association. During discussions, several issues were raised including the use of replicas made by artists in the country seeking repatriation and provided by them to replace the items repatriated from European museums, and also the possible loan of European art works to Third World nations. The British Museum, by virtue of the scale and importance of its collections, has probably been the target for most repatriation requests concerning cultural property in British museums. During the symposium, David Wilson, then the director of the British Museum, emphasised the role of the British Museum as a universal museum 'which was to show the whole of human achievement and the whole of human culture' and has the responsibility for holding in trust, treasures which had been legally acquired 'in the light of the period during which the material was acquired' (ibid: 17). However, he also stated that the British Museum would be able to lend items on long-term loan, and did not rule out the possibility of the British Museum returning an item if it were of 'enormous international religious significance' (ibid: 25).

With demands for repatriation increasing in the post-colonial era, the Museums Association of Great Britain has recently begun to investigate the subject of contested artefacts in museum collections with a view to identifying its role in advising and supporting its member institutions and their staff.

The United States of America

In the United States, significant reforms have been implemented by the Native American Graves Protection and Repatriation Act (NAGPRA) of 1990. NAGPRA places ownership and control of human remains with the Native American population and ultimately it will be they who make decisions concerning disposition and research. However, the Act does make provision for the continuation of research, stating that:

> if the lineal descendant, Indian tribe, or Native Hawaiian organization requests the return of culturally affiliated Native American cultural items, the federal agency or museum shall expeditiously return such items unless such items are indispensable for completion of a specific scientific study, the outcome of which would be of major benefit to the United States. Such items shall be returned no later than 90 days after the date upon which the scientific study is completed.
>
> (US Govt., 1990)

The pressure for a change in the US law has had a profound effect upon practices in many US museums, creating a climate of sympathy and willingness for change amongst many museum anthropologists. Some museums had been engaging in such negotiations for a number of years, even prior to the enactment of NAGPRA. In 1987, the Museum of New Mexico formed a Committee on Sensitive Materials. Following discussions with the Museum's Native American Advisory Committee and public meetings, it was decided that the museum would adopt a policy of contacting Native American tribes to inform them of sensitive materials in the collections and discuss repatriation.

Likewise, the Smithsonian Institution initiated a programme in the 1980s to document the skeletal remains of known individuals or those attributable to specific tribes. The remains of 45 individuals were clearly documented, having originated in the collection of the Army Medical Museum, and tribal officials were notified with a view to contacting descendants and repatriating the remains, if requested to do so. In 1985, the Smithsonian Institution contacted 225 federally recognised tribes, providing them with computer printouts detailing statistical data regarding the North American Indian skeletal collections and details of storage and access arrangements. Of these, only six replied seeking further information and one of those, the Blackfeet of Montana, pursued their request for repatriation, allowing medical research to be completed first (Adams, 1987a: 10–12).

NAGPRA did not include the Smithsonian Institution; it was dealt with separately in the passage of an earlier bill, the National Museum of the American Indian Act, Public Law 101–185, in 1989. This Act authorised the establishment of a new National Museum on the Mall in Washington DC to be devoted to the history and cultures of Native Americans, and instituted a process of identification of Native American human remains in the collections of the Smithsonian Institution (US Govt., 1989). Following this, the Smithsonian Institution established a programme of documentation of the human remains collections, notification to tribal groups, and repatriation of remains, if they had been requested and claim procedures had been satisfied. Staff of the Repatriation Office of the National Museum of Natural History, Smithsonian Institution, are working towards identifying:

> the remains of Native Americans that were collected from battlefields or grave sites by US Army surgeons and explorers of the frontier in the last century with the aim of returning them to 'the appropriate descendant tribes'. As part of this process, the identification and repatriation of the former US Army Medical Museum collection has been the first priority of the Repatriation Office.
>
> (Makseyn-Kelley, 1994)

In 1992 the skeletons of 29 Indians collected from battlefields in 1898 were returned to the Sisseton Dakota Sioux for reburial after the tribe had formally requested their return (Lichtenstein, G., 1992: 142).

With the passage of the Native American Graves Protection and Repatriation Act, all federally funded museums were given five years in which to compile inventories of skeletal remains and associated grave goods, and three years to compile summaries of unassociated grave goods, sacred objects and objects of cultural patrimony. As a result, museums are, with increasing frequency, agreeing to requests for the return of sacred objects and human remains, subject to the tribal claimants producing the necessary evidence to comply with the requirements of the legislation. Some museum curators and anthropologists in the United States are concerned that NAGPRA will open the way to thousands of claims and result in the decimation of the North American ethnographic and archaeological holdings. Staff in other parts of the world share similar fears concerning the possible formalisation and regulation of the repatriation process.

Looking at the issue in terms of statistical probability, it seems likely that a relatively small number of artefacts will be affected by the recent US legislation. Many of the items which formed parts of early collections are poorly documented and therefore individual, or even tribal, links may be impossible to prove. Furthermore, due to the specificity of the definitions used in the legislation, many artefacts will not fall into the appropriate categories. For example, 'sacred objects' refers to 'specific ceremonial objects which are needed by traditional Native American religious leaders for the practice of traditional Native American religions by their present day adherents'. 'Cultural patrimony' is defined as:

> an object having ongoing historical, traditional, or cultural importance central to the Native American group or culture itself, rather than property owned by an individual Native American, and which, therefore, cannot be alienated, appropriated, or conveyed by any individual regardless of whether or not the individual is a member of the Indian tribe or Native Hawaiian organisation and such object shall have been considered inalienable by such Native American group at the time the object was separated from such group.
>
> (US Govt., 1990: sec 2)

The Act legislates for the return of human remains and associated funerary objects when cultural affiliation is established, and for the repatriation of sacred objects and objects of cultural patrimony when requested by a known lineal descendant of the individual who owned the object, or where the item was owned by the tribe as a whole. Likewise, with regard to human remains, the number of individually identifiable human remains is quite small.

Initial estimates suggest that as little as 2 per cent of a museum's collections will be bound by NAGPRA (Sackler, 1993). Peter Welsh (1993) of the Heard Museum believes that a similar figure would apply to the relevant portions of the Heard Museum's collections and does not regret its potential loss: 'These things didn't belong here in the first place. . . . By being here they create a barrier between the institution and the community; the greater loss is the loss of connection with the community.' (See epilogue for update.)

Furthermore, the repatriation process can prove difficult for tribes who have no mechanism for dealing with sacred objects or human remains which may have a limited provenance and which have been desecrated. Even though a burial is identified as that of a Native American, tribal identification is often impossible to prove. As a result, some of the Indian groups prefer to have human remains stay in the museums, as their return would present problems; they might, for instance, be the remains of enemies killed in battle. Therefore to return the remains of an unidentified Indian to a tribe from which they did not come could result in the breaking of taboos and bring about misfortune (Dishta, 1991). The Zuni tribe, when contacted by the Museum of New Mexico with regard to a collection of Zuni human remains, requested that the museum continue to act as custodian of the remains as it was felt by the Zuni that they had lost their cultural identity (Ladd, 1991a). In other instances, tribes have agreed to act as 'hosts' and accept human remains for reburial even though the origins are not known.

However, the issue cannot simply be reduced to statistics and legalities. The issue of retention of human remains is so highly emotive and central to the very spiritual and cultural being of individuals and communities, that it is sometimes difficult to understand how museums can defend the continued holding of such material. Campaigning by indigenous peoples has ensured that the issue has become one of the most contentious and critical to face museum staff in recent years. While federally funded museums in the United States must now address the issues of repatriation as a matter of law, curators in other countries hope to avoid government legislation by developing professional guidelines and practices which adequately address the repatriation issue. In Canada and Australia, in particular, museums have been addressing the issue of human remains in a similar way, but without government legislation, and it is hoped that over the next few years the issue will be dealt with appropriately at a professional level without recourse to law. Indeed, the findings of the Australian Aboriginal and Torres Strait Islander Commission (ATSIC) suggest that museum policies and practices in Australia are generally more advanced than government legislation (ATSIC, 1993a: 13).

Canada

In Canada, museum staff are hopeful that progress can continue to be made without the need for government legislation, and that any developments should address issues not currently covered by legislation. A conference in 1988 entitled *Preserving Our Heritage: A Working Conference Between Museums and First Peoples*, arose out of the events surrounding *The Spirit Sings* exhibition and led to the establishment of a task force, jointly sponsored by the Assembly of First Nations and the Canadian Museums Association. Its mandate was to study access, involvement of Aboriginal peoples in the interpretation process, and the repatriation of human remains and cultural artefacts in consultation with First Peoples and various museum staff, university academics, archaeologists, and cultural, educational, political and governmental organisations. There followed two years of consultation between First Peoples and various individuals and organisations, including over 4,000 invitations for submissions which were sent out to cultural, educational, political and governmental organisations (AFN and CMA, 1992: 2).

The consultative process stimulated discussion of the experiences of individual museums which had been involved in repatriation negotiations during the 1980s or early 1990s, though little publicity had been given to these cases at the time. The task force report, published in 1992, made recommendations concerning strategies for developing partnerships between Native Peoples and museums: 'There is a strong consensus that partnerships should be guided by moral, ethical and professional principles and not limited to areas of rights and interests specified by law' (AFN and CMA, 1992: 4). Speaking at the CMA conference in 1991, Trudi Nicks, co-chair of the task force, commented that the process of dialogue highlighted 'how very important the cultural artefacts that are in museums are to First Peoples. They are sources of pride, self-esteem and continuity with traditional cultures and values' (Nicks, 1991). The recommendations of the task force have been positively received by many within the museum profession and have been substantially adopted by the Canadian federal government.

While acknowledging the wide diversity of cultures and situations throughout the country, the task force report made a number of recommendations, including increased access for First Peoples to collections, exhibitions, photographs, art works, research and archives, for the purposes of viewing, researching, reproduction, ceremonial purposes, as well as access to 'funding sources, policy development and implementation activities, . . . training and employment' (AFN and CMA, 1992: 5). Greater involvement of First Peoples in all aspects of the interpretation process, was recommended, with representation and interpretation conforming 'to an ethic of responsibility to the community represented, as well as to the scholarly or professional ethics of the academic and museum communities'. Also highlighted was the need for the training of non-Native museum staff in order to better understand the First Peoples' communities and develop appropriate professional approaches.

On the subject of repatriation, the report recommended situations in which repatriation should take place with re-interment according to traditional practices. It suggested that museums and First Nations groups should negotiate and agree upon the undertaking of scientific research for a mutually agreed period of time; and also stated that 'the retention of Aboriginal human remains for prolonged periods against the expressed wishes of First Peoples is not acceptable' (ibid: 9). The report recommends that museums enter into negotiations concerning the repatriation, handling and storage of sacred objects and objects of cultural patrimony, and suggests several possible courses of action, including the restitution of objects 'judged by current legal standards to have been acquired illegally' and consideration of restitution in regard to sacred and ceremonial objects of 'ongoing historical, traditional or cultural importance to an Aboriginal community or culture' (ibid: 9). The report also recommends that museums should lend sacred and ceremonial objects for specific occasions, giving consideration to both museum conservation and the perspectives of First Peoples.

Finally, the task force addressed the issue of implementation, calling for federal funding for a number of initiatives over the following five year period. These included assistance with: the funding of new and existing Aboriginal-run cultural centres and museums; the development of 'internship and affirmative action programs at existing museums with cultural patrimony or art collections; the preparation of inventories of ethnographic material in existing museum holdings and dissemination of that information to the appropriate First Peoples; and repatriation negotiations'. Further, they suggest that the principles and recommendations of the task force report form the basis of a set of national guidelines to be developed by the CMA and the AFN, and the establishment of a CMA documentation centre which would assist museums and First Peoples in the implementation of the recommendations.

One of the museums which had previously undertaken the repatriation process was Peterborough Centennial Museum and Archives in Ontario, Canada, which initiated the deaccession and repatriation of the skeletal remains of two individuals in 1983 (Doherty, 1992: 1–7). The remains consisted of the complete skeleton and associated grave goods of a male from the Point Peninsular culture known to have lived in the Trent River system approximately 2,000 years ago, and found under a parking lot in Peterborough in 1960. After excavation and study by staff of the Royal Ontario Museum, the skeleton and grave goods were passed to Peterborough Centennial Museum where they were exhibited in a replica burial display between 1966 and 1983. The other item was the skull of an adolescent female, one of four individuals whose remains were found in 1911 in Smith Township. After years of neglect, on display and in the stores of a small museum in Peterborough, the skull was all that remained of the four skeletons. When this museum closed in the 1950s, the collections were deaccessioned and returned to the original donors; the skull was then given to Peterborough Centennial Museum by the family of the donor.

In 1983, the curator responsible decided that it was no longer appropriate for the material to be displayed. The skeletal material was deteriorating and the display itself was no longer effective: younger children were so frightened by the burial display that it even had to be covered up when primary school children visited the museum. By 1988 staff of the museum had decided, with the agreement of the Board of Museum Management, that the remains should be deaccessioned and repatriated and so they approached the Ojibwa Curve Lake First Nations, the nearest band in the area.

After three years of discussion and negotiation, an agreement was finally drawn up between the band council and the Board of Museum Management. Initially the museum had intended to deaccession and repatriate only the human remains, but they came to recognise that the grave goods were such an integral part of the burial that they had to be included in the agreement. The agreement drawn up allowed the museum staff to document and photograph the process, with a copy to be given to the Curve Lake First Nation. They were also given permission by the Curve Lake Indians to remove small samples for carbon dating if they wished, although this was not deemed necessary, and were able to take casts of the grave goods so that they would be able to have exact replicas of the items for future interpretive use.

The band council arranged for both traditional and Christian ceremonies to be conducted. The remains were transferred to birch bark containers sealed with pine and spruce pitch, traditional sweet grass cleansing ceremonies were carried out at the museum and at Curve Lake, and the two burial ceremonies, Medewewin and Christian, were carried out at the grave-side:

> At the grave-side, an honour song was sung as the burial containers were lifted and placed into their final resting place. The pipe carriers spoke and each dropped tobacco into the grave. All who chose to were invited to drop tobacco into the grave as well. All shared fresh strawberries – which, as the first fruit, are a symbol of birth, – they were also shared with the grave. The traditional ceremony included a reading by a woman of the Medewewin, a song by a Medewewin pipe, a Christian offering, a Christian Hymn in Ojibwe, and concluded with a Christian prayer.
>
> (Doherty, 1992: 5)

The process of repatriation has had benefits for both the Museum and the Curve Lake First Nation. The events of that day have sparked a renewed interest in the cultural traditions of the Medewewin Society who have since been asked to participate in other funeral services. At the request of the donor, the Museum has since repatriated other items to the Curve Lake First Nation including a pipe and a lodge stick. Bill Ramp, Chairman of the Museum Board, has commented that:

> We, at the Museum, were profoundly touched by the generosity with which the people of Curve Lake responded to our overtures. For a very small and long overdue gesture of respect, we received a hand of friendship and gained a renewed appreciation for the vibrant and enduring culture and aspirations of the First Nations. To give a little is to receive a great deal. Perhaps if, as a society, we were to worry a little less about the possible consequences of such giving, we might find that respect and generosity have a way of perpetuating themselves.
>
> (cited in Doherty, 1992: 7)

There are many such examples which demonstrate clearly the positive benefits that emerge when museum staff respond with sensitivity to the views of native people, and the two groups work together in partnership.

Aotearoa New Zealand

Museums in Aotearoa New Zealand hold the most significant collections of Maori material in the world, yet many items of cultural significance are also held in public museums overseas and in private collections. For many years there was concern about the loss of Maori cultural material to purchasers overseas, but the passage of the Antiquities Act in 1975 was an effective aid in addressing the need to halt the export of important cultural material from New Zealand and to retrieve significant items for the benefit of the nation. However, it was also recognised that the existence of Maori cultural material in public collections overseas provided a valuable opportunity for peoples in other societies to appreciate and learn about Maori culture. A subcommittee established by the Council of AGMANZ recommended that financial priority should be given to the conservation and preservation of the material already held in New Zealand's museums, to the purchase of items previously in private collections, and to the acquisition of material from overseas only when of 'major historical significance to the nation as a whole' (Thomson, 1980: 173).

Although opinions vary amongst Maori people about whether or not artefacts in overseas collections should be repatriated, it seems that it is generally felt that the educational opportunities that the artefacts offer for visitors to develop an appreciation of Maori culture warrant their retention overseas. This view lay behind Maori support for *taonga* to be taken overseas in the *Te Maori* travelling exhibition; and the reception given to the exhibition in the United States justified this view. Maori pride in their artistic traditions, and the presence in New Zealand of such a wealth of material, mean that Maoris have not made as much effort as some other cultural groups to seek the repatriation of their cultural material from overseas institutions. However, there have been attempts to obtain the return of human remains (*koiwi tangata*).

The New Zealand government has not formally adopted a policy on the repatriation of Maori human remains from overseas collections, but the Museum of New Zealand *Te Papa Tongarewa* takes an active role in encouraging and facilitating repatriation, and acting as a national repository for Maori human remains. The 'Policy on Human Remains' of the Museum of New Zealand (MoNZ, nd,b) states that decisions to give access to human remains will be made by the National Museum Council in association with the appropriate *iwi* authority; likewise approval for limited destructive analysis to be undertaken by bona fide researchers must also be given.

The subject of Maori human remains came to international attention during the 1980s when tattooed Maori heads were put up for auction. In 1983, a head owned by the Marquis of Tavistock was withdrawn from Sotheby's sale, but the matter drew the attention of the world's press to the possession of Maori tattooed heads in private and museum collections. In 1988, another head was placed in auction with Bonham's and again drew great media attention and opposition from Maori leaders who described it as a 'degrading and deeply offensive desecration'. There was public outrage at the proposed sale; Bernard Levin questioned the morality of the sale of a human head and, as an analogy, referred to the hypothetical auctioning of lampshades made from the flayed skins of Jewish victims of the Nazi regime (Levin, 1988: 14). Following this, the Museum of New Zealand established 'a formally dedicated, sacred tomb' in the basement, which serves as a national repository for human remains. Robin Watt, who first conceived the idea of the tomb, envisaged that it should be 'recognised as a proper burial place for all human remains accepted by the National Museum into its care . . . and provided there were strict controls for access, the remains could be used for bona fide research' (Watt, 1990:98).

Negotiations over the repatriation of *koiwi tangata* were principally handled by the late Maui Pomare, former Chairman of the Museum Board, and he has informally involved the Ministry of Maori Development *Te Puni Kokiri* and the Ministry of Foreign Affairs and Trade *Manatu Aorere*. Cliff Whiting, Director Maori and Bicultural, in the Museum of New Zealand *Te Papa Tongarewa* states that 'the Maori Tribes of New Zealand want all Maori human remains to be returned and to be given back to the descendants for ceremonial burial. If it is not known where they are from they are deposited in our museum in a designated vault' (Whiting, 1994). At the Taonga Maori conference in 1990, Maori participants agreed that *toi moko* or tattooed heads should be returned while Maori *taonga* in overseas collections could be retained by the museums with the condition that Maori visitors would have access. At a conference of southern regional museums in 1993, *Te Runanganui o Tahu*, the *Ngai Tahu* tribal authority, publicised the tribe's policy on heritage issues and human remains (Gillies and O'Regan, 1993). The policy had been formulated by a committee, *Komiti Tuku Iho*, and it identified three goals with regard to *koiwi tangata* in museum collections. Authority and control over Maori human remains were to be 're-vested' to the tribe. The policy recognised that 'scholarly investigation of *koiwi tangata* can further an understanding of the lives of our *tupuna*' (ancestors) (cited in Gillies and O'Regan, 1993: 30) and allowed for the continuation of appropriate academic research – if it was conducted with sensitivity and accountability to the tribe. It also called for the formation of designated rooms *(wahi tapu)* in specified museums in the area, which would be used for the management and research of *koiwi tangata*.

The Scotland Museum and Art Gallery was the first to respond positively to the *Ngai Tahu whanui* policy. The museum has had Maori representatives on its Board of Trustees since 1916 and, in the late 1980s, following discussions with the Maori community, had initiated a policy which enabled Maori skeletal material which was no longer required to be deaccessioned and reburied (Gillies and O'Regan, 1993). The Museum's policy has also provided restricted storage for the remaining Maori skeletal material, and halted the acquisition of any further material to the reference collection. In 1993, the Museum revised its existing policy to take account of the recommendations of the *Ngai Tahu whanui* policy, stating that it agreed 'to place its research collection of Maori human remains under *Ngai Tahu* management and authority (*kaitiakitanga*) as specified in the Foundation Principles and Statement of Jurisdiction of their policy' (cited in Gillies and O'Regan, 1993: 31). Despite this, Dr Schuyler Jones, Director of the Pitt Rivers Museum in Oxford, England, states that he has taken every opportunity to discuss the matter with Maori visitors and found that they are overwhelmingly in support of the tattooed heads being removed from display but retained by the Museum (Jones, 1994).

Australia

In 1973, the Australia Council formed the Aboriginal Arts Board which was composed entirely of Aboriginal people and which received federal funding allocations. This is regarded as being a significant development in the revitalisation and strengthening of Aboriginal culture and, since its formation, the

Australia Council has provided support for many different artistic activities and for the development of Keeping Places and cultural centres (Edwards, 1980: 2). In 1978, Adelaide, Australia, played host to an international meeting, the UNESCO Regional Seminar, 'Preserving Indigenous Cultures: A new role for museums'. This was a significant meeting attended by people involved in the care and interpretation of the cultural heritage of the indigenous peoples throughout the Pacific region, and included many indigenous speakers. The published papers demonstrate the high level of awareness amongst participants of the need to address the issues of indigenous rights in heritage care and interpretation. Various recommendations were made for museum staff to develop new working practices and relationships with the communities whose cultural heritage they hold and interpret. A recommendation was also made for the introduction of legislation to prohibit the removal of sacred objects from their traditional owners (Edwards and Stewart, 1980: 16). The following year, the Conference of Museum Anthropologists was formed to maintain and extend the network of contacts that had been made during the seminar, and to encourage the exchange of ideas and information amongst anthropologists and curatorial staff from many different cultures.

During the 1970s and 1980s, the human remains issue was also being fiercely debated in Australia as Aboriginal Australian activists campaigned for their return for reburial. In 1982, the Australian Archaeological Association (AAA) lent its support to calls for the return to the Tasmanian Aboriginal community of the Crowther collection, held in the collections of the Tasmanian Museum and Art Gallery in Hobart, noting that 'ethical considerations of the manner in which the collection was obtained far outweigh any potential scientific value' (cited in Meehan, 1984). In 1983, the Council of Australian Museum Directors adopted policies which condemned the public display of human remains. Both they and the AAA made clear their support for the repatriation of the skeletal remains of known deceased, but argued for the retention of collections of pre-European material.

Amendments made to the Archaeological and Aboriginal Relics Preservation Act 1972 by the Victorian Government in May 1984 caused an escalation in the debate surrounding the subject of the research potential and possible repatriation of Aboriginal skeletal remains. The AAA formed a Committee on Aboriginal Skeletal Remains which prepared a statement outlining the AAA's position and the heritage and scientific importance of Aboriginal skeletal remains (Thorne *et al.*, 1984). The AAA also recommended that the Victorian Government instigate initiatives which would enable compromise to be reached between Aboriginal concerns about treatment of the dead and scientific concerns for research. They urged the Government to support the construction of Aboriginal Keeping Places for the storage and care of skeletal remains, the training of staff in the skills required for curation of skeletal remains, and consultation and joint research projects by researchers and Aboriginal peoples (Meehan, 1984: 126). The Victorian Aboriginal Legal Service organised an Aboriginal Skeletal Remains Conference in Melbourne to which they invited members of the AAA committee.

Federal legislation, in the form of the Aboriginal and Torres Strait Islander Heritage (Interim Protection) Act, 1984 (amended in 1986), was designed to ensure the preservation and protection of areas and objects in Australia and Australian waters which, according to Aboriginal tradition, are of particular significance to Aboriginal peoples. It required that discoveries of Aboriginal remains (except in Victoria) were to be reported to the Minister for Aboriginal and Torres Strait Islander Affairs so that the appropriate Aboriginal community could be consulted concerning disposition. It also provided for the safekeeping of significant Aboriginal objects which might be threatened by injury or desecration and enabled emergency declarations to be made to protect threatened sites or objects. Part 11a referred specifically to Victorian Aboriginal Cultural Heritage. Here it was stated that if 'no other arrangements can be made to ensure its proper continuing preservation and maintenance, . . . the Minister may . . . compulsorily acquire any Aboriginal cultural property . . . of such religious, historical or cultural significance that it is irreplaceable' and such material 'would be held on trust for the local Aboriginal community or the Aboriginals of Victoria' (Australian Federal Government, 1984: 19).

Many of the major museums in Australia have been responding to Aboriginal concerns for many years and addressing the issues of display, collaborative work, Aboriginal ownership and concepts of restricted knowledge. They are now researching the collections with a view to possible repatriation, and some have already returned substantial collections of human remains. The Australian Museum in Sydney has returned more than one third of the Aboriginal skeletal remains in its collections, primarily to communities in New South Wales and Queensland. A number of carved trees have been returned to the Gunnedah Aboriginal community and a large collection of archaeological material has been transferred temporarily to the Northern Territory Museum in Darwin to be stored there until the completion of a new museum and Keeping Place in Kakadu National Park, at which time some or all of the material will be returned for storage there close to the area from which it originated.

In 1985 the Museum of Victoria in Melbourne returned the remains of 38 unidentified Aboriginal individuals to the Aboriginal people. The remains were reburied with great ceremony at a site in Melbourne, and a plaque placed over the tomb on which were listed the names of the 38 Aboriginal tribes which originally inhabited the state of Victoria. On the plaque were the words 'Rise from this grave, release your anger and pain, as you soar with the winds, back to your homelands. There find peace with our spiritual mother the land, before drifting off into the "Dreamtime"' (Bromilow, 1993: 33).

One of the largest collections of Aboriginal remains was the Murray Black collection of more than 1,600 items excavated in the 1920s. George Murray Black gave his collection to the University of Melbourne in the 1940s. For years Aboriginal communities had been demanding the return of human remains and the Murray Black collection became the subject of a dispute between the University of Melbourne and Victoria Aboriginal Legal Services Co-operative Ltd (VALS). VALS failed to secure the return of the collection, but, following a

Supreme Court ruling, the collection was transferred to the Museum of Victoria. The state government sought changes to the Victorian Aboriginal Relics Act to enable the remains to be returned to the Murray River Aboriginal communities but was defeated in Parliament. However, new federal legislation, in the form of the Aboriginal and Torres Strait Islander Heritage Protection Amendment Act 1987, enabled the repatriation to proceed. Following consultation between the Department of Aboriginal Affairs and the Aboriginal communities, the Murray Black collections were returned to a number of Aboriginal communities in New South Wales and Victoria in 1989. They were then reburied in six locations; those whose place of origin was unknown were buried in two cemeteries designated specifically for unprovenanced remains (Bromilow, 1993: 31).

The reburial of skeletal material is a matter of great concern amongst opponents of repatriation. They argue that the repatriation and reburial of human remains, such as those in the 9–15,000 year old Kow Swamp collection, is an immeasurable loss to science for the study of mankind, and contend that the knowledge gained from research would be of particular benefit to the Aboriginal community (see Mulvaney, 1991; Fagan, 1991). They have also argued that most human remains in museum collections are too old to have any traceable relationship for today's claimants. Yet, native peoples today may perceive a 'spiritual tie, symbolic identification, or psychological relationship' with their unknown ancestors (Davidson, 1990: 7). Henry Cleere, an archaeological heritage consultant and editor of *The European Archaeologist*, 'wholeheartedly support(s) the growing pressure for repatriation' believing that 'the wholesale acquisition of Aboriginal and Native American skeletal material for museum collections or worse is morally indefensible, since these cultures survive in the present-day world'. He differentiates between these collections and those of 'prehistoric burials or Egyptian mummies, [as] the spiritual beliefs underlying the form of disposal of the dead are no longer active in this world' and acknowledges that their potential value for scientific research warrants their continued presence in research collections, though not on public display (Cleere, 1994).

The National Museum of Australia has a policy which differentiates between older and more recent skeletal material, and is actively undertaking the return of remains which are less than 200 years old. This is merely an interim policy which will be reappraised and extended to older material at a future date. In August 1990 ATSIC took the decision that: 'post-white settlement Aboriginal skeletal remains held by collecting institutions' should be returned and that their final disposal – reburial or continued storage under Aboriginal control – be the decision of the Aboriginal community in question. Older skeletal remains would be dealt with on a case-by-case basis taking account of both Aboriginal and scientific interests (AAAC, 1993). (See epilogue for update.)

Aboriginal and Torres Strait Islander skeletal remains are held in more than 180 collecting institutions in 26 countries outside Australia (Bromilow, 1993; Cooper, 1989). Requests for the repatriation of Aboriginal human remains from overseas collecting institutions are usually handled by individuals such as

Michael Mansell, a solicitor with the Aboriginal Legal Services in Hobart, and Bob Weatherall of the Foundation for Aboriginal and Torres Strait Islander Research Action (FAIRA). Such efforts receive the support and financial backing of the Aboriginal and Torres Strait Islander Commission (ATSIC), a statutory authority which was established in 1989 to represent Aboriginal and Torres Strait Islander interests.

ATSIC provides a secretarial amd monitoring role for implementation of the resolutions of the Australian Aboriginal Affairs Council (AAAC) which is composed of Commonwealth, State and Territory government ministers who have responsibility for Aboriginal and Torres Strait Islander issues. They have also played a significant role in the development of policies relating to Aboriginal human remains and material culture in museum collections. An AAAC Task Force, established in 1990, was given the mission 'to consider and develop policy recommendations on the return of Aboriginal and Torres Strait Islander cultural property, leading to a national policy'. The draft policy of the AAAC Task Force on the Protection of Aboriginal and Torres Strait Islander Cultural Property and its Return to Aboriginal and Torres Strait Islander Ownership states that:

> The Commonwealth Government has primary or first responsibility for the return of Aboriginal and Torres Strait cultural material from overseas collecting institutions, and for seeing that such material reaches the relevant Aboriginal and Torres Strait Islander community or individual. The Commonwealth Government's responsibilities in this area will be carried out through the agency of the Aboriginal and Torres Strait Islander Commission (ATSIC).

> (Cited in Foss, 1994)

In 1992, the Council of Australian Governments agreed to 'empower Aboriginal peoples and Torres Strait Islanders to protect, preserve and promote their cultures and heritage, recognising that their unique cultures are Australia's indigenous heritage' (CAG, 1992). In 1993, a Ministerial meeting of the AAAC challenged the concept of state ownership of cultural property when it adopted a set of principles which included recognition of 'Aboriginal and Torres Strait Islander ownership obligations, interests and rights in skeletal remains, artefacts and objects having religious and cultural significance' and called upon governments to 'develop procedures to resolve Aboriginal and Torres Strait Islander ownership of significant cultural property in the possession of the crown'. Also adopted was the commitment to ensure that Aboriginal and Torres Strait Islanders are actively involved in all decision making concerning the preservation, care and possible return of cultural property (AAAC, 1993).

Australian High Commissioners and Heads of Mission have been asked to enter into discussions with overseas governments and museums, emphasising the Australian government's support for repatriation requests made by Australian Aboriginal and Torres Strait Islander peoples seeking the return of skeletal remains and other culturally significant material (Tickner, 1995). The National

Museum of Australia and the Australian Museum in Sydney both act as intermediaries in repatriation negotiations and also serve as secure repositories should the Aboriginal communities concerned wish skeletal remains to continue to be stored.

In 1993, the Council of Australian Museum Associations (CAMA) published *Previous Possessions, New Obligations: Policies for Museums in Australia and Aboriginal and Torres Strait Islander Peoples* which set forth a list of thirteen principles and provided detailed policies designed to guide museums in the formulation of new policies and practices which recognise and respond to the different and varying interests that exist in the cultural heritage of Aboriginal and Torres Strait Islander peoples. In the policy document it is stated that decisions concerning retention, disposition, and intended research, are to be made in consultation with the relevant community (1993b: 11). However, CAMA suggests that the transfer of legal title to all items in collections held by museums would be neither lawful nor feasible (under current circumstances) and, based upon past experiences, would not, in any case, be wanted by many communities (1993b: 6).

As in Canada and the United States, the growth of culturally specific museums and cultural centres is closely linked to repatriation efforts and the increased politicisation of the indigenous communities. The Department of Aboriginal Affairs has noted that 'the success of the repatriation exercise is in part contingent on assurances being given by the Australian Government, that any material returned to Australia would be professionally curated'. It is claimed, therefore, that the growth in interest in Aboriginal Keeping Places had arisen in part from Government efforts to secure the successful repatriation of Aboriginal material from overseas collections (Sampson, 1988: 20).

Developments within the museum profession in Australia suggest that significant changes are taking place and are being instituted nationally through the efforts of organisations such as ATSIC and CAMA, as well as by individuals within the profession. Chris Anderson hopes that Australian museums generally will adopt a proactive stance, rather than resorting to law as has happened in the US:

> If you just hide behind law, your collection will remain sterile and independent of society. . . . We have taken the worst and hardest issues at the interface of Aboriginal peoples and museums and faced them. . . . We have initiated incredibly good interactive relationships with communities.
>
> (Anderson, 1993)

In Australia, New Zealand and North America, much of the impetus for these changes has come from the pressures exerted by the indigenous populations, efforts which have clearly had some success in their own countries. However, when the community is thousands of miles away across the world, the willingness to respond to their wishes may not be so great, and it remains to be seen whether the repatriation policies which are being developed will be extended to address the repatriation requests of indigenous peoples in other parts of the world.

The Museum of New Mexico's policy on collection, display, and repatriation of culturally sensitive materials does not apply solely to Native American collections and issues but to all cultures represented by the collections (Bernstein, 1991a: 3). The Museum of New Mexico consists of four separate buildings and five state monuments with collections covering anthropology, history, folk art and fine art. The Museum is conducting an inventory of all possible sensitive materials in collections including, for example, the Catholic religious art of New Mexico. An exhibition about the Civil War in New Mexico included artefacts from the graves of soldiers. Just as they contact Native American descendants concerning the use of human remains and burial objects, so they attempted, wherever possible, to contact the families or descendants of Civil War dead (Becker, 1991).

The Australian Museum in Sydney applies policies laid down for Australian Aboriginal collections to those from other cultures as well. Should not museums be sensitive to the beliefs of the peoples whose cultures they represent when it is well known that the continued display of such items causes offence? Knowing that sacred objects and human remains are the subjects of great sensitivity and concern, museums should actively take steps to discover the opinions of cultural descendants before displaying such material. When the South Australian Museum in Adelaide hosted the Pacific Arts Symposium in April 1993 they realised that the human skulls on display in the Pacific Gallery might cause offence so they covered them up with a screen and are now making enquiries with various Pacific peoples in order to determine their feelings regarding the continued display of such items in public galleries. Once that is known, the skulls will either be uncovered or removed from display.

Science versus religion

The issues associated with repatriation have divided the profession in a heated debate in which the scientific viewpoint is diametrically opposed to the views of many indigenous peoples. Ronald Grimes (1990: 259) has defined four types of attitudes towards the dead:

> (1) Remains-as-data, the object constituted by scientism. . . . (2) Remains-as-dead-person, that is, one with human rights that exceed the imperatives of research. (3) Remains-as-sacred-memory, which is the conventional, popular religious view. (4) Remains-as-sacred-ancestor, a native view in which remains are more-than-person in that they constitute the seat or home of the spirit.

As Grimes has stated (1986: 313): 'There is no denying that archaeologically gained information about mortuary practice is useful. The question is, Useful to whom?'

The acquisitions and disposals policy of the Marischal Museum in Aberdeen, Scotland, states that resignation of responsibility for any part of the museum's collection would be a demonstration of negligence of understanding of the

242

contribution that the donor has made to history and our world view. However, those in sympathy with the principle of repatriation advocate cultural relativism and respect for alternative world views: 'The feelings of human groups for whom human remains have a symbolic importance, whether for purely religious or for ethnic reasons, must be respected' (Cleere, 1994).

The continuation of angry confrontations between indigenous peoples fighting a spiritual cause, and archaeologists and anthropologists defending their professional research and control of the past, can only result in greater barriers between the two that are destructive to the very work in which the latter are engaged. As Grimes (1986: 313) states: 'However useful the information is to humanistic scholars, its mode of acquisition is an affront to native religious values.' In the past, the concerns of western science have been addressed before those of the dead or their descendants, but resolution of repatriation issues will only be achieved when the validity of alternative world views is acknowledged. The actions and words of indigenous peoples in recent years have drawn attention to this clash of cultural values, and now the continuing rights and interests of indigenous peoples in Canada, the United States, Australia and New Zealand, are beginning to be recognised in government legislation and museum policies concerning cultural heritage. The role of indigenous peoples in preserving and telling their own history in their own way must also be valued and utilised much more.

It is clearly critically important to seek resolution of the current controversies concerning the repatriation of collections of human remains, yet the failure of opponents of reburial to enter into the repatriation debate may well result in the power of decision making being taken from them by legislative changes which could ultimately result in the further loss of scientifically valuable collections. Archaeologist Larry Zimmerman, Organizing Secretary of the World Archaeological Congress's *Intercongress on Archaeological Ethics and the Treatment of the Dead*, has, over the past twenty-five years, become 'a radical spokesman for reburial' who now 'accept(s) reburial as scientifically, professionally, and personally ethical' and believes that reburial should be 'part of our normal practice in the treatment of all human remains' (1994a: 60, 66). Zimmerman claims that he has been moved to this standpoint, in part, by his growing awareness of, and sympathy with, the Indian viewpoint. However, he attributes his own change of viewpoint primarily to the attitudes of his colleagues whom he accuses of academic racism and intransigence, and claims that 'osteology's substantial recent "losses" in the USA are the fault of those who are afraid or refuse to engage in dialogue with either colleagues who might see things differently or the indigenous peoples themselves' (Zimmerman, 1989: 26; 1994a: 60–7). It was this failure to seek and find a compromise path that ultimately led to the passage of the Native American Graves Protection and Repatriation Act.

As a way forward, compromises might be made in order to satisfy repatriation requests while enabling research work to continue, thus satisfying both archaeologists and native peoples. Some repatriation agreements have allowed casts to be taken of bones and skulls, or the retention of small tissue and bone samples to enable further forensic research to be conducted. When Blackfeet remains were returned by the Smithsonian Institution, they informed the tribal representatives of the nature and importance of the research that was being conducted on the skeletal material, illustrating the value this knowledge would have as a contribution to their tribal history and public health. The Blackfeet representatives therefore allowed the research in progress to be completed, casts of the remains to be taken, and other scientific analysis to be conducted as necessary, prior to repatriation and reburial (Adams, 1987a: 12). In Australia, some Aboriginal communities recognise that forensic research can provide greater knowledge of contemporary health problems and evidence to support land claims. As a result, repatriation agreements may allow future research upon human remains which will continue to be stored in secret/sacred stores in state museums or in Aboriginal Keeping Places. In order to ensure that both the interests of science and those of indigenous peoples are satisfied and balanced, it is essential that sincere and meaningful dialogue takes place with each side informing and listening to the other. If this does not happen, the potential losses to all mankind would indeed be profound.

The benefits of repatriation

There are, as we have seen, many categories of objects in museum collections which have been the subject of repatriation requests. Their significance and the reasons why their return is sought are varied. However, it is indisputable that certain objects are required for the practice and perpetuation of religious traditions. Amongst North American Indian communities, for example, much traditional knowledge has already been lost, and that which has endured remains under threat: as elders and religious leaders grow older and less numerous, the knowledge that they hold is in danger of dying with them. Yet that knowledge is vital to ensuring that the cultural revitalisation which is occurring in many native communities should continue to flourish. Native American commentators such as Ray Gonyea (1993) and Rick Hill (1993) have noted a substantial loss of knowledgeable elders and religious leaders over recent years. They have also spoken of the tremendous value gained from the return of precious, religious artefacts and the contribution that this has made to 'the restoration of ancient cycles of spirituality' (Hill, 1993: 10).

Ray Gonyea (Onondaga) and Rick Hill (Tuscarora) are members of tribes of the League of Iroquois, who have recently received wampum and other materials repatriated by Canadian and American museums. Both Gonyea and Hill maintain that the repatriation of sacred artefacts has contributed to an increase in spiritual teaching within their communities. According to Hill, assistant director for public programmes at the National Museum of the American Indian, 'the first impact of repatriation has been the true preservation of knowledge about sacred ways in those communities where objects have been restored' (1993: 10). Hill was shocked, recently, to realise that only two of his people's elders remained. As Hill has recounted, the return of the sacred materials has been timely:

> Those two elders were able to take the sacred objects that we restored to our people and teach them what they could. They have worked tirelessly to teach, to record what they know, and to bring this generation back in touch with the power that used to be our birthright.'
>
> (ibid.: 9–10)

Gonyea has noted that there has been renewed interest in traditional ceremonies associated with the installation of new chiefs, an increase in the number of tribal members attending language and culture classes, and positive changes in the attitudes of women and their status within the Onondaga community.

Gonyea and Hill attribute these changes to the constructive impact that the repatriation of sacred material has had upon community pride and self-esteem. According to Hill, repatriation has created 'a new sense of community . . . the objects themselves confirm the stories that have been heard by native people over the years' (1993: 10). His comments are reinforced by the fundamental principles upon which museums are based: the importance of the object as a tool for research and learning. Education in museums is based upon the premise that the object facilitates learning in a way that secondary source materials cannot. Hill (ibid: 10) explains that:

> since the majority of the cultural patrimony of the Indian nations exists in museums located far from their communities, many young Indians find it hard to understand the beliefs affiliated with the objects . . . without the object, such ritual knowledge had become mere stories told around the community.

Museum staff have also found that the process of entering into repatriation negotiations has brought rewards, disproving those who fear that museums can only lose from repatriation. The consequences of the repatriation process extend far beyond the future of the skeletal remains and sacred objects themselves. The value of such a spirit of collaboration is demonstrated by the experiences of anthropologists and curators who are working closely with communities, accepting the validity of alternative world views and co-operating over sensitive issues such as repatriation. These individuals recognise the benefits to museums and the changing power relationships between museums and indigenous communities. There are many examples of curators who have undertaken dialogue and responded positively to repatriation requests and, as a result, have entered into new relationships with the peoples whose ancestors' remains had previously been viewed, within the museum context, as little more than artefacts. The outcomes demonstrate that flexibility and sympathetic treatment of human remains can pay dividends in other areas of museum work.

Some curators have found that the involvement in the repatriation process has resulted in new discoveries about the collections, greater understanding of cultures and improved relationships leading to collaborative projects. Inviting tribal delegations to examine and comment upon reserve collections or having skeletal remains examined and documented in detail by a physical anthropologist can provide staff with previously unknown information about the collections in their care. When the Heard Museum called in a physical anthropologist to examine their collection of human remains, mainly cremations, he found that two which had been on a list requesting repatriation, were not after all human but were mountain sheep (Welsh, 1993)! As a result of negotiations between Zuni Pueblo and the Museum of New Mexico, several so-called 'sacred' pots and fetish collections were removed from the 'sensitive materials' category after more than sixty years and are once again available to researchers (Bernstein 1991a: 6). Paul Tacon, of the Australian Museum in Sydney, has found that the process of repatriation has led to greater confidence in the museum amongst the Aboriginal communities concerned, which has sometimes resulted in further material being given to the museum, and often to improved working relationships, collaborative research and other projects. 'Instead of closing doors, or losing things, you actually gain and you open doors' (Tacon, 1993).

Chris Anderson, who was involved with proactive custodianship negotiations between the South Australian Museum and Aboriginal communities from 1985 until the late 1990s, has found that these discussions have resulted in 'true social interaction' resulting in joint projects, such as exhibitions; greater understanding and knowledge of material in the collections with detailed cultural histories provided by senior Aboriginal men; and the acquisition of additional material, similar to that returned, given by communities who have developed more trust and respect for the museum. He argues that 'repatriation, under certain circumstances, can represent an important *use* of collections' (Anderson, 1990b: 31).

If museums are to demonstrate that they have shaken off the colonial mantle, they must address fully the issue of repatriation. To have a blanket 'no returns' policy reflects a failure to recognise or acknowledge the relevance of the concepts of spiritual ownership, cultural patrimony and the cultural importance of certain objects to cultures that did not die out in the nineteenth century, as was expected. One of the reasons for acquiring some of the material was to document dying cultures, to preserve for posterity the last remains of the material evidence of dying races. But the cultures did not die: they live and thrive today and their people seek the return of objects which are symbols of cultural identity and survival, potent and necessary ceremonial items and resources for teaching the young and ensuring cultural continuity.

Conclusion
Turning the page

'The philosophy that underlies all our policies [is] that museums aren't really concerned with objects; the objects really just represent people and relationships between people, past and present.'

(Chris Anderson, Director of the South Australian Museum, 1993)

Whereas museums were, in the past, perceived as élitist institutions which served a narrow, ethnically defined audience, today many institutions are developing closer working relationships with the communities whose cultures they interpret, and are proving that museums have a relevant and functional role to play in the contemporary issues which face indigenous and other ethnic groups. Cultural preservation, revitalisation of the arts, increased access to archives and collections, addressing social and political issues and the provision of evidence to support land rights claims: these are some of the ways in which museums and anthropologists are now serving their new audiences.

Preserving cultural heritage

There is no doubt that museums and anthropologists have contributed greatly to the preservation of material culture. Throughout the colonial era, museums accumulated vast collections in order to fulfil their functions of preservation, research and dissemination and these provide a valuable record of cultures as they existed in the past. However, one must question to what extent the anthropological activities of the nineteenth and early twentieth centuries also contributed to the cultural decline experienced by many indigenous peoples, as cultural material was avidly collected in a desperate attempt to salvage as much as possible from tribal peoples who were deemed to be facing extinction. In the most extreme examples, the actions of collectors stripped the communities of many of their cultural treasures and left them with few physical vestiges of their traditional ceremonial ways and material culture. The acquisitive activities of anthropologists and other collectors in their quest for artefacts and information, are a source of continuing anger and bitterness amongst many indigenous peoples today. 'We (Australian Aborigines) are the oldest culture in the world and we have been raped of our history for more than 150 years' (Henrietta Fourmile, cited in Thomas, 1988: 24).

As museum ethnographic collections grew, the movement of information and artefacts was largely one way – from source to collector to museum – there to be displayed and interpreted regardless of the views and sensitivities of the original owners. The benefit was primarily to the recipients of the information, not the givers; but indigenous peoples increasingly raised their voices in protest against traditional museological collecting and display methods and their own exclusion from the interpretive process. Those in the museum profession are finally having to heed their complaints and adopt new approaches, form new relationships and ensure that the collections and activities of museums address the needs of the communities which have given so much in the past. The givers are becoming the recipients, as indigenous and minority peoples discover just how much of their cultural heritage lies within museum walls and seek ways to benefit from those collections. Repatriation is only one aspect of this process; other methods are being developed as museums and communities work together on projects that prove fruitful to both parties.

In recent decades, ethnographic collections have continued to grow, but much more slowly than in the colonial era. The emphasis in recent years has been upon the need to preserve cultural heritage and revitalise or re-establish artistic skills and traditions which suffered serious decline as a result of the impact of colonialism and acculturation. For the indigenous peoples of the United States, Canada and Australia, government policies aimed at assimilation resulted in legislation which attempted to eradicate traditional languages, religious practices, clothing and other forms of cultural expression. The demand for traditionally produced artefacts was reduced; consequently older practitioners ceased to produce work and traditional skills and artistic traditions were not passed on to young people as they had been in the past.

While some of the traditional knowledge was still available through the memories and skills of elders, much has been lost as older members of communities died without having been able to pass their knowledge on to younger members of the community. Collections of material from the eighteenth and nineteenth centuries and earlier, have preserved artefacts and documentary evidence of methods and meanings, providing a visual record of traditional art forms and their social or religious significance. In these circumstances, museum collections may offer, not just the visual evidence of traditional skills and design conventions, but also documentary evidence from anthropological research, recording all aspects of traditional life. There is no doubt that much of this material and knowledge would have been lost due to depopulation and acculturation processes if it had not been collected by anthropologists and others.

While preservation of culture has long been a function of European museums, the role they played in the past was as collectors of artefacts, preservers of evidence of dying cultures. Museums are now proving that they can have relevance to all communities, that they can be givers not just recipients, and can adopt new, more culturally relevant roles in contemporary society. While museological activities in the past have generally focused upon recording traditional technology, social practices and beliefs, and artistic styles and conventions, some museums have begun to adopt a more proactive role in reviving traditions and stimulating artistic production. An additional role they are now playing is that of a resource for those once 'dying', now thriving, cultures.

Over the past 40 years or so, many indigenous peoples have experienced a rediscovery and an increased pride in their cultural heritage, and a desire to preserve traditional skills and knowledge as a means of reclaiming their history and reinforcing their cultural identity. This has combined with growing international interest in indigenous arts and demand for the production of new works, stimulating young artists to learn traditional methods and styles while also developing personal interpretations.

At an international conference in 1978, contributors from throughout the Pacific region presented accounts of the many ways in which museums were being utilised by indigenous peoples, or were contributing to the preservation of their cultures (Edwards and Stewart, 1980). A growing number of indigenous peoples are seeking access to the collections of museums as a source of information about their own histories, cultures and traditional skills and to assist in the preservation or revitalisation of traditions.

Artistic revitalisation

Museums can provide valuable resources for the renewal of dead or dying cultural practices or artistic and technological skills, lost through the colonisation process and the subsequent acquisition of important material culture by collectors and museums. In recent years many indigenous artists have drawn upon these collections in order to re-discover the imagery and technical methodology of the arts in which few of their contemporaries were trained. In the Philippines, a small mobile museum was established during the 1970s to provide a reference collection as part of a craft revitalisation programme aimed at tribal peoples. It was established and maintained by staff of the Museum of Philippine Traditional Cultures and after four years it closed down having successfully served its purpose (Baradas, 1980: 80). Examination of the South Australian Museum's collection of wood-carvings from an area of South Australia enabled an Aboriginal community to revive the traditional practices which had been lost many years before, and it has been noted that Aboriginal users now outnumber white Australian and other researchers utilising the collections (Anderson, 1990a: 177). Revitalisation of traditional arts was also one of the main factors in the establishment of the Tiwi Keeping Place on Bathurst Island in Northern Territory (see Chapter 5).

When the traditional houses of the Canadian Museum of Civilisation's Grand Hall were being constructed in the style of eighteenth- and nineteenth-century Northwest Coast structures, museological records and collections proved invaluable. The Grand Hall contains six houses arranged facing the Ottawa River that can be seen through the vast glass-panelled wall of the Hall, echoing the sea-front positioning of houses in traditional coastal villages. The houses do not, however, attempt to recreate a village; the six houses represent the architectural styles of the six main groups that lived on the Northwest Coast. From south to north the houses represent Coast Salish, Nuu-Chah-Nulth, Central Coast, Nuxalk, Haida and Tsimshian styles. The project was managed by staff from the University of British Columbia Museum of Anthropology but construction work was carried out by native craftsmen. Each house was built by a team of craftsmen from the cultural group represented by the house being built, although not all of them had had the experience of building a traditional style of house before. The designs for the houses were based upon old photographs and archaeological information and adapted to fit into the physical constraints of the Grand Hall. As little information about joining details was available the craftsmen sought solutions to these problems as construction proceeded and received suggestions from village elders. Since the conclusion of the project, the plans have been utilised in some community projects for the building of traditional houses, cultural centres and other buildings (McLennan, 1992).

In North America, the studies and analyses of Northwest Coast Indian art undertaken by Franz Boas (1927) and Bill Holm (1965), have played a significant role in providing material from which native artists of that region could inform themselves (Ames, 1981: 6 and 1993: 59–69). Bill Reid, one of the most prominent artists on the Northwest Coast, has spoken of the value that the collections of the University of British Columbia (UBC) Museum of Anthropology in Vancouver provided as a resource for learning about the artistic traditions of his Haida heritage:

> The museum has provided a training ground for native artists. I unlocked the secrets of traditional designs by studying carefully the old carvings kept there, as well as talking to anthropologists and old people, and reading everything that had ever been written about the art.
>
> (Cited in Coull, 1982: 21)

Museums have also contributed to a revival of traditional practices by establishing programmes of restoration and the re-creation of significant pieces requiring knowledge of traditional skills and artistic conventions. In British Columbia, the UBC Museum of Anthropology and the Royal British Columbia Museum have acted as patrons of the arts through carving programmes involving major artists such as Mungo Martin, Ellen Neel, Bill Reid, Douglas Cranmer, Henry Hunt and his sons (Ames, 1981; Coull, 1982). Both of these museums have been working closely with native carvers since the 1950s when the Kwakwaka'wakw carver Mungo Martin, then aged 70, was encouraged to take up carving once again. He subsequently completed a number of carvings on the campus of the University, including a house frame and eleven totem poles, then spent ten years at the Royal British Columbia Museum as a carver (Coull, 1982: 21).

At UBC, Reid and Cranmer were commissioned to design and carve Haida houses and poles for the Museum of Anthropology and to copy others, so preserving the images and history they document. Over the years, these have been added to with works by other carvers and they now stand behind the museum facing across the waters of the inlet. So successful has the renaissance of totem pole carving been, that many new poles are to be found in native communities, and also in Vancouver and other urban areas, where they are a source of civic pride for all, native and non-native, throughout the province.

While such projects have been of immense value in the revitalisation of North-west Coast arts, if museums merely collected, documented and commissioned examples of past art forms they would be helping to perpetuate a static, unchanging view of Indian art and culture as it was. In the past, museums frequently made the mistake of trying to preserve unchanged the cultures of peoples as represented by eighteenth- and nineteenth-century ethnographic collections, and efforts to revitalise artistic production focused upon copying old artefacts (Doxtator, 1985). Today, however, there is an emphasis upon the need to demonstrate cultural continuity and evolution, and museum anthropologists are contributing to the artistic revival in a more important way: by contributing to the establishment of a market for contemporary art works.

For many years, change in style or content was discouraged and art work which did not conform to tradition was not considered to be 'authentic'. While this is a continuing problem facing Native artists, contemporary art forms are beginning to be appreciated and valued as evidence of the natural process of cultural and creative evolution. Despite stringent financial cutbacks that have affected all areas of museology in recent years, contemporary collecting has enabled some museums to commission new works for the collections, and encouraged the production of contemporary forms of art. Peter McNair, Chief Curator of Ethnology at the Royal British Columbia Museum, has extended the activities of patron of the arts beyond the commissioning of pieces for the museum collection. He has commissioned pieces for potlatches and donated new works to those giving potlatches, thus encouraging an Indian market for new works (Ames, 1981: 12).

Another important area of change is in the categorisation and status of indigenous arts. Exhibitions have been a major vehicle for redefining indigenous arts by presenting exhibitions and research which clearly defined the work as 'fine art' rather than 'ethnography' or 'primitive art' and so have helped to create an international market for new works. Michael Ames (1981), former director of UBC Museum of Anthropology, attributes to Levi-Strauss the first moves to redefine Northwest Coast art as 'fine art' rather than 'primitive art', a concept that was further promoted by museum staff such as Wilson Duff of the Royal British Columbia Museum (formerly the British Columbia Provincial Museum), and Doris Shadbolt of the Vancouver Art Gallery. Exhibitions, such as *People of the Potlatch* (1956), *Arts of the Raven* (1967), *Legacy* (1971), and *Images of Stone BC* (1975), promoted this concept and gave new status to Northwest Coast art. A similar shift in definition has taken place with regard to the arts of other Native American peoples and has been witnessed in exhibitions such as *Sacred Circles* (1976) and *The Spirit Sings* (1988). The arts of Native Americans are now widely collected and regarded as being masterpieces on a par with those of other major artistic traditions of the world, including Europe, Asia and Africa.

The galleries of the Museum of Anthropology at the University of British Columbia, which opened in 1976, were designed to further promote this perspective. Fine pieces of small wood, argillite, bone and ivory in the form of rattles, pipes, jewellery, spoons, combs and so on, are spotlit in a dark Master-piece Gallery, while large monumental pieces such as totem poles, feast bowls and house fronts are positioned in the Grand Hall as pieces of sculpture with minimal labelling. The Museum displays several pieces of work by the late Bill Reid, who was the most prominent Northwest Coast artist of the late twentieth century. His work captures the quintessential and unmistakable qualities of the forms and conventions of Northwest Coast art, yet brings to it a unique and personal view that draws upon and transforms traditional stories and images in a modern form 'freeing his tremendous human and animal subjects from the vertical totem form' (Coull, 1982:21).

Reid's skilful work as a carver and a jeweller ranged from tiny pieces of exquis-ite jewellery, finely worked in precious metals, to large scale sculptural works. These are exemplified by works such as the magnificent and gigantic wood sculpture '*The Raven and the First Humans*' (1980) and the black bronze sculp-ture '*The Spirit of Haida Gwaii*' (1991). '*The Raven and the First Humans*' illustrates the Haida creation story of Raven releasing the First People from a clamshell. The six foot tall wooden sculpture occupies a prominent position in the Museum of Anthropology and is a highlight of the Museum's contemporary Northwest Coast art collection. '*The Spirit of Haida Gwaii*', a bronze sculpture standing outside the Canadian Embassy in Washington DC is in the form of a canoe which is filled with characters from Haida mythology. In other parts of the world, artists have found similar value in museum collections as they peer back into the artistic heritage of their people for, as cultural historian and poet Robert Bringhurst has stated, 'Haida Gwaii is not the only nation whose great-est treasures of art and thought have passed indifferently, like money, through noble and venal, reverent and predatory hands' (Bringhurst, 1991: 8).

Contemporary Native American art forms are diverse in style and content: some are contemporary versions of traditional themes and imagery; some show mod-ern stylistic developments and interpretations which allude to their traditional origins; others incorporate Euro-American artistic styles and techniques in works which articulate indigenous comments upon social and political issues and pro-vide opportunities for Native American artists to present indigenous views of history. During this decade, there have been a number of exhibitions which have provided fine examples of the diversity of styles and the concepts articulated in the work of artists of the Native American fine art movement (Archuleta and Strick-land, 1991; McMaster and Martin, 1992; Roberts, C.A., 1992). Of particular note are the exhibitions: *Shared Visions: Native American Painters and Sculptors in the Twentieth Century* (1991–92), initiated by the Heard Museum, in Phoenix; *The Submuloc Show/Columbus Wohs* (1992–94) organised by Atlatl, a Native American arts organisation based in Phoenix; and *Indigena* (1992–95), initiated by the Canadian Museum of Civilization and curated by two Native staff.

These exhibitions toured to a number of venues and were on show in main-stream museums including the Canadian Museum of Civilization in Hull, the Heard Museum in Phoenix, the Minneapolis Institute of Arts, and the Oregon

Art Institute. However, it is significant that most of the other venues were Indian museums and galleries, or non-Indian museums with a specific interest in Indian arts and art of the American West. It is disturbing that many art museums that were approached rejected any idea of showing *Shared Visions*, perceiving it to be outside their mandate of showing fine art (Pyne, 1991). Such views are a sad reflection of the continuing lack of acceptance of Native American art within the American fine art establishment.

In other parts of the world, too, the creative work of indigenous peoples has been redefined as art and attracted international attention. In New Zealand, the status of Maori *taonga* (cultural treasures) was greatly augmented in the eyes of both Maori and *Pakeha* (non-Maori) following the success of the major international exhibition *Te Maori* which toured to several cities in the United States and New Zealand between 1986 and 1988. Due to the importance of these sacred objects to the Maori people, it was the first time that most of the artefacts had left New Zealand. The Maori people allowed these objects to travel overseas because they recognised that it would provide an opportunity for people to see and appreciate the beauty of Maori artistry and to understand the spiritual qualities associated with the *taonga*. The exhibition tour was most effective in fulfilling this role and also did much to raise awareness of Maori creativity in New Zealand when it returned for a tour of four of the country's major museums (O'Regan, 1994: 101–6).

In Australia, the introduction of the acrylic painting medium in 1971 led to the establishment of the Central Desert painting movement. Symbolic imagery, the manifestation of religious beliefs, has been given permanency through the use of new media and has achieved recognition throughout the international art world. *Dreamings: The Art of Aboriginal Australia* (1988–90), organised jointly by the Asia Society Galleries in New York and the South Australian Museum in Adelaide, was the first international exhibition of Aboriginal art and drew world attention to the richness of Aboriginal artistic expression.

Improving access and sharing information

In the past, the relationship that museums had with indigenous peoples was highly inequitable, serving little or no benefit to the indigenous peoples, but that balance has changed so that there is now developing a more equal partnership in which indigenous communities are able to use museum collections and archives, and indeed the knowledge of anthropologists, to serve their own objectives. From these new relationships are developing new roles for museums and museum anthropologists in which they can play a more central role in dealing with matters of social relevance.

In their attempts to become more inclusive institutions, museums are seeking to attract new audiences and to develop greater relevance to those communities which previously have been the subject of research but have benefited little from that process. In so doing, museums are seeking to increase accessibility to exhibitions, reserve collections and archives, and to create opportunities for indigenous peoples to undertake research into their own cultural heritage. In the first instance this involves improving the physical accessibility of the collections and the storage of data, in order to equip non-specialist visitors with the means to make better use of the vast wealth of information that museums hold. Secondly, it involves the evolution of methods of access which enable those who cannot physically visit the museum to access the collections and databases from afar. This is particularly relevant for indigenous communities whose physical location and cultural and economic circumstances hinder their personal use of the museum. New technologies in the form of computers, CD-ROMs and the information superhighway are providing vast quantities of data, no matter what the location of the museum or the inquirer.

Resulting from the initiatives to increase accessibility, recognition is increasingly being given to the need to address issues of indigenous ownership and rights to knowledge. This has resulted in the development of policies in some museums which contrast sharply with the European beliefs in the freedom and dissemination of information, concepts upon which mainstream museums are based. Access to the collections and the dissemination of information to academic researchers and the general public have been central operating functions of the museum. Now we are witnessing a major change in perceptions and values as museums begin to acknowledge their responsibilities to the traditional owners of objects and knowledge. Access to others may be limited and dependent upon permission being granted by those with ownership rights. Secret/sacred material is no longer a subject of unrestricted research and impartial dissemination with no regard for traditional beliefs or religious restrictions. Traditional owners are becoming co-workers on projects and retain their status as owners of traditional knowledge. They are becoming beneficiaries of museological preservation and research where once they were merely the researchers' informants and subjects with no control over the use to which anthropologists put the results of their research, and little economic or social benefit from such works.

In Canada, the Royal British Columbia Museum has been documenting contemporary Kwakwaka'wakw potlatching on tape and film but, while the museum will have custody of the information, ownership will remain with the Indian people. In New Zealand, museums are seen as custodians of Maori material in their collections; the Maori retain ownership. Australian government policy now recognises that:

> History belongs to the people concerned. As a minimum, Aboriginal and Torres Strait Islander Communities must be given open access and provision of copies of key documentation, including information such as recordings, films, notebooks and photographs, relating to culturally significant material.

(ATSIC, 1993b)

The use of archival material such as this is proving to be of immense value. Anthropologists, recognising the obligation to consult with communities, are now communicating with elders and providing communities with copies of research data. Christopher Chippendale of the Cambridge Museum of Archaeology and Anthropology and Paul Tacon, of the Australian Museum in Sydney, have been conducting a long-term research project in the Northern Territory to study and document rock paintings and record the stories associated with them. This has involved close co-operation between the anthropologists and Aboriginal artists who are advising them on the location and meaning of the rock art sites. During their research trips to rock art sites, they are accompanied by Aboriginal people: elders who can provide historical and cultural interpretations and younger people who can benefit from the opportunity the trips provide to become familiar with some of the remote but significant areas of Aboriginal land. Some of these younger people have been keen to accept the opportunity to receive training in research methodologies.

Tacon has also recently been involved in a training project instigated by an Aboriginal community in the Mann River region of Arnhem Land (Tacon, 1993). Concerned about the threat imposed by mining surveys, and anxious to ensure that the knowledge of the elders is passed on to future generations, the Bawinanga Aboriginal Corporation hired Tacon to provide them with training in appropriate recording methods. After visiting a number of sites with elders, Tacon is able to provide a wider regional framework for the sites pertaining to this community. He then provides basic training in still and video photography, interviewing techniques to obtain the comments of elders concerning sites and paintings, and gives advice on the recording of other relevant information. Those trained will be able to continue this work independently in the future. Although most members of the community live in remote areas on outstations in the Maningrida region, they do have access to computer facilities in Maningrida itself, and the results of this documentation project will be stored on a multimedia database system incorporating still photographs and video footage. This will be stored and managed as part of the existing museum and arts and craft centre.

Upon completion of each season of fieldwork, Tacon and Chippendale present their findings to the community through slides and discussion. They also present to the community plain-English reports complete with a detailed photographic record. Upon completion of his doctoral research, Tacon provided similar material plus a copy of his PhD thesis to the communities concerned.

Research materials provided by the anthropologists are stored in the community libraries and is easily accessible to members of the community. As Tacon points out 'such material includes some of the last thoughts on the rock art by a number of important elders who have since passed away'. This documentation is, therefore, immensely valuable and its return to the community for storage enables tribal knowledge to be preserved for future generations. Tacon is very sensitive to the restricted aspects of some of the material and emphasises that the research is carried out in close co-operation with Aboriginal elders to ensure that secret/sacred information is not divulged or secret/sacred images photographed (Tacon, 1993). Tacon and Chippendale are also proposing to publish a book of rock art photographs resulting from and reflecting this collaboration by presenting the historical data from two viewpoints: the western archaeological perspective alongside the Aboriginal viewpoint. They hope that this book will then be available for purchase in the new Warradjan Aboriginal Cultural Centre in Kakadu National Park.

Opening the archives

In the United States, the American Indian Program of the National Museum of Natural History has been providing Indian communities with documentation relating to the Smithsonian Institution's collections while also facilitating research by tribal members into their tribal history as conveyed by the artefacts and archival materials. The programme was established in 1986 to make the resources of the Smithsonian Institution available to Indian people, particularly those living on reservations or in other rural Indian communities. Consideration was given to applications from individuals of all ages and educational backgrounds who presented worthwhile research proposals concerned with gaining cultural knowledge as represented in the collections. Since its inception, the programme has sponsored more than 68 Indian interns, at a cost of $150,000 per year.

The American Indian Program sponsors a series of tribal catalogues which are intended to provide a comprehensive research catalogue of all of the information in the Museum's collection relating to individual tribes. Members of the tribe concerned carry out the research work and photograph all the objects in the collections. Each catalogue will contain a scholarly article; details of the photographic, archival, and artefact holdings of the museum; and will include a personal name index so that descendants will be able to trace objects that belonged to their ancestors. Compilation of these catalogues will take anything from a few weeks to several years depending upon the size of the collections in the Smithsonian Institution. Research work on the Zuni catalogue has been underway for more than seven years: the collections consist of 20,000 manuscript pages, 6,000 objects and 3,400 photographs (Archambault, 1991). Upon completion, each tribe will be provided with a number of free copies of the catalogue, a set of photographs of the objects, and copies of all historic photographs in the collections. Thus the project furnishes tribes with valuable archival material, and presents training, employment and research opportunities for tribal members.

Perhaps one of the most poignant illustrations of the increased use of anthropological data by indigenous peoples is the value that archive material is proving to have for the 'stolen children': Australian Aboriginal people who were removed from their families in accordance with government policies, and so grew up with little or no knowledge of their families or backgrounds. Between the 1920s and the 1950s detailed records of Aboriginal family histories were compiled as part of a process of recording the genetic histories of Aboriginal peoples and especially those of mixed race. Australian government policy called for the assimilation of Aboriginal peoples and it was considered unsuitable for children of mixed race relationships to be brought up in Aboriginal communities. In order to ensure that they were assimilated into white society, the children of mixed race parents were taken from their Aboriginal families and placed in institutions, adopted into white families, or placed in white homes where they generally served as domestics. These practices continued until the late 1960s; consequently, thousands of Aboriginal people, even today, know little of their family backgrounds.

The South Australian Museum in Adelaide holds the most extensive collection of photographic and genealogical records of Aboriginal people, which includes approximately 5,500 photographs and over 50,000 names (Craig, 1993; Grzybowicz *et al.*, 1990). Most of the material was recorded by Norman Tindale and his colleagues of the South Australian Museum between 1928 and 1957. Tindale began photographing Aboriginal people on missions and government stations and also recorded details of their family histories. These, and other detailed records of Aboriginal histories and culture, were stored in archives mainly in the state capitals. Consequently, genealogical data relating to thousands of Aboriginal families lies in the archives of libraries, museums and other institutions.

Although technically accessible to any inquirer, access and research by most Aboriginal peoples has been inhibited by distance and financial constraints, language and cultural barriers. Furthermore, Aboriginal communities were not given copies of the original documents, nor publications arising from research into their cultures and, as a result, Aboriginal peoples have been largely ignorant of the existence of such information (Fourmile, 1989c).

The discovery of the existence of these records is often greeted with great joy as they offer the potential of tracing lost family members, but this may be tempered with bitterness that Aboriginal people have had no control and little knowledge of these records. Henrietta Fourmile, an Aboriginal lecturer at Brisbane College of Advanced Education, has described how she happened to discover the existence of genealogies, photographs and recordings relating to members of her own family, including family histories dating back to the 1860s. In Fourmile's view, 'Tindale's genealogies, collected over a period of years relate probably to most of the Aboriginal population of Australia. For many Aboriginal people today his genealogies are the essential key to their tribal identity, to ancestral lands, and to finding relatives' (ibid.: 3). She questions the ethics and legality of the control of such information and the motives which may determine funding and control:

> Is it deliberate government policy to limit funds to institutions like the state museums and the [Australian Institute of Aboriginal Studies] so that they are generally unable to compile comprehensive registers and send catalogues or inventories of their collections of our property to us, and thus maintaining our ignorance for political purposes? As we all know, an ignorant population is very susceptible to political manipulation.

(ibid.: 3)

In recent years, a project has been established at the South Australian Museum to remedy this by recording these genealogies in a form more accessible to members of the public, and to facilitate the use of these records by Aboriginal people. Initially funded by grants from the Australian Institute of Aboriginal Studies and the Commonwealth government's Department of Aboriginal Affairs, the Aboriginal Family History Project is now funded by the state government as part of the Department of Arts and Cultural Heritage. The Museum employs two Aboriginal researchers who research, compile and publish family histories, and supply photographs and genealogical information to enquirers. The original records are often in longhand, and need to be computerised, information checked and updated with additional information supplied from other sources such as hospital records, state records of births, marriages and deaths, and the personal knowledge of individuals. Most of the information is published in family histories which are produced at low cost so that they can be purchased by enquirers. For a nominal fee they also supply copies of photographs to enquirers seeking information about relatives whose faces they may never have seen. Researchers and other enquirers who are not family members are instructed to seek written clearance from the families concerned before they can obtain access to photographic records and genealogies in the Museum's holdings.

Staff of the Aboriginal Family History Project are acutely aware of the highly sensitive nature of some of the material and so, to avoid causing offence, they edit the information prior to publication. This is done in consultation with family members who approve draft copies prior to publication. As a result the publications may not contain the full story; information not included in the published family histories may be sought directly from the families. The staff also have to deal sensitively with people seeking information about parents, siblings, or other family members, conscious of the individual's right to privacy and the possibility of causing great anguish in sensitive family circumstances. In this respect the staff work closely with an organisation called Link Up, which assists Aboriginal people in making contact with their natural families and provides counselling to deal with the emotional and psychological turmoil that many experience in their search for their past (Craig, 1993).

The records held in the South Australian Museum cover the whole country but pertain primarily to South Australia and to Western Australia. Staff of the South Australian Museum have been indexing the genealogies from all the states, but Barry Craig, Research Coordinator of the Aboriginal Family History Project, is anxious that appropriate museums or libraries in each state should take responsibility for continuing with the work of checking information, publishing family histories and answering enquiries, integrating the information in the South Australian Museum with other records available locally in each state.

A grant from the Australian National Parks and Wildlife Service (now called the Australian Nature Conservation Agency) enabled the South Australian Museum to employ a member of staff to index the large collection of Western

Australian material. In May 1993, copies of genealogies and photographs of Western Australian Aboriginal people recorded by Tindale, Birdsell and Epling were handed over to the Aboriginal Affairs Planning Authority in Perth, Western Australia, a state government agency staffed by Aboriginal people (Craig, 1995). Information relating to Queensland has been handed over to the State Library in Queensland, ensuring first that they implemented the same restrictions upon the release of data and the need for family members to grant permission for access and research, thus ensuring that ultimate control of the data rests with the families concerned (Craig, 1993). Tindale's material relating to the Aboriginal people of New South Wales has been lodged with the Mitchell Library in Sydney, the State Library of New South Wales. Copies of genealogies and photographs have also been sent to a number of individual communities in New South Wales.

Tindale also compiled genealogical and photographic records of Tasmanian Aboriginal people of Cape Barren Island off the north coast of Tasmania. These were published long ago in the *Records of the Queen Victoria Museum* in Launceston, and complement genealogical material compiled and published by Mollison, of the University of Tasmania. At the request of Aboriginal groups in Tasmania, copies of negatives of the Tindale photographs have been given by the South Australian Museum to the Riawunna Centre for Aboriginal Education at the University of Tasmania, in Launceston, and to the Tasmanian Aboriginal Centre Inc., in Hobart. This will enable them to provide copies of prints to individuals making enquiries about their family members (Craig, 1995).

Museums and land rights

Case studies provide increasing evidence that museums and anthropologists also have a new role to play in the dissemination of information about crucial contemporary issues, such as land claims and hunting and fishing rights. Anthropologists are finding themselves being drawn into political debates concerning indigenous land claims. Aboriginal peoples are finding that anthropological and archaeological records can provide evidence to support their land claims, and so anthropologists are being called upon to provide evidence in court cases to support indigenous land claims by providing valuable information documenting tribal migration and settlement. In Australia, the issue of land rights is one of the greatest areas of conflict between indigenous and non-indigenous Australians. It is a subject which, more than any other, reflects their fundamental differences in concepts of the Creation, land ownership, and utilisation of natural resources. In June 1992, in a landmark decision, the High Court ruled in favour of a Torres Strait Islander, Eddie Mabo, in a land rights claim. The Mabo case was the first time that a judgement had been made on the basis of the invalidity of the concept of *terra nullius* which had held that Australia was a land belonging to no one prior to European settlement, and this opened the way for other Aboriginal peoples to pursue land claims.

The Mabo land claim was taken to the High Court in 1982 by Eddie Mabo and four other plaintiffs from the Murray Islands in the Torres Strait. Ten years later, the High Court found in favour of the plaintiffs ruling that: 'the lands of this continent were not Terra Nullius . . . in 1788. The Meriam people are entitled as against the whole world to possession, use and enjoyment of the lands of the Murray Islands.' (Meriam is another name for the Murray Islanders, particularly those from the island of Mer, and refers to their language, Meriam Mir.) Through reference to the laws of their god Malo, the Islanders were successfully able to prove a traditional system of land ownership, and the High Court judged that Aboriginal title to land had survived European settlement.

In December 1993, the Australian government passed the Native Title or 'Mabo' Bill which became law on 1 January 1994. The bill finally quashed the doctrine of *terra nullius*. It formally acknowledged that Aboriginal peoples have claims to the land and established a judicial system enabling Native title claimants to take their case to state tribunals or federal court. In order to present a case, claimants will have to be able to prove Native title through continuing association or customary usage of the claimed land, an area in which they can be assisted by the evidence of anthropological and archaeological records.

The land rights issue is highly emotive for all concerned and has been subject to misinformation and sensationalism from the press and from those, such as farmers and mining companies, who were fearful of the financial repercussions from successful claims and the loss of leasehold rights. In the months following the High Court ruling, Aboriginal land claims were filed across the country and became the subject of heated debate, particularly when three different Aboriginal groups lodged claims over the Perth metropolitan area. Such was the state of panic amongst the public in the months following the Mabo High Court ruling that some ordinary Australians were fearful of losing their properties or believed that Australia's towns and cities would be returned to Aboriginal ownership. Concerns about the potential for successful land claims upon private land were frequently based upon misinformation, which served only to fuel anger and fear, and ultimately anti-Aboriginal feeling.

Although the legal situation should be somewhat clearer now following the passage of the Land Title Bill (but see epilogue), the relevance of land and sacred sites to Aboriginal peoples remains largely misunderstood by much of the non-Aboriginal Australian population. In part, this stems from the attitudes of many non-Aboriginal Australians who make little effort to understand Aboriginal cultures, see the tribal peoples as lazy, ineffectual and uncaring, and resent even the limited government assistance that Aboriginal peoples have received in the past. It also stems from the highly complex and often secret nature of Aboriginal religious beliefs. Anthropologists, therefore, have another important task: that of informing non-Aboriginal people of the importance of sacred sites to Aboriginal people and providing an explanation of the cultural context and secret nature of many of the sites. Clearly, this is a highly sensitive area of work which requires careful consideration of the information conveyed in order to ensure that no secret material is passed to inappropriate individuals, and to ensure that sacred sites are protected.

The value of controversy

Traditionally museums have tended to avoid dealing with controversial subject matter or taking a proactive stance, but over recent decades there have been increasing calls for museums to address subjects of social concern. Controversial exhibitions, such as those described in part one of this book, mark the sometimes painful steps which must be taken to develop a new museology which is of greater relevance to the cultural needs of both audiences and those whose cultures are represented in the collections. While controversial exhibitions may be perceived to have failed on one level, they can also be seen as landmarks in the development of new exhibition strategies, for they focus attention upon matters of importance to the public, or to specific groups, which may have been neglected or handled in an unsatisfactory manner by curatorial staff in the past. They also illustrate the problems which potentially face those who attempt to challenge conventional practice and popular theories, and highlight the need for consultation and the development of long-term strategies for meeting community needs and expectations. Had the Royal Ontario Museum established a long-term relationship with the local black community, and had the community's cultural needs been adequately addressed through earlier exhibitions and events, the ambitious and sophisticated messages of *Into the Heart of Africa* might well have been better received.

The boycott of *The Spirit Sings* had beneficial repercussions, resulting in significant, positive developments in relations between Canadian museum professionals and First Nations communities. The controversy led to the organisation of *Preserving Our Heritage: A Working Conference Between Museums and First Peoples* held at Carleton University, Ottawa in November 1988, organised jointly by the Assembly of First Nations (AFN) and the Canadian Museums Association (CMA), and funded by the Departments of Communications, Multiculturalism, and the Secretary of State. Delegates and participants felt strongly that there was a need for a task force to explore the issues surrounding the ownership and representation of First Nations' culture and history, and examine ways of developing new partnerships between museums and First Nations in Canada. A national task force on museums and First Peoples was established by the AFN and the CMA, its mission 'to develop an ethical framework and strategies for Aboriginal Nations to represent their history and culture in concert with cultural institutions' (AFN and CMA, 1992). The Working Committees issued four thousand invitations for contributions towards discussion of the issues to a wide range of academics, professional groups, cultural organisations, government agencies, and First Peoples' representatives and communities. Forty-seven submissions were received which provided the views of many participants of museum and community consultations and professional conferences held across the country.

The results of this consultative process were published in the report entitled *Turning the Page: Forging New Partnerships Between Museums and First Peoples* (AFN and CMA, 1992) which included a series of recommendations relating to interpretation, access, repatriation, training, support for community-based cultural institutions, funding, and international collections.

261

The recommendations emphasised the need for the involvement of First Peoples as equal partners in the planning and presentation of exhibitions and programmes relating to their cultures, the care and preservation of collections, and in the research and disposition of human remains. It called for federal funding to support collaborative projects, to support the establishment and running of Aboriginal-run cultural centres and museums, to provide appropriate professional and technical training, to inventory and disseminate information about ethnographic collections, and to monitor future developments. It particularly identified the potential of museums 'to engage with living cultures, not just objects' and 'become forums for discussions of relevant contemporary issues'. Exhibitions provide valuable opportunities for such discussion: they can inform the public and engender debate.

In the permanent Northwest Coast exhibition, the Royal British Columbia Museum provides information concerning the background history of contemporary Native land claims. In London, England, the Museum of Mankind's exhibition *Living Arctic* (1987–8), addressed Native concerns about the effects upon their livelihood and lifestyle of international legislation restricting hunting and fishing. A recent temporary exhibition *Eulachon* (1993), organised by the University of British Columbia Museum of Anthropology, addressed Native fishing rights. During 1993, in the aftermath of the Mabo ruling, the National Museum of Australia presented *Landmarks: People, Land and Political Change*, an exhibition which examined three pieces of legislation which have had enormous political impact within Australia, and 'challenged established ideas about settlement, ownership and use of the land'.

The Canadian museologist, Duncan Cameron (1971), has argued that museums have a social responsibility to present the public with an objective view of controversial subjects. 'There is something missing in the world of museums and art galleries . . . there is a real and urgent need for the re-establishment of the forum as an institution in society.' He called for the creation of 'forums for confrontation, experimentation and debate' as 'related but discrete institutions', arguing that 'the museum as a temple being apolitical, sitting on the fence, unconcerned with social issues,' is unacceptable. 'Where museums, be they of art, history or science, have the knowledge and the resources to interpret matters of public importance, no matter how controversial, they are obliged to do so'. As an example of 'social irresponsibility in museum programming', Cameron cited the concern felt in the 1950s by scientists who were also museum curators regarding pollution. Despite their concern, and the fact that they were actively involved at the international level in discussion about pollution problems, the displays in their natural history museums did not reflect this concern until fifteen to twenty years later when the subject of pollution was becoming generally topical.

Today, it is becoming more widely accepted that museums can provide an important forum for the debate of contemporary issues and some institutions are fulfilling the role of forum as envisioned by Cameron. Science and natural history museums commonly explore controversial issues such as pollution, the fur trade, sharks, endangered species, in an effort to inform and educate the public and actively to alter attitudes and actions. While curators in the field of anthropology have been somewhat more reticent in dealing with controversial subjects, some have been boldly addressing highly emotive and contentious issues.

As we saw in earlier chapters, these efforts have, in some instances, proved controversial and have been subjected to criticism, demonstrations and demands for closure; yet these examples prove how powerful exhibitions can be in raising public awareness of issues and stimulating public debate. Roy Strong has described exhibitions as 'the museum's tongue', stating that:

> 'they can . . . open the eyes of the public to a new aspect of the past or present. They can delight a million visitors with a spectacle of richness and glitter and they can, equally, harrow and upset. . . . Exhibitions have a polemical value . . . (they) should not only caress and console, they should infuriate.
>
> (1983: 78)

As witnessed by the events recounted earlier in the book, exhibitions do, at times, infuriate; and that fury leads to greater thought and discussion, and ultimately to action. While revisionist historical views are not new – they have been the subject of numerous university courses and academic texts over the last twenty to thirty years – they were not widely discussed outside academic circles and certainly did not (and still do not) receive due attention in the primary and secondary school education systems or in public museums. Due to the controversy surrounding the exhibition, *The West as America* succeeded in bringing such perspectives to the attention of the general public and provided endless material for newspaper articles, radio and television programmes.

Likewise, the Cree response to the exhibition *The Spirit Sings* has made more people aware of land rights issues, as was the intention of the demonstrators, but it has also drawn attention to the continuing practice of white curatorial staff interpreting 'the Other'. Painful though such events may be for those most closely involved, they are having a positive effect upon professional awareness of the issues of museum representation and cultural diversity and are helping to achieve progress on the long and painful road towards more inclusive institutions.

Given this potential power to stimulate public debate, we must ask if museums should not be more actively involved in helping to defend the rights of some of the world's minority groups by bringing to public attention some of the issues relating to topics such as Aboriginal land rights or the decimation of the Amazonian rain forest and its effects upon, not just the environment, but the indigenous population. Natural history museums preserve specimens of flora and fauna; but they also take action to protect wildlife and to inform the public of the factors affecting endangered species. Just as natural history museums recognise their responsibility in informing the public of conservation issues, so ethnographic and anthropological museums have a responsibility to inform the public of social and political issues relating to the peoples whose culture they

263

represent in their exhibitions. They should be concerned not just with preserving the material culture of the peoples of the world, but also with informing visitors of the plight of endangered peoples, thereby perhaps helping to preserve the living cultures. The incidence of exhibitions addressing human rights issues is pitifully small. Do museum staff care more about the fate of wildlife and artefacts than they do about other human beings?

Instead of avoiding potentially controversial issues, curators should exploit public interest and the publicity potential of such issues by contributing information and artefacts in displays which are designed to enlighten the public and add to the debate. If a particular country or cultural group is in the news, museums with relevant collections could produce small displays of artefacts relating to that country or culture and provide background facts. Responding in this way to topics of current concern is a practice which few museums undertake, yet it is an approach which was utilised in the Milwaukee Science Museum over 30 years ago. De Borhegyi (1963: 45–57) described how the museum responded to current affairs:

> When Laos was in the headlines, we installed a special short-term exhibit, showing the geography of the country, the linguistic groupings, something of the history, and some Laotian ethnological and art objects. This was a far from comprehensive picture of the area, but it helped the museum visitor to view the current political problem in some kind of context.

The Australian Museum's 'Rapid Response' Project Team, described in Chapter 2, was established on this philosophical basis and provides a valuable means of tackling topical issues and presenting factual data for public consideration, much in the manner of the forum Cameron appealed for in 1971 (Cameron, 1971: 11–24).

Museums in the twenty-first century: artefact- or people-focused?

Many of the examples of museum practice described in this book illustrate positive initiatives which have been taking place in museums in recent years. The new relationships arising out of repatriation negotiations indicate that the curatorial staff involved are now acknowledging and responding sympathetically to the interests of indigenous peoples and their traditions. The successful resolution of repatriation negotiations has often proven to be a valuable process of engendering trust and social interaction between museums and indigenous peoples. Whereas in the past, museums have tended to provide a single authoritative voice; today it is becoming more common to present alternative or multiple perspectives. This affords visitors the opportunity to reflect upon alternative views and provides opportunities for self-representation by peoples who are not normally consulted as part of the interpretive process.

During the era of post-colonialism, museums and communities have begun to enter into collaborative partnerships in research, exhibition presentation, archive acquisition, contemporary collecting, and other areas of museology, and have undertaken projects of primary benefit to the communities, such as medical research leading to improved healthcare, landrights issues and the establishment of community archives, cultural centres and museums. Collaborative activities of this nature have proven beneficial not just to the community but to the museum as well, as they change completely the traditional relationship between the museum anthropologist or ethnographer and the community.

Traditional methods of taking information and artefacts from the community by an outsider, to be presented by and to 'Others', often with little evidence of respect for alternative viewpoints, have resulted in resentment, hostility, and suspicion. Requests for fieldwork are often now regarded with deep suspicion by tribal peoples who are weary of providing material for the academic research and reputations of others, and past experiences have taught them that they receive little in return. The examples given in this chapter demonstrate a few of the ways in which museums and anthropologists can use their knowledge and the collections to actively assist communities in dealing with issues of great concern. This encourages more active participation on the part of the community and can promote mutually beneficial relationships between museums, anthropologists, and the peoples with whom they work.

This does not mean that all museums have adopted such initiatives in research, exhibition presentation, and the provision of visitor services and education programmes. Nor does it mean that bias and stereotyping, romanticism and superficiality no longer occur. There are still great strides to be taken before all museums reflect accurately the true diversity of society, and provide services appropriate to the different cultural groups and of relevance to contemporary society. However, individual cases have done much to bring about a reconciliation of the dichotomy between western concerns with the preservation and reverence of the inviolable object, and Native peoples concerns for people and traditions. It is this interest in people and traditions that needs to be emphasised more. The traditional role of the museum must change, if it is to adapt to the needs of contemporary society, from that of an institution primarily concerned with artefacts and specimens to one which focuses upon people as creators and users of the artefacts in their collections.

Chris Anderson, of the South Australian Museum, feels that the conventional approach to museum curatorship which puts the care of the object before all else must change, believing that a curator working with indigenous secret/sacred material needs to be 'a people-person, not an object-person' with, potentially, a division of labour between those dealing with the basic curation of the collections and those involved in research and interaction with communities. Out of this has grown 'a philosophy that underlies all our policies, that museums aren't really concerned with objects; the objects really just represent people and relationships between people, past and present' (Anderson, 1993). This philosophy is reflected in the development of interdisciplinary projects which, for example, portray science as culturally defined, merging anthropology and natural history, focusing upon the ways in which people have viewed, used, portrayed and interacted with their environment.

265

At the seminar *Preserving Indigenous Cultures: A New Role for Museums* held in Adelaide in 1978, David Baradas, formerly director of the Museum of Philippine Traditional Cultures, suggested that museums in 'technologically developed areas' are 'artefact-focused', while 'developing or traditional area museums' are 'context-focused' (1980: 79). The context in which western museums and their collections were established has changed, and museums must also change in response to the contemporary contexts of the objects – the lost heritage of peoples still fighting for cultural autonomy and self-determination in the post-colonial era.

It is time that museums undertook a re-appraisal of the fundamental philosophies upon which they currently operate, to re-evaluate and re-focus their roles in the light of contemporary social thinking, so reflecting in their policies and practices the recognition of other peoples' world views and rights with regard to the ownership, representation and interpretation of material culture. Perhaps in this way they could become the context- and people-focused museums that Anderson and Baradas speak of.

Epilogue

Since this book was first published in 1996 there have been a number of significant developments, most notably relating to repatriation and restitution issues. These developments will be reported in this epilogue which will review the situation in Canada, Australia and the United Kingdom and provide an update of the United States Native American Graves Protection and Repatriation Act outlining the situation ten years after the legislation was implemented.

International treaties and activities

Issues of repatriation and restitution have become the focus of scrutiny by museums, professional organisations and governments. Across the globe, looting and the illicit trafficking of cultural property continue to cause the destruction of archaeological sites and the loss of cultural heritage. Efforts by government agencies and by international organisations such as ICOM and UNESCO continue to be directed at halting the destruction and loss of material by ratification and enforcement of international treaties designed to protect the cultural heritage and halt the illicit exportation of art works and antiquities. In its battle against the illicit trade in art and artefacts, UNESCO has been highlighting the damage that is being done to the cultural heritage of countries which are at particular risk of the looting of archaeological sites and the theft and export of works of art. Through publications and internet sites they have been publicising thefts and threats or actual damage to cultural heritage sites, and continuing to solicit governments to adopt international protocols designed to halt the illicit trade and to protect cultural heritage. The 1970 UNESCO Convention on the Means of Prohibiting and Preventing the Illicit Import, Export, and Transfer of Ownership of Cultural Property now has 92 States Parties, including the UK which signed the UNESCO Convention in March 2001, following recommendations made by the Illicit Antiquities Research Centre (Brodie *et al.* 2000: 6) and by a Ministerial Advisory Panel on Illicit Trade (DCMS, 2000: 23). New Zealand has not yet signed. The 1995 UNIDROIT Convention came into force in 1998 after Romania became the fifth country to ratify or accede to it. By 20 April 2000, another seven countries had joined them; but Britain, Canada, USA, Australia and New Zealand are not amongst them.

Ninety-five countries are now Parties to the 1954 Hague Convention on the Protection of Cultural Property in the Event of Armed Conflict; but the USA and Great Britain are not amongst them. A Second Protocol to the 1954 Hague Convention was adopted on 26 March 1999. This seeks to address the various arguments made against the First Protocol and to provide greater protection for cultural property than it was able to afford. The new protocol requires occupying powers to prohibit and prevent the illicit export, removal or change of ownership of cultural property and defines new crimes in relation to the protection of cultural property. It directs that an act of hostility against cultural property may only be made as an 'imperative military necessity'. This is defined as an occasion when 'that cultural property has, by its function, been made into a military objective; and there is no feasible alternative available to obtain a similar military advantage to that offered by directing an act of hostility against that objective'. It also strengthens and clarifies the sections dealing with conflicts within nations. The protocol will have to be ratified by individual states and supported by the introduction of national laws, but there is also a provision for universal international jurisdiction enabling crimes to be prosecuted in other countries than those in which they were committed (UNESCO, 1999).

The campaign to locate and return works of art stolen by the Nazis during the Holocaust and the Second World War has recently drawn particular attention to the losses suffered by Jewish families and others who were the victims of the Nazi regime. Between 1933 and 1945, the Nazis carried out the largest programme of systematic looting the world has seen. Beginning in the late 1930s with the persecution of the Jews, the Nazis began plundering art works and antiques, a programme that continued in the occupied countries across Europe. The stolen art works were to be transported to the Reich for Hitler's planned Führermuseum in Linz or to the private collections of Hermann Göering and other high-ranking Nazis.

Although the Allies undertook a programme of restitution at the end of the war, portions of the Nazi collection fell into the hands of the Soviets and others. Indeed, the Soviet Union had its own programme of art acquisition undertaken by teams of military personnel and art specialists specifically assigned to this task. Nazi loot stolen from Jewish homes and from private and public buildings in the occupied countries has become scattered across Europe and North America, although the bulk remains in collections or secret stores in the former Soviet Union. For decades, efforts have been made by Jewish organisations to have the stolen art works restored to their rightful owners or their descendants but have largely failed, until recently, due to lack of knowledge of the whereabouts of the works. Hundreds of stolen art works have remained lost to their owners and some may now be in the collections of some of the world's most respected institutions. However, the issue is being addressed by major museums in North America and Europe in which staff have been undertaking reviews of their collections to confirm the provenance of works acquired since 1933 and identify whether any were indeed stolen during the Holocaust or the war.

Whilst these developments are significant, there are many other issues concerning the return of cultural property still to be addressed. *Making Representations* is primarily concerned with the issues associated with the continued holding, care and display of collections of antiquities and ethnographic material acquired in past centuries, matters which continue to pose ethical and legal challenges for those involved in museum collection management. Here, too, there have been further developments during the past five years.

The International Council of Museums (ICOM) Ethics Committee is proposing certain revisions to its code of ethics which reflect the increasing awareness within the museum sector of the concerns, beliefs and wishes of indigenous peoples in relation to the care of their cultural heritage. The proposed revisions include an addition to the section dealing with conservation and restoration warning that 'the restoration of sacred objects may be unacceptable to the communities which produced them and have on-going associations with them'. In the section dealing with human remains and material of ritual significance, the term 'ritual' is replaced by the word 'sacred'. The proposed revisions include directions to museums that collections of human remains and sacred objects 'should always be available to qualified researchers and educators, but not to the morbidly curious', and that 'research and care of such collections should be carried out in a manner acceptable not only to fellow professionals but also to those of various beliefs, including particular members of the community, ethnic or religious groups concerned'. It also adds that

> Although it is occasionally necessary to use human remains and other sensitive material in interpretative exhibits, this must be done with tact and with respect for the feelings for human dignity held by all peoples . . . Furthermore, requests for removal from public display of human remains or material of sacred significance must be addressed expeditiously with respect and sensitivity. Requests for the return of such material should be addressed similarly. Museum policies should clearly define the process for responding to such requests.
>
> (ICOM, 2000)

At an international level, recognition has been growing of the need to assert and protect the human rights of indigenous peoples and to provide protection for indigenous intellectual and cultural property rights. This has been facilitated in large measure through the efforts of indigenous and Third World peoples and through the activities of the United Nations and its agencies including the United Nations' Commission on Human Rights, the United Nations' Educational, Scientific and Cultural Organisation (UNESCO), the United Nations' Working Group on Indigenous Populations (WGIP), and the United Nations' World Intellectual Property Organization (WIPO). These efforts have seen the setting of standards and drafting of international agreements such as the UN Draft Declaration on the Rights of Indigenous Peoples (UNWGIP, 1993) and the Mataatua Declaration on Cultural and Intellectual Property Rights of Indigenous Peoples (Commission on Human Rights, 1993).

In Australia and in other countries, the issue of intellectual property rights and their infringement, has been highlighted by a number of legal cases brought against individuals, governments or commercial organisations involving the appropriation by non-Aborigines of Aboriginal designs and images. This is an issue which is of increasing concern and complexity; as the World Wide Web, digital imaging and storage and retrieval systems become more sophisticated they offer increasing opportunities for making collections more accessible and provide individuals with opportunities for marketing their work as never before. These technologies offer tremendous potential for increased dissemination of information and access to images of collections around the world. In the US, for example, the Arctic Studies Center and the repatriation office of the National Museum of Natural History used video teleconferencing facilities to link museum staff in Washington, DC with elders of the Tlingit and Haida Tribes in Juneau, Alaska. The elders were able to observe on-screen images of the beautiful objects made by their tribal ancestors and now held in the museum collections, and provide many insightful comments based upon their memories, experiences, and indigenous knowledge. Such projects provide further examples of the benefits of the collaborative procedures now being employed in some museums and illustrate the value of new technologies in increasing access to collections. Simultaneously, however, these technologies also greatly increase the threat of appropriation of art work, images and other forms of indigenous cultural property. So, while information and communications technologies provide the potential means to resolve some of the issues of accessibility highlighted by demands for repatriation, they also offer the potential for further abuses of indigenous people's rights and the continued appropriation of their cultural property, now in the virtual realm.

All of these issues have been the subject of extensive debate over the past few years and the following text will outline recent developments in heritage protection and repatriation issues in the countries dealt with earlier in Part 3 of this book.

United Kingdom

Repatriation has, in the past, been seen by the UK government as a matter to be dealt with by museums, not government; however, recent developments have thrust the issue onto the political and cultural agenda in the UK. In October 1999, the Culture, Media and Sport Committee of the House of Commons announced that it would conduct an inquiry into the return and illicit trade of cultural property (House of Commons, 1999). In February 2000, the Committee announced its terms of reference and took oral evidence at a series of sessions held between March and June. Their report was published in July 2000 (House of Commons, 2000). Although illicit trafficking and spoliation were the main subjects of their enquiries, broader issues of repatriation were also examined, and the Committee took evidence relating to indigenous concerns over the holding of human remains and cultural property in museum collections. These matters had also become the subject of scrutiny by the main professional organisations in Britain.

During the 1990s, the Museums Association had been examining the issue of repatriation and the policies and experiences of their members with the intention of identifying how they might provide support to museum staff. To this end, the Museums Association commissioned the author to undertake research on their behalf (Simpson, 1994b; 1997). Chapter 9 of this book (pp. 224–6) includes a description of the first stage of the Museums Association's fact-finding mission, when they commissioned research on the policies and experiences of museums in dealing with requests for repatriation of human remains from their collections. The results of this work were published in an article entitled 'Burying the Past' which appeared in the July 1994 issue of *Museums Journal*. Recognising the need to address the broader repatriation issues involved in other areas of museum collections, the Museums Association then commissioned the author to undertake further research. This time the subject was contested items in museum collections dealing with all other types of material including archaeological and ethnographic material, natural history specimens, social history collections, and so on, but excluding human remains except where these have been modified in some way and incorporated into an ethnographic artefact.

Two surveys were conducted. One focused upon the attitudes of individual staff members to repatriation and the reasons they considered to be the most compelling for retention or return. It was sent to those holding individual membership of the Museums Association and included individuals representing all staff levels and disciplines, including full-time post-holders, freelance staff, and volunteers. The second survey sought information relating to the policies of museums with regard to repatriation and the actual experiences, if any, that they had of receiving and dealing with such requests. This survey form was sent to museums and other collecting institutions that were members of the Museums Association. The research project also involved the collection of data relating to the policies of various professional organisations in Britain with an interest in the issue of repatriation, including the Museums Association, the Museums and Galleries Commission (now replaced by Resource: The Council for Museums, Archives and Libraries), the Museum Ethnographers' Group, and the Society of Museum Archaeologists. This was compared with similar data gathered from professional organisations and government agencies in other European countries.

The results of this research project were published in a report entitled *Museums and Repatriation: An Account of Contested Items in Museum Collections in the UK, with Comparative Material from Other Countries* (Simpson, 1997) which was launched in November 1997 at a seminar held in the Museum of London. Copies of the full report are available from the Museums Association but a brief outline of the findings is given below.

One of the most significant facts to emerge was the extremely high number of respondents who accepted that, in certain circumstances, repatriation was a feasible action for museums to take in response to repatriation requests. The survey questionnaire sent to individual MA members suggested a number of contexts in which an item might be returned and asked respondents to indicate which they felt were valid reasons for an item to be returned. Of the 123 respondents, only three were categorically opposed to repatriation. The vast majority of respondents (97.6 per cent) accepted the notion of repatriation and acknowledged the validity of a number of arguments for the return of cultural property. Respondents placed most importance upon the significance of an item as part of the cultural heritage of a living people (75 per cent) or its requirement for use in the continuing religious practices of a living people (65.8 per cent).

'The item is a significant part of the cultural heritage of a living people' was acknowledged by 75 per cent of respondents as an acceptable reason for return; while 65.8 per cent agreed that, if an item is required by a living culture for the practice of continuing religious traditions, then this would be acceptable as a reason for return. Less importance was given to the status of an object as being of a secret/sacred nature with viewing restricted, for example, to the uninitiated. Nevertheless almost half of the respondents (49.2 per cent) regarded this as an acceptable argument for return, with a similar number (50.8 per cent) agreeing that a reason for repatriation could be that an item was communally owned and should not have been given away or sold by any individual. If the item was endangered at the time of removal but can now be well cared for by those seeking repatriation, 62.2 per cent of respondents agreed that it might be appropriate to repatriate. The continued preservation of items in 'a museum or secure storage facility' was a primary consideration for 69.2 per cent. Just over half (54.2 per cent) felt that an acceptable reason for repatriation could be that the item was removed at a time when the collector and the culture of origin were at war or in conflict. Removal from a grave or other burial site was the least acceptable reason for repatriation (43.3 per cent).

The results of the institutional survey showed only 17 out of 164 museums had received requests for repatriation, of which nine had repatriated items. However, it should be noted here that some of the nation's largest museums, and those museums that have had the most direct involvement in repatriation discussions in the past, did not participate in the research. The British Museum, for example, declined to contribute to the research project but recently submitted a memorandum to the House of Commons Select Committee on Cultural Property: Return and Illicit Trade in which it is stated that the Museum has over the past 30 years (1970–99) received twenty-seven foreign requests for repatriation whose nature and source vary considerably. 'Some bids have been government to government, some have been government to British Museum, others have been less formal, involving individual politicians, cultural leaders or museum services' (BM in House of Commons, 2000: vol 2: 219). Despite the restrictions on disposition imposed by the British Museum Act, there have been a few cases of items being repatriated in the past.

Comparison of the results from the two surveys provide clear evidence that although there is sympathy for the issues which motivate requests for repatriation, the views of individual staff remain, for the most part, untested by experience. The results also highlighted the fact that a dichotomy exists between institutional policies in museums in the UK and the personal views of the staff who work within them. In the attitude survey of museum staff, there was almost unanimous agreement that repatriation from museum collections was acceptable in certain circumstances, yet only 5.5 per cent of the museums that responded to the survey had a written policy relating to repatriation. Consequently, a tension may exist between the individual staff member's professional responsibilities to enforce museum policy, and their personal views. This tension has been articulated by Dr Schuyler Jones, former director of the Pitt Rivers Museum. During the 1990s, he was involved in the negotiations over a claim made by the Zuni Indians of New Mexico in the USA, for the return of a war god which the Zuni were claiming as authentic, despite it having been made by an American anthropologist, Frank Cushing (Coote, 1997). Dr Schuyler Jones stated that as an anthropologist he sympathised with the Zuni's request, but as a museum director he had to protect the integrity of the museum's collections (Jones, S., 1996).

While repatriation is not an issue that has directly affected most museums in Britain, it is nevertheless a subject of considerable interest within the museum profession and it was clear from the comments made by respondents that many museum staff feel ill-equipped to deal with requests. Repeatedly, respondents indicated that they felt that there was a lack of guidance from the government agencies and professional organisations responsible for museums in the UK. They emphasised their wish to know much more about this complex subject and the need for guidance should they ever be faced with such a request.

Additional research involved the collection of data from professional organisations in the UK and Europe to ascertain the level of professional guidance currently available to museum staff and to relate this to the broader context of policies and practices in other European countries. This showed that British organisations such as area museum councils, the Museums Association, the Museum and Galleries Commission, and the Museum Ethnographers Group provide little guidance to members concerning the repatriation of cultural property. Most referred to the Museum Association's Code of Practice for Museum Governing Bodies, which itself made little reference to repatriation per se. There was even less evidence of professional guidance in other European countries. As discussed earlier, it was also clear that existing international treaties on the illicit trade in cultural property have little, if any, relevance to demands for repatriation of material acquired during the colonial era.

Contemporary politics and cultural ideologies will doubtless ensure that repatriation requests increase in future as indigenous communities seek to regain control of their cultural heritage and the historical record. It was recognition of this factor and of the need to support their membership, that motivated the Museums Association to commission research into repatriation issues in the United Kingdom. The recommendations made to the Museums Association in the report suggested five possible courses of action that would provide muscum staff with greater access to information and guidance on repatriation issues, and ensure that repatriation enquiries were dealt with in a professional yet sensitive manner.

The first recommendation made in the report, and the one that was most important and urgent, was that a set of guidelines should be prepared. These would provide museum staff with a set of principles and issues that they would need to consider when responding to a repatriation request. There can be no simple formula for responding to repatriation requests and each artefact needs to be considered on a case-by-case basis. It was therefore suggested that these guidelines should be informative but non-prescriptive, designed to raise issues for consideration in each individual case. It was proposed that the principles of the guidelines should reflect the concerns of all parties and encourage museums to be sensitive to the interests of donors, researchers and other members of the public, as well as to the traditional owners of items in the collections.

In November 1998, the Museums and Galleries Commission, in a joint initiative with the Museums Association and the National Museum Directors' Conference, commissioned Jane Leggett, a British Museum consultant based in New Zealand, to undertake the task of writing the guidelines. A steering group was established to oversee this process and consisted of senior staff from eight museums and representatives of the three afore-mentioned organisations, including the author as one of the Museums Association representatives. The guidelines, entitled *Restitution and Repatriation: Guidelines for Good Practice* (Leggett, 2000), were published by the MGC in March 2000.

Drawing upon the research and case studies in the MA's report *Museums and Repatriation* and other recent examples, Leggett drew up a detailed framework of issues to be considered and actions to be taken by governing bodies, museum directors and staff when they receive a repatriation claim. The guidelines are not prescriptive in terms of outcome. They provide a checklist of issues to be considered and differing viewpoints to be heard, and suggest a series of steps which museum staff might follow in progressing through the complexities of responding to a claim. Indeed, the MGC points out that the guidelines

> do not instruct museums on whether or not to return objects from their collections. The MGC believes that responsibility for decisions on such requests should lie with museums' governing bodies, which are best placed to examine the validity and consider the merits of each request.
>
> (MGC, 1999)

In responding to a request for the repatriation of an item, the guidelines advise museum staff to explore and clarify the status of those making the repatriation request, and to understand the reasons for the request being made. Here, the guidelines include such motivations as cultural renewal, respect for human remains or sacred objects, completion of burial rites, retrieval of property that was wrongfully taken, research requirements, museum collection acquisition, and also commercial advantage or political motivation at a national or local level. The publication includes case studies of recent requests to illustrate the variety of cases received. The guidelines direct those handling requests to consider the interests of all parties and balance the needs of museums, museum visitors and researchers and also those of the requesting parties. Staff are also asked to consider the future of the material if it is retained and if it is returned, and to consider alternative forms of resolution. Guidance is given on managing the decision-making process and the announcement of the decision through sensitive and appropriate communications with those directly concerned, and advises museums to manage carefully the public announcements and media coverage.

The production of the MGC's guidelines was a very significant development in British museological policy providing for the first time clear guidance for museums in responding to requests and in handling all aspects of the decision-making process and the repatriation, if a decision to return was taken. The guidelines have been well received within the museum profession and were commended by members of the Museums Standing Advisory Group on Repatriation and Related Cultural Property Issues and by the House of Commons Select Committee which recently reported on the subject of cultural property (House of Commons, 2000, xxxiv; and vol 2: 99).

As illustrated by the research, repatriation is an issue of which most museum staff have had little or no direct experience. To date, requests for the repatriation of artefacts originating from overseas have largely been addressed to major collecting institutions, particularly national museums such as the British Museum, the Museum of Natural History, and the Victoria and Albert Museum. Requests for human remains have been made primarily to large research institutions known to hold substantial collections of skeletal material, such as the Natural History Museum, the Royal College of Surgeons, and the University of Edinburgh. However, there have been instances where the return is sought from other sources of the remains of known individuals and there have also been instances of general repatriation requests being made to all museums across the country which hold ethnographic collections.

In 1996 the late Bernie Grant, formerly a Labour MP, wrote to a number of museums around the UK requesting the return of Benin 'bronzes' and other items which had been taken from Benin City during the British Punitive Expedition in 1897. His assistance in this matter was apparently sought by the Oba of Benin and was supported by the West African Museums Programme (WAMP) and the African Reparations Movement (UK). The recent centennial of the event highlighted the issue of Benin artefacts being held in overseas museums and became the focus of the campaign at that particular time. A major exhibition of African art at the Royal Academy was also targeted as a means of highlighting the circumstances under which some items in museum collections were acquired. On their website, the African Reparations Movement showed images of African artefacts that were included in the exhibition. ARM claimed that many of them had been acquired by theft and displayed their photographs emblazoned in red lettering with the word 'Stolen!' (ARM, 1996).

In 1999, David Devenish, then the acting director of the embryonic National Museum of the Cook Islands, sent a general request to museums holding ethnographic collections. He sought the return of, or information pertaining to, material originating from the Cook Islands. One British museum has returned material while others have provided documentation, photographs and offered to lend material.

Other repatriation requests have been made to British museums on a regional basis; that is, museums or cultural organisations requesting the return of an item from another part of the country. Recent cases include the Stone of Destiny, which for five centuries had resided under the coronation throne in

Westminster Abbey in London since its theft from Scotland in 1296. Its theft had long been the subject of resentment amongst Scots and its return to Scotland in 1996 was warmly welcomed. Another request has been made to Glasgow Museums by a Community Council in Scotland for the return of the remains of the 'Covenanter', although the identification of the body as that of a Covenanter is disputed.

One of the case studies cited in *Museums and Repatriation* concerned the return from the collection of Exeter Museum in England, of a bracelet and necklace that had belonged to Truganini. She was an important figure in Tasmanian Aboriginal history and was perceived by colonialists to be the 'last full-blooded Tasmanian Aborigine'. After her death in 1876, her skeleton hung for many years on display in Hobart Museum where it was scrutinised by curious settlers. It remained there for over ninety years until it was removed and placed in a coffin in the basement and then returned to the Tasmanian Aboriginal community after legislative changes in 1974 and 1976.

In 1994, staff of Exeter Museum contacted the Tasmanian Aboriginal community to inform them of their holding of Truganini's bracelet and necklace. Knowing the tragic events suffered by Truganini and her people during the nineteenth century, and recognising the importance of the items, they felt that the Tasmanian Aboriginal community should be notified of their presence in Exeter Museum. Negotiations took place and it was agreed that the jewellery would be returned to the care of the Tasmanian Aboriginal community for safekeeping in their Cultural Centre. Following this, Tasmanian Aboriginal Centre (TAC) representatives were for some time unable to undertake the journey to England to formally receive the items. However, in November 1997 representatives of the TAC and the Tasmanian Aboriginal community travelled to England to collect Truganini's necklace and bracelet and return them home.

This trip provided the Tasmanian Aboriginal representatives with the opportunity to present a paper at the conference launching the MA report *Museums and Repatriation*. It was a chance to address British Museum staff directly and speak to them forcibly of Tasmanian Aboriginal continuity, to assert their rights and their cultural identity. Many books speak of the extinction of the Tasmanian Aboriginal race and describe Truganini as the last 'full-blooded' female Tasmanian Aborigine. Robert Brain, for example, in his 1972 text *Into the Primitive Environment*, describes Truganini as 'the last Tasmanian of all' (Brain, 1972: 26). Her description in these terms has led to a common belief that Tasmanian Aborigines are extinct, a concept which is passionately repudiated by present-day Tasmanian Aborigines. In a powerful and moving presentation, the TAC speaker, Caroline Spotswood, spoke forcibly about the lack of recognition of Tasmanian Aboriginal continuity, the loss of their material culture, and the continued retention in museum collections of human remains and historical material relating to Tasmanian Aboriginal history and culture. She described the response by one museum director who 'refused to return remains, telling Tasmanian Aboriginal lawyer Michael Mansell, that it was a "fact" that Tasmanian Aborigines were extinct' (Spotswood *et al.*, 1997: 1).

Despite attitudes like this, Tasmanian Aboriginal human remains had been returned from several museums in the United Kingdom and the TAC had also begun campaigning for the return of cultural material. They found, however, that many museums had refused their requests, claiming that they were prohibited by legislation from returning items. In Australia, the TAC had successfully claimed human remains from museum collections, but had found some museums less co-operative when requests were made for items of cultural property and was particularly critical of the South Australian Museum in Adelaide. The TAC paper also criticised the policy in museums which

> endorses the return of remains and secret/sacred objects only, and proposes all sorts of collaborative arrangements for other, utilitarian, cultural items. The museums' focus has shifted from ownership to custodianship of indigenous material. The museums will not give up this custodianship; their strong view of themselves as the proper carers of objects persists. In all cases, the museum keeps the pieces and the owners get to use it in specified ways, with the proviso that they show adequate care.
>
> (ibid: 6)

Later that week, Ms Spotswood accompanied Tasmanian Aboriginal elders as they travelled to Exeter where they formally received the bracelet and necklace.

Another repatriation case that was described in *Museums and Repatriation* and which has since been resolved, was the request that was made for the return of a Lakota Ghost Dance shirt from Kelvingrove Museum in Glasgow, Scotland. Public opinion proved strong in support of repatriation when the future of the Ghost Dance shirt was debated at a public meeting in Glasgow in November 1998.

Followers of the nineteenth-century Native American Ghost Dance Religion believed that they would succeed in driving out the white men and wore Ghost Dance shirts that they believed would protect them from the white man's bullets. Among the followers of this religion were more than 250 men, women and children of the Lakota Sioux who were massacred by the Seventh Cavalry at Wounded Knee in 1890. The Ghost Dance shirt in the collection of the Kelvingrove Museum was acquired by the museum from a member of Buffalo Bill's Wild West show when it visited Glasgow in 1892; he claimed that it had been removed from the body of one of the Lakota Sioux killed at Wounded Knee.

In 1992, the shirt was seen in a display case in the Kelvingrove Museum by a Cherokee lawyer. This led to a formal request being submitted to the museum in 1994 by the Wounded Knee Survivors' Association. They sought the return of the shirt and four other Lakota items, although they later rescinded their claim for the other items in order to pursue the claim for the shirt. The request was originally refused on the basis that the shirt was not unique and there were several others in the US, some of which had already been returned to the Lakota. The Kelvingrove shirt was the only one in the UK and it was felt by museum staff that the shirt provided a potent vehicle for telling the story of the massacre of Wounded Knee to museum visitors in Scotland. However, following the MA seminar *Point of No Return?: Museums and Repatriation* in

November 1997 which launched the report *Museums and Repatriation*, Kelvingrove Museum reviewed its policy on repatriation and a member/officer group was established to consider individual requests for repatriation in the future.

The matter of the Ghost Dance shirt was re-examined early in 1998 and a public hearing took place in November of that year. Of the 150 written submissions considered, only six argued for the retention of the shirt in Glasgow (Glasgow City Council, 1998: 2). Presentations were given by museum staff and by members of the Lakota Sioux. The official museum view was that the museum had legal ownership of the shirt and was under no legal obligation to return it; however, Mark O'Neill, head of curatorial services, explained in his presentation that the decision should be made upon consideration of humanitarian concerns.

> If museums represent our better selves, our humane values, then we have to admit to the possibility that there may be other values, which are more important than that of possession. Possession is not an absolute value. If our values lead us to preserve an object because of what it tells us about the history of a particular human group, then it is inconsistent not to give that group the respect of at least taking their views seriously. The objects we preserve and the stories they tell reflect our values, what we stand for, how we wish to see ourselves, what we wish to bring with us into the future. Contrary to popular beliefs, museums are not in fact about the past, but about the present and the future.
>
> (O'Neill, 1998: 1)

After consideration of all the submissions, Glasgow City Council's Arts and Culture Committee took the decision to return the shirt to the Lakota Sioux. This was on condition that the shirt would be displayed in a place where the story of the Lakota Sioux and the shirt's history in Glasgow can be told. As part of the agreement, it was determined that the shirt may be taken back to Glasgow for public display at times agreed to by both Glasgow City Council and the Wounded Knee Survivors' Association. The Council and the Association would also explore opportunities for developing educational and cultural links. The City Council made clear that the decision to return the shirt does not bind the Council to return other artefacts from its museums. The repatriation of the shirt does not, therefore, represent a precedent for Glasgow Museums or other museums in the UK, as each museum will consider every request individually and reach decisions based upon their own assessments of the case.

At the hearing in Glasgow, Marcella LeBeau, a Lakota tribal elder and great-granddaughter of one of the survivors of the massacre at Wounded Knee, presented Glasgow City Council with a replica shirt that she had made. Today, this shirt is on display in the Kelvingrove Museum with the full story of the terrible events of December 1890. The display also details the history, acquisition and repatriation of the original Ghost Dance shirt and the donation by the Lakota of the new shirt.

The original Ghost Dance shirt was formally handed over to the Wounded Knee Survivors' Association in a ceremony in Glasgow and when it was returned to South Dakota, a spiritual ceremony called the Wiping of Tears was held at the site of the mass grave of the Wounded Knee victims. Initially, the shirt will form part of an exhibition at the Cultural Heritage Center in Pierre, South Dakota, and later will be placed on permanent display in a museum which is to be built at Wounded Knee to commemorate the massacre of 1890.

The procedures which Glasgow City Council adopted in handling this repatriation request were commended by members of the House of Commons Review Committee which examined cultural property issues in 2000; in particular they praised the extensive public consultation undertaken and the holding of a public hearing (House of Commons, 2000: xxxv–xxxvi).

While the production of the MGC's repatriation and restitution guidelines provides practical advice to museum staff in the procedural aspects of handling a claim, there is, nevertheless, still a need for staff to gain more information concerning the broad range of issues and contexts that may be encountered. Other recommendations that were made in *Museums and Repatriation* focused further upon the dissemination of knowledge concerning repatriation issues. They made reference to specific case studies drawing upon the experiences and views of those involved, as well as information concerning care and storage of artefacts. Specifically, these additional recommendations called for the establishment of a reference file of relevant literature pertaining to repatriation issues, including case studies, literature, official reports, policy documents, statements from tribal councils, etc. While there is now a substantial body of literature on repatriation, much of it is in the form of conference papers, small-circulation professional journals, foreign journals, and the documentation of museums and museum organisations in other parts of the world. Much of this material is held only in university libraries and museums, or in the private collections of researchers and, as such, can be difficult to access. The collection of such material in one accessible location could greatly increase its availability.

It was recommended that such a file should

> be comprehensive and should illustrate the perspectives of traditional owners and museum staff, opponents and proponents of repatriation. This file of information would enable enquirers to inform themselves more fully of the facts of repatriation, the complexity of issues involved, and the views and experiences of indigenous peoples, museum staff and others.
>
> (Simpson, 1997: 95–6)

Suitable material for inclusion would be: case studies of repatriation requests including information relating to the sources and foundations of requests, how they were handled, the outcomes and benefits, as well as the problems encountered. Also, examples of collecting practices, research methods and interpretative practices which help to address issues raised by contested artefacts; and statements, articles, letters etc., reflecting the views of traditional owners concerning the significance of certain items and methods of handling, storing, and displaying material.

It was also suggested that sources of expert advice should be identified, both in the UK and overseas, including individuals from the museum sector, academic institutions and indigenous communities.

> Those who have had experience of handling repatriation requests and developing closer working relationships with communities in other parts of the world would be able to provide valuable advice. Likewise, museum staff, art historians, anthropologists, natural historians, and academics with specialist knowledge can provide insight into the nature of specific items. In addition, the contributions which can be made by indigenous peoples should not be overlooked.
>
> (ibid: 96)

Indeed, great effort should be made to involve indigenous peoples in the process of increasing professional awareness of the complexity of repatriation issues and the seeking of resolutions, as well as providing greater insight into the cultural significance and curatorial requirements of artefacts such as sacred, or otherwise sensitive, material.

At a more formal level, it was suggested that an advisory body should be established to handle or advise on repatriation negotiations. To determine the feasibility, potential role and activities of such a body, it was suggested that advice might be sought from the American Indian Ritual Object Repatriation Foundation (AIRORF) in New York. This US-based organisation was established in 1991 to advise and assist with negotiations between collectors and Native Americans in cases in which the return of a sacred object is sought or offered (see page 223). Anne Cassidy, executive director of AIRORF, has welcomed the suggested establishment of an advisory body in the UK, saying

> even when both parties involved in a return are willing participants, it is extremely helpful to have someone in between to anticipate the expectations of either side, and to maintain the continuity of the interaction. In addition, there are many questions – legal, ethical, procedural, and factual – that come up during repatriation. An advisory body could conceivably develop enough information and experience to provide real help to institutions and individuals grappling with the complexities of repatriation.
>
> (Cassidy, 1999)

In response to these recommendations and those made by the Illicit Antiquities Research Centre in Cambridge in their report *Stealing History: The Illicit Trade in Cultural Material* (Brodie *et al.*, 2000), the possible establishment of a European cultural property advisory centre is being explored by Resource, the Council for Museums, Archives and Libraries.

The recommendations made in *Museums and Repatriation* also suggested that the MA should organise conferences or focus groups to enable representatives of museums to discuss repatriation. This last suggestion was initiated with the organisation, by the Museums Association, of a national conference held in the Museum of London in 1997, to launch the report and provide delegates with first-hand accounts of the handling and outcomes of recent repatriation requests which were described in the report. These cases illustrated the regional and international contexts in which repatriation requests may feature and illustrated a spectrum of outcomes.

The results of the MA research project highlighted the lack of repatriation policies or procedural guidance within British museums or available from the governmental or professional organisations with responsibility for museums. In response, the National Museum Directors' Conference in conjunction with the Museums and Galleries Commission and the Museums Association established the Museums Standing Advisory Group on Repatriation and Related Cultural Property Issues in 1999. While the group will be a forum for the exchange of information and views on restitution and repatriation, one of its initial tasks was to consider and respond to the recommendations made in *Museums and Repatriation*. In particular, they would examine suggestions for the establishment of a reference file of relevant literature pertaining to repatriation issues, and identification of sources of expert advice within museums, academic institutions and indigenous communities.

The Museums Standing Advisory Group submitted evidence to the House of Commons Select Committee which was established to examine issues associated with repatriation and restitution. In their evidence, they emphasised the complexity and breadth of the repatriation issues and commended the MGC's publication of *Restitution and Repatriation: Guidelines for Good Practice* as providing a consistent framework for museum staff to follow in handling a request. They also recommended that the British Government accede to the UNIDROIT (1995) and UNESCO (1970) Conventions or 'at the very least to consider what equivalent measures might be put in place'.

The Select Committee received submissions and heard oral evidence from numerous organisations and individuals. They represented the antiquities and art trades, auction houses, museums and galleries in Britain and Europe, the Italian Carabinieri, the Metropolitan Police Service, the National Criminal Intelligence Service, HM Customs and Excise, Native American tribes, Australian Aboriginal organisations, the Ambassador of the Arab Republic of Egypt, Prince Edun Akenzua of Benin, and the Ethiopian World Federation Incorporated.

In July 2000, the Select Committee published its report in which it was recommended that the Home Office establish 'a national database of stolen cultural property and cultural property exported against the laws of countries concerned under national police control' and ensure that it is 'compatible with the wider international development of a database of stolen and illegally exported cultural property' (ibid: xv–xvii). The Committee took evidence concerning international legislation and considered possible courses of action regarding new domestic legislation and UK ratification of international treaties (ibid: xvii–xxviii). They recommended that the Government 'introduce legislation creating a criminal offence of trading in cultural property in designated categories from designated countries which has been stolen or illicitly excavated in or illegally exported from those countries after the entry into force of the legislation' (ibid: xxix). If these recommendations were implemented, they did not feel that the United Kingdom should sign the 1970 UNESCO Convention, although this was later done on the recommendation of a Ministerial Advisory Panel on Illicit Trade (DCMS, 2000: 23). The Committee welcomed the publication of the MGC's guidelines and commended the procedures previously adopted by Glasgow City Council for handling claims (ibid: xxxiv–xxxvi). While ruling out the introduction of legislation which would give greater powers of disposal generally to the directors and governing bodies of national museums, the Committee felt that, where a special case could be made, it would be appropriate for new primary legislation to be enacted if sanctioned by Parliament.

The Committee considered that cultural property taken during the Holocaust and the Second World War was worthy of special treatment. The Committee emphasised very strongly the need for the removal of legislative barriers in cases where a claim has been upheld and restitution is proposed. The Committee recommended that the Department for Culture, Media and Sport should set out its strategy for assisting non-national museums with the undertaking of provenance research relating to the period 1993–45. They also recommended that the DCMS should begin cross-party consultations to secure agreement for legislation which would enable the trustees or boards of national museums to return to their rightful owners, any objects which the Spoliation Advisory Panel views as being wrongfully taken during the period 1933–45. (ibid: xlvii–l).

With regard to access to museum collections and documentation, the Committee directed that information should not be

> unreasonably withheld from those with a legitimate interest, including claimants and potential claimants [and that] in setting priorities for the conduct of research on collections and making information about these collections accessible, museums should give consideration to the interests of originating communities.
>
> (ibid: xxxiv)

The Committee agreed with arguments that human remains should be seen as an issue distinct from the broader issues of repatriation of cultural property and felt that the MGC guidelines on restitution and repatriation did not give enough weight to the issue of human remains. They recommended that

> the Department for Culture, Media and Sport initiate discussions with appropriate representatives of museums, of claimant communities and of appropriate Governments to prepare a statement of principles and accompanying guidance relating to the care and safe-keeping of human remains and to the handling of requests for return of human remains.
>
> (ibid: xlii)

Furthermore, they recommended that the DCMS should 'seek commitments from all holding institutions in the United Kingdom about access to information on holdings of indigenous human remains for all interested parties, including potential claimants' (ibid: xlii).

The issue of the repatriation of human remains is becoming less controversial as collecting institutions recognise the rights of the descendants to claim the remains of their ancestors. The Parliamentary Review Committee's finding on human remains endorses the policies that have been developing in recent years within the Museums Association, and in some museums and universities, as well as the Foreign Office. In recent years there have been a number of repatriations, including the return of a second large collection from the University of Edinburgh.

The University of Edinburgh, which previously held the largest known collection of Aboriginal remains in the UK, has recently returned large numbers of remains held in its anatomy collection for around 100 years. In 1991, the University handed over the remains of 307 Aboriginal bodies from its anatomy collection. Tasmanian Aboriginal hair samples were returned to a delegation from the Tasmanian Aboriginal Centre in 1997. Three Aboriginal skulls were returned by the University in 1999 and were subsequently buried in South Australia and, in June 2000, the remains of 330 Aborigines were returned to two South Australian tribes. The University's policy

> is governed by the principle that, subject to appropriate safeguards, it will return human remains from its historic anatomy collection, when requested, to appropriate representatives of cultures for which such remains continue to have particular significance. It is the University's wish that all returned human remains be passed to representatives of the people legitimately entitled to receive them, so that they can be held or disposed of in accordance with the customs and beliefs of these people.
>
> (University of Edinburgh, 1997)

In 1997, the skull of a Nyungar Aborigine called Yagan, a nineteenth-century Aboriginal resistance fighter, was returned to Australia after it was exhumed from a cemetery in England. In 1833, Yagan had been murdered by white bounty hunters and his head and skin removed from his body. The head later came to be in the collection of Liverpool Museum where it was displayed for many years but in 1964 it was buried in a pauper's grave in Everton Cemetery in Liverpool, England. The request for the exhumation of Yagan's skull was supported by the Foreign Office and then endorsed by the Home Office. The proposal to exhume the skull caused some controversy as the bodies of 21 stillborn children had since been buried in the ground above. However, the skull was eventually retrieved by scientists who conducted a geophysical survey using electromagnetic and ground penetrating radar equipment to locate the exact position of the metal box containing the skull. They were then able to dig down beside the grave and excavate the box from the side, thereby leaving the graves of the children undisturbed. The whereabouts of the rest of Yagan's remains are unknown.

USA: NAGPRA update

When the Native American Graves Protection and Repatriation Act was introduced in 1990, there was considerable division within the ranks of museum professionals, archaeologists and other scientists whose work involved the study of Native American artefacts, archaeological sites and human remains. Some felt that the legislation gave special privileges to Native Americans. However, in introducing NAGPRA legislation, the US Congress did not seek to afford special privileges to Native Americans but rather sought to rectify failures and omissions in existing federal legislation and the resulting differentials in the treatment of Native Americans, their cultural property and their burial sites. Tim McKeown, who as Team Leader of the US National Parks Service has been closely involved in repatriation negotiations and their implementation, is emphatic about this point.

> As civil rights legislation, Congress wished to acknowledged that over the nation's history, Native American human remains and funerary objects suffered from differential treatment as compared with the human remains and funerary objects of other groups. They also wanted to recognise that the loss of sacred objects by Indian tribes and Native Hawaiian organisations to unscrupulous collectors negatively impacted Native American religious practice. As Indian law, Congress founded their efforts on an explicit recognition of tribal sovereignty and the government-to-government relationship between the United States and Indian tribes. As property law, the Congress wanted to highlight the failure of American law to adequately recognise traditional concepts of communal property still in use by some Indian tribes. Lastly, as administrative law, Congress would direct the Department of the Interior to implement Congress' mandate, including the promulgation of regulations to ensure due process, awarding of grants, and assessment of civil penalties.
>
> (McKeown, 2001: 1)

So, what has been the impact of the NAGPRA legislation in its first ten years? It has provided a mechanism for consultation between federal land managers and Indian tribes and Native Hawaiian organisations to protect human remains and cultural items from burial sites which are or might be excavated or found on federal or tribal lands. It also established procedures enabling lineal descendants or affiliated tribes or Native Hawaiian organisations to repatriate human remains and certain categories of material (associated grave goods, sacred objects and objects of cultural patrimony). With regard to existing museum collections, it has established consultation procedures in the compilation of inventories and required museums to respond to repatriation requests according to the regulations of the legislation.

NAGPRA inventories of human remains and associated grave goods were completed by museums in consultation with Indian tribes and Native Hawaiian organisations. Federal funding was made available to assist Indian tribes, Native Hawaiian organisations and museums in completing the inventories. Since these funds were made available in 1994, the National Park Service has awarded 178 grants to Indian tribes, Alaskan Native villages and corporations, and Native Hawaiian organisations, totalling $9.75 million; and 114 grants totalling $5.55 million have been made to museums (NPS, 2000).

Upon completion, a Notice of Inventory Completion is published indicating that a museum or Federal agency has made a determination of cultural affiliation for Native American human remains and associated funerary objects in their possession or control. The notices represent determinations made by institutions and Federal agencies and provide enough detail to enable individuals, Indian tribes and Native Hawaiian organisations to determine an interest in claiming the remains or objects. The notices do not necessarily indicate whether repatriation has occurred or will occur. By 16 November 2000, 820 museums and federal agencies had completed inventories and 411 Notices of Inventory Completion had been published in the Federal Register listing 22,261 human remains and 446,243 associated funerary objects (McKeown, 2000).

Prior to the passage of NAGPRA, estimates of the number of individuals represented in collections of human remains put the figure at around 200,000. These early estimates seem to be confirmed by the evidence so far available based upon museums' responses to NAGPRA regulations (NAGPRA Review Committee, 1999: 4). Tim McKeown suggests that of these at least 50,000 will be culturally unidentifiable, basing his estimate upon the experience of the National Park Service of whose holdings of 5,996 human remains, 25 per cent were listed as culturally unidentifiable (McKeown, 2000).

NAGPRA summaries relate to holdings of unassociated funerary objects, sacred objects and objects of cultural patrimony; 1,042 Federal agencies and museums have submitted summary information. When a museum or Federal agency has received, reviewed, and accepted a claim by a tribe for sacred objects, unassociated funerary objects, or objects of cultural patrimony, a Notice of Intent to Repatriate is posted. The notices represent active repatriation claims by tribes for the objects indicated. Since 1990, 165 notices of intent to repatriate have been published, consisting of 50,887 unassociated funerary objects, 893 sacred objects, 237 objects of cultural patrimony, 383 items which fall into both categories of sacred object and object of cultural patrimony (ibid.).

Under the NAGPRA regulations, two notices must be placed two weeks apart in newspapers announcing the excavation or discovery of human remains or cultural items on Federal or tribal lands. Copies of published Notices of Disposition are also sent to the National NAGPRA programme. In ten years, there have been 27 notices, relating to 75 human remains, 46 funerary objects, no sacred objects, and five objects of cultural property (ibid.). The publication of the notices does not mean that a decision has been made concerning the finds, but is a last means of communication with any individual, Indian tribe or Native Hawaiian organisation which may have been omitted from the consultation process. The notice announces that particular lineal descendants, Indian tribes or Native Hawaiian organisations have a right to claim the remains or items. A Review Committee was established to resolve disputes, although its recommendations are not binding. To date around ten cases have been submitted to the Review Committee for consideration; in only four cases has the process been completed and the stage been reached at which final recommendations are issued.

NAGPRA makes illegal the act of trafficking in Native American human remains and cultural items. In ten years, three individuals have been convicted after pleading guilty to charges relating to the illegal trafficking of Native American human remains. Another seven individuals have been convicted of illegal trafficking of cultural items, one of these was convicted twice. Of these eight cases, six convictions resulted from guilty pleas. There have been a further eight civil cases filed in the Federal court involving NAGPRA regulations as they relate to excavation and discovery and six civil cases involving NAGPRA collections provision (McKeown, 2000; NPS, 2000).

Hartman Lomawaima (Hopi), associate director of Arizona State Museum, University of Arizona, feels that

> NAGPRA has made people stop and think before taking action. People who are in the marketplace and deal with human remains as well as sacred objects [now] think about the consequences. With regard to museums, what's coming out is a much richer ethnographic record because of this partnership between museum specialists and Native Americans . . . I also believe that [NAGPRA] has created other interesting linkages between Indian nations and branches of the federal government. There's been a lot of interaction consultation [sic] between Forest Service representatives, Bureau of Land Management, Bureau of Reclamation, and so on, more than ever before.
>
> (Lomawaima in AAM, 2000: 44)

Barbara Isaac, assistant director of the Peabody Institute of Archaeology and Ethnology, Harvard University, says

> There's been much more of a shift in the perception by museum staff of their responsibilities to other communities. There's an enhanced sensitivity in our concern for other communities . . . I don't think now that we would dream of putting on an exhibit without the full involvement of the Native community.
>
> (Isaac in AAM, 2000: 49, 68)

In McKeown's view, the legislation may not be perfect but

> Taken together, the system of subject parties, parties with standing, purview, and processes outlined by the statute provide a workable compromise for resolving the complex and potentially contentious issues surrounding the disposition of Native American human remains and cultural items that are excavated or discovered on Federal or tribal lands or held in Federal or museum collections . . . Returning control of these human remains and funerary objects to lineal descendants, Indian tribes, and Native Hawaiian organisations remedies years of unequal treatment. Acknowledging the communal property systems traditionally used by some Indian tribes not only returns those objects of cultural patrimony to their rightful owners, but reinforces the complex social webs in which they serve. Neither idea is very new, both reflecting the guarantee of equal protection under the law imagined by America's founding fathers and codified in the Constitution of the

United States. In some ways it is sad that a law is needed to remind us of those ideals.

(McKeown, 2000)

Australia

Australia's human rights record in relation to Aboriginal communities is very poor and has been criticised by the United Nations Committee on the Elimination of Racial Discrimination (CERD) and by Amnesty International (UN, 2000a,b,c). Nevertheless, there has been some progress in increasing government and public awareness and acknowledgement of past and present inequalities and racist policies which have had a devastating effect on many Aboriginal people. In the early 1990s, a number of initiatives and legislative changes suggested that indigenous land rights, cultural heritage issues and other areas of inequity were being positively addressed and the concerns and rights of Aboriginal and Torres Strait Islander communities were to be reflected in future policies and practices.

The Royal Commission's 1991 *Report into Aboriginal Deaths in Custody* highlighted the high number of deaths amongst Aboriginal prison inmates and amongst those being held on remand or in police custody (RCIADIC, 1991). The Mabo decision in 1992 and the 1993 Native Title Act (see pages 259–60) were landmarks in the Aboriginal land rights campaign giving recognition, for the first time, to prior occupation of Australia by Aboriginal and Torres Strait Islanders and acknowledging their claims to certain areas of land. In 1993, the Council of Australian Museum Associations (now Museums Australia) published its policy document *Previous Possessions, New Obligations* (see page 241) and ATSIC published a *Draft National Policy for the Return of Aboriginal and Torres Strait Islander Cultural Property* which was adopted in 1998.

Also in 1993, the Commonwealth Government established the Heritage Collections Committee. Amongst other things, this Committee established Australian Museums Online, an Internet site that provides information about collections in over 830 museums and galleries throughout Australia. In December 1996, the Cultural Ministers Council agreed to form a Heritage Collections Council to replace and build on the work of the Heritage Collections Committee and to broaden community access to museum collections including Aboriginal keeping places. The Council comprised representatives from, and was jointly funded by, Federal, State and Territory governments and the museums sector. The Heritage Collections Council was given the task of achieving set objectives by the year 2001. These included identification of significant Australian heritage items overseas for repatriation; placement of 80 per cent of Australia's heritage collections on the Australian Museums Online Internet site; implementation of a national conservation strategy; and provision of assistance for a programme of thematic exhibitions telling Australia's story.

These developments represent significant progress but, unfortunately, a change in government has resulted in a reduction in the commitment to Aboriginal affairs. Amendments and further legislation combined with inaction or ineffective implementation of legislation and recommendations made in official reports has resulted in erosion of some of the hard-won progress.

Following the WIK decision in which it was determined that the rights of pastoral leaseholders could co-exist with Native Title rights, the 1993 Native Title Act was amended in 1998. Later that year, the United Nations' Committee on the Elimination of Racial Discrimination (CERD) found that the 1998 Native Title Amendment Act discriminated against indigenous Australians and, in November 1999, Australia was reported to the General Assembly for failing to address breaches of the *Convention on the Elimination of all Forms of Racial Discrimination* which Australia signed in 1966 and ratified in 1975 when it passed the Racial Discrimination Act. In March 2000, CERD urged the Australian Government to ensure that there was no further erosion of the rights of Aboriginal people and to adopt more affirmative action on racial discrimination. The Committee expressed concern about the Australian Government's policy on land rights and the Native Title Amendment Act of 1998. They also criticised the discriminatory approach to law enforcement practised under the Mandatory Sentencing Laws in Western Australia and Northern Territory, and recommended that the Australian government seek effective measures to address the socio-economic marginalization of Aboriginal peoples (UN, 2000a,b,c).

The Aboriginal Deaths in Custody report attested to the inequity in arrest practices of the police force and the sentencing policies of the Australian courts and made 339 recommendations relating to the criminal justice system, Aboriginal socio-economic and educational disadvantage and the over-representation of Aboriginal individuals in custody. However, critics claim that the recommendations are not being adequately implemented or not operating effectively. In March 1992, Amnesty International sent a memorandum to the Federal and State governments expressing concern about the high incidence of Aboriginal deaths in custody. In a report in 1997, Amnesty International reinforced that concern stating that 'the rate of Aboriginal deaths in custody remains at the same high level'. It continued: 'in some cases ill-treatment, or lack of care amounting to cruel, inhuman or degrading treatment may have contributed to a death in custody' (Amnesty International, 1997). In March 2000, the United Nations' Committee on the Elimination of Racial Discrimination (CERD) criticised the continuing inequitable treatment of Aboriginal Australians in the Federal and State judicial systems.

In 1997, the Human Rights and Equal Opportunity Commission (HREOC) released *Bringing Them Home: Report of the National Inquiry into the Separation of Aboriginal and Torres Strait Islander Children from Their Families*. This report exposed the appalling actions of previous governments which, for purposes of racial integration and cultural assimilation, removed Aboriginal children from their natural parents and placed them in missions, children's homes, or with white Australian families. This policy continued from 1910 until 1970 and the report states that 'Nationally we can conclude with confidence that between one in three and one in ten Indigenous children were forcibly removed from their families and communities in the period from approximately 1910 until 1970' (HREOC, 1997). Thousands of Aboriginal people still seek contact with their blood relatives and many suffer the psychological effects of this forced removal or from abuses suffered afterwards. Many others are unaware of their Aboriginality. In November 1999, the Senate passed a motion to address a range of matters highlighted in the report. The motion called for the Legal and Constitutional References Committee to inquire and report on matters including: processes to increase support and family reunions for members of the stolen generation; recording of stories of those affected by forced removal; education for the whole community about this part of Australia's history; and ways to implement an alternative dispute resolution tribunal for those affected by forced removal.

Reconciliation

In 1991, the Federal Government established the Council for Aboriginal Reconciliation comprising 25 community leaders drawn from Aboriginal and Torres Strait Islander communities and representatives from business and other sectors. The purpose of the Council was to generate public support and national commitment for the reconciliation process and achieve the vision of 'A united Australia which respects this land of ours; values the Aboriginal and Torres Strait Islander heritage; and provides justice and equity for all'. The Council for Aboriginal Reconciliation and its enabling legislation, the Council for Aboriginal Reconciliation Act 1991, expired on 1 January 2001 and their work is now being continued by Reconciliation Australia, an independent non-government foundation (Reconciliation Australia 2000). One of the most controversial aspects of the reconciliation process has been the subject of a government apology to the Aboriginal people for past injustices. The national parliament adopted a 'Statement of Regret' in 1999 but has refused to say 'sorry'. Public opinion in Australia is split on the issue, with some non-Aboriginal Australians fearing that a government apology would open the way for liability claims. Others feel that the Australian government's failure to make an apology for past injustices against Aboriginal populations is jeopardising the process of reconciliation.

As well as the issue of an official government apology, the reconciliation process encompasses a range of issues including socio-economic disadvantage, cultural recognition, education, land rights, intellectual property rights and cultural heritage. In the context of this book and its study of museum politics, the most relevant of these are the issues relating to cultural heritage and intellectual property rights.

Intellectual property rights and cultural heritage issues

In the mid-1990s, ATSIC funded the Indigenous Cultural and Intellectual Property Project through the Australian Institute of Aboriginal and Torres Strait Islander Studies (AIATSIS). An indigenous lawyer, Terri Janke, undertook the work and produced two reports. First, a discussion paper *Our Culture; Our*

289

Future: Proposals for the Recognition and Protection of Indigenous Cultural and Intellectual Property was launched in July 1997 in paper form and on the Internet with an invitation for submissions. In June 1998, her final report was published. *Our Culture: Our Future – Report on Australian Indigenous Cultural and Intellectual Property Rights* makes many recommendations, including legislative intervention to protect Indigenous intellectual and cultural property rights (Janke, 1998).

In June 1999, the Council for Aboriginal Reconciliation published a draft *Declaration for Reconciliation* and devised a series of national strategies to advance reconciliation. The four strategies are: the Strategy to Promote the Recognition of Aboriginal and Torres Strait Islander Rights; the Strategy for Economic Independence; the Strategy to Sustain the Reconciliation Process; and the Strategy to Address Aboriginal and Torres Strait Islander Disadvantage (CAR, 1999).

The National Strategy to Promote the Recognition of Aboriginal and Torres Strait Islander Rights seeks recognition and protection of the cultures, heritage and languages of Aboriginal and Torres Strait Islander peoples and their intellectual property rights. This includes 'all types of artistic works, ecological and biological knowledge, ceremonies, spiritual knowledge and objects, including sacred and historical sites, ancestral remains and languages' (CAR, 2000, 4ii). It points out that 'The cultures and beliefs of Aboriginal and Torres Strait Islander peoples are still living despite many efforts to change them . . . [Culture] is diverse and dynamic and reflects politics, histories, stories, songs, ceremonies, traditions and relationships to land'. It declares that 'it is the right of Aboriginal and Torres Strait Islander peoples to enjoy their distinct cultures and to see these cultures acknowledged and respected by all Australians' and asserts that 'Recognition and protection of Indigenous cultures and heritage is essential for achieving reconciliation' (CAR, 2000).

To achieve these goals, the Council seeks the introduction of community education programmes to promote respect for Indigenous intellectual property and the development by ATSIC and AIATSIS of codes of practice for the protection of intellectual property rights. It calls on Commonwealth, State and Territory governments to work with indigenous representatives to develop legislation to protect indigenous intellectual property and to assist relevant community groups to work with Aboriginal and Torres Strait Islander peoples to develop projects which record, recognise and protect local aspects of Indigenous culture, heritage or language. It also asks the Commonwealth Government to assist indigenous communities to document their traditional environmental management knowledge and technologies to ensure its transfer to subsequent generations. It also requests that all Australian museums improve processes for recording and obtaining information about indigenous intellectual property.

The Council for Aboriginal Reconciliation endorses the UN's *Draft Declaration on the Rights of Indigenous Peoples* and the Strategy declares that

> Aboriginal and Torres Strait Islander people have the right to our unique cultural traditions and customs. This includes aspects of our cultures such

as designs, ceremonies, performances and technologies. We have the right to own and control our cultural and intellectual property, including our sciences, technologies, medicines, knowledge of flora and fauna, designs, arts and performances. Our cultural property taken without consent shall be returned to us . . . Aboriginal and Torres Strait Islander peoples have the right to our spiritual and religious traditions. This includes the right to preserve and protect our sacred sites, ceremonial objects and the remains of our ancestors.

(CAR, 2000)

Heritage protection

The Aboriginal and Torres Strait Islander Heritage Protection Act 1984 was introduced to provide a mechanism for the protection of areas or objects of cultural significance which are under threat of injury or desecration. This Commonwealth legislation was intended to complement the heritage protection legislation in the States and Territories and to be used only in circumstances in which State legislation proved ineffective. However, in their Annual Report 1996–7, the Aboriginal and Torres Strait Islander Council (ATSIC) expressed concern about deficiencies in State Government legislation and 'the degree to which Indigenous heritage legislation is being amended, reviewed or administered by a number of States'. It stated that as a result 'Indigenous people . . . increasingly view the operations of the Commonwealth's Aboriginal and Torres Strait Islander Heritage Protection Act 1984 as an avenue for primary protection, rather than a last resort' (ATSIC, 1997: 11). Shortcomings of the legislation were highlighted by Federal and High Court judgments, and led the Commonwealth Government to undertake a review of the Act which was carried out by Justice Elizabeth Evatt. Her report was submitted in 1996 and made a number of recommendations designed to increase the effectiveness of the Commonwealth legislation and create greater uniformity in the laws of the States and Territories.

In 1998, the Act was amended, largely as a result of several cases that were perceived to have highlighted deficiencies in the legislation. One of the most notable was that of Hindmarsh Island Bridge in South Australia. In 1993, construction of the bridge was halted as a result of protests by white conservationists and unionists, and members of the Ngarrindgeri Aboriginal community who had occupied the area for thousands of years before white settlement. The Ngarrindgeri protesters argued that construction would damage or destroy burial sites and sites used for secret women's business. In May 1994, the then Commonwealth Minister for Aboriginal Affairs, Robert Tickner, issued a 30-day emergency protection declaration under the Aboriginal and Torres Strait Islander Heritage Protection Act 1984. He then commissioned Professor Cheryl Saunders to prepare a report into the matter. This drew upon testimony offered by Ngarrindgeri women attesting to the importance of the area for secret women's business. As a result, Tickner issued a 25-year heritage protection declaration prohibiting bulldozing, excavation and other work related to the construction of the bridge. This decision was, however, overturned by a Judicial Review.

291

In 1995 it was alleged that the secret women's business had been fabricated. The South Australian Government established a Royal Commission to inquire into the allegation. A Royal Commission's report found that the claim of the secret women's business was a fabrication designed to obtain a heritage protection declaration prohibiting construction of the Hindmarsh Island Bridge under the Aboriginal and Torres Strait Islander Heritage Protection Act 1984 (Australian Parliamentary Library, 1996). An appeal by the Minister was dismissed but not on the merits of the application for the protection declaration. Instead, the Court was concerned about procedural matters, most notably that the Minister had not considered the contents of an attachment to the Saunders report which contained an account of the secret women's business. The envelope was marked 'confidential' and directed that the contents should be read only by women. By failing to read this and relying merely upon the existence of such an account, the Court found that the Minister had failed to comply with the preconditions required for him to exercise his power in issuing a heritage protection declaration. The Federal Government then passed the Hindmarsh Island Bridge Act 1996 that removed the heritage protection measures in relation to the Hindmarsh Island Bridge area and allowed construction of the bridge to proceed.

ATSIC asserts that the 1998 Aboriginal and Torres Strait Islander Heritage Protection Act has weakened the position of indigenous peoples. In its Annual Report of 1997–8, ATSIC states that

> This Bill does not reflect many of Evatt's recommendations, and would effectively allow the Commonwealth to withdraw from protecting Indigenous heritage. Instead State/Territory heritage legislation would be accredited after certain 'minimum standards' are met, and the Commonwealth's involvement limited to cases involving 'the national interest'.
>
> (ATSIC, 1998: 5)

ATSIC is seeking amendment of the bill.

Although, authorities have moved some way towards recognising customary law, the differences in legal concepts enshrined in the two systems cannot always be easily resolved (Ellicott, 1986; McLaughlin, 1996). Western legal systems, such as that of contemporary Australia, place great emphasis upon evidence substantiated by written documentation or witness statements. Traditional Aboriginal practices, however, place great significance on secret/sacred knowledge, and customary law within Aboriginal communities prohibits disclosure of such information.

Elizabeth Evatt notes that the Hindmarsh Island case

> reflects the fundamental differences between the introduced common law system and the legal system of the Indigenous oral culture. This latest episode in the Hindmarsh Bridge saga has provided graphic illustration as to how little our apparently beneficial legislation has accommodated to the realities of Aboriginal culture. I hope that one outcome of this episode may be that a completely new approach is adopted in relation to Aboriginal heritage issues.
>
> (Evatt, cited in Goldflam, 1997)

As Russell Goldflam points out, the Aboriginal and Torres Strait Islander Heritage Protection Act

> is an enactment of one legal system which is yet to formally recognise the existence of another, parallel legal system in this country. And until that recognition is attained, the Act can never guarantee the right of Indigenous Australians to protect and preserve their cultural property according to their traditional laws.
>
> (Goldflam, 1997)

In other areas of heritage preservation, the establishment of Keeping Places has continued with Commonwealth funding administered by ATSIC. ATSIC's Heritage Protection programme is used to assist in the establishment and operation of cultural centres and keeping places, including projects involving some of the state museums working in consultation with Aboriginal communities to facilitate the establishment of keeping places. The programme also provides workshops, meetings, conservation training, and technical assistance in establishing and maintaining keeping places and in operating keeping places and heritage centres effectively. ATSIC funding also provides support for national and state-wide projects such as the South Australian Museum's travelling exhibition programme which takes exhibitions to remote communities, and the preservation and promotion of indigenous heritage in Victoria by the Koori Heritage Trust. It also enabled the South Australian Museum to further develop its family history information services.

Repatriation of Aboriginal remains and cultural property

It is estimated that 7,200 ancestral remains and about 11,000 objects of restricted men's business are still held in museums around Australia. In addition, there are unknown quantities of objects associated with Aboriginal women's secret/ sacred business, and restricted business objects from the Torres Strait Islands. The Australian Government policy states that it supports the view 'that indigenous people have the primary interest in the protection, safekeeping and return of human remains relating to their community' (House of Commons, 2000: 381). It has provided funding to assist with repatriation efforts and to facilitate the documentation and identification of unprovenanced ancestral remains.

Responsibility for the protection and return of cultural property within Australia, including the return of indigenous human remains, is administered by the Department of Communications, Information Technology and the Arts (formerly the Australian Cultural Development Office) through its Return of Indigenous Cultural Property programme. Commonwealth funding from the DCITA and from ATSIC finances programmes is available to assist museums and universities holding collections of human remains with the preparation of documentation relating to these collections. It has also enabled consultation and research to take place and assists communities who request the return of indigenous remains. Commonwealth funding also financed two projects undertaken through the South Australian Museum. The Custodianship of Sacred Objects

Project involved the compilation of a database of objects used in restricted men's business (see page 222). The National Skeletal Provenancing Project, undertaken by Dr Colin Pardoe and Deanne Hanchant, involved consultation with communities and the documentation and identification of unprovenanced ancestral remains held in museums (Hanchant, 2001).

The ATSIC Heritage Protection programme works towards achieving the return of human remains and significant cultural property to their communities of origin, and has facilitated the identification and protection of grave sites. In 1993, a *National Policy on the Protection and Return of Significant Cultural Property to Aboriginal and Torres Strait Islander People* was prepared for ATSIC by the Aboriginal Affairs Council. It was amended and adopted in 1998.

In November 1997, the Museums Standing Committee on Museums and Indigenous Peoples formed a working party to formulate a national plan to resolve the issues surrounding collections of secret/sacred objects and ancestral remains. Their work represents a collaborative effort between the Federal and State/Territory governments and the museums sector. Together they drew up the *Strategic Plan for the Return of Indigenous Ancestral Remains* which was endorsed by the Australian Cultural Ministers Council in February 1998. A target date of 2001 was set for completion of the task. The plan, which focuses on government-funded museums and does not apply to holdings overseas, has three main objectives. First, the identification, where possible, of the origins of ancestral remains held in museums; second, to provide notification to communities of holdings of ancestral remains in museums; and third, to facilitate repatriation of ancestral remains where it is culturally appropriate to do so and when requested by the appropriate community (Australian Government, 2000: 381). Work on the identification and documentation of this material will involve close collaboration with Aboriginal communities and final decisions regarding repatriation or retention by the museum will be made by the communities.

The logistics of the tasks identified in the Strategic Plan are complex. National and state museums hold collections representing communities from across the nation, potentially involving around 800 Aboriginal communities. This limited time frame worried indigenous advisors who expressed concern that the sensitivity of this task and the need to determine and observe cultural protocols is such that it could not be undertaken within such a relatively short time frame. They emphasised the need for sensitivity when approaching communities and individuals on such matters, and strongly recommended a longer time period for completion of this task to allow it to be undertaken with due consideration and in accordance with indigenous protocols.

The Australian Government has also now adopted a policy whereby it will make official representation to foreign governments seeking the return of Aboriginal human remains held in museums and other collecting institutions overseas. The Aboriginal and Torres Strait Islander Commission is the Commonwealth Government's key agency in administering efforts to identify and seek the repatriation of indigenous human remains from overseas. ATSIC continues to actively seek the return of Aboriginal human remains from overseas collections and to help communities respond to offers from overseas museums and other holding institutions to return indigenous human remains. The Foundation for Aboriginal and Islander Research Action (FAIRA), with the aid of government grants, has also been active in this area. Lyndon Ormond-Parker, a FAIRA researcher, recently completed a survey of museum, university and other collections in the UK and Europe to identify holdings of Aboriginal human remains (Ormond-Parker, 1997 and House of Commons, 2000).

In early 2000, the Australian Government submitted evidence to the British Government's Parliamentary Review Committee on Cultural Property outlining their policy on the repatriation of the remains of Aboriginal and Torres Strait Islanders.

> The Australian Government supports the view that indigenous people have the primary interest in the protection, safekeeping and return of human remains relating to their community . . . Given its particular significance, the Australian Government sees the issue of repatriation of indigenous human remains as distinct from the broader issue of the repatriation of cultural property.
>
> (House of Commons, 2000: 381)

In the submission, the Australian Government therefore stated that it 'makes no comment or any representation in relation to cultural property more generally' (ibid: 381).

The Australian Government submission noted the sensitivity and complexity of the issue, and the diversity of views within the Aboriginal community concerning the handling and ultimate fate of repatriated human remains. The submission

> does not advocate an immediate large-scale repatriation of indigenous human remains from British collections. This would be an inappropriate and impractical goal . . . Rather the Government is seeking to develop a co-operative approach to identifying indigenous remains in British holding institutions, identifying indigenous interests in these remains and examining opportunities and systems for repatriation.
>
> (ibid: 385)

In July 2000, Australian Prime Minister John Howard issued a joint statement with British Prime Minister Tony Blair in which they announced that both governments 'agree to increase efforts to repatriate human remains to Australian indigenous communities' (Howard, 2000).

While these developments in repatriation policics are broadly welcomed, those most closely involved in the documentation of ancestral remains urge caution and sensitivity. The target date of 2001 for completion of the repatriation project has been criticised as undesirable and potentially damaging in view of the sensitive nature of the subject and the need to involve communities and families in the discussions and decision-making process.

The amended ATSIC *Policy for the Protection and Return of Significant Cultural Property* allows for the return of inadequately provenanced cultural property and enables ATSIC to fund small delegations to travel overseas to retrieve remains. ATSIC has established an Advisory Committee to investigate whether a national organisation should handle all repatriation matters on behalf of mainland Aboriginal communities, with the Tasmanian Aboriginal Council to deal with Tasmania. In addition, they are also investigating the feasibility of a national repository or Keeping Place for human remains which would also undertake research and co-ordinate repatriations. 'Storage in museums is generally unacceptable to Aboriginal people, who would prefer a community-managed facility' (ATSIC, 1998: 7). Only then, they believe, would the remains be cared for in an appropriate manner. The concept of a national repository or National Keeping Place for unprovenanced human remains has also been challenged by some. The return of the ancestral remains from Edinburgh and the future return of remains from Australian museums has highlighted the problem of how to manage the return of unprovenanced human remains. Many Aboriginal communities are unwilling to accept the burial of unprovenaced remains in their area or 'country', believing that they should be buried in their own country.

At present, the National Museum of Australia has a special facility which acts as a repository for collections of remains until they are returned to the community. However, the continued presence of collections of ancestral remains in museums is unacceptable to many indigenous people who believe that, if the decision-making process and care of the collections remains in the control of museums, scientific research on the remains will continue without the consent of Aboriginal people.

Canada

In Canada, repatriation and other matters relating to museums and First Nations have been the subject of considerable discussion within the museum profession and in consultation with First Nations. Initially, more inclusive practices were largely undertaken on a voluntary basis by those with sensitivity to the issues and a desire to see change, but were more widely adopted as the virtues and equity of these methods were recognised.

The launch in 1992 of the report *Turning the Page: Forging New Partnerships Between Museums and First Peoples* (AFN and CMA, 1992) undertaken by a task force jointly sponsored by the Assembly of First Nations and the Canadian Museums Association provided further impetus for change on a wider level (see pages 231–3, 261–2). With regard to repatriation, the report made several recommendations. It called for museums and First Nations to negotiate over the return of human remains and engage in discussions with First Nations concerning the handling, storage or repatriation of sacred objects and cultural patrimony. These recommendations were voluntarily introduced within the Canadian museum sector, although the task force also recommended that the CMA and AFN should produce a set of national guidelines and establish a documentation centre to assist museums and First Nations in the implementation of the recommendations.

In addition to the non-legislative efforts to address the repatriation issue, there have also been treaty negotiations taking place between First Nations and federal and provincial governments. These negotiations have been undertaken to resolve claims over a number of issues including land rights, hunting and fishing rights, and the management and control of cultural heritage. The Nisga'a of British Columbia have concluded the process with the ratification of a treaty agreed by the Nisga'a nation and the governments of British Columbia and Canada. Other First Nations communities are also engaging in treaty negotiations. As of 31 January 2000 there were 51 other First Nations participating in the BC treaty process in 42 sets of negotiations (some negotiations involve two or more First Nations) (British Columbian Treaty Commission, 2000).

The Nisga'a live in the Nass River region and, like other tribes of the Northwest Coast, lived by hunting and fishing prior to the arrival of white settlers. The Nisga'a have a rich artistic tradition which was manifest through the production of totem poles, house posts, ceremonial clothing, masks, head-dresses, rattles, and highly decorated utilitarian items such as boxes, bowls, spoons, etc. As in other parts of the world, cultural material was removed from the Northwest Coast by a variety of means including trade, purchase and theft but, in addition, the banning of the potlatch led to the confiscation of cultural property from tribes on the Northwest Coast (see pages 153–7). This, combined with the salvage collecting of the late nineteenth century, resulted in the loss by Indian tribes of a great deal of their material culture.

The process towards the settlement of the Nisga'a Treaty began over 110 years ago when the Nisga'a chiefs travelled to Victoria seeking treaty negotiation and the recognition of land title and self-governance. Legislation introduced by the Canadian government in 1927 prohibited any further discussions or claims until 1951 when the Parliament repealed legislation prohibiting the potlatch and group discussion of land claims. In 1968, the Nisga'a initiated legal action on the question of land rights and entered into negotiations with the Canadian government in 1976. In 1990, the British Columbian government joined negotiations and the following year a framework was agreed by all three parties. The Nisga'a Agreement in Principle was signed in 1996 and the Final Agreement initialled in 1998. After the introduction of necessary Provincial and Federal legislation, the Nisga'a Treaty was ratified on 13 April 2000 and received Royal Assent.

The treaty comprises a land claim agreement and other matters relating to fishing, hunting, wildlife, environmental protection, government, and cultural heritage and artefacts. Under the treaty, approximately 300 Nisga'a artefacts will be returned by the Canadian Museum of Civilization (CMC) and the Royal British Columbia Museum (RBCM). The treaty requires that the artefacts be returned within a period of five years, or sooner if requested by the Nisga'a nation; otherwise an alternative time period can be agreed by the Nisga'a nation and the museums. The CMC must return all Nisga'a artefacts of a religious nature. The Nisga'a nation and the museum will share possession of the remaining collection and will negotiate and try to reach custodial agreement in respect of these artefacts. In defining the parameters of such custodial agreements, the treaty directs that they respect Nisga'a laws and practices relating to Nisga'a artefacts as well as complying with Federal and Provincial laws and the statutory mandate of the CMC. The Royal British Columbia Museum must return 50 per cent of their Nisga'a collection representing all types of artefacts. Both museums will retain collections 'to celebrate and share Nisga'a culture and heritage'(Government of British Columbia, 1998).

* * * * *

It is clear that repatriation is a dynamic area of museology and that developments witnessed over the past decade will continue to evolve as those involved work through the issues. Museums in Western countries are gradually adopting more responsive and even proactive repatriation policies which recognise the legitimacy of indigenous claims to certain categories of material and to items taken under questionable circumstances.

Resolution of repatriation claims and other conflicts over museological practice often involves compromise on both sides, although increasingly museum policy is encompassing the rights of the peoples whose cultures had previously been the subject of study and interpretation but whose voices were rarely heard and whose property rights were not acknowledged. While discussions about repatriation previously focused upon the legal ownership of objects, there is now acknowledgement that the issues associated with repatriation of cultural property are far more complex than simple legal arguments based upon property law. They involve recognition of indigenous or customary laws; raise questions of ethics of acquisition, ownership and custodianship; and encompass basic concepts of human rights relating to freedom of religious expression, protection of cultural heritage, recognition of their diverse cultural identities and other rights embodied in the UN's Declaration on the Rights of Indigenous Peoples. Several of the articles of this declaration relate directly to museological practice.

> *Article 12* Indigenous peoples have the right to practise and revitalise their cultural traditions and customs. This right includes the right to maintain, protect and develop the past, present and future manifestations of their cultures, such as archaeological and historical sites, artefacts, designs, ceremonies, technologies and visual and performing arts and literature, as well as the right to the restitution of cultural, intellectual, religious and spiritual property taken without their free and informed consent or in violation of their laws, traditions and customs.

> *Article 13* Indigenous peoples have the right to manifest, practise, develop and teach their spiritual and religious traditions, customs and ceremonies; the right to maintain, protect, and have access in privacy to their religious and cultural sites; the right to the use and control of ceremonial objects; and the right to the repatriation of human remains.

States shall take effective measures, in conjunction with the indigenous peoples concerned, to ensure that indigenous sacred places, including burial sites, be preserved, respected and protected.

(UNWGIP, 1993)

Embodied in these articles, are the concepts that relate directly to the past collecting practices of museums and the current repatriation issue. The interpretative and exhibiting aspects of museology are encompassed in the rights asserted in articles 14 and 16:

Article 14   Indigenous peoples have the right to revitalize, use, develop and transmit to future generations their histories, languages, oral traditions, philosophies, writing systems and literatures, and to designate and retain their own names for communities, places and persons.

States shall take effective measures, whenever any right of indigenous peoples may be threatened, to ensure this right is protected and also to ensure that they can understand and be understood in political, legal and administrative proceedings, where necessary through the provision of interpretation or by other appropriate means.

Article 16   Indigenous peoples have the right to have the dignity and diversity of their cultures, traditions, histories and aspirations appropriately reflected in all forms of education and public information.

States shall take effective measures, in consultation with the indigenous peoples concerned, to eliminate prejudice and discrimination and to promote tolerance, understanding and good relations among indigenous peoples and all segments of society.

(UNWGIP, 1993)

Respect for the rights of traditional owners of artefacts in museum collections and collaboration in the custodianship and interpretation of cultural property will ensure that museums in the future do not give priority to the objects to the exclusion of the religious and cultural values and wishes of traditional owners. This would ensure that museums become more community-oriented and people-focused.

In the past, those who made and used the artefacts which fill the museums' stores and galleries were the subjects and the informants of anthropologists and curators, providing the material for the curators and designers to create exhibitions for the visitors, students and researchers who used the museums. Today, museums are consulting and working with communities, involving them in the processes of exhibition production and interpretation and the storage and care of collections and providing a richer experience and greater understanding by staff and visitors. Furthermore, the descendants of the makers and users of those artefacts are now also amongst the visitors, curators, designers, students and researchers, and are establishing their own museums, cultural centres and Keeping Places. As a result of these developments, museums and galleries are richer and more diverse in the styles, content and perspectives of their interpretations

299

and activities. As people-centred institutions, they will provide the curators, designers, visitors and researchers with a far richer experience and greater understanding of the objects and their status, meaning and importance in differing cultural contexts. Simultaneously, they will develop into inclusive institutions which truly reflect and respect the knowledge, values, and rights of the world's diverse cultures.

Appendix
Interviews

My thanks are given to the following individuals whom I interviewed during the course of research for this and a second forthcoming book, or who otherwise assisted with my visits. My apologies to anyone whose name has accidentally been omitted from this list.

Charles Hunt, Aberdeen University Anthropological Museum, Aberdeen, Scotland.

Charles Brass and April Whitt, Adler Planetarium, Chicago, Illinois, USA.

Jack Franklin, Anthony Ng, Pearl Robinson and Richard Watson, Afro-American Historical and Cultural Museum, Philadelphia, Pennsylvania, USA.

Chris Steiner, Albuquerque Museum, New Mexico, USA.

Elizabeth A. Sackler, Founder and President, American Indian Ritual Object Repatriation Foundation, New York, USA.

Ann Prewitt, Stanley Freed and Beth Steinhorn, American Museum of Natural History, New York, USA.

Nancy Long and Curtis Tate, Arkansas Historical Restoration, Little Rock, Arkansas, USA.

Ramona Austin and Esther Grisham, Art Institute of Chicago, Chicago, Illinois, USA.

Tom McKinney, Ataloa Lodge, Muskogee, Oklahoma, USA.

John Coster, Wendy Johnstone, Karen McKay, Roger Neich, Stuart Park, Mick Prendergast and Te Warena Taua, Auckland Institute and Museum, Auckland, New Zealand.

Tamsin Donaldson, Australian Institute of Aboriginal and Torres Strait Islander Studies, Canberra, ACT, Australia.

Des Griffin, Janelle Hatherly, Paul Tacon, Helen Slarke and Lula Saunders, Australian Museum, Sydney, Australia.

Pat Bakunas, Balzekas Museum of Lithuanian Culture, Chicago, Illinois, USA.

Dolores Calaf, Joan Lester, Laura Miyamura, Joanne Rizzi, Jeri Robinson, Pat Steuert, Leslie Swartz and Linda Warner, Boston Children's Museum, Boston, Massachusetts, USA.

Michael O'Hanlon, British Museum, London, England.

Prof. Michael Day, British Museum of Natural History, London, England.

Gavin Brookes, Wanganui, New Zealand.

Sonnet Takahisa and Debra Schwartz, Brooklyn Museum, Brooklyn, New York, USA.

Betty Schmidt and Jeannette Taylor, Campbell River Museum, British Columbia, Canada.

Jeffrey Freedman, Ban Seng Hoe, Robert Klymasz, Suzanne Leboeuf, Gerald McMaster, David Perry, Nancy Ruddell and Leslie Trotter, Canadian Museum of Civilization, Hull, Quebec, Canada.

Helen Parker, Capitol Children's Museum, Washington, DC, USA.

Margie Douthit, Cherokee Historical Association, Cherokee, North Carolina, USA.

Mac Harris, Cherokee National Museum, Tahlequah, Oklahoma, USA.

Amina Dickerson and Susan Tillett, Chicago Historical Society, Chicago, Illinois, USA.

Darchelle Garner and Dianne Sautter, Chicago Children's Museum, Chicago, Illinois, USA.

Mary Lui, Chinatown History Museum (now Museum of Chinese in the Americas), New York, USA.

Jan Gilliam, Peggy McDonald Howells, Helen Philips and Robert Watson, Colonial Williamsburg, Virginia, USA.

Carolyn Blackmon, Calvin Gray, Karen Hutt, Janet Kamien, JoEllen McKillop, Phyllis Rabineau, Michael Spock, John Terrell and Jim Vanstone, Field Museum of Natural History, Chicago, Illinois, USA.

Geoff Clark, Framlingham Aboriginal Land Trust, Victoria, Australia.

Roxanne Fea, Hawke's Bay Cultural Trust, Napier, New Zealand.

Mary Brennan, Gina Laczko, Gloria Lomahaftewa, Anne Marshall, Martin Sullivan and Peter Welsh, Heard Museum, Phoenix, Arizona, USA.

Elaine Peters, Him Dak Ak-Chin Ecomuseum, Ak-Chin, Arizona, USA.

Rick Hill, Institute of American Indian Arts, Santa Fe, New Mexico, USA.

Anastasia Bergh, Jamestown Settlement Museum, Virginia, USA.

Jim Berg, Koorie Heritage Trust, Melbourne, Victoria, Australia.

Darlene Hochman and Eve Hope, 'Ksan Indian Village Museum and the Northwestern National Exhibition Centre, 'Ksan, Hazelton, British Columbia, Canada.

Marian Andrew and Dora Sewid Cook, Kwagiulth Museum, Cape Mudge, Quadra Island, British Columbia, Canada.

Dr Johanna Miller-Lewis, Little Rock, Arkansas, USA.

Mina McKenzie, Greg McManus, Manawatu Museum, Palmerston North, New Zealand.

David Butts, Massey University, Palmerston North, New Zealand.

Deborah Haase, McLellan Galleries, Glasgow, Scotland.

Carlos Tortolero and Helen Valdez, Mexican Fine Art Center Museum, Chicago, Illinois, USA.

Marie Boland, Viv Szekeres, Kaye Frearson and Kate Walsh, Migration Museum, Adelaide, South Australia.

Lazar Brkich, Vivian Corres, Claudia Jacobsen, James Kelly, Mary Korenic, Carter Lupton, Nancy Lurie, Barry Rosen and George Ulrich, Milwaukee Public Museum, Milwaukee, Wisconsin, USA.

Troy Brown and Susan Vogel, Museum of African Art, New York, USA.

Monica Fairburn and Maurice Nobles, Museum of Afro American History, Boston, Massachusetts, USA.

Ken Blankenship and Joan Greene, Museum of the Cherokee Indian, Cherokee, North Carolina, USA.

Bernice Murphy and Collete Warbuck, Museum of Contemporary Art, Sydney, Australia.

Steven Becker, Bruce Bernstein, Edmund Ladd, Carol Cooper and Pearl Sunrise, Museum of Indian Arts and Culture, Museum of New Mexico, USA.

Charlene Cerny, Helen Lucero and Barbara Mauldin, Museum of International-al Folk Art; Museum of New Mexico, USA.

Neil Anderson, Alan Baker, Ken Gorbey, Arapata Hakiwai, Gary Morgan, Bet-ty Rewi, Cheryll Sotheran, Pat Stuart, Megan Tamati-Quennell, Tim Walker, John Walsh and Irihapeti Walters, Museum of New Zealand, Wellington, New Zealand.

Selina Bernard, Maryanne McCubbin, Rose Price-Reed, Melanie Raberts, Gaye Sculthorpe, Sandra Smith and Louise Whiting, Museum of Victoria, Melbourne, Victoria, Australia.

Margaret Brandl, National Gallery of Art, Canberra, ACT, Australia.

Lorraine Coutts and Luke Taylor, National Museum of Australia, Canberra, ACT, Australia.

Alan Downer, Navajo Nation Historic Preservation Department, Window Rock, Arizona, USA.

Harry Walters, Ned A. Hatathli Museum, Navajo Community College, Tsaile, Arizona, USA.

Zoya Kocur, New Museum of Contemporary Art, New York, USA.

Portia Hamilton-Sperr and Cynthia Primas, Museums in the Life of a City, The Philadelphia Initiative for Cultural Pluralism, Philadelphia, Pennsylvania, USA.

Amy Jared, Philadelphia Art Museum, Philadelphia, Pennsylvania, USA.

Jonah Roll, Philadelphia Civic Center, Philadelphia, Pennsylvania, USA.

Bill Ward, Philadelphia Maritime Museum, Philadelphia, Pennsylvania, USA.

Kathryn Blake and Jan Krulick, Phoenix Art Museum, Arizona, USA.

Karen Atwood, Kris Kelly, John Kemp, Liz Lodge, Nanepashemet and the interpreters, Plimoth Plantation, Plymouth, Massachusetts, USA.

George Rivera, Poeh Center, Pueblo of Pojoaque, Santa Fe, New Mexico, USA.

Maui Pomare, Wellington, New Zealand.

Pat Ray, Rotorua, New Zealand.

Nigel Holman, Red Rock Museum, New Mexico, USA.

John Perry and Paul Tapsell, Rotorua Museum of Art and History, Rotorua, New Zealand.

Lynne Kurylo, Richard Lahey, Ron Miles and Trudi Nicks, Royal Ontario Museum, Toronto, Ontario, Canada.

Louise Evans and Victoria Pirie, Russell Cotes Art Gallery and Museum, Bournemouth, England.

Celia Thompson, Sarjeant Art Gallery, Wanganui, New Zealand.

Jack Grist, Shepparton International Village, Victoria, Australia.

Smithsonian Institution, Washington, DC, USA:

- Zora Martin-Felton and Steven Newsome, Anacostia Neighborhood Museum.
- Vera Hyatt, International Gallery.
- Claudine Brown, National African American Museum Project.
- Edward Lifschitz and Sylvia Williams, National Museum of African Art.
- William Truettner, National Museum of American Art.
- Heather Smith and Spencer Crew, National Museum of American History.
- Elaine Gurian and Clara Sue Kidwell, National Museum of the American Indian.
- Joallyn Archambault, Margery Gordon, Aleta Inglero, Ivan Karp, Laura McKie, Ang Robinson and Robert Sullivan, National Museum of Natural History.
- Harry Jackson, National Portrait Gallery, Smithsonian Institution.
- Nancy Fuller, Native American Museums Programme.
- Tom Lowderbaugh, Office of Elementary and Secondary Education.
- Lauryn Guttenplan Grant, Office of the General Counsel.
- Brian LeMay, Office of International Relations.

Chris Anderson, Philip Clarke, Barry Craig, Sally Fieldhouse, Lorraine McLaughlin, Chris Reebeck, South Australian Museum, Adelaide, South Australia.

Susan Marcus, Spertus Museum, Chicago, Illinois, USA.

Doreen Mellor, Tandanya National Aboriginal Cultural Institute, Adelaide, Australia.

Michael Mansell, Tasmanian Aboriginal Centre Inc., Hobart, Australia.

Patricia Sabine, Tasmanian Museum and Art Gallery, Hobart, Australia.

Jennifer Evans and Cherie Meecham, Te Awamutu District Museum, Te Awamutu, New Zealand.

Anita Jacobsen, Lower East Side Tenement Museum, New York, USA.

Elwood Green, Native American Center for the Living Arts (The Turtle), Niagara Falls, New York, USA.

Linda Manz, U'mista Cultural Centre, and Dan Cranmer, Alert Bay, Cormorant Island, British Columbia, Canada.

Ngahuia Te Awekotuku, University of Auckland, New Zealand.

Jill Baird, Miriam Clavir and Anne Stevenson, University of British Columbia Museum of Anthropology, Vancouver, BC, Canada.

Rebecca Buck, Pamela Hearne, Mary Day Kent, and Gillain Wakely, University of Pennsylvania Museum of Archaeology and Anthropology, Philadelphia, Pennsylvania, USA.

Lynn Maranda, Vancouver Museum, Vancouver, British Columbia, Canada.

Barbara Moke-Sly, Michelle Orgad, Sally Parker and Bruce Robinson, Waikato Museum, Hamilton, New Zealand.

Michelle Horwood, Wanganui Museum, Wanganui, New Zealand.

Joan Maynard, Weeksville Society, Brooklyn, New York, USA.

Steve Rogers, Wheelwright Museum, Santa Fe, New Mexico, USA.

Tom Hill, Woodland Cultural Centre, Brantford, Ontario, Canada.

Bonnie Wuttunee-Wadsworth.

Otto Lucio and Rose Wyaco, Zuni Museum Project; Joseph Dishta and the Zuni Tribal Council, Pueblo of Zuni, New Mexico.

Bibliography

AAAC (1993) 'Recommended national policy on the protection and return of significant Aboriginal and Torres Strait Islander cultural property', Australian Aboriginal Affairs Council, October.

AAM (1941) 'Plains Indian Museum at Browning dedicated', *Museum News* 19(6), 15 September: 1, 7.

—— (1972) *Museums: Their New Audience*, a report to the Department of Housing and Urban Development by a Special Committee of the American Association of Museums, Washington, DC: American Association of Museums.

—— (1984) *Museums for a New Century*, a report of the Commission on Museums for a New Century, Washington, DC: American Association of Museums.

—— (1991) 'Your vantage point: consensus shouldn't be an excuse to avoid controversy', *Museum News* 70(6): 83–4.

—— (2000) 'NAGPRA at 10: examining a decade of the Native American Graves Protection and Repatriation Act', *Museum News*, September/October: 42–9, 67–9, 71–5.

AAMA (1989) *A Decade of Devotion: African American Museums Association 1978–1988*, Washington, DC: African American Museums Association.

AAMA/AASLH (nd) *Profile of Black Museums: A Survey Commissioned by the African American Museums Association*, Washington, DC/Nashville, Tennessee: African American Museums Association and the American Association for State and Local History.

Abrams, G.H.J. (1994) 'The case for wampum: repatriation from the Museum of the American Indian to the Six Nations Confederacy, Brantford, Ontario, Canada', in F.E.S. Kaplan (ed.)

Museums and the Making of 'Ourselves', Leicester and London: Leicester University Press.

Acle, A. (1989) 'Native Americans protest exhibit', *The Gainesville Sun*, 8 December: 1B.

Adams, R.M. (1987a) 'Statement by Robert McCormick Adams, Secretary, Smithsonian Institution, before the Select Committee on Indian Affairs', United States Senate, Washington, DC, 20 February 1987.

Adams, R.M. (1987b) 'Statement by Robert McCormick Adams, Secretary, Smithsonian Institution, before the Committee on Rules and Administration and the Select Committee on Indian Affairs', United States Senate, Washington, DC, 12 November 1987.

AFN and CMA (1992) *Turning the Page: Forging New Partnerships Between Museums and First Peoples*, Ottawa: Assembly of First Nations and the Canadian Museums Association.

Agyeman, J. (1993) 'Alien species', *Museums Journal* 93(12): 22–3.

Ak-Chin (1987) 'Ak-Chin Indian community: water settlement celebration', 9 January 1988. Maricopa, Arizona: Ak-Chin Indian Community.

Alexander, E.P. (1979) *Museums in Motion: An Introduction to the History and Function of Museums*, Nashville: AASLH.

Ambler, M. (1991) 'The nation's first tribal college', *Native Peoples* 4(2): 22–3.

Ames, M.M. (1981) 'Museum anthropologists and the arts of acculturation on the Northwest Coast', *BC Studies* 49: 3–14.

—— (1990) 'Cultural empowerment and museums: opening up anthropology through collaboration', in S. Pearce (ed.) *Objects of Knowledge*, London and Atlantic Highlands: The Athlone Press.

305

—— (1993) *Cannibal Tours and Glass Boxes: The Anthropology of Museums*, Vancouver: UBC Press.

Amnesty International (1993) *Australia: A Criminal Justice System Weighted Against Aboriginal People*, New York: Amnesty International.

Amnesty International (1997) *AUSTRALIA. Deaths in custody: How many more?* ASA 12/04/1997, dated 01/07/1997. Online. Available http:www.amnesty.org/ailib/index (accessed 19 November 2000).

Anderson, C. (1988) Comments on 'Aboriginal Keeping Places' document from DAA, *COMA Bulletin of the Conference of Museum Anthropologists* 20: 24–6.

—— (1990a) 'Australian Aborigines and museums – a new relationship', *Curator* 33(3): 165–79.

Anderson, C. (1990b) 'The economics of sacred art: the uses of a secret/sacred collection in the South Australian Museum', *COMA Bulletin of the Conference of Museum Anthropologists* 23: 31–41.

—— (1990c) 'Repatriation, custodianship and the policies of the South Australian Museum', *COMA Bulletin of the Conference of Museum Anthropologists* 23: 112–15.

—— (1990d) 'Repatriation of cultural property: a social process', *Museum* 165(1): 54–5.

—— (1991a) 'Aboriginal people and museums: restricting access to increase it', in S. Tonkin (ed.) *Something for Everyone, Access to Museums*, the 1991 Conference of the Council of Australian Museum Associations: 189–93.

—— (1991b) 'The custodianship of sacred objects project: an overview', *Records of the South Australian Museum* 25(1): 111–12.

—— (1993) Interview with Chris Anderson, Head of the Division of Anthropology (now Director), South Australian Museum, Adelaide, 22 July 1993.

Anderson, D. (1992) 'Beyond museums: objects and cultures', *Journal of Education in Museums* 13: 9–12.

Anderson, R. (1992) 'Thinking big at the BM', *Museum Development*, December: 31–7.

Anon. (1969) 'Metropolitan guard injured by vandal writing obsenity', *New York Times*, 2 February 1969: 74.

AP (Associated Press) (1991) 'Woman who bought Indian masks plans to return them to tribes', *Rocky Mountain News*, 5 June 1991.

Archambault, J. (1991) Interview with Joallyn Archambault, National Museum of Natural History, Smithsonian Institution, 2 May 1991.

Archuleta, M. and Strickland, R. (1991) *Shared Visions*, New York: The New Press.

Arden-Hopkins, J. (1988) *Home at last*, published by the Steuben Courier-Advocate.

ARM (1996) *Hijacked African Treasures*. Online. Available http:www.arm.arc.co.uk (accessed 31 July 1996).

Arnold, D. (1990) 'Indian artifacts: where do they rightfully belong?', *The Boston Globe*, Monday 2 April: 27–8.

Arnold, M. (1969) 'Paintings defaced at Metropolitan; one a Rembrandt', *New York Times*, Friday 17 January.

Art-Talk (1991) 'Indian art at auction shows market strength – and one buyer's character', *Art-Talk*, August/September: 51.

Asante, M.K. (1990) 'Arrogance of white culture ignores African achievement', *Now* 9(43).

Aspinall, P. (1993) 'Preface' in A. Hakiwai and J. Terrell, *Ruatepupuke: A Maori Meeting House*, (draft version), Chicago: Field Museum of Natural History.

Atkinson, J. (1985) 'The Shepparton Aboriginal Keeping Place', *COMA Bulletin of the Conference of Museum Anthropologists* 16: 9–10.

ATSIC (1993a) 'Policy development and Aboriginal and Torres Strait Islander cultural property', Canberra: Aboriginal and Torres Strait Islander Commission, Issues Paper No. 3, October.

—— (1993b) 'Discussion papers: attachment a: issues arising from the consultation by ATSIC on a proposed policy', Canberra: Aboriginal and Torres Strait Islander Commission.

—— (1997) *ATSIC Annual Report 1996–7*, Canberra: Aboriginal and Torres Strait Islander Commission. Online. Available http:www.atsic. gov.au (accessed 15 June 2000).

—— (1998) *ATSIC Annual Report 1997–8*, Canberra: Aboriginal and Torres Strait Islander Commission. Online. Available http:www. atsic.gov.au (accessed 15 June 2000).

Austin, J.F. (1982) 'Their face to the rising sun: trends in the development of black museums', *Museum News* 60(3): 28–32.

Australian Parliamentary Library (1996) 'Hindmarsh Island Bridge Bill 1996', *Bills Digest*, 50 1996–97, Canberra: Department of the Parliamentary Library. Online. Available http:www.aph.gov.au/library (accessed 17 November 2000).

Bacone (nd.a) 'Ataloa', information sheet produced by Ataloa Art Lodge of Bacone College, Muskogee, Oklahoma.

—— (nd.b) 'Bacone College: a unique and historic mission', Bacone College leaflet, Muskogee, Oklahoma.

Balasegaram, M. (1990) 'A show of heads and skulls', *Sunday Star Plus*, 4 November.

Baradas, D.B. (1980) 'Developing or traditional area museums', in R. Edwards and J. Stewart (eds) *Preserving Indigenous Cultures: A New Role For Museums*, papers from a regional seminar held in Adelaide, Australia, 10–15 September 1978, Canberra, Australia: Australian Government Publishing Service: 79–80.

Barley, N. and Sandaruppa, S. (1991) *The Torajan Ricebarn*, British Museum Occasional Paper 72, Department of Ethnography, London: British Museum.

Becker, S. (1991) Comments made in presentation during a session entitled 'Communities in Collaboration Part 2', at the annual conference of the American Association of Museums, May.

Bell, J. (1991) 'The West: a realist's guide to the American frontier', *Museum and Arts Washington*, March/April: 70.

Berndt, R.M. (1981) 'A long view: some personal comments on land rights', *AIAS Newsletter* No. 16, September.

Bernstein, B. (1991a) 'Communities in collaboration: repatriation means collaboration', paper presented at the American Association of Museums Annual Meeting, Denver, Colorado, 22 May.

—— (1991b) Interview with Bruce Bernstein, Assistant Director of the Museum of Indian Arts and Culture, Museum of New Mexico, Santa Fe, June.

Berry, S. (1995) Letter from Dr Susan Berry, Curator of Ethnology, Provincial Museum of Alberta, 21 July.

Biddle, L. (1977) 'Keeping tradition alive', *Museum News* 55(5), 35–42.

Blair, B. (1979a) 'American Indians vs. American museums: a matter of religious freedom, part 1', *American Indian Journal* 5(5):13–21.

—— (1979b) 'American Indians vs. American museums: a matter of religious freedom, part 2', *American Indian Journal* 5(6):2–6.

Blankenship, K. (1996) Interview with Ken Blankenship, Director of the Cherokee National Museum in Cherokee, Oklahoma, 24 July.

Blankenship, K., Volkert, J. and King, D. (1993) *Exhibit Concept for the Museum of the Cherokee Indian* (draft), 2 May.

Boas, F. (1927) *Primitive Art*, Oslo: H. Aschehoug and Co., Reprinted by Dover in 1955.

Bolton, L. (1988) Comments on Department of Aboriginal Affairs Policy Paper on Aboriginal Keeping Places, *COMA Bulletin of the Conference of Museum Anthropologists* 20: 27–8.

Bolton, L. and Specht, J. (1985) *Polynesian and Micronesian Artefacts in Australia: An Inventory of Major Public Collections*, UNESCO.

Borthwell, D. (1994) Personal correspondence with the author, 18 June.

Bouchard, M. (1993) 'Museums without walls: ecomuseums in the Keewatin, Northwest Territories', *History News* 48(6): 24–5.

Bourne, R. (1985) 'Are Amazonian Indians museum pieces?' *New Society*, 29 November, 380–1.

Brain, R. (1972) *Into the Primitive Environment: survival on the edge of our civilization*, London: George Philip.

Brascoupé, S. (ed.) (1981) *Directory of North American Indian Museums and Cultural Centers*, Niagara Falls: North American Indian Museums Association.

Bringhurst, R. (1991) *The Black Canoe: Bill Reid and the Spirit of Haida Gwaii*, Seattle: University of Washington Press and Vancouver/Toronto: Douglas and McIntyre.

Brinkley-Rogers, P. (1991) '"Gesture of heart": buyer to return masks to tribe', *Arizona Republic*, May 23.

British Columbian Treaty Commission (2000) 'Status report as of January 31, 2000', *British*

Columbia Treaty Commission Newsletters, updated February 2000 edition. Vancouver: British Columbia Treaty Commission. Online. Available http:www.bctreaty.net (accessed 1 June 2000).

British Museum (1985) 'North American artists to demonstrate their work at the Museum of Mankind', News release 7/85, issued by the Press and Information Office of the British Museum, London, April.

Brodie, N., Doole, J. and Watson, P. (2000) *Stealing History: The Illicit Trade in Cultural Material,* Cambridge: The McDonald Institute for Archaeological Research.

Brody, H. (1987) *Living Arctic: Hunters of the Canadian North,* London: Faber and Faber.

Bromilow, G. (1993) 'Finders Keepers?' *Museums Journal* 93(3): 31–4.

Brookes, G. (1993) Interview with Gavin Brookes, Maori Anglican missionary involved in the development of a *marae* museum in Koriniti near Wanganui on New Zealand's North Island, 19 June.

Broun, E. (1991) 'The story behind the story of the West as America', *Museum News* 70(5).

Brown, C. (1990) 'Museums' roles in a multicultural society', closing keynote address at 'Building Partnerships: Museums and Their Communities', a training congress for museum professionals, 26–9 June 1990, Office of Museum Programs, Smithsonian Institution, Washington, DC.

—— (1993) 'Community focused museums: reflecting the reality of a plurality', *Orator* 1(4).

Brown, E. (nd) Introduction and Mission Statement, Chicago: Chicago Historical Society.

Buyer, R. (1991) 'Under The Turtle's Shell', *The Buffalo News Magazine,* 10 May: 8–12.

CAG (1992) 'National commitment to improved outcomes of programs and services for Aboriginal Peoples and Torres Strait Islanders', Council of Australian Governments, 7 December.

CAMA (1993a) *New Obligations: Policies for Museums in Australia and Aboriginal and Torres Strait Islander Peoples,* Council of Australian Museum Associations, May.

—— (1993b) *Previous Possessions, New Obligations: Policies for Museums in Australia and Aboriginal and Torres Strait Islander Peoples,* Melbourne: Council of Australian Museum Associations, 1 December.

Cameron, D.F. (1971) 'The Museum, a temple or the forum', in *Curator* 14(1) 11–24.

Cannizzo, J. (1989) *Into the Heart of Africa,* exhibition catalogue, Toronto: Royal Ontario Museum.

—— (1990a) 'Artistry of the "Unknown Continent"', *Archaeology,* March/April: 48–51.

—— (1990b) 'Into the heart of a controversy', *The Toronto Star,* Tuesday 5 June.

—— (1991) 'Exhibiting Cultures: "Into the Heart of Africa"', *Visual Anthropology Review* 7(1): 150–60.

Cannon-Brookes, P. (1990) 'Into the Heart of Africa', *International Journal of Museum Management and Curatorship,* Sept, 9(3): 292–7.

CAR (1999) *Draft Document for Reconciliation,* Barton, ACT: Council for Aboriginal Reconciliation. Online. Available http:www.reconciliation.org.au/docrec (accessed 10 November 2000).

—— (2000) *National Strategy to Promote Recognition of Aboriginal and Torres Strait Islander Rights,* Barton, ACT: Council for Aboriginal Reconciliation. Online. Available http:www.reconciliation.org.au/docrec (accessed 12 November 2000).

Carpenter, C.H. (1981) 'Secret, precious things: repatriation of potlatch art', *Artmagazine,* May/June: 64–70.

Carrier, J. (1991) 'The Colorado: a river drained dry', *National Geographic,* June, 179(6): 4–35.

Cassidy, A.W. (1999) Letter to the author from Anne W. Cassidy, Executive Director of the America Indian Ritual Object Repatriation Foundation, 5 November, 1999.

Caygill, M. (1992) *The Story of the British Museum,* London: British Museum Press.

Chamberlin, R. (1983) *Loot! The Heritage of Plunder,* London: Thames and Hudson.

Chew, F. (1990) 'Museum-in-process', *Bu Gao Ban* 7(1): 2.

Childs, E.C. (1980) 'Museums and the American Indian: legal aspects of repatriation', *Council for Museum Anthropology Newsletter* 4(4):4–27.

Chin, C. (1991) 'Aiming at the Year 2000', *Bu Gao Ban* 8(1): 2.

Clark, G. (1993) Interview with Geoff Clark, Chairman of the Framlingham Aboriginal Land Trust, July.

Clarke, J. (nd) Personal correspondence from J. Clarke, Curator of Anthropology, Tasmanian Museum and Art Gallery to the author.

Clay, W. (1994) 'Update: our family and cultural heritage', in *Orator* 2(1), Spring.

Cledhill, R. (1990) 'Aboriginal skulls are returned', *The Times*, 18 June.

Cleere, H. (1994) Personal correspondence to the author from Henry Cleere, Archaeological consultant and editor of *The European Archaeologist*, 22 March.

Clifford, J. (1988) *The Predicament of Culture: Twentieth-Century Ethnography, Literature, and Art*, Cambridge, Mass. and London: Harvard University Press.

Clifford, J. (1991) 'Four Northwest Coast museums: travel reflections', in I. Karp and S.D. Lavine (eds) *Exhibiting Cultures*, Washington, DC: Smithsonian Institution Press.

—— (1992) 'Museums in the Borderlands', in *Different Voices*, New York: Association of Art Museum Directors.

CNHS (1976) *Tsa-La-Gi (Its History Through July 1976)*, Tahlequah: The Cherokee National Historical Society, Inc.

—— (1995) *Cherokee National Historical Society Mission Statement*, Tahlequah: Cherokee National Historical Society, Inc.

Cocks, R. (1993) Letter from Dr Robin Cocks, Keeper of Palaeontology, The Natural History Museum, London, to Maurice Davies, Editor of the *Museums Journal*, Museums Association, London, 23 November.

Cole, D. (1985) *Captured Heritage*, Seattle and London: University of Washington Press.

Cole, D. and Chaikin I. (1990) *An Iron Hand Upon the People*, Vancouver and Toronto: Douglas and MacIntyre; Seattle: University of Washington Press.

Commission on Human Rights (1993) *Mataatua Declaration on Cultural and Intellectual Property Rights of Indigenous Peoples*. Adopted at the First International Conference on the Cultural and Intellectual Property Rights of Indigenous Peoples held in Whakatana, Aotearoa, New Zealand, 12–18 June 1993. Commission on Human Rights, Sub-Commission of Prevention of Discrimination and Protection of Minorities Working Group on Indigenous Populations. Online. Available http:www.ankn.uaf.edu (accessed 26 November 2000).

Connor, W.P. (1982) *History of Cherokee Historical Association 1946–82*, Cherokee: Cherokee Historical Association.

Cooper, A. and Liu, M. (1991) 'Salvaging the past', *Museum News*, 70(6): 50–2.

Cooper, C. (1989) *Aboriginal and Torres Strait Islander Collections in Overseas Museums*, Canberra, Aboriginal Studies Press, The Institute Report Series.

Coote, J. (1997) 'The Zuni War God at the Pitt Rivers Museum, University of Oxford and its Contested Status', a paper presented at the Museums Association seminar 'Point of No Return? Museums and Repatriation', held at the Museum of London, 4 November 1997.

Coull, C. (1982) 'Carving out its own legend: UBC's Museum of Anthropology', in *Beautiful British Columbia* 24(2):16–23.

Craig, B. (1993) Interview with Barry Craig, Research Coordinator, Aboriginal Family History Project, South Australian Museum, Adelaide, Australia, 23 July.

—— (1995) Personal correspondence to the author from Barry Craig, Research Coordinator, Aboriginal Family History Project, South Australian Museum, Adelaide, Australia, 26 April.

Crean, S. (1990) 'Africa exhibit added insult to original injury', *Toronto Star*, 6 Sept: A25.

Crook, J.M. (1972) *The British Museum*, London: Allen Lane.

CTA (nd) 'Would the ROM mount an exhibit of the Nazi perspective of the holocaust ???', Toronto: Coalition for the Truth About Africa.

Da Breo, H.A. (1989/90) 'Royal spoils: the museum confronts its colonial past', *FUSE*, Winter.

Daes, E.-I. (1995) *Discrimination against Indigenous Peoples: Protection of the Heritage of Indigenous Peoples*, Final Report of the Special Rapporteur, Mrs Erica-Irene Daes in conformity with Sub-Commission resolution 1993/44 and decision 1994/105 of the Commission on Human Rights, Geneva, 47th Session, E/CN.4/Sub.2/1995/26.

—— (1995) *Protection of the Heritage of Indigenous People*, Final Report of the UN Special Rapporteur to the Sub-Commission on Prevention of Discrimination and Protection of Minorities, E/CN.4/Sub.2/1995/26, Document 95–12808, 21 June 1995. Geneva: Office of the United Nations High Commissioner for Human Rights.

Davidson, G.W. (1990) 'The human remains controversies', *The Dodge Magazine* 82(4): 4–7, 24–5.

Davies, B. (1979) 'Museums and Native American rights', *Proceedings of the Mountain-Plains Museums Conference*, 135–42.

Day, M. (1989) *The Vermillion Accord*, adopted by the World Archaeological Congress, First Intercongress on the Disposition of the Dead, Vermilllion, South Dakota, August.

—— (1990) 'Archaeological ethics and the treatment of the dead', *Anthropology Today* 6(1), February: 15–16.

DCMS (2000) *Report of the Ministerial Advisory Panel on Illicit Trade*. London: Department for Culture, Media and Sports.

de Blavia, M.G. (1985) 'The Barquisimeto: invent or drift', *Museum* 148: 224–9.

de Borhegyi, S.F. (1963) 'Visual communication in the Science Museum', *Curator* 6(1): 45–57.

Deloria, V. (1973) *God is Red*, New York: Grossett and Dunlop.

DeLuca, R. (1983) ' "We hold the rock!" The Indian attempt to reclaim Alcatraz Island', *California History* 62(1): 2–23.

Dillenburg, E. (nd) *The Morning Star Controversy*, a Field Museum document compiled by E. Dillenburg, Chicago: Field Museum.

Dishta, J. (1991) Presentation during session entitled 'Communities in collaboration' at the American Association of Museums, annual conference in Denver, Colorado, May.

Doherty, K. (1992) *The Peterborough Precedent*, a presentation at Queen's University Conservation Training Programme, 9 May.

Douthit, M. (1995) Interview with Margie Douthit, Marketing Director for 'Unto These Hills' and Oconaluftee Indian Village, Cherokee Historical Association, Cherokee North Carolina, 24 July.

Doxtator, D. (1985) 'The idea of the Indian and the development of Iroquoian museums', *Museum Quarterly*, Summer: 20–6.

—— (1992) *Fluffs and Feathers: An exhibit on the Symbols of Indianness*, a resource guide, Brantford, Ontario: Woodland Cultural Centre.

Drainie, B. (1991) 'ROM adds insult to injury in debacle over African show', *Globe and Mail*, 6 April.

Duncan, C. and Wallach A. (1980) 'The universal survey museum', *Art History* 3(4), 448–69.

Duroux, M. (1985) 'Establishing a Keeping Place', *COMA Bulletin of the Conference of Museum Anthropologists* 16 June: 7–8.

Echo-Hawk, W.R. (1985) *Sacred Material and the Law*, paper presented at the Buffalo Bill Historical Center, Plains Indian Museum's Ninth Annual Plains Indian Seminar: 'The Concept of Sacred Materials and Their Place in the World', September.

—— (1988) Testimony of Walter R. Echo-Hawk before the Senate Select Committee on Indian Affairs on a Substitute Bill (Amendment No. 2124) for S.187, the 'Native American Museum Claims Commission Act', 29 July.

Echo-Hawk, W.R. and Echo-Hawk, R.C. (1991) 'Repatriation, reburial and religious rights', in C. Vecsey (ed.) *Handbook of American Indian Religious Freedom*, New York: Crossroad Publishing Co. 63–80.

Edwards, E. (1988) 'Representation and reality: science and the visual image', in H. Morphy and E. Edwards (eds) *Australia in Oxford*, Oxford: Pitt Rivers Museum.

Edwards, R. (1980) 'Shepparton Aboriginal Arts Council Co-operative limited Aboriginal Keeping Place', *COMA, Bulletin of the Council of Museum Anthropologists*, 5: 11–15.

Edwards, R. and Stewart, J. (eds) (1980) *Preserving Indigenous Cultures: A New Role For Museums*, papers from a regional seminar held in Adelaide, Australia, 10–15 September 1978; Canberra, Australia: Australian Government Publishing Service.

Eisterhold, G.L. (1992) 'National Civil Rights Museum', *Museum News*, 71(5): 52–3.

Ellis, R. (1990) 'A decade of change: black history at Colonial Williamsburg', *Colonial Williamsburg*, Spring.

Ellicott, R.J. (1986) *The Recognition Of Aboriginal Customary Laws*, The Law Reform Commission, Report No. 31, Canberra: Australian Government Publishing Service. Online. Available http:www.alrc.gov.au (accessed 8 November 2000).

Elliott, J. and Kinard, J.R. (1972) *Museums and Their New Audience*, a report to the Department of Housing and Urban Development by a special committee of AAM, Washington, DC: American Association of Museums.

Fagan, B. (1991) Editorial, *Antiquity* 65 (247): 188–90.

Farb, P. (1978) *Man's Rise to Civilization: The Cultural Ascent of the Indians of North America*, New York: Dutton.

Feldman, E.P. (1981) *The Birth and the Building of the DuSable Museum*, Chicago: DuSable Museum Press.

Fenton, W.N. (1971) 'The New York State wampum collection: the case for the integrity of the cultural treasures', *Proceedings of the American Philosophical Society* 115: 437–61.

Ferguson, T.J. (1979) *Handling of Sacred Articles and Sacred Sites*, paper presented at the American Indian Museums Association (AIMA), 1st National Conference, in Denver, Colorado, 30 April–3 May. Edited by M. Risser, reproduced and distributed under the auspices of the Office of Museum Programs, Native American Museum Training Program, Smithsonian Institution, Washington, DC.

—— (1991) 'Return of War Gods sets example for repatriation', *Zuni History*, Part 2: 13.

Ferguson, T.J. and Eriacho, W. (1990) 'Ahayu:da Zuni war gods: cooperation and repatriation', *Native Peoples*, Fall: 6–12.

Ferguson-Acosta, D. (1990) *Report of the Symposium on African American and Latino Museums and their Collections*, held in the Mexican Fine Arts Center Museum, Chicago, Illinois, May.

Fforde, C. (1992) 'English collections of human remains: an introduction', *World Archaeological Bulletin* 6, 1–4.

Fforde, C., Hubert, J., Turnbull, P. and Hanchant, D. (2001) (eds) *The Dead and Their Possessions: Repatriation in Principle, Policy and Practice*, London: Routledge.

File, N. and Power, C. (1995) *Black Settlers in Britain 1555–1958*, Oxford: Heinemann.

Finster, D. (1975) 'Museums and Medicine Bundles', *The Indian Historian* 8 (4), Fall: 40–48.

Flood, R.S. (1995) *Lost Bird of Wounded Knee: Spirit of the Lakota*, New York: Scribner.

Floyd, C. (1984) 'Chinatown', *History News* 39(6), 6–11.

Foner, E. and Wiener, J. (1991) 'Fighting for the West', *The Nation*, 29 July–5 August: 163–6.

Forbes, J.D. (1964) *The Indian in America's Past*, New York: Prentice-Hall.

Ford, A.J. (1982) 'Their face to the rising sun: trends in the development of black museums', *Museum News* 60(3): 29–32.

Foss, P. (1994) Personal correspondence from Hon. Peter Foss, MLC, Minister for Health, the Arts, Fair Trading; Government of Western Australia, to the author in a letter dated 27 May.

Fourmile, H. (1987) 'Museums and Aborigines: a case study in contemporary scientific colonialism', *Praxis M* 17: 7–11.

—— (1989a) 'Aboriginal heritage legislation and self-determination', *Australian–Canadian Studies* 7(1 and 2): 45–61.

—— (1989b) 'The Aboriginal art market and the repatriation of Aboriginal cultural property', *Social Alternatives* 8(1): 19–22.

—— (1989c) 'Who owns the past? – Aborigines as captives of the archives', *Aboriginal History* 13(1 and 2) 1989: 1–8.

—— (1990a) 'Possession is nine-tenths of the law – and don't Aboriginal people know it!' *COMA Bulletin of the Conference of Museum Anthropologists* 24: 57–67.

—— (1990b) 'The case for independent but complementary Aboriginal cultural institutions', in Australia Council for the Arts *Extending Parameters*: a selection of papers delivered at the Extending Parameters Forum, held at the Queensland Art Gallery, 21–3 February: 35–40.

Frampton, E. (1994) 'End to chapter of history', *Mid Somerset Series*, 28 July: 24–5.

Fraser, P. and Visram, R. (1988) *Black Contribution to History*, London: Geffrye Museum.

Freedman, J. (1990) 'Bringing it all back home; a commentary on *Into the Heart of Africa*', *Museum Quarterly* 18(1): 39–43.

Frisbie, C.J. (1987) *Navajo Medicine Bundles or Jish: Acquisition, Transmission, and Disposition in the Past and Present*, Albuquerque: University of New Mexico Press.

Fryer, P. (1984) *Staying Power – The History of Black People in Britain*, London: Pluto Press.

Fulford, R. (1991) 'Into the Heart of the Matter', *Rotunda* 24 (1): 19–28.

Fuller, N. (1991a) 'Ak-Chin Him Dak – a new model for community heritage management opens to the public', *Cultural Resources Management* 14(5): 36–43.

—— (1991b) Interview with Nancy Fuller, Research Program Manager, Office of Museum Programs, Smithsonian Institution, Washington, DC.

Fuller, N. (1992) 'The museum as a vehicle for community empowerment: the Ak-Chin Indian Community Ecomuseum Project', in I. Karp, C.M. Kreamer and S.D. Lavine (eds) *Museums and Communities*, Washington, DC: Smithsonian Institution Press.

Fuoco, S.W. (1979) 'Islanders celebrate potlatch after 57 years', *The Vancouver Sun*, Saturday 30 June.

Gaither, B. (1990) 'Museums and values for tomorrow', opening keynote address at 'Building Partnerships: Museums and Their Communities', a training congress for museum professionals, June 26–9, Washington, DC: Office of Museum Programs, Smithsonian Institution.

Gale, F. (1982) 'Community involvement and academic response: the University of Adelaide Aboriginal Research Centre', in *Aboriginal History* 6(2): 130–4.

Gathercole, P. and Lowenthal, D. (eds) (1994) *The Politics of the Past*, London: Routledge.

Gbadamosi, G. (1990) 'So much misery condensed', *Museums Journal* 90(9): 25.

Gifford, A., Brown, W. and Bundey, R. (1989) *Loosen the Shackles: First Report of the Liverpool 8 Inquiry into Race Relations in Liverpool*, London: Karia Press.

Gillies, K. and O'Regan, G. (1993) 'Murihiku resolution of Koiwi Tangata Management', *New Zealand Museums Journal* 24(1): 30–1.

Glasgow City Council (1998) Report to Arts and Culture Committee of 19 November 1998 by the Working Group on the Repatriation of Artefacts: Lakota Ghost Dance Shirt.

GLC (1986) *A History of the Black Presence in London*, London: Greater London Council.

Glueck, G. (1969a) '"J'accuse, Baby!" she cried', *New York Times*, Sunday 20 April.

—— (1969b) 'Into the mainstream, everybody', *New York Times*, 15 June, ll,: 24.

Goldflam, R. (1997) 'Noble Salvage: Aboriginal Heritage Protection And The Evatt Review', *Indigenous Law Bulletin*, 3 (88). Online. Available http:www.austlii.edu.au/au/journals/ILB (accessed 19 September 2000).

Gonyea, R.W. (1993) 'Give me that old time religion', *History News* 48(2): 4–7.

Goodman, A.H. and Armelagos, G.J. (1985) 'Disease and death at Dr. Dickson's mound', *Natural History* 9: 12–18.

Government of British Columbia (1998) *Nisga'a Final Agreement*, Victoria: Government of British Columbia, Ministry of Aboriginal Affairs. Online. Available http:www.aaf.gov.bc.ca (accessed 3 May 2000).

Graburn, N.H.H. and Lee, M. (1988) '*The Living Arctic*, doing what *The Spirit Sings* didn't', *Inuit Art Quarterly*, Fall: 10–13.

Graves, M. (1980) *United Indians of All Tribes Foundation: A Ten Year History, March 8, 1970–March 8, 1980*, Seattle: UIATF.

Griffin, G. (1994) 'Curators' committee: the AMIE awards', *Museum News* 73(1): 26.

Griffin, L. (1993) 'Listening to different voices', *MUSE* June–July: 3.

Grimes, R. (1990) 'Breaking the glass barrier: the power of display', *Journal of Ritual Studies* 4(2): 239–62.

—— (1986) 'Desecration of the dead: an inter-religious controversy', *American Indian Quarterly* Fall: 305–18.

Grzybowicz, N., Kartinyeri, D. and Craig, B. (1990) 'The Aboriginal Family History Project at the South Australian Museum', in *COMA Bulletin of the Conference of Museum Anthropologists* 23 April: 12–18.

Haas, J. (1991) Paper presented in a session entitled 'Museums and Native people: establishing a dialogue', at the AAM Annual Conference in Denver, Colorado, 19–23 May.

Hakiwai, A. (1993) Interview with Arapata Hakiwai, Curator of Maori Collections, Auckland Museum, New Zealand.

Haldane, W. (1984) 'The museum and its relevance in a multicultural society', *Agmanz Journal* 15(4): 26–7.

Halpin, M. (1988) 'The Spirit Sings: artistic traditions of Canada's First Peoples', *Culture* VIII (1): 89–93.

Hamilton-Sperr, P. (1991a) Interview with Portia Hamilton-Sperr, Director of the Philadelphia Initiative for Cultural Pluralism, Pennsylvania, USA, 12 August.

—— (1991b) *Museums in the Life of a City, 2nd Interim Report due July 15th 1991*, Philadelphia: Philadelphia Initiative for Cultural Pluralism.

—— (1992a) *Museums in the Life of a City, 3rd Interim Report due July 24th 1992*, Philadelphia: Philadelphia Initiative for Cultural Pluralism.

—— (1992b) *Museums in the Life of a City, Final Report 1989–1992*, Philadelphia: Philadelphia Initiative for Cultural Pluralism, December.

Hamilton-Sperr, P. and Primas, C. (1990) 'Museums in the Life of a City: The Philadelphia Initiative for Cultural Pluralism'. *Bulletin*, May.

Hammil, J. and Cruz, R. (1994) 'Statement of American Indians Against Desecration before the World Archaeological Congress', in R. Layton, (ed.) *Conflict in the Archaeology of Living Traditions*, London: Routledge.

Hanchant, D. (2001) 'Australia's skeletal provenancing project: an archival researcher's point of view', in Fforde *et al.* (eds) *The Dead and Their Possessions: Repatriation in Principle, Policy and Practice*, London: Routledge.

Hanson, J.A. (1980) 'The reappearing Vanishing American', *Museum News* 59(2): 44–51.

Harper, K. (1989) *Give Me My Father's Body*, Iqaluit: Blacklead Books.

Harris, O. and Gow, P. (1985) 'The British Museum's representation of Amazonian Indians', *Anthropology Today* 1(5): 1–2.

Hemming, S. (1992) 'Chinese homes', *Journal of Education in Museums*, 13: 33–4.

Herle, A. (1992) 'Cultural exchange between Naga people and CUMAA', *MEG News* July: 4.

—— (1993) 'Shaman insights', *Museums Journal* 93(12): 24.

Hildred, A. (1995) Telephone conversation with Alexandra Hildred, Head of Research, Mary Rose Trust, Portsmouth, England on 24 January.

Hill, R. (1977) 'Reclaiming cultural artefacts', *Museum News* 55(5): 43–6.

—— (1990) 'Beyond repatriation', *History News* 48(2): 9–10.

Hiller, S. (1992) *The Myth of Primitivism*, London: Routledge.

Hinsley, C.M. (1981) *Savages and Scientists*, Washington, DC: Smithsonian Institution Press.

Hitchcock, A. (1976) 'Tribal cultural centers: an attempt to salvage cultural heritage', papers from two conferences: San Antonio, Texas, October 1976: and Mexico City, December 1976: Texas Historical Foundation.

Hobhouse, H. (1985) *Seeds of Change*, London: Sidgewick & Jackson.

Holbert, G. (1989) 'Mexican Museum celebrates "Day of the Dead"', *Chicago Sun-Times*, 20 October: 53.

Holm, B. (1965) (1991, 13th edn) *Northwest Coast Indian Art: An analysis of Form*, Thomas Burke Memorial Washington State Museum, Monograph No. 1, Seattle and London: University of Washington Press.

Hooper, J. (1992) 'Stuffed Bushman stays the course for Olympics', *The Guardian*, 21 May.

Hopkins, K.R. (1970) 'Is confrontation in your future?', *Curator* Xlll/2: 120–4.

Horse Capture, G.P. (1981) 'Some observations on establishing tribal museums', AASLH Technical Leaflet 134, *History News* 36(1).

—— (1991) 'An American Indian perspective', in H.J. Viola and C. Margolis (eds) *Seeds of Change: Five Hundred Years Since Columbus*, Washington, DC: Smithsonian Institution Press pp. 186–207.

—— (1992) 'Survival of culture', *Museum News* 70(1): 49–51.

Horwood, M. (1995) Personal correspondence to the author from Michelle Horwood, Curator, Whànganui Museum, New Zealand, dated 14 June.

House of Commons (1999) *Committee decides in principle to conduct inquiry into The Return of Cultural Property*. Press Notice No. 31 of Session 1998–99. London: House of Commons.

—— (2000) *Cultural Property: Return and Illicit Trade. Culture, Media and Sport Committee, Seventh report. Session 1999–2000. Volume 1: Report and Proceedings of the Committee. Volume 2: Minutes of Evidence. Volume 3: Appendices to the Minutes of Evidence*, London: The Stationery Office Limited.

Houtman, G. (1985) 'Survival International: going public on Amazonian Indians', *Anthropology Today* 1(5): 2–4.

Howard, J. (2000) *Joint Statement with Tony Blair on Aboriginal Remains*. Media Release from the Office of the Prime Minister of Australia, Canberra, 4 July 2000.

HREOC (1997) *Bringing Them Home: Report of the National Inquiry into the Separation of Aboriginal and Torres Strait Islander Children from Their Families*. Human Rights and Equal Opportunity Commission. Online. Available http:www.hreoc.gov.au/publications (accessed 10 November 2000).

Hubert, H. (1985) 'Ecomuseums in France: contradictions and distortions', *Museum* 148: 186–90.

Hubert, J. (1994) 'A proper place for the dead: a critical review of the "reburial" issue', in R. Layton (ed.) *Conflict in the Archaeology of Living Traditions*, London: Routledge.

Hudson, K. (1992) 'The dream and the reality', *Museums Journal* 92(4): 27–31.

Hume, C. (1990) 'ROM critics confusing content with the context', *The Toronto Star*, 19 May.

Hustito, C. (1991) 'Why Zuni War Gods need to be returned', *Zuni History*, Section 2: 12.

Hutterer, K.L. (1995) Personal correspondence to the author from Karl L. Hutterer, Director of the Thomas Burke Memorial Washington State Museum of Natural and Cultural Heritage, Seattle, 14 November.

ICOM (1986) *ICOM Code of Professional Ethics*, Paris: International Council of Museums. Online. Available http:www.icom.org (accessed 23 November 2000).

—— (2000) *Revision of the ICOM Code of Professional Ethics, 2nd June 2000*, Paris: International Council of Museums. Online. Available http:www.icom.org (accessed 23 November 2000).

Impey, O. and MacGregor, A. (1985) *The Origins of Museums: The Cabinet of Curiosities in 16th and 17th Century Europe*, Oxford: Clarendon Press.

Indigenous 500 Committee (1992) 'Strengthening the spirit', papers of *The Indigenous Peoples of the Americas International Conference*, held in Ottawa-Hull, 11–14 November.

Janke, T. (1998) *Our Culture: Our Future – Report on Australian Indigenous Cultural and Intellectual Property Rights*, Sydney: Aboriginal and Torres Strait Islander Commission (ATSIC) and the Australian Institute of Aboriginal and Torres Strait Islander Studies (AIATSIS) Online. Available http:www.icip.lawnet.com.au (accessed 29 May 2000).

Jaume, D., Pons, G., Palmer, M., McMinn, M., Alcover, J.A. and Politis, G. (1992) 'Racism, archaeology and museums: the strange case of the stuffed African male in the Darder Museum, Banyoles (Catalonia), Spain', *World Archaeological Bulletin* 6, 113–18.

Jenness, A., Rizzi, J. and Chiu, F. (nd) *The Multicultural Program*, leaflet produced by the Boston Children's Museum, Boston, Massachusetts.

Jimenez, G. (1987) 'Muralists bare soul of Mexican community', *Chicago Sun-Times*, 31 July.

Jones, D. (1987) 'Exhibition review of *Hidden Peoples of the Amazon*', *Museum Ethnographers Group Newsletter* 20: 103–10.

—— (1992) 'Dealing with the past', *Museums Journal* 92 (1): 24–7.

Jones, S. (1994) Letter to the author from Dr Schuyler Jones, Director of the Pitt Rivers Museum in Oxford, 1 July.

—— (1996) Interview with Dr Schuyler Jones, Former Director of the Pitt Rivers Museum, Oxford, 19 September 1996.

Karp, I. and Lavine, S. (eds) (1991) *Exhibiting Cultures: The Poetics and Politics of Museum Display*, Washington, DC and London: Smithsonian Institution Press.

Karp, I., Kreamer, C.M. and Lavine, S. (eds) (1992) *Museums and Communities: The Politics of Public Culture*, Washington, DC and London: Smithsonian Institution Press.

Kimber, R.G. (1980) 'Desecration of Aboriginal sites and sacred objects in central Australia', *The Artifact* 5: 79–91.

Kinard, J.R. (1972) 'Intermediaries between the museum and the community', in ICOM, *The Museum in the Service of Man Today and Tomorrow: The Museum's Educational and Cultural Role*, Ninth General Conference Papers, Paris: International Council of Museums.

—— (1985) 'The neighbourhood museum as a catalyst for social change', *Museum* 148, 37(4): 217–23.

Kinard, J.R. and Nighbert, E. (1972) 'The Anacostia Neighborhood Museum, Smithsonian Institution, Washington, DC', *Museum* 24(2): 102–9.

King, D.H. (1976) 'History of the museum of the Cherokee Indian', *Journal of Cherokee Studies*, 1(1): 60–4.

King, J.C.H. (1989) *Living Arctic: Hunters of the Canadian North*, Ottawa: Indigenous Survival International and London: Museum of Mankind.

Klymasz, R. (1991) Interview with R. Klymasz, Curator, East European Programme, Canadian Museum of Civilization, 10 July.

Knowles, L. and M. van Helmond (1991) 'Staying power', *Museums Journal* 91(4): 16.

Koorie Heritage Trust (1991) *Koorie*, North Melbourne: Creative Solutions.

Krzysztof, P. (1990) *Collectors and Curiosities: Paris and Vienna 1500–1800*, Cambridge: Polity Press.

'Ksan Association (nd) ''*Ksan*, a guide to the 'Ksan Historic Indian Village', Hazelton, British Columbia: 'Ksan Association.

Kwasnik, E. (1994) *A Wider World: Collections of Foreign Ethnography in Scotland*, Edinburgh: National Museums of Scotland.

Ladd, E. (1991a) 'Repatriation – Zuni Sensitive Material: a case study', a paper presented, and answers to questions, at the session *Communities in Collaboration, Part 2*, at the AAM Annual Meeting in Denver, Colorado on 22 May.

—— (1991b) Interview with Edmund Ladd, Curator of Ethnology, Museum of Indian Arts and Culture, Museum of New Mexico, Santa Fe, June.

Leggett, J. (2000) *Restitution and Repatriation: Guidelines for Good Practice*, London: Museums and Galleries Commission.

Lester, J. (1991) Interview with Joan Lester, Chief Curator, Boston Children's Museum, Boston, Massachusetts, May.

Levin, B. (1988) 'Foul deeds of desecration', *The Times*, 6 June: 14.

Lichtenstein, G. (1992) 'Who Owns the Past?' *Diversion*, January.

Longman, P. (1994) Letter to the author from Peter Longman, Director of the Museums and Galleries Commission, London, 7 January.

Lowenthal, D. (1985) *The Past is a Foreign Country*, Cambridge, New York and Melbourne: University of Cambridge Press.

Lucs, S. (1990) 'Another look at . . . Into the Heart of Africa', *Museum Quarterly* 18(3): 35–9.

Lumley, R. (ed.) (1988) *The Museum-Time Machine*, London and New York: Routledge.

Lusaka, J. (1993) 'Laying the Foundation', *Orator* 1(3): 1–2.

—— (1995) 'Directors of African American museums tell stories of struggle and success', *Orator* 3(1): 5, 10.

Lyons, O.R. (1987) *Haudenosaunee testimony concerning S.1722*, presented by Oren R. Lyons, Faithkeeper, Onondaga Nation, Fire Keepers of the Haudenosaunee also known as the Six Nations Iroquois Confederacy to the US Select Committee on Indian Affairs, during its consideration of a bill to establish a National Museum of the American Indian, November.

McCormack, P.A. (1991) 'Reconstituting a Natoas bundle: a Provincial Museum of Alberta – Peigan collaborative project', a paper submitted to the 1991 Task Force on Museums and First Peoples.

McDermott, M. (1995) 'Of blankets and bonnets: The Ataloa Art Lodge', *Oklahoma Today* 45(3): 51–7.

MacDonald, G.F. (1993) 'Changing relations between Canada's Museums and First Peoples', paper prepared for a lecture tour, Australia, July.

MacDonald, S. (1990) 'Telling white lies', *Museums Journal* 90(9): 32–3.

McEwan, C. (1994) *Ancient Mexico in the British Museum*, London: British Museum Press.

McGreevy, S.B. (1987a) 'Journey toward understanding: Mary Cabot Wheelwright and Hastiin Klah', *The Messenger*, 2nd quarter: 1–3.

—— (1987b) 'Journey toward understanding: a museum evolving', *The Messenger*, 3rd quarter: 1–4.

McKeown, C.T. (2001) 'Implementing a "True Compromise": The Native American Graves Protection and Repatriation Act after Ten Years', in Fforde *et al.* (eds) *The Dead and Their Possessions: Repatriation in Principle, Policy and Practice*, London: Routledge.

McKinney, T. (1995) Interview with Tom McKinney, Museum Coordinator, Ataloa Art Lodge, Bacone College, Muskogee, Oklahoma, on 11 July.

McLaughlin, R. (1996) 'Some Problems and Issues in the Recognition of Indigenous Customary Law', *Indigenous Law Bulletin*, 3(82). Online. Available http:www.austlii.edu.au/au/journals/ILB (accessed 8 November 2000).

McLennan, B. (1992) Personal correspondence to the author from B. McLennan, 7 April.

McMaster, G. (1990) 'Problems of representation: our home, but the natives' land', *Muse*, Autumn: 35–8.

McMaster, G. and Martin, L. (eds) (1992) *Indigena: Contemporary Native Perspectives in Canadian Art*, Tortola: Craftsman House.

McNeill, J. (1991) Letter for publication, issued by the Office of the Director, Royal Ontario Museum, 1 March.

McNulty, R.H. (1992) 'Times of change', in P. Hamilton-Sperr, *Museums in the Life of a City, Final Report 1989–1992*, Philadelphia: Philadelphia Initiative for Cultural Pluralism, December, p. 33.

Maddra, S. (1996) 'The Wounded Knee Ghost Dance Shirt', *Journal of Museum Ethnography*, 8: 41–56.

Makseyn-Kelley, S.A. (1994) Personal correspondence from S.A. Makseyn-Kelley, Repatriation Office, NMNH, Smithsonian Institution, 14 April.

Mansell, M. (1993) Interview with Michael Mansell, Legal Adviser, Tasmanian Aboriginal Legal Centre, Hobart, Tasmania, Australia.

Marrie, A. (1985) 'Killing me softly: Aboriginal "art" and western critics', *Art Network* 14: 17–21.

—— (1989) 'Museums and Aborigines: a case study in internal colonialism', *Australian–Canadian Studies* 7(1 and 2): 63–80.

Martza, B. (1991) 'On the trail of the Zuni War Gods', *Zuni History*, Section 2: 12.

Masters, K. (1991) 'Senators blast Smithsonian for "political agenda"', *Washington Post*, 16 May: D1 & D9.

Maynard, J. (1988) 'The Weeksville Society "Save the Memories of Self" 1968–98', in *The Weeksville Society celebrates its 20th Annniversary*, Gala celebration programme, New York: The Weeksville Society.

—— (1994) 'Where children's dreams became reality: the Society for the Preservation of Weeksville and Bedford-Stuyvesant History', in B.L. Savage, *African American Historic Places*, Washington, DC: The Preservation Press.

Maynard, J. and Cottman, G. (1983) *Weeksville Then and Now*, New York: the Society for the Preservation of Weeksville and Bedford-Stuyvesant History.

Mead, S.M. (1983) 'Indigenous models of museums in Oceania', *Museum* 138, 23(2): 98–101.

—— (ed.) (1985) *Te Maori*, Auckland: Heinemann.

Meehan, B. (1984) Letter to Mr Evan Walker, Minister for Planning and Environment, Government of Victoria, from Dr Betty Meehan, President AAA for the AAA Committee on Aboriginal Skeletal Remains, 10 August.

Meehan, B. and Bonnam, J. (1986) *The National Inventory of Aboriginal Artefacts*, Fitzroy: the Council of Australian Museum Directors.

MEG (1991) 'Recommendations on professional guidelines concerning the storage, display, interpretation and return of human remains in ethnographical collections in United Kingdom Museums', adopted at Museum Ethnographers Group Annual General Meeting, 23 May 1991.

Megaw, R. (1988) *Nothing To Celebrate? Australian Aboriginal political art and the bicentennial*, Bedford Park: The Flinders University of South Australia.

Megaw, R., Giles, K. and Megaw, J.V.S. (1988) *The Cutting Edge: New Art from the Third and Fourth Worlds*, catalogue of an exhibition presented for NADOC Week 1988, Experimental Art Foundation and Flinders University of South Australia.

Mehmood, T. (1990) 'Trophies of plunder', *Museums Journal* 90(9): 27–30.

Merriman, N. (1991) *Beyond the Glass Case*, Leicester, London and New York: Leicester University Press.

Messenger, P.M. (1989) *The Ethics of Collecting Cultural Property: Whose Culture? Whose Property?*, Albuquerque: The University of New Mexico Press.

Metz, H. (1993) 'Remains to be seen: relic repatriation fuels Native American activists', *Student Lawyer* 21(8): 40–2.

MFACM (1991) Information booklet published by the Mexican Fine Arts Center Museum, Chicago, Illinois.

MGC (1999) *Restitution: Introduction*, London: Museums and Galleries Commission. Online. Available: http:www.museums.gov.uk (accessed 10 July 2000).

Migration Museum (1992) *The Forum: Community Access Gallery*, Adelaide: Migration Museum.

—— (1993) *Collecting the Evidence of South Australia's Immigration and Settlement History*, Adelaide: Migration Museum.

—— (nd) *Information notes: staff culture*, Adelaide: Migration Museum.

Milanich, J.T. (1989) 'A lesson for the Columbian Quincentenary', a paper submitted for publication in the *Gainesville Sun*, 9 December.

Milanich, J.T. and Milbrath, S. (eds) (1989) *First Encounters*, Gainesville: University of Florida Press.

Milbrath, S. and Milanich, J.T. (1990) *First Encounters: An exhibit guide*, Gainesville: Florida Museum of Natural History.

—— (1991) 'Columbian conflict', *Museum News* 70(5): 34–7.

Miller, L. (1995) Personal correspondence from Lynette Miller, Curator of the Wheelwright Museum of the American Indian, 19 April.

Molleson, C. and Cox, M. with Waldron, A.H. and Whittaker, D.K. (1993) *The Spitalfields Project: Vol 2. The Anthropology: The Middling Sort*, York: Council for British Archaeology.

MoNZ. (nd.a) *Museum of New Zealand Te Papa Tongarewa Interpretive Plan: A Conceptual Framework for Exhibitions*, Wellington: Museum of New Zealand Te Papa Tongarewa.

—— (nd.b) *Museum of New Zealand Te Papa Tongarewa Policy on Human Remains*, Wellington: Museum of New Zealand Te Papa Tongarewa.

Moore, D.R. (1985) 'A project for a Torres Strait Islands Museum and Culture Centre', *COMA Bulletin of the Conference of Museum Anthropologists*, 16: 32–8.

Moore, G. (1993) Correspondence to the author from George J. Moore, Research Intern, American Indian Ritual Object Repatriation Foundation, New York.

Moore, S. (1994) 'Federal Indian burial policy: historical anachronism or contemporary reality?', in R. Layton, *Conflict in the Archaeology of Living Traditions*, London: Routledge.

Morison, P. (1990) 'Museums face up to grave issues', *Financial Times*, 7 December.

Morphy, H. (1986) 'Reflections on representations', *Anthropology Today* 2(2): 24–6.

Moser, B. (1986) 'Amazonian Indians', letter published in *Anthropology Today* 2(1): 26.

Mulvaney, D.J. (1991) 'Past regained, future lost: the Kow Swamp Pleistocene burials', *Antiquity* 65(246): 12–21.

Mundine, J. (1990) 'A memorial for the dead', in *Artlink* 10(1 and 2): v-vi.

—— (nd) 'Aboriginal Memorial', a pamphlet produced by Ramingining Arts, Australia.

Murray, D. (1904) *Museums, Their History and Their Use*, Glasgow: MacLehose.

Museum of New Mexico (1991) *Museum of New Mexico Policy on Collection, Display, and Repatriation of Culturally Sensitive Materials*, Museum of New Mexico, Santa Fe, USA.

Myers, P. (1980) 'Tiwi Keeping Place, Ngaripuluwamigi Nguiu, Bathurst Island, Northern Territory', in R. Edwards and J. Stewart (eds) *Preserving Indigenous Cultures: A New Role For Museums*, papers from a regional seminar held in Adelaide, Australia, 10–15 September 1978, Canberra, Australia: Australian Government Publishing Service: 63–6.

Myles, K. (1976) 'Museum development in African countries', *Museum* 28(4): 196–202.

Nabais, A. (1985) 'The development of the Ecomuseum in Portugal', *Museum* 148: 186–90.

NAGPRA Review Committee (1999) *Report to Congress on 1998 Activities, August 1999*. Online. Available http:www.cr.nps.gov/nagpra/review (accessed 23 October 2000).

NAIMA (1980) *North American Indian Museum By-laws*, Niagara Falls: North American Indian Museums Association.

NARF (1979) *AIRFA: Task Force report*, report concerning Native American religious freedom submitted to US Congress by the Native American Rights Fund, February.

Newsome, S. (1995) 'Letter from the project Director', *Orator* 3(2): 1.

Nicholson, J. (1985) 'The museum and the Indian community: findings and orientation of Leicestershire Museums Service', *MEG Newsletter* 19: 3–14.

—— (1989) 'Whose story? The control and display of ethnic minority heritage in museums in Britain', in *Presenting Ethnic Heritage or: Breaking the Hall of Mirrors*, the papers of a one day conference on 'Presenting Ethnic Heritage' held at St Mary's College on 4 March.

Nicks, T. (1991) Tape transcription: 'Task force on museums and First Peoples interim report/discussion', CMA Conference, Hamilton, Ontario.

Nisga'a Tribal Council (1998) *Understanding the Nisga'a Treaty*, British Columbia: Nisga'a Tribal Council. Online. Available http:www.ntc.bc.ca (accessed 3 May 2000).

NMAH (1990) *Resource Guide – American Indian Sacred Objects, Skeletal Remains, Repatriation and Reburial*, Washington, DC: Smithsonian Institution.

NMAI (1992) *Collections Policy*, Washington, DC: National Museum of the American Indian, Smithsonian Institution.

NMGM (1994) Press release of the National Museums and Galleries on Merseyside, *Transatlantic Slavery: Against Human Dignity. Progress Report and Background Information*, 1 February.

NMNH (1994) *Collection Practices on the Frontier in the 1860s* (excerpt from Repatriation Office Case Report No. 94–003), National Museum of Natural History, Washington, DC: Smithsonian Institution

Noble, J.V. (1971a) 'Drug scene in New York', *Museum News* 50(3): 10–15.

—— (1971b) 'Museum prophecy: the role of museums in the 1970s', *Curator* 14(1): 69–74.

Nooter, P. (1991) 'Review of African Reflections', *African Arts* 24(3): 76–9.

NPS (1995) *Briefing Statement: Museum Exhibits – Trail of Tears National Historic Trail*, National Park Service, Southwest Regional Office.

—— (2000) *NAGPRA Grants*, Washington, DC: National Park Service. Online. Available http:www.cr.nps.gov/nagpra/grants (accessed 19 November 2000).

NYCHP (1990) 'Artifacts drive', *Bu Gao Ban* 7(1): 11.

O'Biso, C. (1987) '*First Light: A Magical Journey*', New York: Paragon House.

O'Keefe, P.J. (1995) 'First international conference on the cultural and intellectual property rights of indigenous peoples', *International Journal of Cultural Property*, 2(4): 382–7.

O'Mara, M. (1993) Personal correspondence to the author from Margaret O'Mara, Department of National Heritage, 21 December.

O'Neill, M. (1998) Presentation by Mark O'Neill, Head of Curatorial Services, Glasgow Museums and Art Galleries to Ghost Dance Shirt Hearing, Burrell Lecture Theatre, 13 November 1998.

O'Regan, S. (1994) 'Maori control of the Maori heritage', in P. Gathercole and D. Lowenthal (eds) *The Politics of the Past*, London: Routledge, 95–106.

Orator (1995) 'Update: Rep. Lewis and Sen. Simon introduce museum's legislation to the 104th session of Congress', *Orator* 3(1).Washington, DC: National African American Museum Project, Smithsonian Institution.

Ormond-Parker, L. (1997) 'A Commonwealth Repatriation Odyssey', *Indigenous Law Bulletin* 3(90): 9–12. Online. Available http:www.austlii.edu.au/au/journals/ILB (accessed 19 September 2000).

Ottenberg, S. (1991) 'Into the heart of Africa', *African Arts* 24(3): 79–82.

Paleopathology Association (1986) Statement on the Ethical Treatment of Human Remains, adopted at the Thirteenth Annual Meeting of the Paleopathology Association on 13 April, in Albuquerque, New Mexico.

Parker, P.L. (ed.) (1990) *Keepers of the Treasures: Protecting Historic Properties and Cultural Traditions on Indian Lands*, a report on tribal preservation funding needs submitted to Congress. National Park Service, United States Department of the Interior, Washington, DC, May.

Pearce, S.M. (ed.) (1989) *Museum Studies in Material Culture*, London and Washington, DC: Leicester University Press and Smithsonian Institution Press.

—— (ed.) (1990) *Objects of Knowledge*, London: Athlone Press.

—— (1992) *Museums, Objects and Collections: A Cultural Study*, London: Leicester University Press.

Peirson Jones, J. (1989) 'The challenge of ethnic interpretation and the American experience', in *Presenting Ethnic Heritage or: Breaking the Hall of Mirrors*, the papers of a one day conference on Presenting Ethnic Heritage held at St Mary's College on 4 March.

Peters, E. (1993) Interview with Elaine Peters, museum assistant, Ak-Chin Him Dak Indian Community Ecomuseum, Arizona, 11 May.

Peterson II, J.E. (1990) 'A conflict of values: legal and ethical treatment of American Indian remains', *Death Studies* 14(6): 519–54.

Poovaya Smith, N. (1990) 'Bring out your wares', *Museums Journal* 90(9): 34–5.

Porter, L. (1989) 'Indian activist decries new exhibit', *The Tampa Tribune*, 8 December: 1.

Powers, K. (1995) 'Collectors: museum founder Paul W. Stewart preserves the legacy of black cowboys', *Orator* 3(1): 3–4.

PPDR (1991) 'Analysis of visitor attitudes about Africa for the Africa exhibit: Field Museum of Natural History', unpublished report of research conducted by People, Places and Design Research, Northampton, Massachusetts.

Pridmore, J. (1992) 'Dickson Mounds: closing a window on the dead', *Archaeology* 45(4): 18–19.

Primas, C. (1991) Interview with Cynthia Primas, Assistant Director of the Philadelphia Initiative for Cultural Pluralism, 12 August.

Pyne, L. (1991) 'Thundering Heard: Indians' fine work deserves place at best art museums', *The Phoenix Gazette*, Thursday 25 April: E1 and 4.

Ramamurthy, A. (1990) 'Museums and the representation of black history: introduction', *Museums Journal* 90(9): 23.

RCIADIC (1991) *Aboriginal Deaths in Custody* (5 volumes), Canberra: Royal Commission on Aboriginal Deaths in Custody. Online. Available http:www.austlii.edu.au/au/special/rsproject/rsjlibrary/rciadic (accessed 22 October 2000).

Reconciliation Australia 2000. Corroboree 2000: Towards Reconciliation. Online. Available http: www.reconciliation.org.au/towards//index.html (accessed 14 April 2001).

Reeve, J. and Adams, M. (1993) *The Spitalfields Project. Vol 1. The Archaeology: Across the Styx*, York: Council for British Archaeology.

Reeve, J. and Bateman, P. (1991) 'From the Arctic to the Middle East: three multicultural programmes at the Museum of Mankind', *Journal of Education in Museums* 12: 14–17.

Richardson, L. (1994) 'The acquisition, storage and handling of Aboriginal skeletal remains in museums: an indigenous perspective', in R. Layton (ed.) *Conflict in the Archaelogy of Living Traditions*, London: Routledge.

Ringle, K. (1991) 'Political correctness: art's new frontier', *The Washington Post*, 31 March: G1, G4.

Rivard, R. (1985) 'Ecomuseums in Quebec', *Museum* 148: 202–5.

Robbins, M.W. (1971) 'The neighborhood and the museum', *Curator* 14(1): 63–8.

Roberts, C. (1992) 'The demography and palaeopathology of past populations', *World Archaeological Bulletin* 6, 98–103.

Roberts, C.A. (1992) *The Submuloc Show/Columbus Wohs. A Visual Commentary on the Columbus Quincentennial from the Perspective of America's First People* (exhibition catalogue), Phoenix: Atlatl.

Roberts, J.W. (1990) 'Laying a foundation for new understandings of American culture', keynote speech for launching of the Philadelphia Initiative for Cultural Pluralism, July.

Rodgers, M.W. (1994) Personal correspondence from Mark W. Rodgers, Director, Office of Government Relations, Smithsonian Institution, to the author, 27 July.

Roe, P. (1980) 'How important are museum sites and buildings in preserving our culture?', in R. Edwards and J. Stewart (eds) *Preserving Indigenous Cultures: A New Role For Museums*, papers from a regional seminar held in Adelaide, Australia, 10–15 September 1978, Canberra, Australia: Australian Government Publishing Service, pp. 53–4.

Rose, W. (1990) 'For some it's a time of mourning', *The New World* 1: 4.

Roth, E. (1991) 'Success stories', *Museum News* 70(1): 41–5.

—— (1992a) 'First peoples, first steps', *Museum News* 71(4): 30–2.

—— (1992b) 'Repatriation saga', *Museum News* 71(6): 12–13.

Royal Ontario Museum (nd) *Into the Heart of Africa*, publicity leaflet, Toronto: Royal Ontario Museum.

Ruffins, F.D. (1991a) 'Mythos, memory, and history: African American preservation efforts, 1820–1990', in I. Karp, C.M. Kreamer and S.D. Lavine (eds) *Museums and Communities: The Politics of Public Culture*, Washington, DC: Smithsonian Institution Press.

—— (1991b) 'Towards a collecting policy for the museum', in Smithsonian Institution, *African American Institutional Study Final Report*, Smithsonian Institution, Washington, DC: 15–20.

Sackler, E. (1993) Founder and director of the American Indian Ritual Object Repatriation Foundation (AIRORF), New York; interview with the author, Tuesday 3 August.

Sackler, E., Sullivan, M. and Hill, R. (1992) 'Three voices for repatriation', *Museum News* 71(5): 58–61.

Sampson, C. (1988) 'Aboriginal Keeping Places', *COMA Bulletin of the Conference of Museum Anthropologists* 20: 20–1.

Science Museum of Minnesota (1992) Press statement on the American Indian Movement (Minneapolis) protest incident, Friday 29 May.

—— (1993) 'Protest and the Columbus Quincentennial: a museum/community dialogue on "the teachable moment", a submission in the crisis management category for large institutions', 12 February, Science Museum of Minnesota.

Sewell, M.C. (1991) 'When two cultures collide', *Museum News*, September/October: 38–42.

Sewid-Smith, D. (1979) *Prosecution or Persecution*, Cape Mudge: Nu-yum-balees Society.

Shein, B. (1987) 'Playing, pretending, being real', *Canadian Art*, Spring.

Shelley, H.C. (1911) *The British Museum: Its History and Treasures*, Boston, Mass.: L.C. Page.

Silverman, R.A. (1987) 'Review of Baldwin, J. *et al. Perspectives: Angles on African Art*', *African Arts* 21(1): 19–24.

Simpson, M. (1989) 'Visions of other cultures: current practices in Dutch museum education', *Journal of Education in Museums* 10, 31–6.

—— (1991) ' "To see ourselves as others see us": images of Africa in four Dutch museums', *Journal of Museum Ethnography* 3, 55–72.

—— (1992a) *Black History – Whose Perspective?* An unpublished report to the National Museums and Galleries on Merseyside, April.

—— (1992b) 'Celebration, commemoration or condemnation?', *Museums Journal* 92(3): 28–31.

—— (1994a) 'A grave dilemma: Native Americans and museum in the USA', *Journal of Museum Ethnography* 6: 25–37.

—— (1994b) 'Burying the past', *Museums Journal* 94(7): 28–32.

—— (1997) *Museums and Repatriation: An Account of Contested Items in Museum Collections in the UK, with Comparative Material from Other Countries*, London: Museums Association.

Slarke, H. (1995) Personal correspondence from Helen Slarke, Manager, Our Place, Australian Museum, Sydney, to the author, 6 May.

Small, P. (1990) 'Aboriginal remains to make final journey', *Scotland on Sunday*, 12 August.

Smidt, D. (1980) 'Papua New Guinea: the National Museum and Art Gallery', in R. Edwards and J. Stewart (eds) *Preserving Indigenous Cultures: A New Role For Museums*, papers from a regional seminar held in Adelaide, Australia, 10–15 September 1978, Canberra, Australia: Australian Government Publishing Service: 154–7.

Smith, W. (1990) 'The Dickson controversy: two heritages in conflict', *Chicago Tribune*, Sunday 11 February.

Smithsonian Institution (1991) *African American Institutional Study Final Report*, Washington, DC: Smithsonian Institution.

—— (1994) 'Directory of museums and cultural centers of America's indigenous peoples', American Indian Museum Studies Program, Office of Museum Programs, Smithsonian Institution, Washington DC.

—— (nd) 'Funding sources for American Indian, Alaska and Hawaii native museums and cultural centers', American Indian Museum Studies Program, Center for Museum Studies, Smithsonian Institution, Washington, DC.

Southworth, E. (1993) 'A special concern', *Museums Journal* 93(7): 23–5.

Southworth, E., Taubman, A., Tibbles, A. and Knowles, L. (1993) 'Developing dialogue', *Museums Journal* 93(9):19–21.

Specht, J., Gordon, P., Attenbrow, V., Tacon, P., Wakeln-King, Z., Bonshek, L. and Graham, J. (1991) 'Working together on issues of access: indigenous peoples and the Australian Museum', in S. Tonkin (ed.) *Something for Everyone: Access to Museum*, papers of the 1991 Conference of the Council of Australian Museum Associations, University of Adelaide, South Australia.

Spitalfields Centre (1983) Information notes, London: Spitalfields Centre for the Study of Minorities.

Sponholtz, E. (1988) Head-Smashed-In Buffalo Jump Interpretive Centre, *MUSE* 6(3): 8–9.

Spotswood, C. *et al.* (1997) *Free Exchange or Captive Culture? The Tasmanian Aboriginal Perspective on Museums and Repatriation*, Hobart: Tasmanian Aboriginal Centre.

Staunton, I. and McCartney, M. (eds) (1981) *Lost Heritage*, a report on a symposium on the return of cultural property held at the Africa Centre, London, 21 May, London: The Africa Centre and the Commonwealth Arts Association.

Steuert, P. (1993) *Opening the Museum: History and Strategies Towards a More Inclusive Institution*, Boston: The Children's Museum.

Stevens, E. (1975) 'Black arts centers', *Museum News* 53(6): 19–24.

Strong, R. (1983) 'The museum as communicator', *Museum* 138, 35(2): 75–81.

Stocking, G.W. (1985) *Objects and Others: Essays on Museums and Material Culture*, Madison: University of Wisconsin Press.

Sturtevant, W.C., Collier, D., Dark, P., Fenton, W.N. and Dodge, E.S. (1970) Letter written on behalf of the Committee on Anthropological Research in Museums (CARM) of the American Anthropological Association to the Honorable Nelson A. Rockefeller, Governor of New York, and The Regents of the University, 23 February.

Suetopka-Thayer, R. (1986) *Repatriation considerations and the American Indian*, a paper presented at the conference 'Creating a Museum in an Indigenous Community', organised by Swedish UNESCO and the SAAMI Ecomuseum, at Jokkmokk, Sweden, 26 June.

Sugarman, A. (1992) 'The Treasures of America . . . LOOTED!', *Condé Nast Traveler*, July: 80–5, 120–4.

Suina, R. (1979) 'Indian Pueblo Cultural Center', in M. Risser (ed.) Papers presented at the First International Conference of the American Indian Museums Association (AIMA), held in Denver, Colorado, 30 April–3 May: 6–7. Reproduced and distributed under the auspices of the Office of Museum Programs, Native American Museums Training Program, Smithsonian Institution, Washington, DC.

Sullivan, M. (1992) 'Return of the sacred wampum belts of the Iroquois', *The History Teacher* 26(1): 7–14.

—— (1993) Personal correspondence from Martin Sullivan, Director of the Heard Museum, Phoenix, Arizona, to the author, 26 November.

—— (1995) Personal correspondence from Martin Sullivan, Director of the Heard Museum, Phoenix, Arizona, to the author, 5 December.

Szekeres, V. (1992) 'From the Director', *Migration News 1992*, Adelaide: The Migration Museum.

Tacon, P. (1993) Research Scientist, Anthropology, Australian Museum, Sydney; interview with the author, 9 July.

—— (1995) Personal correspondence from Paul Tacon, Research Scientist, Anthropology, Australian Museum, Sydney, to the author, 4 May.

Tandanya (nd) 'Tandanya Information', Adelaide: National Aboriginal Cultural Institute Incorporated.

Tawadros, G. (1990) 'Is the past a foreign country?', *Museums Journal* 90(9): 30–1.

Taylor, L. (1993) Senior curator, National Museum of Australia; interview with the author, 5 July.

Tchen, J.K.W. (1992) 'Creating a dialogic museum: the Chinatown History Museum Project', in I. Karp, C.M. Kreamer and S.D. Lavine (eds) *Museums and Communities: The Politics of Public Culture*, Washington, DC: Smithsonian Institution Press.

Te Aku Graham, B. (1995) 'Trafficking authenticity: aspects of non-Maori use of Maori cultural and intellectual property', *New Zealand Museums Journal* 25(1): 31–4.

Terrell, J. (1993) 'We want our treasures back', *Museums Journal* 93(3): 34–6.

Thomas, N. (1991) *Entangled Objects: Exchange, Material Culture, and Colonialism in the Pacific*, Cambridge, Mass. and London: Harvard University Press.

Thomas, S. (1988) 'Henrietta fights for her history', *The Courier-Mail*, Tuesday 15 November, 1988, Brisbane, Australia.

Thomsett, S. (1985) 'The Australian Museum's training programme for community museums, 1982–84', *COMA Bulletin of the Conference of Museum Anthropologists* 16: 39–46.

Thomson, K.W. (1980) 'Retrieving cultural property: the role of the New Zealand Government', in R. Edwards and J. Stewart (eds) *Preserving Indigenous Cultures: A New Role For Museums*, papers from a regional seminar held in Adelaide, Australia, 10–15 September 1978, Canberra, Australia: Australian Government Publishing Service: 169–74.

Thorne, A., Meehan, B., Golson, J. and White, N. (1984) 'Australian Aboriginal skeletal remains: their heritage and scientific importance', position paper of the Australian Archaeological Association, *Australian Archaeology* 19: 128–33.

Throckmorton, A. (nd) American Indian exhibit at the Chicago Field Museum. A letter to the Field Museum, Chicago, Illinois, USA.

Tickner, R. (1995) Letter to the author from the Hon. Robert Tickner, MP, Minister for Aboriginal and Torres Strait Islander Affairs, Canberra, ACT, Australia, 19 May.

Tivy, M. (1993) 'Passing the point of no return', *Museums Journal* 93(3): 25–8.

TMAG (nd) *Anthropology Department Collecting Policy*, Hobart, Australia: Tasmanian Museum and Art Gallery.

Todd, P. (1990) 'African exhibits inspire awe and anger', *Toronto Star*, Monday 7 May: A6.

Tonkin, S. (ed.) *Something for Everyone: Access to Museum*, papers of the 1991 Conference of the Council of Australian Museum Associations, University of Adelaide, South Australia.

Tortolero, C. (1991) Interview with Carlos Tortolero, Executive Director of the Mexican Fine Arts Center Museum, Chicago, Illinois.

Trescott, J. (1994) 'Museum bill dies in Senate', *Orator* 2(4): 1–2.

Trope, J.F. and Echo-Hawk, W.R. (eds) (1992) 'Symposium: The Native American Graves Protection and Repatriation Act of 1990 and state repatriation-related legislation', *Arizona State Law Journal*, Spring.

Truettner, W. (ed.) (1991) *The West As America: Reinterpreting Images of the Frontier*, Washington and London: Smithsonian Institution Press.

Ubelaker, D.H. and Grant, L.G. (1989) 'Human skeletal remains: preservation or reburial?', *Yearbook of Physical Anthropology* 32: 249–87.

U'mista (nd) 'The Potlatch', information leaflet from U'mista Cultural Centre, Alert Bay, BC.

UN (2000a) *United Nations Press Release. 21 March 2000, afternoon*. 56th session of the Committee for the Elimination of Racial Discrimination. Online. Available http:www.unhchr.ch/index (accessed 16 November 2000).

—— (2000b) *United Nations Press Release. 22 March 2000, morning. Asks for More Affirmative Action by the Government to Decrease Racial Discrimination*. 56th session of the Committee for the Elimination of Racial Discrimination. Online.

Available http:www.unhchr.ch/index (accessed 16 November 2000).

—— (2000c) *United Nations Press Release. 24 March 2000, morning*. 56th session of the Committee for the Elimination of Racial Discrimination. Online. Available http:www.unhchr.ch/index (accessed 16 November 2000).

UNESCO (1999) *Second Protocol to the Hague Convention of 1954 for the Protection of Cultural Property in the Event of Armed Conflict*, The Hague: United Nations. Online. Available http:www.unesco.org/culture/legalprotection (accessed 21 November 2000).

UNWGIP (1993) 'The UN draft declaration on the rights of indigenous peoples'. UN Doc. E/CN.4/Sub.2/1993/29, Annex I of *Discrimination Against Indigenous Peoples: Report of the Working Group on Indigenous Populations on its eleventh session*. Geneva: Office of the United Nations High Commissioner for Human Rights, 23 August 1993. Online. Available http:www.cwis.org (accessed 23 June 2000).

University of Edinburgh (1997) *Return of Tasmanian Aboriginal Remains*. Online. Available http:www.cpa.ed.ac.uk/news/latest/archive (accessed 19 November 2000).

Vargas, M.G. (1990) 'Guatemala', essay in the catalogue to accompany the exhibition '*Vestido Con El Sol: Traditional Textiles From Mexico – Guatemala – Panama*', at the Mexican Fine Arts Center Museum in Chicago, 8 June–16 September.

Vecsey, C. (ed.) (1991) *Handbook of American Indian Religious Freedom*, New York: Crossroad.

Vergo, P. (ed.) (1991) *The New Museology*, London: Reaktion Books.

Visram, R. (1986) *Ayahs, Lascars and Princes: Indians in Britain*, 1700–1947, London: Pluto Press.

Visram, R. and Fraser, P. (1988) *The Black Contribution to History*, London: Geffrye Museum/Centre for Urban Educational Studies.

WAC (1990) 'W.A.C. First Code of Ethics', *Anthropology Today* 6(6): 24.

Wallace, N.M. (1981) 'The anthropologist's role in land rights claims', *The Artefact* 6(3 and 4): 3–9.

Wallach, A. (1991) '3 Indian masks, many owners', *Newsday*, 23 May.

Wallulatum, N. (1987) Testimony of Nelson Wallulatum, religious leader and chief of the

Wasco Tribe, and Tribal Council member, the Confederated Tribes of the Warm Springs Reservation of Oregon on S. 187, The Native American Cultural Preservation Act, before the Select Committee on Indian Affairs, United States Senate, 20 February.

Walters, H. (1991) Interview with Harry Walters, Director of the Ned Hatathli Museum, Navajo Community College, Tsaile, Arizona.

Wari, K.R. (1980) 'The function of the National Cultural Council in co-ordinating cultural development in Papua New Guinea', in R. Edwards and J. Stewart (eds) *Preserving Indigenous Cultures: A New Role For Museums*, papers from a regional seminar held in Adelaide, Australia, 10–15 September 1978, Canberra: Australian Government Publishing Service.

Watt, R.J. (1990) 'Museums as sacred repositories for human remains: the New Zealand experience', *COMA Bulletin of the Conference of Museum Anthropologists* 24: 97–104 proceedings of the Conference held at the National Centre for Cultural Heritage Science Studies, University of Canberra, November–December.

WCIP (World Council of Indigenous Peoples) (1990) 'The sacred and the profane: the reburial issue as an issue', *Death Studies* 14(6): 501–17.

Webster, G.C. (1988) 'The "R" word', *Muse*, 6(3): 43–6.

Welsh, P.H. (1992) 'Repatriation and cultural preservation: potent objects, potent pasts', *University of Michigan Journal of Law Reform* 25(3 and 4).

—— (1993) Director of Research and Chief Curator, Heard Museum, Phoenix, Arizona. Interview with the author, May.

West, M.K.C. (1981) 'Keeping Place vs. museum – the North Australian example', *COMA Bulletin of the Conference of Museum Anthropologists* 7: 9–14.

White, L. (1991) 'Staying power', *Museums Journal* 91(4): 16–17.

Whiting, C. (1994) Personal correspondence from Cliff Whiting, Director, Maori and Bicultural, Museum of New Zealand *Te Papa Tongarewa* to the author 31 July.

Willis, A. and Fry, T. (1988) 'Ethnocentrism, art and the culture of domination', *Praxism M* 20: 16–22.

Wilson, D.M. (1981) Comments made during the symposium 'Lost Heritage', in I. Staunton and M. McCartney (eds) *Lost Heritage*, a report on a symposium on the return of cultural property held at the Africa Centre, London, 21 May, London: The Africa Centre and the Commonwealth Arts Association.

—— (1990) *The British Museum: Purpose and Politics*, London: British Museum Publications.

Winter, I. J. (1992) 'Change in the American Art Museum', in Association of Art Museum Directors *Different Voices*, New York: Association of Art Museum Directors.

Wissler, C. (1911) 'Ceremonial bundles of the Blackfoot Indians', *Anthropological Papers, American Museum of Natural History*, Vol. VII.

—— (1918) 'Blackfoot Sun Dance', *Anthropological Papers, American Museum of Natural History*, Vol. XVI.

Wittlin, A.S. (1949) *The Museum - Its History and Its Tasks in Education*, London: Routledge Kegan Paul.

Worthington, P. (1990) 'Reverse racism on display', *The Toronto Sun*, 7 June: 11.

Wright, R. (1991) Presentation in the session 'Bringing the museum and the Native American community together' at the American Association of Museums' Annual Conference: 'Forces of Change' held in Denver Colorado, 19–23 May.

Yu, J. (1990) 'Looking backwards into the future', *Bu Gao Ban* 7(1), 1, 4, 5.

Yunupingu, G. (1993) 'The black/white conflict', in B. Luthi (ed.) *Aratjara: Art of the First Australians*, Dusseldorf: Kunstsammlung Nordrhein-Westfalen.

Zimmerman, L.J. (1989) 'An opinion about some of the challenges and opportunities for archaeology and the osteological sciences offered at the WAC Inter-Congress', *World Archaeological Bulletin*, November: 23–8.

—— (1994a) 'Made radical by my own: an archaeologist learns to accept reburial', in R. Layton (ed.) *Conflict in the Archaeoogy of Living Traditions*, London: Routledge.

—— (1994b) 'Human bones as symbols of power: aboriginal American belief systems towards bones and "grave-robbing" archaeologists', in R. Layton (ed.) *Conflict in the Archaeology of Living Traditions*, London: Routledge.

Legislation and treaties

INTERNATIONAL TREATIES

EC (1993) *Council directive 93/7EEC of 15 March 1993 on the return of cultural objects unlawfully removed from the territory of a Member State*, Official Journal of the European Communities, No. L 74/74.

UNESCO (1970) *The Convention on the Means of Prohibiting and Preventing the Illicit Import, Export, and Transfer of Ownership Cultural Property*, adopted by the General Conference at its sixteenth session, Paris, 14 November.

UNIDROIT (1995) *Final Act of the Diplomatic Conference for the adopting of the draft UNIDROIT Convention on the International Return of Stolen or Illegally Exported Cultural Objects*, done at Rome, 24 June, 1995.

United Nations (1999) *Second Protocol to the Hague Convention of 1954 for the Protection of Cultural Property in the Event of Armed Conflict.*

United Nations Working Group on Indigenous Populations (1993) *United Nations Declaration on the Rights of Indigenous Peoples*

LEGISLATION: COMMONWEALTH GOVERNMENT OF AUSTRALIA

Commonwealth Government of Australia (1984) Aboriginal and Torres Strait Islander Heritage (Interim Protection) Act, no. 79. 25 June.

Commonwealth Government of Australia (1986) Aboriginal and Torres Strait Islander Heritage (Interim Protection) Amendment Act, no. 83. 24 June.

Commonwealth Government of Australia (1987) Aboriginal and Torres Strait Islander Heritage Protection Amendment Act.

Commonwealth Government of Australia (1975) Racial Discrimination Act.

Commonwealth Government of Australia (1998) Aboriginal and Torres Strait Islander Heritage Protection Act.

Commonwealth Government of Australia (1998) Native Title Amendment Act.

Victorian Government, Australia (1972) Archaeological and Aboriginal Relics Preservation Act, Melbourne, Australia.

Victorian Government, Australia (1984) Archaeological and Aboriginal Relics (Amendment) Act. Melbourne, Australia.

LEGISLATION: UNITED STATES OF AMERICA

US Govt. (1906) Antiquities Act, 16 USC 432.

US Govt. (1975) Indian Self-Determination and Education Assistance Act. Public Law 93–638. 25 USCA, 4 January.

US Govt. (1978a) American Indian Religious Freedom Act. Public Law 95–341, 95th Congress. 92 Stat. 469, 11 August.

US Govt. (1978b) Senate Report No. 95–709 (Select Commission on Indian Affairs), 21 March.

US Govt. (1979) Archaeological Resources Protection Act. Public Law. 96–95, 93 Stat. 721; 16 USC, 31 October.

US Govt. (1989) National Museum of the American Indian Act. Public Law 101–185, 101st Congress, 28 November.

US Govt. (1990) Native American Grave Protection and Repatriation Act. Public Law 101–601, 25 USC 3001 et seq., 16 November.

US Govt. (1968) The National Trails System Act. Public Law 90–543, 16 USC 1241 et seq., 2 October.

US Govt. (1994) The National Trails System Act (amended). Public Law 103–437, 2 November.

Index